Numerical Simulation and Methods in Computational Fluid Dynamics

Numerical Simulation and Methods in Computational Fluid Dynamics

Guest Editor

Sebastian A. Altmeyer

MDPI

Basel • Beijing • Wuhan • Barcelona • Belgrade • Novi Sad • Cluj • Manchester

Guest Editor
Sebastian A. Altmeyer
Castelldefels School of
Telecommunications and
Aerospace Engineering
(EETAC)
Universitat Politècnica de
Catalunya (UPC)
Barcelona
Spain

Editorial Office
MDPI AG
Grosspeteranlage 5
4052 Basel, Switzerland

This is a reprint of the Special Issue, published open access by the journal *Mathematics* (ISSN 2227-7390), freely accessible at: https://www.mdpi.com/journal/mathematics/special_issues/R865XYC2A4.

For citation purposes, cite each article independently as indicated on the article page online and as indicated below:

Lastname, A.A.; Lastname, B.B. Article Title. *Journal Name* **Year**, *Volume Number*, Page Range.

ISBN 978-3-7258-6059-3 (Hbk)
ISBN 978-3-7258-6060-9 (PDF)
https://doi.org/10.3390/books978-3-7258-6060-9

Contents

About the Editor

Sebastian A. Altmeyer

Sebastian A. Altmeyer is a Serra Húnter associate professor at the School of Telecom and Aerospace Engineering at Universitat Politècnica de Catalunya (UPC). He received two Pre-Diplomas (B.Sc. degree) in Mathematics and Physics in 2004, a Diploma (M.Sc degree) in Physics in 2007, and a Ph.D. degree in Theoretical Physics at the University of Saarland (Germany). Thereafter, he worked as a Postdoctoral Researcher in the Department of Mathematics at Kyungpook National University (South Korea), the Max Planck Institute for Dynamics and Self-Organization (Germany), and the Institute of Science and Technology (Austria). He joined the UPC as a Serra Húnter Fellow (tenure track) in 2017, where he was established as an Associate Professor in 2022. He has carried out research and academic activities for more than 15 years at different institutions and, to date, has published more than 50 papers.

His main research interest is in computational fluid dynamics with an emphasis on complex systems, non-linear dynamics, pattern formation, computational methods, and bifurcation theory, as well as prototypical systems such as Taylor–Couette flow and pipe flow. He is also interested in complex fluids like ferrofluids. The key goal of his simulations is to obtain physical insight into complex fluids to understand complex flow physics and modeling requirements, as well as to explore their potential use for flow control. Recently, his research area has expanded into the aerodynamics and aero-space sector with a focus on numerical simulations using genetic codes for optimal aerodynamics and mission design and efficiency.

mathematics

MDPI

Article

Effect of an Applied Magnetic Field on Joule Heating-Induced Thermal Convection

Anupam M. Hiremath [1], Harunori N. Yoshikawa [2,3] and Innocent Mutabazi [1,*]

1 Université Le Havre Normandie, Normandie Université, LOMC CNRS UMR 6294, 76058 Le Havre, France; anupam-mahantayya.hiremath@etu.univ-lehavre.fr
2 Faculty of Science and Engineering, Doshisha University, Kyoto 602-0321, Japan; hayoshik@mail.doshisha.ac.jp
3 Université de Côte d'Azur, INPHYNI CNRS UMR 7010, 06100 Nice, France
* Correspondence: innocent.mutabazi@univ-lehavre.fr

Abstract: Thermal convection induced by internal heating appears in different natural situations and technological applications with different internal sources of heat (e.g. radiation, electric or magnetic fields, chemical reactions). Thermal convection due to Joule heating in weak electrical conducting liquids such as molten salts with symmetric thermal boundary conditions is investigated using linear stability analysis. We show that, in the quasi-static approximation where the induced magnetic field is negligible, the effect of the external magnetic field consists of the delay in the threshold of thermal convection and the increase in the size of thermoconvective rolls for an intense magnetic field. Analysis of the budget of the perturbations' kinetic energy reveals that the Lorentz force contributes to the dissipation of the kinetic energy.

Keywords: thermal convection; Joule heating; Chebyshev polynomials; collocation method; Lorentz force

MSC: 80; 76

1. Introduction

Recent technological developments in metallurgy include the design of concentrated solar panels associated with thermal energy storage and in nuclear engineering where molten salt reactors appear to be a promising issue [1–6], have increased the demand for efficient heat exchangers that can operate at very high temperatures. For high-temperature operations, most of the fluids tend to evaporate or might need a huge amount of pressure to increase their boiling points. One method to overcome these challenges is the utilization of molten salts. Solid at room temperature, salts cannot transfer heat by convection and hence they need to be preheated above their melting point but kept under the boiling point in order to produce convective motion inside them. Due to their large thermal capacity and higher boiling points, molten salts are widely employed for thermal transfer at high temperatures and in recent applications, they are used as electrolytes for energy storage systems such as liquid metal battery [7–10].

Salts are typically inorganic ionic mixtures of fluorides, chlorides, carbonates, etc. Depending on the application, molten salts can be made of binary such as LiCl, or ternary molecules such as NaCl-NaI. Due to the strong ionic bonds between the atoms, a huge amount of heat is required to bring them to a liquid state. Hence, molten salts need to be maintained at high temperatures to keep them in a stable liquid state. Due to their low electrical and thermal conductivities, the application of an electrical current generates the Joule heating in the molten salts. This internal heating can trigger thermal convective motions in the molten salts and modify the heat transfer coefficient with their container.

Thermal convection induced by internal heating has been investigated by many authors [11–22] because this phenomenon is encountered in many engineering situations where internal heating can be induced by viscous heating or by dielectric heating or any other localized internal heat sources. It occurs also in Earth's mantle where convective motions are sustained by radiogenic heating throughout the mantle itself and by the conduction from the underlying hot outer core due to internal radiation. In the upper atmosphere, thermal convection is driven by radiative cooling and by heating from the lower atmosphere and the Earth's surface [14]. In an astrophysical context, nuclear burning processes occur in thin shells at some distance from the center of the star leading to compressible thermoconvective motions in the star [17]. Molten salts are also used as electrolytes between electrodes in thermal batteries used in military applications for guided missiles but also as primary power sources for radar and electronic packages for nuclear weapons [21] However, convection induced by internal heating has received much less attention than Rayleigh–Bénard convection induced by a constant temperature gradient imposed at the plates bounding the fluids [23,24].

The conduction state induced by internal heating has a parabolic temperature profile compared to the linear profile of the conduction state induced by fixed temperature difference. Linear stability analysis has been performed by different authors using different kinematic and thermal boundary conditions [11–13,17] to predict the threshold of thermal convection induced by internal heating. Numerical simulations have been performed to estimate the hydrodynamic field and the heat transfer coefficient associated with internal heating [14–16]. Sparrow et al. [11] were the first to tackle the problem of thermal convection induced by internal heating in a fluid between two parallel plates with different thermal boundary conditions, using a semi-analytical method. They found that the threshold of thermal convection decreases with the magnitude of the internal heat source. The same problem was revisited by Kulaki et al. [12,13] who performed a more exhaustive linear stability analysis and energetic analysis and obtained more accurate results on the critical parameters of thermal convection induced by internal heating. The implication of internal heating in the astrophysical environment and in geophysics was developed by Strauss [17] and by Goluskin et al. [14]. Another type of internal heating induced by a high-frequency electric field in dielectric liquids under microgravity conditions was investigated by Yoshikawa et al. [18] who showed also that the temperature of the conducting state has a parabolic profile and determined the critical parameters for thermo-electro-convection induced by the dielectrophoretic buoyancy force. Thermal convection induced by Joule-heating from magnetic fields has also been investigated in more complex flow systems such as generalized Couette flow of Jeffrey fluid [19] or in a cylindrical annulus with different magnetic configurations [20]. The estimate of convective flows and heat transfer induced by internal heating was performed in direct numerical simulations by Goluskin et al. [14,16]. A recent work by Wang et al. [25] developed the unifying theory of scaling laws of turbulence in thermal convection induced by internal heating. All these studies have confirmed that, due to the parabolic temperature profile of the conduction state, thermal convection induced by internal heating appears for lower value of the Rayleigh number compared to the threshold of Rayleigh–Bénard convection induced by an imposed constant temperature gradient.

In most geophysical and astrophysical situations but also in technological applications, the magnetic field has a strong impact on the thermal convection in fluids. The effect of the magnetic field on Rayleigh–Bénard convection has been theoretically predicted by Chandrasekhar [23] who showed the delay of the threshold of thermal convection in a liquid layer under a magnetic field. This effect has been confirmed by further studies on higher regimes of thermoconvection [26]. However, to our best knowledge, for internal heating-induced convection in a horizontal liquid layer, the effect of the magnetic field has received less attention if any.

We have performed linear stability analysis to investigate the effect of magnetic field on the thermal convection induced by Joule heating in an electrolyte-type liquid crossed by a stationary homogeneous current for different kinematic and thermal boundary conditions. We have performed the energetic budget to identify the contribution of each force in the temporal evolution of the kinetic energy of perturbations close to the onset and we found that the Lorentz force acts as a dissipative force and delays the threshold to thermal convection induced by internal heating.

The paper is organized as follows. In Section 2, we formulate the problem of thermal convection induced by Joule heating. The results of the linear stability are presented in Section 3 and discussed in Section 4. The last Section consists of the Conclusion.

2. Problem Formulation

We consider a liquid layer of poor electrical and thermal conductivities, confined between two infinite horizontal plates located at $z = \pm d/2$ in a Cartesian coordinates system (Figure 1). The liquid is considered as incompressible and Newtonian with the density ρ, the thermal expansion coefficient α, the kinematic viscosity ν, the specific heat capacity c_p, the thermal conductivity $\lambda = \rho c_p \kappa$ (where κ is the thermal diffusivity) and the electrical conductivity σ.

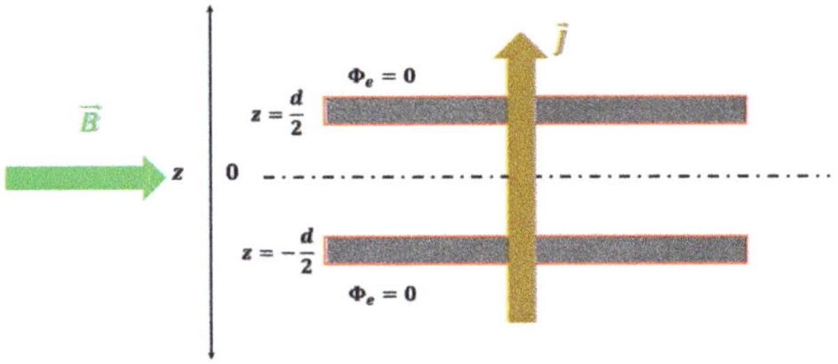

Figure 1. Liquid layer between two electrically conducting plates ($\Phi_e = 0$) located at $z = \pm d/2$ where Φ_e is the electric potential.

A uniform current I of density $\vec{J} = (I/S)\vec{e}_z$ applied across the fluid layer (of cross-section area S) generates a Joule heat in the liquid because of its weak electrical conductivity. The density q of the Joule heat flux across the liquid layer is

$$q = \frac{J^2}{\sigma} \tag{1}$$

2.1. Conduction State Induced by Internal Joule Heating

The stationary conduction state induced by Joule heating in a liquid layer confined between two horizontal infinite plates is characterized by the temperature profile $T(z)$ which satisfies the following heat equation

$$\frac{d^2T}{dz^2} + \frac{J^2}{\lambda\sigma} = 0 \tag{2}$$

To allow the heat exchange with the environment, we impose the Robin boundary conditions which are hybrid thermal boundary conditions combining both the Neumann and the Dirichlet conditions at the plates:

$$\begin{cases} \dfrac{dT}{dz} = -h(T - T_\infty) \qquad \text{at } z = \dfrac{d}{2} & \text{(3a)} \\ \dfrac{dT}{dz} = h(T - T_\infty) \qquad \text{at } z = -\dfrac{d}{2} & \text{(3b)} \end{cases}$$

where h is the heat exchange coefficient which incorporates both the convective and radiative heat transfer and T_∞ is the temperature in the bulk of the environment away from the plates. Choosing d and ΔT as characteristic length and temperature, respectively, (i.e., $z = dz'$, $T - T_\infty = \Delta T\,\Theta$), the Joule heating yields the temperature scale $\Delta T = J^2 d^2/\lambda\sigma$. The stationary heat equation and the Robin boundary conditions in dimensionless form become

$$\begin{cases} \dfrac{d^2\Theta}{dz^2} + 1 = 0 & (4a) \\ \dfrac{d\Theta}{dz} = -Bi\,\Theta \quad \text{at } z = \dfrac{1}{2} & (4b) \\ \dfrac{d\Theta}{dz} = Bi\,\Theta \quad \text{at } z = -\dfrac{1}{2} & (4c) \end{cases}$$

where $Bi = hd/k$ is called Biot number. From now, z is the dimensionless vertical coordinate. The conducting state induced by Joule heating in the liquid layer is thus described by a symmetric quadratic temperature profile

$$\Theta(z) = -\frac{1}{2}\left(z^2 - \frac{1}{4} - \frac{1}{Bi}\right) \quad (5)$$

The maximum temperature $\Theta_{max} = 1/(2Bi)$ is reached at the mid-plane $z = 0$ of the liquid layer and it is very sensitive to the heat exchange coefficient, i.e., to Bi [13]. For isothermal boundary conditions (Neumann conditions), i.e., for $Bi \to \infty$, we recover the temperature profile already obtained in previous studies [13,14]. The temperature profiles of the conducting state induced by the Joule heating are plotted in Figure 2. They differ from each other by the quantity Θ_{max} and they can be represented by a single curve $\Theta^*(z)$ (Figure 2b) defined as

$$\Theta^*(z) = \Theta(z) - \Theta_{max} \quad (6)$$

The symmetry of the temperature profiles with respect to the mid-plane of the liquid layer is due to the boundary conditions where the heat exchange coefficients between the plates bounding the liquid with the bulk environment are assumed to be identical. If they are different, the symmetry of the conduction state is broken, and the temperature profiles are asymmetric with coefficients containing the Biot numbers Bi_l of each plate l ($l = 1$: lower plate, $l = 2$: upper plate).

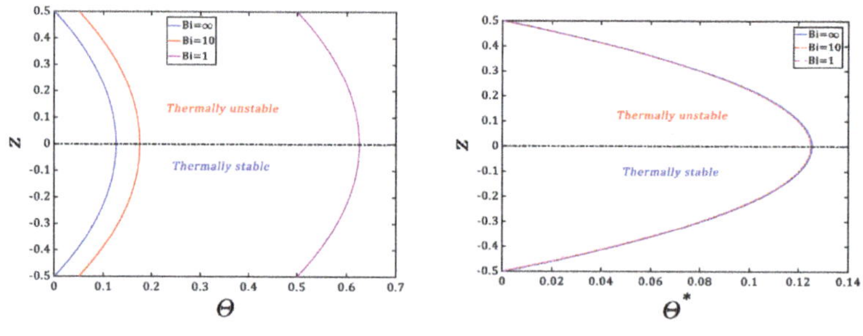

Figure 2. Temperature profiles of the conduction state in Joule heated liquid with Robin boundary condition: (**a**) for different values of Bi. (**b**) for the scaled conduction state Θ^* where all the considered boundary conditions merge into a single curve.

2.2. Driving Forces and Control Parameters

The internal Joule heating induces a temperature gradient and thus the Archimedean buoyancy $\Delta\rho g (= -\alpha\Delta T\rho_0 g)$ within the liquid layer where ρ_0 is the liquid density at the reference temperature T_0. The lower layer of the liquid is thermally stable while the upper one is thermally unstable. We need to estimate the magnitude of the internal heating, i.e., the magnitude of the applied current required to trigger thermal convection in the liquid layer. The Archimedean buoyancy will overcome the thermal diffusion and viscous dissipation if the Archimedean time scale τ_A is much smaller than the combined visco-diffusive timescale $\sqrt{\tau_\nu \tau_\kappa}$ in the liquid. The Archimedean timescale for a buoyant liquid particle to rise the distance $d/2$ is $\tau_A = \sqrt{d/[2g\alpha(\Delta T)_{max}]}$. The timescales for viscous dissipation and thermal diffusion of the buoyant particle which rises the same distance $d/2$ are $\tau_\nu = d^2/4\nu$ and $\tau_\kappa = d^2/4\kappa$, respectively. The temperature profile Θ^* in Figure 2b yields $(\Delta T)_{max} = \Delta T/8$. Thus, the magnitude of the Archimedean buoyancy can be estimated by the Rayleigh number defined as follows

$$Ra = \frac{\tau_\nu \tau_\kappa}{\tau_A^2} = \frac{1}{64}\frac{\alpha g J_0^2 d^5}{\rho c_p \nu \kappa^2 \sigma} = GrPr \tag{7}$$

where $Pr = \nu/\kappa$ is the Prandtl number and $Gr = U_{th}\, d/\nu$ is the Grashof number sometimes called the thermal Reynolds number if the characteristic thermal velocity of the buoyant particle under the action of Joule heating is introduced:

$$U_{th} = \frac{1}{64}\frac{\alpha g J_0^2 d^4}{\rho c_p \kappa \nu \sigma} \tag{8}$$

The second driving force in a liquid layer crossed by an electric current density $\vec{J}$ and an applied horizontal magnetic field $\vec{B}$ is the Lorentz force density $\vec{F} = \vec{J} \times \vec{B}$. For weakly electrically conducting liquids $\sigma \approx \mathcal{O}(10^2)$ S/m and for thermal convective velocities at laboratory scales $V \approx \mathcal{O}(10^{-2})$ m/s, the magnetic fields induced by the current density $\vec{J}$ and the drift Maxwell current $\vec{J}_d = \mu\epsilon\partial D/\partial t$ due to time variations of the electric field are so weak that they can be neglected in the so-called "quasi-static approximation" [27]. Here, μ and ϵ represent the magnetic permeability and the electrical permittivity of the liquid. The electric field $\vec{E}$ is thus stationary and it can be written as $\vec{E} = -\vec{\nabla}\Phi_e$ where Φ_e is the electric potential chosen to vanish at the bounding plates at $z = \pm d/2$ (Figure 1). The density current in the liquid is given by Ohm law

$$\vec{J} = \sigma\left(\vec{E} + \vec{u} \times \vec{B}\right) \tag{9}$$

where $\vec{u}$ is the velocity induced in the liquid. The stationarity of the applied current density $\left(\vec{\nabla}.\vec{J} = 0\right)$ leads to the Poisson equation relating the electric potential to the magnetic field:

$$\Delta\Phi_e = \nabla.\left(\vec{u} \times \vec{B}\right) \tag{10}$$

In the quasi-stationary approximation [27], the electric field in the conducting state is homogeneous and the electric potential satisfies the Laplace equation: $\nabla^2\Phi_e = 0$. This means that the electric field between the plates is homogeneous. The Ohm law becomes

$$\vec{J} = \sigma\left(-\vec{\nabla}\Phi_e + \vec{u} \times \vec{B}\right) \tag{11}$$

To estimate the magnitude of the Lorentz force acting in the liquid, we introduce the Hartmann number Ha which is the ratio of the magnitude B_0 of the applied magnetic field to the intrinsic magnetic field of the liquid B_i

$$Ha = \frac{B_0}{B_i}\ ,\quad B_i = \frac{1}{d}\sqrt{\frac{\rho\nu}{\sigma}} \tag{12}$$

The Hartmann number is often defined as the ratio between the characteristic length of the flow d and the Hartmann length l_{Ha}, i.e.,

$$Ha = \frac{d}{l_{Ha}} \quad , \quad l_{Ha} = \frac{1}{B_0}\sqrt{\frac{\sigma}{\rho\nu}} \tag{13}$$

The quantity $Q = Ha^2$ is called the Chandrasekhar number.

To make the governing equations dimensionless, we use the liquid layer thickness d as the characteristic scale for space coordinates, i.e., $\vec{r} = d\,\tilde{\vec{r}}$ and the viscous diffusion velocity $d/\tau_\nu = \nu/d$ as a characteristic velocity, i.e., $\vec{u} = (\nu/d)\,\tilde{\vec{u}}$ because we have chosen the viscous time as the characteristic timescale, i.e., $t = \tau_\nu\,\tilde{t}$. The dynamics of the liquid subject to Joule heating can be uniquely determined by four independent dimensionless control parameters given in Table 1. The Biot number Bi characterizes the heat exchange between the liquid and its environment, the Prandtl number Pr determines the thermo-viscous diffusive nature of the liquid, the Rayleigh number Ra measures the magnitude of the Archimedean buoyancy compared to the viscous dissipation and thermal diffusion, the Hartmann number Ha is the ratio between the Lorentz force and the viscous dissipation. The Grashoff number Gr is not an independent control parameter, it is sometimes used instead of Ra.

Table 1. List of independent control parameters.

Control Parameters	Symbol
Biot umber	Bi
Prandtl number	Pr
Rayleigh number	$Ra = GrPr$
Hartmann number	Ha

2.3. Linearized Equations for Internal Heating-Driven Convection

As of now, all variables are dimensionless, for simplicity, we have dropped the tildes above variables $t, \vec{u}, \vec{r}$. We superimpose to the conduction state small perturbations of the temperature field θ', of the electric potential Φ', of the generalized pressure H' and the velocity $\vec{u} = (u, v, w)$. We assume the validity of the Boussinesq approximation. Linearization of the momentum, energy and electric potential equations near the base state yield the following equations in non-dimensional form [7,27]:

$$\begin{cases} \vec{\nabla}.\vec{u} = 0 & \text{(14a)} \\ \dfrac{\partial \vec{u}}{\partial t} = -\vec{\nabla}H' + \sqrt{\dfrac{Pr}{Ra}}\Delta\vec{u} + \theta'\vec{e}_z & \\ \qquad\qquad + Ha^2\sqrt{\dfrac{Pr}{Ra}}\left[\left(-\nabla\Phi' + \vec{u}\times\vec{B}\right)\times\vec{B}\right] & \text{(14b)} \\ \dfrac{\partial\theta'}{\partial t} + w\dfrac{d\Theta}{dz} = \dfrac{1}{\sqrt{Ra.Pr}}\Delta\theta' & \text{(14c)} \\ \Delta\Phi' = \nabla.\left(\vec{u}\times\vec{B}\right) & \text{(14d)} \end{cases}$$

The second term in Equation (14b) is due to the viscous dissipation, the third term is the Archimedean buoyancy and the last term represents the Lorentz force. The temperature field is coupled to the velocity field via Equation (14b) and Equation (14c). In the quasi-stationary approximation, the perturbation $\vec{b}$ of the magnetic field is neglected [27].

Two different kinematic boundary conditions are imposed on the fluid, i.e., the no-slip boundary condition where the velocity perturbations vanish at the walls and the free-slip boundary condition where the normal stress vanishes at the walls. The free-slip boundary conditions read

$$\frac{\partial u}{\partial z} = \frac{\partial v}{\partial z} = w = \Phi' = 0 \qquad \text{at } z = \frac{1}{2}, -\frac{1}{2} \tag{15}$$

The no-slip boundary conditions are

$$u = v = w = \Phi' = 0 \qquad \text{at } z = \frac{1}{2}, -\frac{1}{2} \tag{16}$$

The thermal boundary conditions stem from boundary conditions (3):

$$\begin{cases} \dfrac{\partial \theta'}{\partial z} = -Bi\,\theta' & \text{at } z = \dfrac{1}{2} \quad (17a) \\ \dfrac{\partial \theta'}{\partial z} = Bi\,\theta' & \text{at } z = -\dfrac{1}{2} \quad (17b) \end{cases}$$

2.4. Normal Mode Expansion and Numerical Method

In the present study, we choose the horizontal axes in such a way that the magnetic field is applied along the horizontal axis $\vec{e}_x$ and its non-dimensional form is $\vec{B} = (1,0,0)$. The infinitesimal perturbations $\vec{\Psi}(t,x,y,z) = (u', v', w', H', \theta', \Phi')^t$ are expanded as normal modes

$$\vec{\Psi}(t,x,y,z) = \vec{\hat{\Psi}}(z)e^{st+i(k_x x + k_y y)} \tag{18}$$

where $\vec{\hat{\Psi}}(z) = (\hat{u}(z), \hat{v}(z), \hat{w}(z), \hat{H}(z), \hat{\theta}(z), \hat{\Phi}(z))^t$ is the structure-function of the perturbations, the quantity $s = s_r + is_i$ is a complex temporal growth rate with s_r and s_i being the real growth rate and the frequency of the perturbations, respectively. As the system is assumed infinite in the horizontal plane, the wave numbers k_x and k_y are real. Substitution into the linearized Equation (14) yields the following system of equations of the complex amplitudes $\vec{\hat{\Psi}}$:

$$\begin{cases} 0 = ik_x\hat{u} + ik_y\hat{v} + D\hat{w} & (19a) \\ s\hat{u} = -ik_x\hat{H} + \sqrt{\dfrac{Pr}{Ra}}\hat{\Delta}\hat{u} & (19b) \\ s\hat{v} = -ik_y\hat{H} + \sqrt{\dfrac{Pr}{Ra}}\hat{\Delta}\hat{v} - Ha^2\sqrt{\dfrac{Pr}{Ra}}\left[D\hat{\Phi} + \hat{v}\right] & (19c) \\ s\hat{w} = -D\hat{H} + \sqrt{\dfrac{Pr}{Ra}}\hat{\Delta}\hat{w} + \hat{\theta} + Ha^2\sqrt{\dfrac{Pr}{Ra}}\left[ik_y\hat{\Phi} - \hat{w}\right] & (19d) \\ s\hat{\theta} = -\hat{w}D\Theta + \dfrac{1}{\sqrt{Ra.Pr}}\hat{\Delta}\hat{\theta} & (19e) \\ 0 = \hat{\Delta}\hat{\Phi} + D\hat{v} - ik_y\hat{w} & (19f) \end{cases}$$

with the operators $D = \frac{d}{dz}, \hat{\Delta} = k_x^2 + k_y^2 + D^2$. The boundary conditions develops into,

$$\begin{cases} \text{No-slip boundary conditions :} & (20a) \\ \qquad \hat{u} = \hat{v} = \hat{w} = \hat{\Phi} = 0 \qquad \text{at } z = \dfrac{1}{2}, -\dfrac{1}{2} & \\ \text{Free-slip boundary conditions :} & (20b) \\ \qquad D\hat{u} = D\hat{v} = \hat{w} = \hat{\Phi} = 0 \qquad \text{at } z = \dfrac{1}{2}, -\dfrac{1}{2} & \\ \text{Thermal boundary conditions :} & (20c) \\ \qquad D\hat{\theta} = -Bi\,\hat{\theta} \quad \text{at } z = \dfrac{1}{2} \text{ and } D\hat{\theta} = Bi\,\hat{\theta} \quad \text{at } z = -\dfrac{1}{2} & \end{cases}$$

Besides the four control parameters given in Table 1, the system of linearized Equation (19) together with the boundary conditions (20) contains 10 dimensionless variables. The system of Equation (14) can be written in a matrix form as follows :

$$\overline{\overline{A}}\vec{\hat{\Psi}} = s\overline{\overline{B}}\vec{\hat{\Psi}} \tag{21}$$

where the expressions of the matrices $\overline{\overline{A}}$ and $\overline{\overline{B}}$ can easily be derived from the system of Equation (19). The system of Equation (21) is an eigenvalue problem with the eigenvalue s and the structure-function of the perturbations $\vec{\hat{\Psi}}$ is the eigenvector. The eigenvalue s is searched as a function of the control parameters and of the wave numbers of the perturbations

$$s = f(Ra, Pr, Ha, k_x, k_y) \tag{22}$$

We are interested in the determination of the threshold of thermal convection, so we look for marginal perturbations for which $s_r = 0$. The marginal state is thus represented by the hypersurface $f(Ra, Pr, Ha, k_x, k_y, s_i) = 0$. We fix Pr and Ha and the hypersurface is reduced to a marginal stability curve $\tilde{f}(Ra, k) = 0$ for stationary perturbations where $k = \sqrt{k_x^2 + k_y^2}$.

In order to determine the marginal stability curve, we use the following numerical scheme. The system of equations of complex amplitudes (19) and the boundary conditions (20) are discretized using the Chebyshev spectral method. The Chebyshev variable ξ is related to the vertical coordinate z as follows,

$$\xi = 2z \tag{23}$$

where $\xi \in [-1, 1]$. Discretization is conducted along a vertical direction $z = z_i (i = 3, 4, 5, ..., N)$ corresponding to collocation points $\xi_i = \cos(i\pi/N)$. The highest order of Chebyshev polynomials is needed to ensure the convergence is set to $N = 60$.

Marginal stability curves for which $s_r = 0$ are plotted in the plane (k, Ra) and their lowest minimum determines the critical parameters (k_c, Ra_c) of thermal convection.

3. Results

In the absence of the magnetic field, the critical modes are invariant with respect to rotation of the wavenumber vector $\vec{k}$ in the plane (k_x, k_y): the critical patterns can either be rolls of the y axis with wavevector $\vec{k} = (k, 0)$ or of the x axis with wavevector $\vec{k} = (0, k)$; they can be square patterns with wavevector $\vec{k} = \sqrt{2}(k, k)/2$ or hexagonal patterns with a more complex combination of wavenumbers k_x and k_y such that the velocity and temperature fields must be invariant for rotation by $\pi/3$ about the origin and they must be periodic in the x- and y-directions [23]. Nonlinear stability analysis shows that for Rayleigh–Bénard convection, square patterns are not stable while rolls and hexagons are stable [28,29]. The Lorentz force due to the magnetic field breaks this invariance. Here, we have assumed that the perturbations are two-dimensional, i.e., $k_y = 0$, so that we have $\hat{u} = -d\hat{\psi}/dz, \hat{w} = ik\hat{\psi}$. We first present results the threshold Ra_c and critical wavenumber k_c of thermal convection for different values of Bi and the eigenfunctions $\hat{\theta}(z), \hat{\psi}(z)$ in the absence of the magnetic field, and then we analyze the effect of the magnetic field (i.e., of Ha) on the critical parameters (Ra_c, k_c) of the convection induced by Joule heating.

3.1. Threshold of Internal Heating-Induced Convection

We have computed the marginal stability curves for free-slip and no-slip boundary conditions and for different values of the Biot number Bi (Figure 3). The critical modes are stationary, i.e., $s_r = 0, s_i = 0$ and they are independent of Pr. The threshold of Joule heating-induced convection between two horizontal plates is lower than the one of the classic Rayleigh–Bénard convection with a constant temperature gradient between the plates. This is due to the quadratic profile of the temperature field of the conduction state. We recover the results of previous studies [11–13,17].

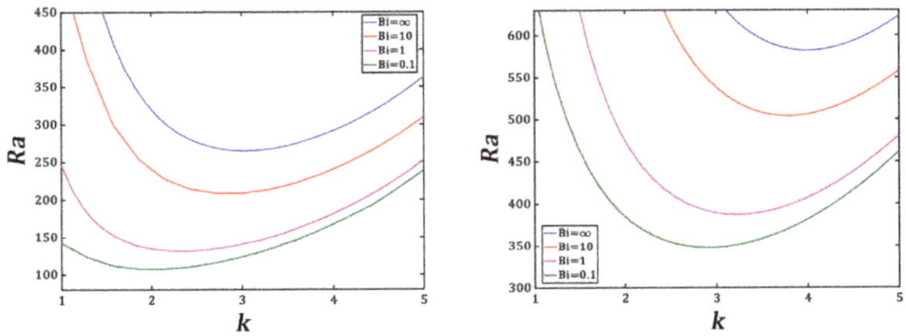

(**a**) (**b**)

Figure 3. Stability curves for $s_r = 0$ in the plane (k, Ra) (**a**) free-slip and (**b**) no-slip boundary condition.

Table 2 presents the critical parameters (k_c, Ra_c) for chosen values of Bi. For $Bi \to \infty$ corresponding to isothermal boundary conditions, the threshold is the highest for both types of kinematic boundary conditions. This suggests that the heat exchange between the liquid layer and the environment favors the occurrence of Joule heating-induced convection. The effect of the Biot number on the size of thermoconvective cells induced by internal heating is significant: thermoconvective cells have a smaller size for isothermal boundary conditions than in the presence of heat exchange with the environment. For a fixed value of Bi, we recover the result that the free-slip conditions favor the convection as in the case of the classic Rayleigh–Bénard convection. In Figure 4, we have plotted the vertical profiles of the temperature perturbation $\hat{\theta}(z)$ and of the vertical velocity component $\hat{w}(z)$.

Table 2. Critical values for thermal convection induced due to internal heating for (**a**) free-slip and (**b**) no-slip boundary conditions.

Bi	Ra_c	k_c
	(a)	
∞	265.5	3.027
10	208	2.857
1	131.15	2.344
0.1	106.75	2.008
	(b)	
∞	583.20	3.998
10	503.85	3.784
1	387.2	3.246
0.1	348.0	2.902

The vertical profile of the temperature $\hat{\theta}(z)$ and of the vertical velocity component $\hat{w}(z)$ in Figure 4 show that the temperature and velocity perturbations perturbations penetrate into the lower stable part of the liquid. However, the upper part of the liquid layer is more active than the lower part as the last one is thermally stable. The eigenfunctions of the temperature field to which we have superimposed the velocity vectors and the stream functions $\psi(x,z) = const$ of the critical states are plotted in Figure 5. The cores of the stream functions are also located in the thermally unstable zone of the liquid layer.

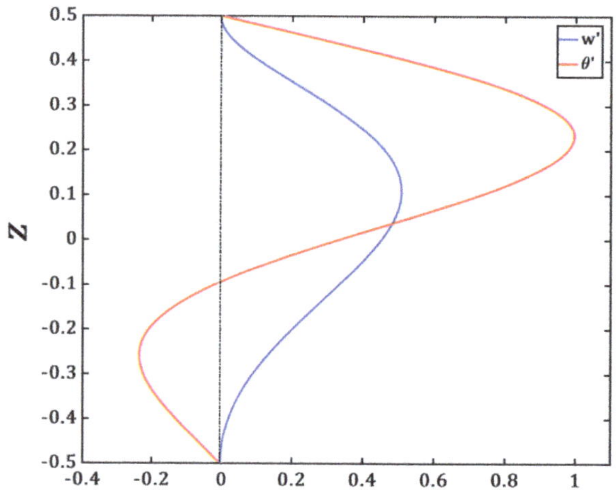

Figure 4. Profiles of the temperature perturbation $\hat{\theta}(z)$ and the axial velocity $\hat{w}(z)$ for isothermal no-slip condition $Bi = \infty$ in the absence of the magnetic field ($Ha = 0$).

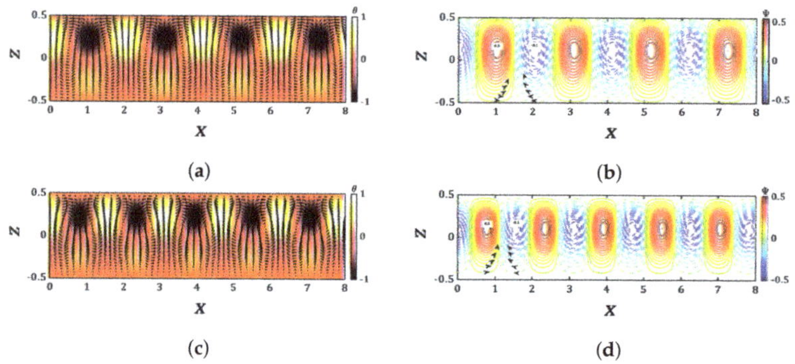

Figure 5. Isotherms and stream functions for isothermal boundaries ($Bi \to \infty$): (**a**,**b**) for free-slip boundary conditions and (**c**,**d**) for no-slip boundary conditions. Yellow and black zones in (**a**,**c**) correspond to hot and cold zones, respectively. Red color and blue color in (**b**,**d**) correspond to anticlockwise and clockwise vortices, respectively. Black arrows indicate the vortices' orientation.

3.2. Effect of the Magnetic Field on Internal Heating Induced Convection

Different studies on thermal convection have shown that the vertical magnetic field delays the occurrence of the Rayleigh–Bénard convection with a decrease in cell size [23]. In the present study, we analyze the effect of the horizontal dimensionless magnetic field $\vec{B} = (1, 0, 0)$ on the threshold of internal heating-driven convection. We have solved the eigenvalue problem for different values of the Hartmann number Ha and plotted in Figure 6 the critical parameters (Ra_c, k_c) as functions of Ha. The critical modes are stationary for all values of Ha and the threshold is independent of Pr. The effect of the magnetic field on the threshold of thermal convection induced by Joule heating becomes significant for $Ha > 1$ where the threshold Ra_c and the critical wavelength ($\sim 1/k_c$) start to increase for all values of the Biot number Bi. For both types of kinematic boundary conditions with imposed isothermal boundaries, the variations $Ra_c(Ha)$ can be approximated by quadratic polynomials. For free-slip boundary conditions,

$$Ra_c = 1.649Ha^2 + 22.12Ha + 222.6 \tag{24}$$

For no-slip boundary conditions,

$$Ra_c = 1.771Ha^2 + 39.9Ha + 493.7 \quad (25)$$

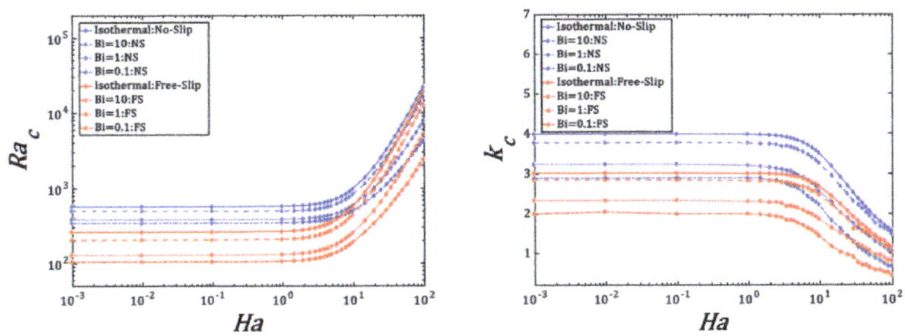

(a) (b)

Figure 6. (**a**) Variation of Ra_c as a function of Ha for different boundary conditions and (**b**) variation of the critical wave number.

The stabilization effect of the magnetic field on thermal convection becomes significant when the applied field B_0 becomes larger than the characteristic intrinsic magnetic field B_i which depends on the properties and of the thickness of the liquid according to the relation (12). The isotherms and stream functions of the critical modes for $Bi = 1, Ha = 50$ are plotted in Figure 7. They illustrate the increase in the wavelength of the thermoconvective cells compared to the case without the magnetic field shown in Figure 5.

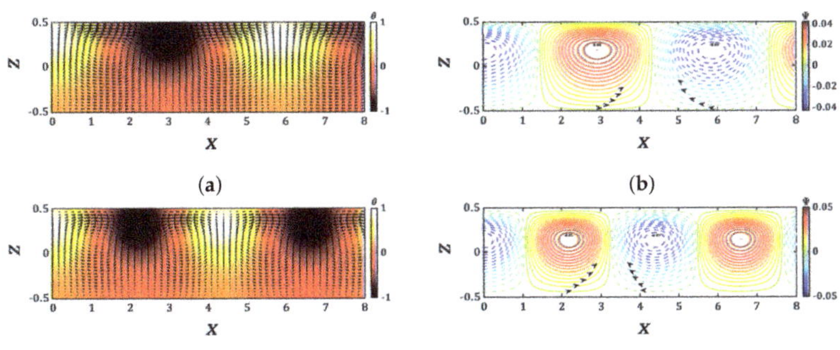

(a) (b) (c) (d)

Figure 7. Isotherms and stream functions for $Bi = 1$ and $Ha = 50$: (**a**,**b**) for free-slip boundary conditions and (**c**,**d**) for no-slip boundary conditions. Yellow and black zones in (**a**,**c**) correspond to hot and cold zones, respectively. Red color and blue color in (**b**,**d**) correspond to anticlockwise and clockwise vortices, respectively. Black arrows indicate the vortices' orientation.

4. Discussion

We have revisited the linear stability of thermal convection induced by Joule heating in a liquid layer crossed by a homogeneous current of intensity I and bounded by two infinite horizontal plates that exchange heat with the environment. We have confirmed the results from previous studies [11–13,17] which have shown that the heat exchange between the liquid and the environment favors the appearance of thermal convection by the energy input into the liquid.

We have neglected the induced currents and magnetic fields in the liquid. The applied horizontal magnetic field delays the occurrence of thermal convection as in the case of Rayleigh-Bénard convection. In order to explain this result, we have derived from the system of Equation (14), the equation of the energy budget of the perturbations

$$\frac{dK}{dt} = B + D + L \tag{26}$$

where $K = \int \vec{u}^2 d^3\vec{r}$ is the kinetic energy, $B = \int w\theta' d^3\vec{r}$ is the power of the Archimedean buoyancy, $D = \sqrt{\frac{Pr}{Ra}} \int (\vec{u}.\nabla^2\vec{u}) d^3\vec{r} < 0$ [30] is the dissipation due to viscosity and $L = -Ha^2\sqrt{\frac{Pr}{Ra}} \int (v^2 + w^2) d^3\vec{r} < 0$ is the power performed by the Lorentz force in which we have neglected the power produced by the perturbation of the electric field. The Lorentz force contributes to the dissipation of the kinetic energy of the perturbations and thus, it delays the thermal convection.

Molten salts are used in some microfluidic systems used in aeronautics and in electronic circuitries [31]. They also have found a new application in the design of liquid metal batteries which consist of three superimposed liquid layers where an electrolyte is sandwiched between two liquid metals serving as electrodes [10,32]. These liquid layers are crossed by an electric current which induces a Joule heating in the electrolyte because of its low electrical conductivity compared to the liquid metals. To control the thermoconvective motion in liquid metal batteries where this motion can induce short-circuit and then damage the battery, the application of the magnetic field in the appropriate direction seems to be a solution to suppress or delay the thermoconvective motion in the battery.

From the critical values Ra_c, one can estimate the critical current J_{0c} required to trigger thermal convection induced by Joule heating in a liquid layer of thickness d using the relation (7) between the control parameter Ra and the applied current J:

$$J = 8\sqrt{\frac{\sigma\lambda\nu\kappa Ra}{\alpha g d^5}} \tag{27}$$

Table 3 yields the values of the critical current J_c for a thickness $d = 10^{-2}$ m of the $LiCl - KCl$ molten salt with properties [7] : $\alpha = 2.93 \times 10^{-4}$ (1/K), $\lambda = 0.42$ (W/mK), $\sigma = 170$ (S/m), $\nu = 0.71 \times 10^{-6}$ (m^2/s), $\kappa = 2012 \times 10^{-7}$ (m^2/s).

Table 3. Critical value of current density to trigger convection for $d = 10^{-2}$ m.

	Ra_c	J_c (A/m^2)
No-slip	583.207	1184.10
Free-slip	265.505	799.06

Figure 8 shows the variation of critical current density J_{0c} that has to be applied to avoid convective motions as a function of the applied magnetic field B_0. These calculations have been made for different thicknesses of the molten salt layer.

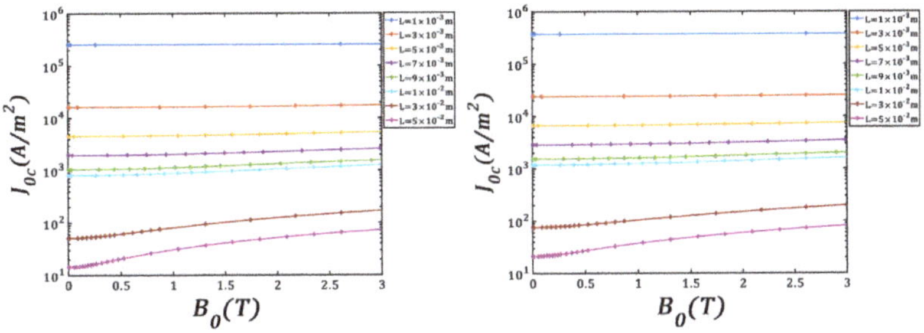

(a) (b)

Figure 8. Variation of the critical current density J_{0c} as a function of applied horizontal magnetic field B_0 for different layer thickness, isothermal boundaries: (**a**) free-slip boundary and (**b**) no-slip boundary.

5. Conclusions

Thermal convection induced in a liquid layer confined between two infinite horizontal plates and subject to Joule heating by a homogeneous current has been revisited for different kinematic and thermal boundary conditions. The application of the horizontal magnetic field leads to the delay of thermal convection and to the increase in the wavelength of the thermoconvective cells. The energy budget shows that the Lorentz force produces a negative power and so it contributes, together with viscous forces, to the dissipation of the kinetic energy of thermoconvective perturbations induced by Joule heating in the liquid layer.

Author Contributions: Methodology, A.M.H., H.N.Y. and I.M.; Software, A.M.H., H.N.Y. and I.M.; Validation, A.M.H., H.N.Y. and I.M.; Formal analysis, A.M.H., H.N.Y. and I.M.; Investigation, A.M.H., H.N.Y. and I.M.; Resources, H.N.Y. and I.M.; Data curation, A.M.H., H.N.Y. and I.M.; Writing—original draft, A.M.H., H.N.Y. and I.M.; Writing—review & editing, H.N.Y. and I.M.; Supervision, H.N.Y. and I.M.; Project administration, I.M.; Funding acquisition, I.M. All authors have read and agreed to the published version of the manuscript.

Funding: This research was funded by French National Research Agency (ANR) through the Program Investissements d'Avenir (Grant ANR-10 LABX-09-01, LabEx EMC^3/project HILIMBA) and Région Normandie (Réseau d'Intérêt Normand—Label d'Excellence).

Data Availability Statement: The data will be made available by the authors on request.

Conflicts of Interest: The authors declare no conflicts of interest.

References

1. Kuchibhotla, A.; Banerjee, D.; Dhir, V. Forced convection heat transfer of molten Salts: A review. *Nucl. Eng. Des.* **2020**, *362*, 110591. [CrossRef]
2. Jeong, Y.S.; Seo, S.B.; Bang, I.C. Natural convection heat transfer characteristics of molten salt with internal heat generation. *J. Therm. Sci.* **2018**, *129*, 181–192. [CrossRef]
3. Zhang, S.; Sun, X.; Domniguez-Ontiveros, E.E. Numerical study on convective heat transfer and friction characteristics of molten salts in circular tubes. *Ann. Nucl. Energy* **2020**, *142*, 107375. [CrossRef]
4. Fiorina, C.; Cammi, A.; Luzzi, L.; Mikityuk, K.; Ninokata, H.; Ricotti, M.E. Thermal-hydraulics of internally heated molten salts and application to the Molten Salt Fast Reactor. *J. Phys. Conf. Ser.* **2014**, *501*, 012030. [CrossRef]
5. Nunes, V.M.B.; Queirós, C.S.; Lourenço, M.J.V.; Santos, F.J.V.; De castro, C.A.N. Molten salts as engineering fluids—A review: Part I. Molten alkali nitrates. *Appl. Energy* **2016**, *183*, 603–611. [CrossRef]
6. Turchi, C.S.; Vidal, J.; Bauer, M. Molten salt power towers operating at 600–650 C: Salt selection and cost benefits. *Sol. Energy* **2018**, *164*, 38–46. [CrossRef]
7. Shen, Y.; Zikanov, O. Thermal convection in a liquid metal battery. *Theor. Comput. Fluid Dyn.* **2016**, *30*, 275–294. [CrossRef]
8. Köllner, T.; Boeck, T.; Schumacher, J. Thermal Rayleigh-Marangoni convection in a three-layer liquid-metal-battery model. *Phys. Rev. E* **2017**, *95*, 053114. [CrossRef]

9. Personnettaz, P.; Beckstein, P.; Landgraf, S.; Köllner, T.; Nimtz, M.; Weber, N.; Weier, T. Thermally driven convection in Li||Bi liquid metal batteries. *J. Power Sources* **2018**, *401*, 362–374. [CrossRef]
10. Kelley, D.H.; Weier, T. Fluid Mechanics of Liquid Metal Batteries. *Appl. Mech. Rev.* **2018**, *70*, 020801. [CrossRef]
11. Sparrow, E.M.; Goldstein, R.J.; Jonsson, V. Thermal instability in a horizontal fluid layer: Effect of boundary conditions and non-linear temperature profile. *J. Fluid Mech.* **1964**, *18*, 513–528. [CrossRef]
12. Kulacki, F.A.; Goldstein, R.J. Thermal convection in a horizontal fluid layer with uniform volumetric energy sources. *J. Fluid Mech.* **1972**, *55*, 271–287. [CrossRef]
13. Kulacki, F.A.; Goldstein, R.J. Hydrodynamic instability in fluid layers with uniform volumetric energy sources. *Appl. Sci. Res.* **1972**, *31*, 81–109. [CrossRef]
14. Goluskin, D.; Spiegel, E.A. Convection driven by internal heating. *Phys. Lett. A* **2012**, *377*, 83–92. [CrossRef]
15. Goluskin, D. Internally heated convection beneath a poor conductor. *J. Fluid Mech.* **2015**, *771*, 36–56. [CrossRef]
16. Goluskin, D.; der Poel, E.P.V. Penetrative internally heated convection in two and three dimensions. *J. Fluid Mech.* **2016**, *791*, R6. [CrossRef]
17. Strauss, J.M. Penetrative convection in a layer of fluid heated from within. *Astrophys. J.* **1976**, *209*, 179–189. [CrossRef]
18. Yoshikawa, H.N.; Kang, C.; Mutabazi, I.; Zaussinger, F.; Haun, P.; Egbers, C. Thermoelectrohydrodynamic convection in parallel plate capacitors under dielectric heating conditions. *Phys. Rev. Fluids* **2020**, *5*, 113503. [CrossRef]
19. Mng'ang'a, J.; Onyango, E.R.; Chilingo, K.J. Joule heating and induced magnetic field on magnetohydrodynamic generalized Couette flow of Jeffrey fluid in an inclinded channel with Soret and Dufour effects. *Int. J. Ambient. Energy* **2024**, *45*, 2305328. [CrossRef]
20. Muhammad, M.Y.; Lawan, M.A.; Gambo, Y.Y. Heat absorption effect of magneto-natural convection flow in a vertical concentric annulus with influence of radial and induced magnetic field. *Sci. Rep.* **2024**, *14*, 15165.
21. Guidotti, R.A.; Masset, P. Thermally activated ("thermal")battery technology. Part I: An overview. *J. Power Sources* **2006**, *161*, 1443–1449. [CrossRef]
22. Masset, P.; Guidotti, R.A. Thermally activated ("thermal")battery technology. Part II: Molten salts electrolytes. *J. Power Sources* **2007**, *164*, 397–414. [CrossRef]
23. Chandrasekhar, S. *Hydrodynamic and Hydromagnetic Stability*; Oxford University Press: Oxford, UK, 1961.
24. Mutabazi, I.; Wesfreid, J.E.; Guyon, E. *Dynamics of Spatio-Temporal Cellular Structures: Henri Bénard centenary Review*; Springer: Berlin/Heidelberg, Germany, 2006.
25. Wang, Q.; Lohse, D.; Shishkina, O. Scaling in internally heated convection: A unifying theory. *Geophys. Res. Lett.* **2020**, *10*, 1029. [CrossRef]
26. Aurnou, J.M.; Olson, P.L. Experiments on Rayleigh–Bénard convection, magnetoconvection and rotating magnetoconvection in liquid gallium. *J. Fluid Mech.* **2001**, *430*, 283–307. [CrossRef]
27. Davidson, P.A. *An Introduction to Magnetohydrodynamics*; Cambridge University Press: Cambridge, UK, 2001.
28. Busse, F.H. Non-linear properties of thermal convection. *Rep. Prog. Phys.* **1978**, *41*, 1929–1967. [CrossRef]
29. Manneville, P. *Dissipative Structures and Weak Turbulence*; Academic Press: Cambridge, MA, USA, 1990.
30. Eckhardt, B.; Grossmann, S.; Lohse, D. Torque scaling in turbulent Taylor–Couette flow between independently rotating cylinders. *J. Fluid Mech.* **2007**, *581*, 221–250. [CrossRef]
31. Caraballo, A.; Galán-Casado, S.; Caballero, A.; Serena, S. Molten salts for sensible thermal energy storage: A review and an energy performance analysis. *Energies* **2021**, *14*, 1197. [CrossRef]
32. Kim, H.; Boysen, D.A.; Newhouse, J.M.; Spatocco, B.L.; Chung, B.; Burke, P.J.; Bradwell, D.J.; Jiang, K.; Tomaszowska, A.A.; Wang, K.; et al. Liquid Metal Batteries: Past, Present, and Future. *Chem. Rev.* **2013**, *113*, 2075–2099. [CrossRef]

mathematics

Article

Convective Heat Transfer in Uniformly Accelerated and Decelerated Turbulent Pipe Flows

Ismael Essarroukh and José M. López *

Department of Mechanical, Thermal, and Fluid Engineering, Edificio de Ingenierías UMA, University of Malaga, Arquitecto Francisco Peñalosa, 6, Campanillas, 29071 Málaga, Spain
* Correspondence: jose.lopez@uma.es

Abstract: This study presents a detailed investigation of the temporal evolution of the Nusselt number (Nu) in uniformly accelerated and decelerated turbulent pipe flows under a constant heat flux using direct numerical simulations. The influence of different acceleration and deceleration rates on heat transfer is systematically studied, addressing a gap in the previous research. The simulations confirm several key experimental findings, including the presence of three distinct phases in the Nusselt number temporal response—delay, recovery, and quasi-steady phases—as well as the characteristics of thermal structures in unsteady pipe flow. In accelerated flows, the delay in the turbulence response to changes in velocity results in reduced heat transfer, with average Nu values up to 48% lower than those for steady-flow conditions at the same mean Reynolds number. Conversely, decelerated flows exhibit enhanced heat transfer, with average Nu exceeding steady values by up to 42% due to the onset of secondary instabilities that amplify turbulence. To characterize the Nu response across the full range of acceleration and deceleration rates, a new model based on a hyperbolic tangent function is proposed, which provides a more accurate description of the heat transfer response than previous models. The results suggest the potential to design unsteady periodic cycles, combining slow acceleration and rapid deceleration, to enhance heat transfer compared to steady flows.

Keywords: unsteady flow; Nusselt number; turbulent pipe flow; heat transfer; direct numerical simulation; flow acceleration; flow deceleration

MSC: 76-10

1. Introduction

Understanding the heat transfer characteristics of unsteady turbulent pipe flows is crucial for optimizing a wide range of industrial and technological processes. These include exhaust systems in internal combustion engines; heating, ventilation, and air conditioning (HVAC) systems; aerospace propulsion; chemical reactors; and biomedical technology applications. In recent decades, there has been growing interest in the potential of unsteady periodic pipe flows to enhance convective heat transfer compared to steady flows at the same Reynolds numbers. In particular, pipe flow driven by pulsations has attracted significant attention. Numerous experimental studies (Dec et al. [1], Habib et al. [2], Barker and Ffowcs Williams [3], Elshafei et al. [4], Patel and Attal [5], Simonetti et al. [6], Brahma and Singh [7]) and computational fluid dynamics (CFD) analyses (Wang and Zhang [8], Elshafei et al. [9], Nishandar et al. [10]) have investigated how pulsation parameters, such as amplitude, frequency, and mean Reynolds number, affect heat transfer. Despite extensive research, the effects of these parameters remain unclear, and contradictory findings continue to challenge the development of reliable predictive models.

Investigations have shown that pulsation can increase, decrease, or have no effect on heat transfer relative to steady conditions, depending on the pulsation control parameters. It is generally accepted that enhancing heat transfer requires the pulsation amplitude to exceed the mean velocity, leading to flow reversal (Dec et al. [1], Patel and Attal [5], Simonetti et al. [6], Brahma and Singh [7], Wang and Zhang [8]). However, it is still uncertain whether this condition alone is sufficient or if additional factors play a role in determining the heat transfer enhancement. When the pulsation amplitude is below the mean velocity, researchers have observed slight reductions (Habib et al. [2], Elshafei et al. [4,9]) in heat transfer, as well as cases where heat transfer remains similar to steady-flow conditions (Barker and Ffowcs Williams [3], Elshafei et al. [4,9], Nishandar et al. [10]).

Unlike amplitude, there is no consensus on how pulsation frequency affects heat transfer. Some studies indicate that heat transfer increases with higher pulsation frequencies (Dec et al. [1], Patel and Attal [5]), while others report that significant changes only occur at optimal or resonant frequencies (Habib et al. [2], Simonetti et al. [6], Wang and Zhang [8]). In contrast, numerous studies have found that varying the pulsation frequency has little to no significant effect (Barker and Ffowcs Williams [3], Elshafei et al. [4], Brahma and Singh [7], Elshafei et al. [9], Nishandar et al. [10]). There is currently no theory that explains the differing results reported in these experiments and simulations

Similarly, the influence of the mean Reynolds number on heat transfer remains contentious. While most studies have not detected significant effects from variations in the Reynolds number (Barker and Ffowcs Williams [3], Elshafei et al. [4], Brahma and Singh [7], Elshafei et al. [9], Nishandar et al. [10]), some have observed that heat transfer enhancement due to pulsation increases with the mean Reynolds number up to a threshold, beyond which further increases yield no significant changes (Patel and Attal [5], Wang and Zhang [8]).

While the effects of pulsatile flows on heat transfer have been extensively studied, much less attention has been given to non-periodic unsteady flows, such as uniformly accelerated and decelerated flows. Understanding the heat transfer characteristics of these flows is important not only due to their broad industrial and civil engineering applications but also because unsteady periodic flows are composed of alternating acceleration and deceleration phases. Thus, investigating the heat transfer behavior during these individual phases could provide valuable insights into unresolved questions regarding heat transfer in pulsatile flows.

To date, only the laboratory experiments conducted by Shiibara et al. [11] and Nakamura et al. [12] have explored the effects of acceleration or deceleration on heat transfer in turbulent pipe flow. Using high-speed infrared thermography, these studies reported on the temporal response of the Nusselt number and thermal structures when flow speed changed abruptly (Shiibara et al. [11]). Based on these observations, a model was proposed to characterize this temporal response (Nakamura et al. [12]). Their results indicated a time delay in the heat transfer response to changes in velocity, resulting in lower heat transfer during acceleration and higher heat transfer during deceleration compared to steady conditions. However, the experimental setup did not allow control over the acceleration and deceleration rates (denoted by the parameter α), so they were unable to explore the effects of varying α.

To address this gap, the present work uses direct numerical simulations (DNS) to systematically investigate the impact of α on the temporal evolution of the Nusselt number in turbulent pipe flow under constant heat flux. DNS captures all relevant scales of motion and avoids the approximations of turbulence models, allowing for a detailed examination of flow structures and heat transfer mechanisms. However, due to its high computational cost, DNS has not been previously used to study heat transfer in unsteady flows.

This study contributes to the field in two significant ways. First, the simulations offer the first numerical verification of the experimental findings, confirming the existence of three phases in the Nusselt number evolution—delay, recovery, and quasi-steady phases—as well as the characteristics of the thermal structures during these phases. The results further show that, for the parameters investigated, accelerated flows may reduce heat transfer by up to 48% compared to the steady conditions, while decelerated flows may increase it by up to 42%. These findings suggest that unsteady periodic flow cycles, composed of alternating slow acceleration and rapid deceleration phases, could be designed to achieve greater heat transfer efficiency compared to steady flows.

Second, it is found that the experimental model for the temporal response of the Nusselt number is accurate only for high values of $|\alpha|$. For moderate or small $|\alpha|$, the model fails to capture the response accurately. To address this limitation, a new model based on a hyperbolic tangent function is proposed, which accurately describes the temporal response of the Nusselt number across a broad range of α values.

2. Materials and Methods

2.1. Governing Equations and Dimensionless Parameters

The hydrodynamically and thermally developed flow of an incompressible fluid through a straight, horizontal pipe of a constant cross-sectional area is analyzed (Figure 1). The fluid properties, including density ρ, kinematic viscosity ν, thermal conductivity κ, specific heat at constant pressure C_p, and thermal diffusivity λ_t, are assumed to be constant. The fluid motion is described by the continuity and momentum equations in cylindrical coordinates (r, θ, z). The mean bulk velocity $v_{b,m}$ of the acceleration or deceleration period (definition is given below), the pipe diameter D, the dynamic pressure $\rho v_{b,m}^2$, and the advective time scale $D/v_{b,m}$ are used as characteristic scales for velocity, length, pressure, and time, respectively. These considerations lead to the following non-dimensional forms of the momentum and continuity equations:

$$\frac{\partial \mathbf{v}}{\partial t} + (\mathbf{v} \cdot \nabla)\mathbf{v} = -\nabla p + \frac{1}{Re_m}\nabla^2 \mathbf{v}, \tag{1}$$

$$\nabla \cdot \mathbf{v} = 0, \tag{2}$$

where $\mathbf{v} = (v_r, v_\theta, v_z)$ represents the velocity field in cylindrical coordinates, t denotes time, p is the non-dimensional pressure, and

$$Re_m = \frac{v_{b,m} D}{\nu}, \tag{3}$$

is the mean Reynolds number.

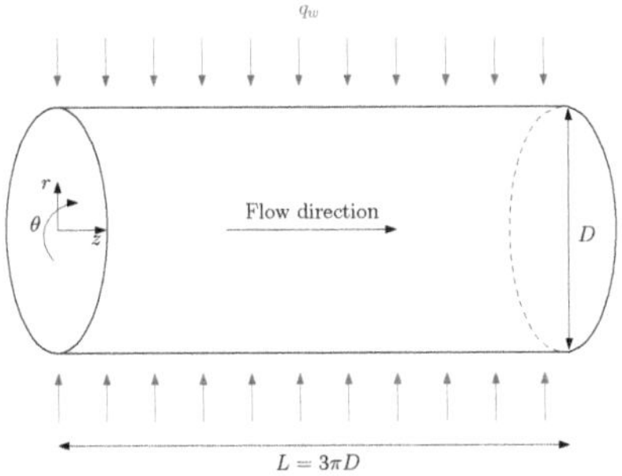

Figure 1. Schematic of the pipe flow configuration and the coordinate system used in the simulations. A constant and uniform heat flux per unit area, q_w, is applied along the pipe surface, as indicated by the red arrows.

Periodic boundary conditions are applied in the axial and azimuthal directions, whereas no-slip conditions at the pipe wall and regularity conditions at the axis are imposed in the radial direction.

This study examines flows that are uniformly accelerated or decelerated. To model this behavior, the non-dimensional bulk velocity $v_b(t)$ is updated at each time step according to the equation

$$v_b(t+\delta t) = v_b(t) + \alpha \delta t, \tag{4}$$

where δt is the time step size, and α represents the non-dimensional rate of acceleration or deceleration, defined as

$$\alpha = \frac{dv_b}{dt}, \tag{5}$$

The updated bulk velocity is enforced using the equation

$$v_b(t+\delta_t) = \frac{1}{A}\int v_z dA, \tag{6}$$

where A denotes the cross-sectional area of the pipe. The variation in the bulk velocity implies that the Reynolds number continuously changes during flow acceleration or deceleration. The characteristic Reynolds number in these cases is calculated using the mean bulk velocity, defined as $v_{b,m} = \frac{v_{b,init}+v_{b,end}}{2}$, where $v_{b,init}$ and $v_{b,end}$ indicate the bulk velocity at the beginning and end of the acceleration or deceleration phase.

The external surface of the pipe is subjected to a constant and uniform heat flux per unit area, denoted by q_w. In this analysis, the effects of gravitational buoyancy are neglected, which allows us to treat the temperature T as a passive scalar. Viscous dissipation and internal heat generation are also neglected. Consequently, the temporal evolution of T is governed by the advection–diffusion equation, given in its dimensional form by

$$\frac{\partial T}{\partial t} + \mathbf{v}\cdot\nabla T = \kappa \nabla^2 T. \tag{7}$$

Fluid properties are evaluated at the mean bulk temperature, denoted as T_b, which is defined as the volumetric flow rate weighted average temperature across the cross-sectional area of the pipe [13]:

$$T_b = \frac{\int_A \langle v_z\rangle^t \langle T\rangle^t dA}{\int_A \langle v_z\rangle^t dA}, \tag{8}$$

where $\langle . \rangle^t$ denotes time averaging. An energy balance conducted over a thin section of the pipe reveals a linear axial variation in T_b, characterized by the following rate of change:

$$\frac{dT_b}{dz} = \frac{4q_w}{\rho C_p v_{b,m} D}. \tag{9}$$

This scenario prevents the use of periodic boundary conditions in the axial direction. In line with previous studies [14–16], this limitation is addressed by replacing temperature variable T with the dimensionless temperature difference $\phi = \frac{T_b(z)-T(r,\theta,z,t)}{T_{ref}}$, where the reference temperature is defined as $T_{ref} = \frac{q_w}{\rho C_p v_{b,m}}$. This modification eliminates the axial temperature gradient $\frac{d\langle\phi\rangle^t}{dz} = 0$, thus permitting the use of periodic boundary conditions.

The reformulated equation, expressed in non-dimensional terms using the previously defined scales, is

$$\frac{\partial \phi}{\partial t} + \mathbf{v}\cdot\nabla\phi - 4v_z = \frac{1}{Re_m Pr}\nabla^2\phi, \tag{10}$$

where Pr is the Prandtl number, defined as

$$Pr = \frac{\nu}{\lambda_t}, \tag{11}$$

Periodic boundary conditions are used in the axial and azimuthal directions, with regularity conditions at the pipe axis and a prescribed heat flux, often termed the isoflux condition [14], applied at the pipe wall. The isoflux condition is expressed in non-dimensional form as

$$\left.\frac{\partial \phi}{\partial r}\right|_{r=1/2} = -Re_m Pr. \tag{12}$$

An additional condition is required to ensure the uniqueness of the solution for Equation (10) [14]. It is imposed that the volumetric flow rate weighted average of ϕ over the entire pipe volume must be zero:

$$\int_V \phi v_z \, dV = 0. \tag{13}$$

To quantify convective heat transfer in accelerated or decelerated flows, the instantaneous Nusselt number is employed, which measures the relative importance between convective and conductive heat transport in the fluid:

$$Nu(t) = \frac{h(t)D}{\kappa} = \frac{q_w D}{\kappa \langle (T_w(t,\theta,z) - T_b(z) \rangle^{\theta,z}}, \tag{14}$$

where T_w is the wall temperature, and $\langle . \rangle^{\theta,z}$ denotes averaging over the axial and azimuthal directions. With the non-dimensionalization carried out in this study, the instantaneous Nusselt number is expressed as

$$Nu(t) = -\frac{Re_m Pr}{\langle \phi_w(t,\theta,z) \rangle^{\theta,z}}. \tag{15}$$

Table 1 provides a summary of the dimensionless numbers that arise in the mathematical formulation of the problem, distinguishing between the control parameters (input parameters) and those derived from the simulation results (output parameters). For the control parameters, the values used in this study are also presented.

Table 1. Summary of the dimensionless numbers arising in the formulation of the problem.

Dimensionless Number	Symbol	Equation	Character	Value/s
Mean Reynolds number	Re_m	(3)	Input parameter	6400
Acceleration/Deceleration rate	α	(5)	Input parameter	$0.0015 \leq \lvert\alpha\rvert \leq 2$
Prandtl number	Pr	(11)	Input parameter	0.7
Nusselt number	Nu	(14)	Output parameter	-

2.2. Methodology and Numerical Code

The results presented in this paper were obtained from direct numerical simulations of the equations and boundary conditions outlined in Section 2.1. These simulations were performed using the open-source code NSPipeFlow [17], which has been recently extended to support non-isothermal flow simulations. The updated version of the code has been validated against previously published data in [14,16]. This enhanced version of the code is made publicly available in conjunction with this paper and is accessible in the repository [18].

The spatial discretization of the flow variables is performed using eighth-order central finite differences on a Gauss–Lobatto–Chebyshev grid in the radial direction, combined with Fourier–Galerkin expansions in the two homogeneous directions, θ and z. The Fourier–Galerkin expansions for the dimensionless velocity, pressure, and temperature fields are given by

$$\mathbf{v}(r,\theta,z) = \sum_{l=-L}^{L} \sum_{n=-N}^{N} \hat{\mathbf{v}}(r,n,l) e^{i(n\theta + lk_z z)}, \tag{16}$$

$$p(r,\theta,z) = \sum_{l=-L}^{L} \sum_{n=-N}^{N} \hat{p}(r,n,l) e^{i(n\theta + lk_z z)}, \tag{17}$$

$$\phi(r,\theta,z) = \sum_{l=-L}^{L} \sum_{n=-N}^{N} \hat{\phi}(r,n,l) e^{i(n\theta + lk_z z)}. \tag{18}$$

Here, n and l represent the Fourier mode numbers in the azimuthal and axial directions, respectively, and k_z is the axial wavenumber, which defines the axial length of the computational domain as $L_z = 2\pi/k_z$. The coefficients $\hat{\mathbf{v}}(r,l,n)$, $\hat{p}(r,l,n)$, and $\hat{\phi}(r,l,n)$ are complex spectral coefficients. The values of N and L specify the spectral resolution in the θ and z directions, respectively.

Substituting these expansions into Equations (1) and (10) yields a set of $(2N+1) \times (2L+1)$ independent equations, each associated with a specific (n,l) pair. Solving this system enables the determination of the spectral coefficients. The time integration of these equations is carried out using a second-order accurate predictor–corrector scheme based on the Crank–Nicolson method [19]. To facilitate understanding of this algorithm, it is useful to define $N_{\hat{\mathbf{v}}} = -(\hat{\mathbf{v}} \cdot \nabla)\hat{\mathbf{v}}$ y $N_{\hat{\phi}} = -(\hat{\mathbf{v}} \cdot \nabla)\hat{\phi} + 4\hat{v}_z$ and to rewrite Equations (1) and (10) as

$$(\frac{\partial}{\partial_t} - \frac{1}{Re_m}\nabla^2)\hat{\mathbf{v}} = -\nabla\hat{p} + N_{\hat{\mathbf{v}}}, \tag{19}$$

$$(\frac{\partial}{\partial_t} - \frac{1}{PrRe_m}\nabla^2)\hat{\phi} = N_{\hat{\phi}}. \tag{20}$$

Additionally, a pressure Poisson equation must be included, which is obtained by taking the divergence of Equation (19), along with the incompressibility condition

$$\nabla^2 \hat{p} = \nabla \cdot N_{\hat{\mathbf{v}}}. \tag{21}$$

In all these equations, the hat symbol indicates that the variables are spectral coefficients. The predictor step provides the initial estimates of the velocity and temperature fields at time step $q+1$ using data from time step q, and is formulated as

$$\nabla^2 \hat{p}_1^{q+1} = \nabla \cdot N_{\hat{\mathbf{v}}}^q, \tag{22}$$

$$(\frac{1}{\delta_t} - \frac{c}{Re_m}\nabla^2)\hat{\mathbf{v}}_1^{q+1} = -\nabla\hat{p}_1^{q+1} + N_{\hat{\mathbf{v}}}^q + (\frac{1}{\delta_t} - \frac{(1-c)}{Re_m}\nabla^2)\hat{\mathbf{v}}^q, \tag{23}$$

$$(\frac{1}{\delta_t} - \frac{c}{PrRe_m}\nabla^2)\hat{\phi}_1^{q+1} = N_{\hat{\phi}}^q + (\frac{1}{\delta_t} - \frac{(1-c)}{PrRe_m}\nabla^2)\hat{\phi}^q, \tag{24}$$

where δ_t is the time step size, and c is a constant that sets the implicitness of the scheme (set to 0.5 in our simulations). These initial estimates, $\hat{\mathbf{v}}_1^{q+1}$ and $\hat{\phi}_1^{q+1}$, are then iteratively refined through a correction process. During each iteration, the non-linear terms are updated, and the velocity and temperature fields are refined by solving

$$\nabla^2 \hat{p}_{j+1}^{q+1} = \nabla \cdot N_{\hat{\mathbf{v}}_j}^{q+1}, \tag{25}$$

$$(\frac{1}{\delta_t} - \frac{c}{Re_m}\nabla^2)\hat{\mathbf{v}}_{j+1}^{q+1} = -\nabla\hat{p}_{j+1}^{q+1} + cN_{\hat{\mathbf{v}}_j}^{q+1} + (1-c)N_{\hat{\mathbf{v}}}^q + (\frac{1}{\delta_t} - \frac{(1-c)}{Re_m}\nabla^2)\hat{\mathbf{v}}^q, \tag{26}$$

$$(\frac{1}{\delta_t} - \frac{c}{PrRe_m}\nabla^2)\hat{\phi}_{j+1}^{q+1} = cN_{\hat{\phi}_j}^{q+1} + (1-c)N_{\hat{\phi}}^q + (\frac{1}{\delta_t} - \frac{(1-c)}{PrRe_m}\nabla^2)\hat{\phi}^q, \tag{27}$$

where $j = 1, 2, \ldots$

The iteration terminates once $\|\hat{\mathbf{v}}_{j+1}^{q+1} - \hat{\mathbf{v}}_{j}^{q+1}\| \leq 10^{-6}$ and $\|\hat{\phi}_{j+1}^{q+1} - \hat{\phi}_{j}^{q+1}\| \leq 10^{-6}$, with convergence typically achieved after one corrector iteration. The additional cost of evaluating advective terms twice per time step is offset by the larger δt permitted by this scheme compared to other conventional methods.

To solve the pressure Poisson Equation (21), a homogeneous Neumann boundary condition, $\frac{\partial \hat{p}}{\partial_r} = 0$, is used at the pipe wall. Consequently, the velocity field obtained from (19) does not satisfy the divergence-free condition. This condition is subsequently enforced through influence matrices, a technique that ensures machine-level accuracy (typically of the order 10^{-16}) and avoids the need for artificial pressure boundary conditions.

The code employs a hybrid MPI-OpenMP approach for parallelization, enabling efficient scaling across thousands of processors. For further details about the parallelization strategy and code functionalities, the reader is referred to [17] and the references therein.

All results presented in this article correspond to uniformly accelerated or decelerated flows, where the initial and final Reynolds numbers are $Re_{init} = 3200$ and $Re_{end} = 9600$, respectively, for accelerations, and vice versa for decelerations. The mean Reynolds number in all cases is therefore $Re_m = 6400$. Within this range of Reynolds numbers, the flow is always turbulent under constant flow rate conditions. Figure 2 displays two examples of the temporal evolution of the instantaneous Reynolds number, $Re(t) = \frac{v_b(t)D}{\nu}$. For accelerated flows (Figure 2a), the instantaneous Reynolds number increases linearly from $Re = 3200$ to $Re = 9600$. A steady phase is then simulated, where the flow rate remains unchanged to monitor the stabilization of flow characteristics at $Re = 9600$. Similarly, for decelerated flows (Figure 2b), the instantaneous Reynolds number decreases linearly from $Re = 9600$ to $Re = 3200$, followed by a steady phase to examine stabilization at the lower Reynolds number. In all cases, Pr is set to 0.7. The initial conditions for these simulations are calculated from constant-flow rate simulations at $Re = 3200$ and $Re = 9600$.

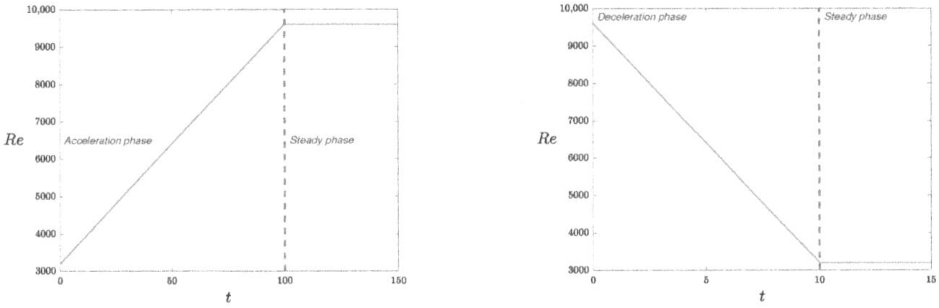

(**a**) (**b**)

Figure 2. Variation of the instantaneous Reynolds number with time in simulations, where (**a**) the flow is uniformly accelerated with $\alpha = 0.01$ from $Re_{init} = 3200$ to $Re_{end} = 9600$, followed by a steady phase, and (**b**) the flow is uniformly decelerated with $\alpha = -0.1$ from $Re_{init} = 9600$ to $Re_{end} = 3200$, followed by a steady phase.

To examine how acceleration or deceleration rates affect convective heat transfer, simulations were conducted with $|\alpha|$ values ranging from 0.0015 to 2.

The simulations were carried out in a pipe of an axial length $3\pi D$, using 128 radial nodes, 121 azimuthal Fourier modes, and 400 axial Fourier modes. To confirm the resolution adequacy, additional simulations were performed using twice the number of radial nodes and 1.5 times the Fourier modes in both the azimuthal and axial directions. These tests revealed no significant quantitative differences, validating the initial grid size. The time step size was set to $\delta_t = 5 \times 10^{-3}$ for $|\alpha| < 0.01$ and $\delta_t = 10^{-3}$ for $|\alpha| \geq 0.01$. All simulations were conducted on the Picasso supercomputer at the University of Málaga using 128 processors per simulation, resulting in durations ranging from 3 to 6 days depending on the value of α.

3. Results

3.1. Temporal Variation in the Nusselt Number in Uniformly Accelerated Flows

This section examines the behavior of convective heat transfer in a uniformly accelerated flow. Figure 3a illustrates the temporal evolution of instantaneous Nusselt number Nu (solid black line) at a moderate acceleration rate of $\alpha = 0.02$. It also presents the corresponding quasi-steady Nusselt number values obtained from the empirical Gnielinski correlation (red dashed line). Three distinct phases can be identified in the temporal variation in Nu. In the initial phase (Phase 1), which lasts up to $t \approx 27$, Nu remains nearly unchanged. This is followed by a growth phase (Phase 2), which is characterized by three sub-stages with different growth rates: a slow increase from $t \approx 27$ to $t \approx 35$, a more rapid increase from $t \approx 35$ to $t \approx 50$, and finally, a gradual approach to the quasi-steady value, which is reached around $t \approx 61$. In the last phase (Phase 3), Nu fluctuates around the quasi-steady value.

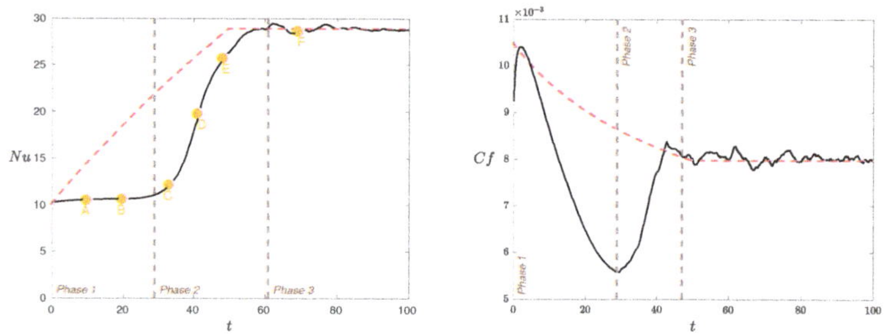

(a) (b)

Figure 3. Temporal variation in Nusselt number Nu (**a**) and friction coefficient c_f (**b**) in a uniformly accelerated flow with a moderate acceleration rate, $\alpha = 0.02$. The red dashed lines represent the corresponding quasi-steady values, calculated using the Gnielinski correlation for Nu and the Blasius formula for c_f. The brown vertical dashed lines delineate the distinct phases, each characterized by different behaviors. The points in the left panel correspond to the time instants for which flow patterns are shown in Figure 4.

The qualitative behavior of the Nu response shown in Figure 3a is in agreement with experimental observations [11,12], even though those studies were conducted at higher acceleration rates. It is also consistent with the established descriptions of turbulence behavior in unsteady flows [20,21]. These descriptions propose that the response of turbulence to changes in the mean velocity occurs in three stages.

The initial stage, often referred to as the delay phase, corresponds to Phase 1 in Figure 3a. This phase is characterized by the phenomenon of frozen turbulence, where turbulent stresses respond with a delay to changes in mean velocity. Due to this delay, the intensity of the turbulent stresses remains largely unchanged despite the variation in the instantaneous Re. Consequently, the convective heat transfer carried by these stresses remains nearly constant, resulting in the almost invariant Nu observed during this initial stage.

Once the turbulent fluctuations respond to the velocity change, the turbulence intensity increases (second stage), leading to the growth in Nu observed in Phase 2. Eventually, the turbulence intensity stabilizes at the quasi-steady condition (third stage), similar to how Nu stabilizes in Phase 3. These latter two stages are typically referred to as the recovery stage and quasi-steady stage, respectively.

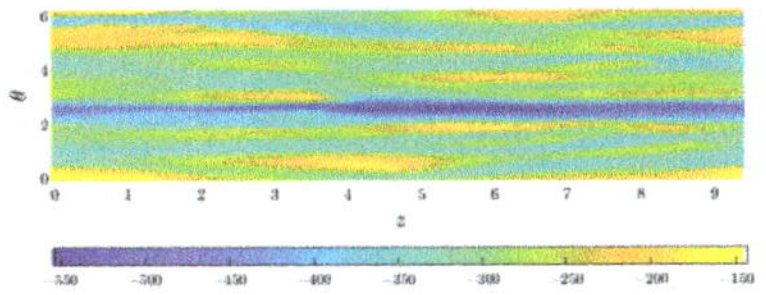

(a) ϕ at $t = 10.0$ (point A)

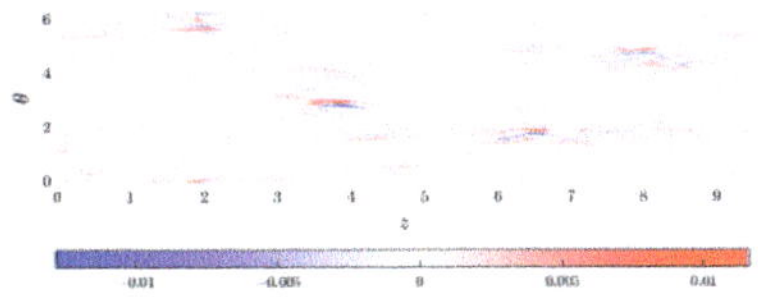

(b) v_r at $t = 10.0$ (point A)

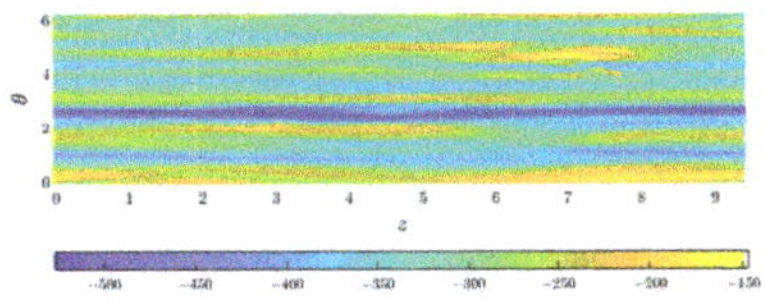

(c) ϕ at $t = 20.0$ (point B)

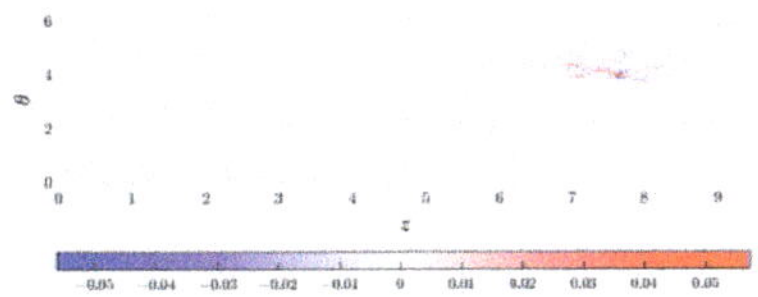

(d) v_r at $t = 20.0$ (point B)

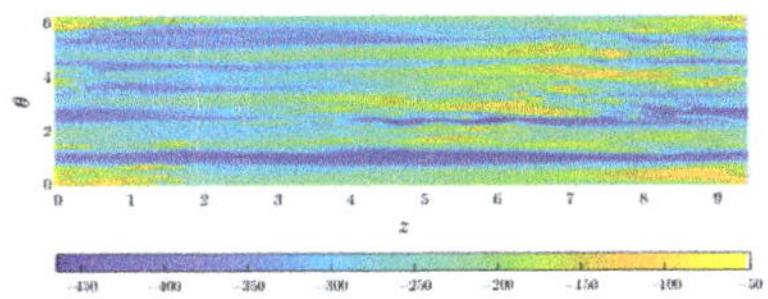

(e) ϕ at $t = 33.5$ (point C)

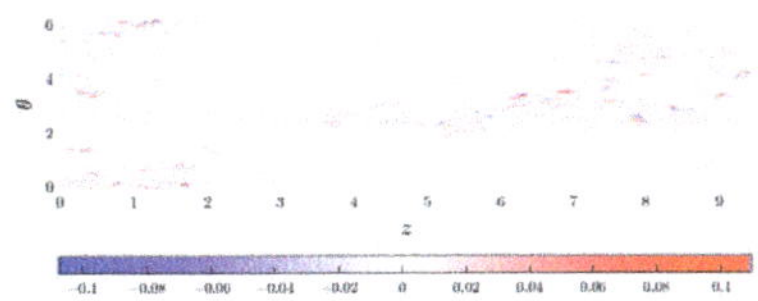

(f) v_r at $t = 33.5$ (point C)

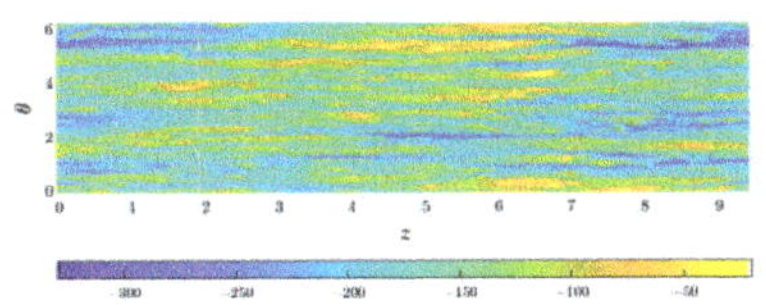

(g) ϕ at $t = 41.5$ (point D)

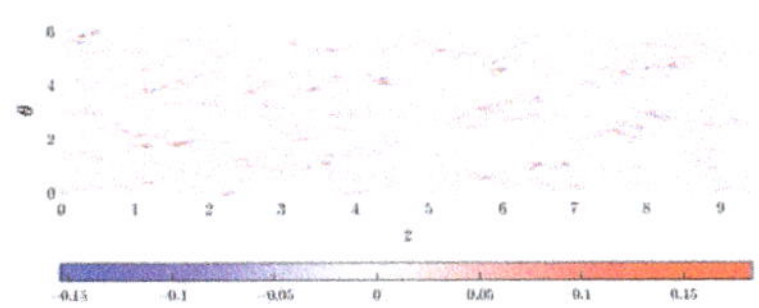

(h) v_r at $t = 41.5$ (point D)

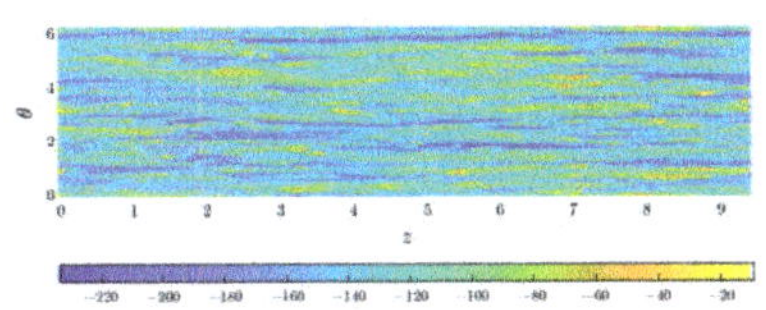

(i) ϕ at $t = 48.5$ (point E)

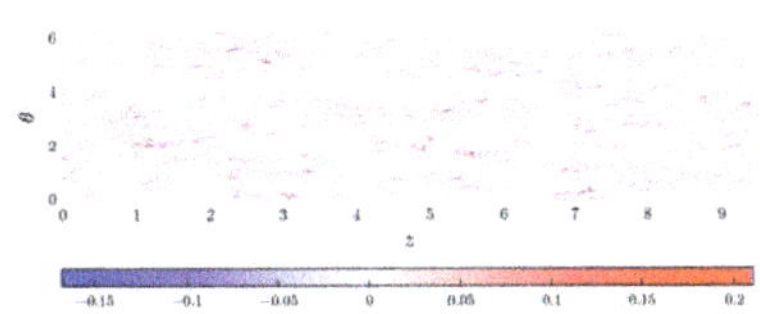

(j) v_r at $t = 48.5$ (point E)

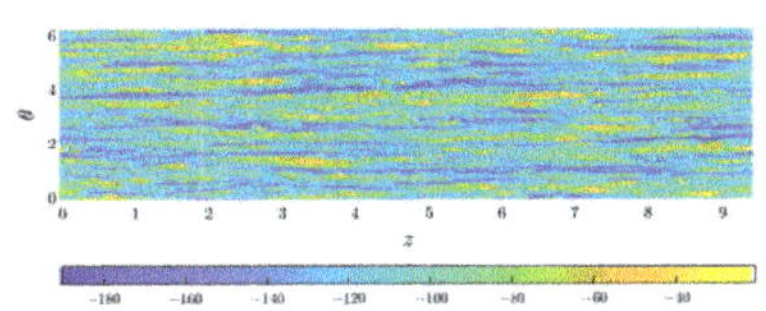

(k) ϕ at $t = 71.5$ (point F)

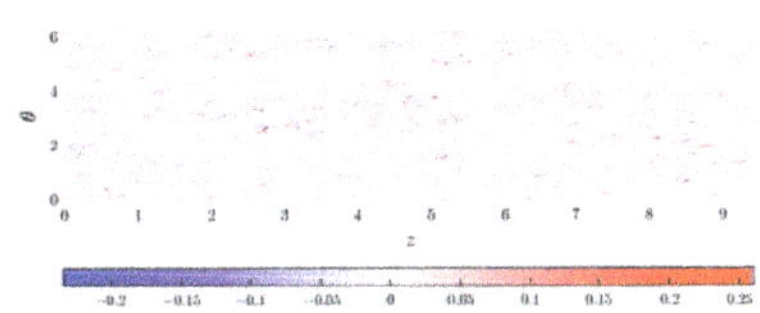

(l) v_r at $t = 71.5$ (point F)

Figure 4. Instantaneous snapshots of the temperature difference with respect to bulk temperature ϕ (**left panels**), and radial velocity v_r (**right panels**), illustrating the evolution of these structures in the near-wall region under uniform flow acceleration with $\alpha = 0.02$. The structures are depicted in a cylindrical section (z, θ) at a radial location of $r/D = 0.49$. The flow direction is from left to right. From top to bottom, each row corresponds to the structures at points A to F as denoted in Figure 3a.

A key result of the delayed response of convective heat transport to changes in the mean velocity is that, during acceleration, the instantaneous Nu is always less than or equal to the quasi-steady Nu. This delay causes the average Nu for a uniformly accelerated flow to be lower than that of a steady flow at the mean Reynolds number (in this study, $Re_m = 6400$). For the specific case shown in Figure 3a, the average Nu is 13.7, while the Nu for a steady flow at $Re = 6400$ is 20.32, indicating a 32.6% reduction from the steady value. A detailed quantitative study on the reduction or increase in Nu relative to the steady case, as a function of the α values, is provided in Section 3.4.

Comparing the temporal response of Nu with that of the friction coefficient c_f for the same case, shown in Figure 3, provides useful insights. The friction coefficient is calculated using the Fanning equation $c_f(t) = \frac{\tau_w(t)}{2v_b(t)^2}$, where $\tau_w(t)$ denotes the instantaneous wall shear stress, and $v_b(t)$ is the instantaneous bulk velocity. The figure also includes quasi-steady values (red dashed line), which, for this range of Re values, are well approximated by the empirical Blasius formula $c_f(t) = 0.079Re(t)^{-0.25}$. The temporal variation in c_f observed in the simulation qualitatively matches the previous findings [22], showing the three stages of the turbulence response in unsteady flows: delay, recovery, and quasi-steady phases. However, two important differences are noted between the temporal responses of Nu and c_f.

The first difference occurs during the initial delay phase. Here, c_f initially shows a slight increase above the quasi-steady value caused by the high inertia needed to start accelerating the flow. This is followed by a significant decrease, reaching values approximately 40% lower than the quasi-steady case. This behavior contrasts with Nu, which remains constant during this phase. This observation deviates from the widely accepted Colburn analogy [23], which posits a proportional relationship between c_f and Nu. While this analogy has been extensively validated in steady flows, the comparison in Figure 3 suggests that the relationship between these two quantities is more complex in unsteady flows.

The second difference is observed during the recovery phase. In this stage, c_f rapidly increases due to the rise in turbulent stresses, surpassing the quasi-steady value and reaching a relative maximum at $t \approx 43$. Subsequently, c_f decreases and stabilizes around the steady value at $t \approx 48$. In contrast, the growth rate of Nu is much more gradual, resulting in a considerably longer recovery phase compared to c_f.

An important aspect investigated in the experiments of [11,12] is the spatiotemporal characteristics of heat transfer in unsteady flows. Specifically, they examined the evolution of the spatial distribution of the instantaneous convective heat transfer coefficient near the pipe wall, as the flow was accelerated or decelerated. To compare their observations with the simulation results, Figure 4 illustrates the spatial distribution of the temperature difference relative to the bulk temperature, ϕ (left panels), near the pipe wall at various time instants during acceleration. Notably, this quantity is proportional to the convective heat transfer coefficient, and therefore, its spatiotemporal characteristics are analogous.

In the color scale used to depict ϕ structures, dark blue represents regions of higher temperature, while yellow indicates areas of lower temperature within the section shown. Note that negative values of ϕ indicate a temperature higher than the bulk temperature, which is typically observed near the wall. To aid in the interpretation of the physical processes driving the evolution of these thermal structures, the evolution of the radial velocity, v_r (right panels), is also shown in Figure 4. The color maps for v_r employ a blue-to-red scale, where negative values (blue) correspond to radial flow toward the pipe center, and positive values (red) correspond to radial flow toward the wall.

During the early delay phase, ϕ structures appear as elongated streaks aligned with the flow direction (Figure 4a). These streaks show alternating regions of high and low temperature in the azimuthal direction and have slight modulations that appear to be associated with localized areas of significant radial velocity (Figure 4b). These areas are remnants of the initial steady turbulent state. As the flow accelerates, these regions do not regenerate and gradually dissipate. This characteristic is evident in Figure 4d, where significant radial velocity gradients are only observed in a small area near the outlet section of the pipe.

Without vortices to redistribute momentum and heat, the streaky structures of ϕ lose the weak modulation observed in the early stages of the acceleration, becoming almost parallel and more elongated, often spanning the entire computational domain (Figure 4c). It is important to note that although some structures span the entire pipe length, suggesting that the axial domain used in the simulations may be insufficient to capture the full physics of the problem, additional simulations with extended pipe lengths were conducted and revealed no significant differences from the results obtained with the present configuration.

At the beginning of the recovery phase (point C in Figure 3a), regions of significant radial velocity begin to emerge across a large portion of the section (Figure 4f). The heat transport associated with these fluctuations causes the streaky structures to start oscillating and breaking down into smaller structures (Figure 4e). In areas where the radial velocity remains near zero, the ϕ structures continue to form elongated streaks aligned with the flow direction.

As the recovery phase progresses, and the Nusselt number growth rate increases (point D in Figure 3a), radial velocity structures have spread almost entirely along the pipe's axial length (Figure 4h). Consequently, the elongated streaks from earlier moments transform into shorter streaks that eventually break down into structures with varied spatial scales (see Figure 4g,i). Toward the end of the recovery phase, the ϕ (Figure 4i) and v_r (Figure 4j) structures become nearly identical to those observed in the steady case (Figure 4k and Figure 4l, respectively).

The magnitude of ϕ substantially decreases during the recovery phase, indicating that as the flow becomes more turbulent, mixing is enhanced near the wall, leading to temperatures closer to the bulk temperature. A smaller value of ϕ corresponds to a higher Nu, consistent with the evolution of this parameter shown in Figure 3a. Conversely, the magnitude of v_r increases during the recovery phase, rising from very low values in the delay phase (often referred to as the relaminarization phase due to the low fluctuation intensity) to the typical levels seen in fully developed turbulent flow.

The evolution of the ϕ structures depicted in this figure closely resembles the instantaneous convective heat transfer coefficient patterns reported by Nakamura et al. (see Figure 4 in [12]) for experiments in a similar Reynolds number range, further confirming the high fidelity of the simulations in reproducing the experimental results.

3.2. Temporal Variation in the Nusselt Number in Uniformly Decelerated Flows

This section examines the evolution of the Nusselt number in uniformly decelerated flows. Figure 5a illustrates the temporal response of Nu for a simulation with a deceleration rate of $\alpha = -0.02$, matching the magnitude used for the uniformly accelerated case in Section 3.1. The three phases identified for uniformly accelerated flows are also present in decelerated flows.

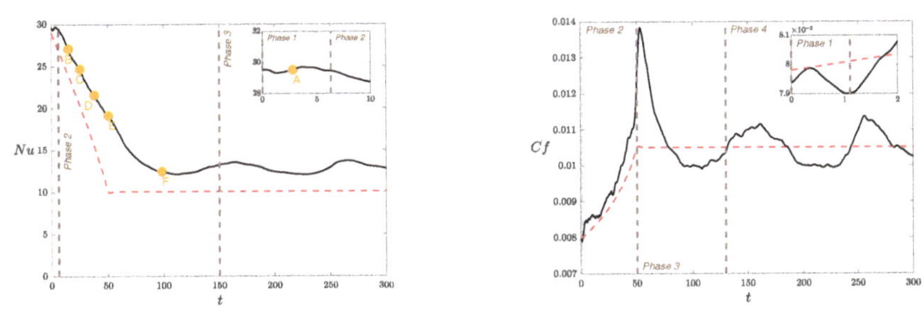

(a) (b)

Figure 5. Temporal variation in Nusselt number Nu (**a**) and friction coefficient c_f (**b**) in a uniformly decelerated flow with a moderate acceleration rate, $\alpha = -0.02$. The red dashed lines represent the corresponding quasi-steady values, calculated using the Gnielinski correlation for Nu and the Blasius formula for c_f. The brown vertical dashed lines delineate the distinct phases, each characterized by different behaviors. The points in the left panel correspond to the time instants for which flow patterns are shown in Figure 6.

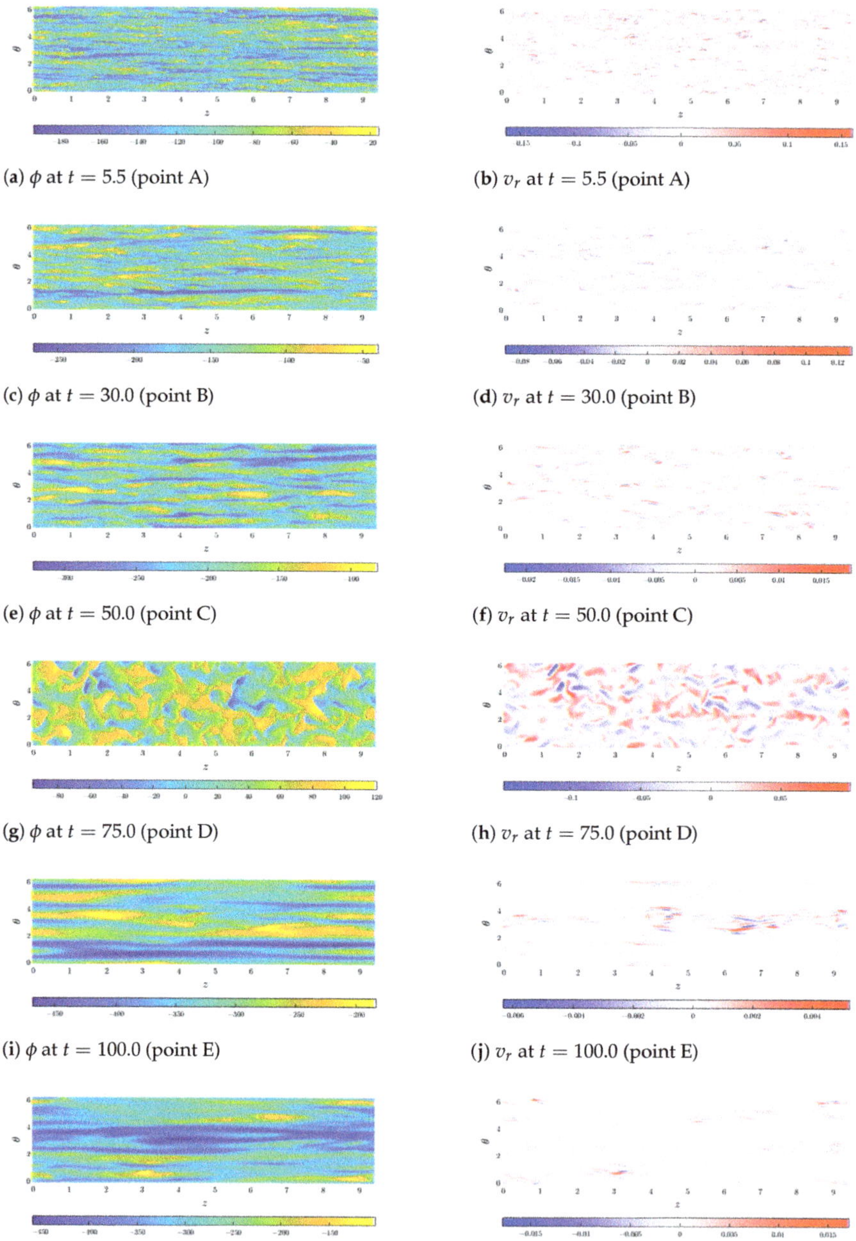

(**a**) ϕ at $t = 5.5$ (point A) (**b**) v_r at $t = 5.5$ (point A)

(**c**) ϕ at $t = 30.0$ (point B) (**d**) v_r at $t = 30.0$ (point B)

(**e**) ϕ at $t = 50.0$ (point C) (**f**) v_r at $t = 50.0$ (point C)

(**g**) ϕ at $t = 75.0$ (point D) (**h**) v_r at $t = 75.0$ (point D)

(**i**) ϕ at $t = 100.0$ (point E) (**j**) v_r at $t = 100.0$ (point E)

(**k**) ϕ at $t = 196.0$ (point F) (**l**) v_r at $t = 196.0$ (point F)

Figure 6. Instantaneous snapshots of the temperature difference with respect to the bulk temperature, ϕ (**left panels**), and the radial velocity, v_r (**right panels**), illustrating the evolution of these structures in the near-wall region under uniform flow deceleration with $\alpha = -0.02$. The structures are depicted in a cylindrical section (z, θ) at a radial location of $r/D = 0.49$. The flow direction is from left to right. From top to bottom, each row corresponds to the structures at points A to F as denoted in Figure 5a.

Initially, there is a delay phase (Phase 1), during which Nu remains approximately constant despite a decrease in instantaneous Re (see inset in the figure). This phase is significantly shorter than in the uniformly accelerated case. Here, the delay phase extends to $t \approx 6$, accounting for 12% of the deceleration period, whereas it covered nearly 50% of the acceleration period in the accelerated flow.

Following the delay phase, the recovery phase (Phase 2) begins, during which Nu decreases from its initial value to levels consistent with the final condition. Unlike the recovery phase in accelerated flows, where the intensity of turbulent fluctuations increases towards the quasi-steady level, in decelerated flows, the intensity of these fluctuations decreases to match the lower mean flow velocity. However, this decrease occurs more slowly than in the quasi-steady case (dashed red line), leading to greater convective heat transport and consequently higher Nu compared to the quasi-steady case. This implies an increase in the intensity of turbulent fluctuations during the initial part of the recovery phase.

The exact cause of this increase is not entirely clear, but it may be associated with the presence of inflection points in the velocity profile, a characteristic feature of decelerated flows. These inflection points can induce instantaneous linear instabilities [24,25], potentially providing the energy needed for the transient increase in turbulence intensity.

The decrease in Nu continues until $t \approx 110$, extending well beyond the duration of the deceleration period. This is followed by a slight increase, leading to the quasi-steady phase (Phase 3), during which Nu oscillates slightly around a steady value. Notably, there is an offset between this steady value and the quasi-steady value predicted by the Gnielinski correlation. This offset is expected, as the correlation is known to deviate from the experimental values when Re approaches the transitional regime. As in the uniformly accelerated case, the three phases observed in the Nu response to deceleration are consistent with the experimental observations in [11,12].

In contrast to the acceleration case, Nu values during deceleration are always above or equal to those of the quasi-steady case, resulting in a net increase in heat transfer compared to the steady case when the flow is driven at the mean Re. For this specific case, the average Nu during deceleration is 24.68, while, as noted earlier, Nu corresponding to the steady case for Re = 6400 is 20.32. This leads to a net increase in Nu of 21.45%.

A comparison of the temporal evolution of Nu and c_f throughout the deceleration phase (Figure 5b) reveals significant differences in their respective responses. The temporal response of c_f can be divided into four distinct stages.

In the initial phase, c_f undergoes a slight decrease due to the adverse pressure gradient applied to decelerate the flow. This phase is brief, lasting only until $t \approx 1$, which is six times shorter than the delay phase observed in the temporal response of Nu. Following this initial decrease, a second phase begins, characterized by a rapid recovery to values exceeding the quasi-steady level. During this phase, c_f follows the same trend as the quasi-steady value but its magnitude remains slightly higher. This behavior supports the hypothesis of a local instability that transiently increases turbulence levels during flow deceleration. The onset of this second phase could therefore be linked to the initiation of this instability.

The third phase starts at the end of the deceleration period ($t = 50$) and extends to $t \approx 140$. During this phase, c_f exhibits a pronounced overshoot above the quasi-steady value due to the significant inertia of the fluid. After reaching this maximum, c_f gradually decreases to values below the steady case before stabilizing.

In the fourth and final phase, c_f oscillates around the steady value. Notably, as in the case of uniformly accelerated flow, c_f reaches this final phase before Nu stabilizes.

As discussed in the previous section, the qualitative differences in some phases of the Nu and c_f temporal responses suggest that the physical mechanisms governing the instantaneous values of these parameters in unsteady flows may differ. This observation raises questions about the applicability of the Colburn analogy for unsteady-flow conditions.

The evolution of the ϕ structures near the wall during uniform deceleration (left panels of Figure 6) shows significant differences compared to the case of uniform acceleration depicted in Figure 4. As in Figure 4, the evolution of v_r is shown alongside the ϕ structures, using the same color palettes.

During the delay phase (illustrated in Figure 6a,b for $t \approx 5.5$), both the ϕ and v_r structures remain similar to the initial steady turbulent state. The thermal structures are primarily organized into streaks, alternating regions of high (blue) and low (yellow) temperatures in the azimuthal direction, which coexist with smaller structures.

Comparing the ϕ structures with the v_r distribution reveals that regions with smaller structures align with areas where the radial velocity is more pronounced. These regions are identified in Figure 6b as spatially localized regions with closely spaced high positive (dark red) and negative (dark blue) radial velocities in the azimuthal direction.

A significant change observed during the transition to the recovery phase is the elongation of the v_r structures (Figure 6d). Regarding the ϕ structures, fewer small structures are observed (Figure 6c), and the streaky structures exhibit several clear differences compared to the previous phase: a marked increase in both the axial length and azimuthal width of the structures, and the onset of a certain undulation. This undulation is consistent with the emergence of a secondary instability as previously speculated, which enhances turbulence levels and causes Nu to rise above the quasi-steady value.

As time progresses and the deceleration period nears its end, the width of the ϕ structures continues to grow, and their undulation becomes more pronounced due to fluctuations extracting energy from the secondary instability (Figure 6e). An increase in the magnitude of ϕ is also evident, consistent with the decrease in Nu that results from the diminishing intensity of turbulent fluctuations as the instantaneous Re decreases. This substantial reduction in turbulent fluctuation intensity is clearly visible in Figure 6f. Additionally, this figure shows that the distribution of v_r remains similar to that at the start of the recovery phase, though the azimuthal length of the structures has significantly increased.

The transition between the deceleration phase and the subsequent steady phase is marked by a clear change in the topology of the structures (Figure 6g,h). The elongated streaks observed in earlier stages are replaced by irregular structures with a large azimuthal length, similar to the "mottled structure" observed experimentally in [11,12]. This change likely results from streak collapse due to the local secondary instability during the recovery phase.

Notably, up to this point, the ϕ structures consistently displays negative values near the wall, indicating higher temperatures than the bulk temperature. However, Figure 6g shows that some thermal structures now have positive values, indicating temperatures lower than the average. This change indicates significant heat and momentum transport from the central part of the pipe, where the temperature is lower, to the wall, which is also consistent with the substantial increase in c_f relative to the steady value observed in Figure 5b during the third phase of the temporal response of this parameter. This increase in c_f is also consistent with the substantial rise in the magnitude of v_r observed in Figure 6h.

As Nu approaches the end of the recovery phase, the turbulent fluctuations arising from the secondary instability gradually dissipate, and the ϕ structures revert to streaks aligned with the flow direction but with a significantly larger azimuthal length than during the initial deceleration stages (Figure 6i). This feature is again consistent with the experimental observations in [11,12]. The evolution of the structures during this stage is similar to what occurs during the frozen turbulence phase when the flow accelerates. Initially, the intensity of turbulent fluctuations remains at very low levels for some time (Figure 6j), giving rise to ϕ streaks that extend axially across the entire computational domain, along with smaller streaks that emerge from the breakup of larger streaks in regions where v_r is significant. Eventually, the intensity of turbulent fluctuations increases to adapt to the final steady state (Figure 6l), and the thermal structures take on the characteristic distribution of a steady turbulent flow, exhibiting a pattern of streaks of various sizes alternating high and low temperatures in the azimuthal direction (Figure 6k).

3.3. Characterization of the Temporal Variation in the Nusselt Number as a Function of Acceleration or Deceleration Rate

This section examines the temporal characteristics of the Nu variation as a function of the acceleration or deceleration rate α and introduces a simple model that satisfactorily reproduces the Nu response across a wide range of α values.

Figure 7 presents the temporal evolution of Nu for uniformly accelerated flows, covering α values spanning three orders of magnitude. Two distinct behaviors emerge depending on the magnitude of α.

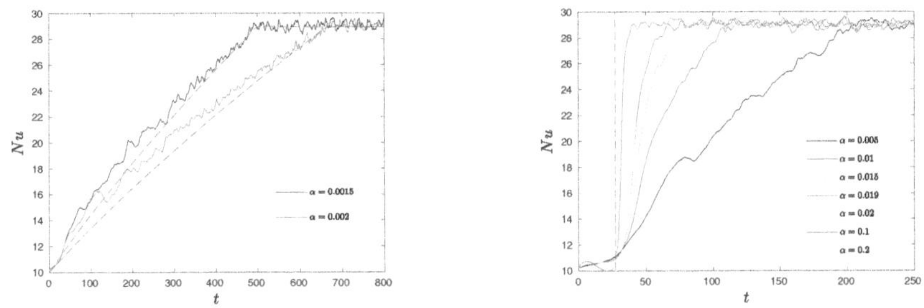

(a) (b)

Figure 7. Temporal response of the Nusselt number in uniformly accelerated flows as a function of the acceleration rate α. (**a**) Cases where $\alpha \leq 0.002$, showing the Nusselt number increasing in a quasi-steady manner. The red dashed lines represent the quasi-steady values of the Nusselt number calculated using the semi-empirical Gnielinski correlation. (**b**) Cases where $\alpha > 0.002$, with the evolution of the Nusselt number following the qualitative description provided in Section 3.1. The brown dashed line indicates the transition between the delay and recovery phases.

For very small values ($\alpha \leq 0.002$, Figure 7a), Nu increases quasi-steadily over time. The change in the mean flow velocity is slow enough for the turbulent fluctuations to adjust almost instantaneously to the evolving flow conditions. As a result, the Nu value corresponding to each instantaneous Re value closely matches that of a steady flow at the same Re. In these cases, the Gnielinski correlation (indicated by the red dashed lines in the figure) provides a good estimate of the Nu evolution. Initially, the correlation slightly underestimates Nu because the instantaneous Re is close to transitional values, where this semi-empirical correlation is known to be less accurate. However, as time progresses and the instantaneous Re moves further from the transitional regime, Nu converges with high precision to the value predicted by the Gnielinski correlation.

For $\alpha > 0.002$ (Figure 7b), the evolution of Nu follows the three phases described in Section 3.1. The delay phase (demarcated by the brown dashed line) lasts until $t \approx 27$ in all cases, demonstrating that its duration is independent of α. However, the range of Re values encompassed during this phase expands as α increases due to the more rapid change in mean velocity, which results in a higher Re by the end of the delay phase. When α exceeds 0.02, the transition time between the initial and final Re values becomes shorter than the delay phase, causing this phase to extend beyond the acceleration period. Despite this, the qualitative behavior of the Nu evolution is consistent with that observed at lower α values, with the notable exception that the increase in Nu and its approach to quasi-steady values occur while the flow is already being driven at a constant Re.

The most significant effect of increasing α is the faster growth in Nu during the recovery phase. As α increases, this increase becomes increasingly sharper until $\alpha \approx 0.1$. Beyond this point, further increases in α have minimal impact on the recovery phase, and the temporal evolution of Nu is practically identical in all cases as observed for $\alpha = 0.1$ and $\alpha = 0.2$.

The dependence of the Nu temporal response with α in uniformly decelerated flows, illustrated in Figure 8, reveals two significant differences compared to the uniformly accelerated case. The first is that, for low deceleration rates, no quasi-steady variation in Nu is observed. Even at the lowest deceleration rate considered ($\alpha = -0.0015$), shown in Figure 8a, the three phases described in Section 3.2 are still present. After the delay phase, which extends until $t \approx 10$ (see the inset in the figure), Nu decreases to values close to those predicted by the Gnielinski correlation but progressively deviates as time advances. This deviation can be attributed to two factors. First is the presence of a secondary instability that increases turbulence levels and convective heat transfer beyond what would exist in a quasi-steady state. Second, as the instantaneous Re approaches transitional values, the Gnielinski correlation becomes less accurate. The first factor explains the early-stage deviations, while the second factor accounts for deviations later in the deceleration and during the quasi-steady phase that follows.

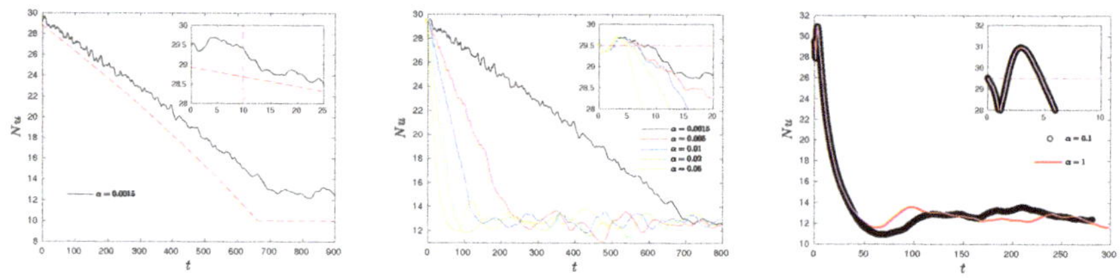

(a) (b) (c)

Figure 8. Temporal response of the Nusselt number in uniformly decelerated flows as a function of the deceleration rate, α. (**a**) The behavior for the lowest deceleration rate considered, $\alpha = -0.0015$, along with the quasi-steady Nusselt number values calculated using the semi-empirical Gnielinski correlation (red dashed line). (**b**) presents a comparison of several cases where $0.0015 \leq |\alpha| \leq 0.02$. (**c**) The response for very rapid decelerations, $|\alpha| \geq 0.04$. In all panels, an inset highlights the details of the initial delay phase.

The second notable difference is the dependence between the delay phase duration and α. As the magnitude of α increases, the delay phase shortens (see inset of Figure 8b). However, this trend does not hold across the entire range of α values studied. For rapid decelerations as shown in Figure 8c, the delay phase stabilizes at $t \approx 5$. The variation in the delay phase duration observed for $0.0015 \leq |\alpha| \leq 0.02$ may be linked to the onset of the secondary instability. As the magnitude of α increases, the instability sets in earlier, causing variations in the turbulent fluctuations level and the associated convective transport. As a result, Nu deviates from its initial value earlier. However, for rapid decelerations, the transition between the initial and final states occurs so quickly that the onset of instability is similar regardless of the value of α. This could explain why the duration of the delay phase becomes independent of α at higher deceleration rates.

Similar to accelerated flows, the Nu values during the recovery phase vary more sharply as the deceleration rate increases (Figure 8b), until reaching a limit at $\alpha = -0.04$. Beyond this threshold, further increases in α do not significantly affect the temporal response of Nu (Figure 8c).

The evolution of thermal structures during both acceleration and deceleration is qualitatively similar to the structures described in Sections 3.1 and 3.2. The exception is the quasi-steady cases for uniformly accelerated flows, where the thermal structures exhibit the characteristic pattern of turbulent flow: streaks of varying sizes coexisting with smaller structures that become finer as the instantaneous Re increases.

Nakamura et al. [12] propose a model to characterize the temporal variation in Nu in unsteady flows upon sudden acceleration (deceleration), assuming an exponential growth (decay) of Nu during the recovery phase. This model is based on two parameters: the delay phase duration Δt_d and a parameter τ, which controls the steepness of the exponential growth (decay). According to this model, the instantaneous Nu is given by the following piecewise function:

$$Nu(t) = \begin{cases} Nu_{init} & \text{if } t \leq \Delta t_d \\ Nu_{end} - (Nu_{end} - Nu_{init}) \exp\left(-\frac{t-\Delta t_d}{\tau}\right) & \text{if } t > \Delta t_d, \end{cases} \tag{28}$$

where Nu_{init} and Nu_{end} represent the Nu values corresponding to the initial and final Re values in steady-flow conditions. When applied to the simulation data for uniformly accelerated flows, this model accurately reproduces the Nu response for high acceleration rates (Figure 9a). However, for moderate α values (Figure 9b) and quasi-steady cases (Figure 9c), the model fails to adequately predict the Nu growth.

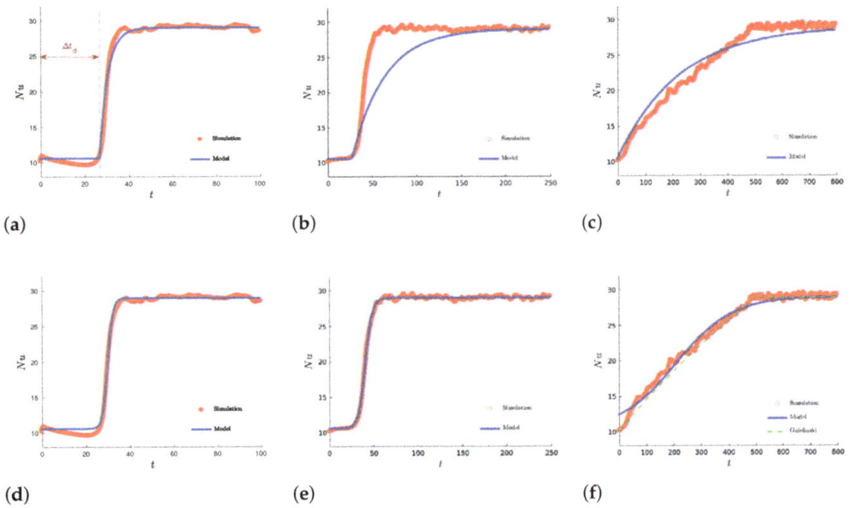

Figure 9. Characterization of the temporal response of the Nusselt number in uniformly accelerated flows. The upper panels illustrate the performance of the model proposed by Nakamura et al. [12] when fitted to our data. (**a**) Results for $\alpha = 1$, representing rapid accelerations; (**b**) data for $\alpha = 0.02$, corresponding to moderate acceleration rates; and (**c**) data for $\alpha = 0.002$, where the Nusselt number evolves in a quasi-steady manner. The lower panels demonstrate the performance of the model proposed in this study. For comparison, the same α values as in the upper panels are used: (**d**) $\alpha = 1$, (**e**) $\alpha = 0.02$, and (**f**) $\alpha = 0.002$.

To address this limitation, a new model is proposed, where the Nu growth is modeled using a hyperbolic tangent function. In this model, the temporal variation in Nu is expressed as

$$Nu(t) = 0.5(Nu_{init} + Nu_{end}) + 0.5(Nu_{end} - Nu_{init}) \tanh\left(\frac{t - t_{inf}}{s}\right). \tag{29}$$

This model also introduces two parameters: t_{inf}, which marks the inflection point of the Nu growth curve, and s, which controls the steepness of the curve, similar to τ in the previous model. As shown in the lower panels of Figure 9, the proposed model accurately estimates the Nu response across the entire range of α values. For high α values, the new model matches the accuracy of the exponential model (Figure 9d). However, unlike the exponential model, it also accurately predicts the Nu variation for moderate α values (Figure 9e).

Even for low α values, where Nu varies quasi-steadily, the proposed model provides a reasonable estimate, with only a slight overestimation during the initial phase. In quasi-steady cases, the Gnielinski correlation (shown as a green dashed line in Figure 9e) remains the most accurate predictor of Nu values.

The variation in the model parameters t_{inf} and s with α is presented in Figure 10. The parameter t_{inf}, shown in Figure 10a, decreases with increasing α and eventually stabilizes at an approximately constant value for $\alpha > 1$. This behavior is well described by an exponential function with three parameters (blue line in the figure):

$$t_{inf} = 0.2\alpha^{-1.1} + 29 \tag{30}$$

The variation in s, displayed in Figure 10b, exhibits two distinct phases. For low to moderate values of α (up to $\alpha \approx 0.02$), s decreases sharply as α increases. However, beyond this threshold ($\alpha > 0.02$), the decrease becomes much more gradual. The variation in s across the entire range of α is well approximated by the following function (again represented by the blue line in the figure):

$$s = 0.5(0.33\alpha^{-1.04} + 0.175\alpha^{-0.54} - 9.76) + 0.5(0.175\alpha^{-0.54} - 0.33\alpha^{-1.04} + 13.96)\tanh\left(\frac{\alpha - t_{inf}}{s}\right) \tag{31}$$

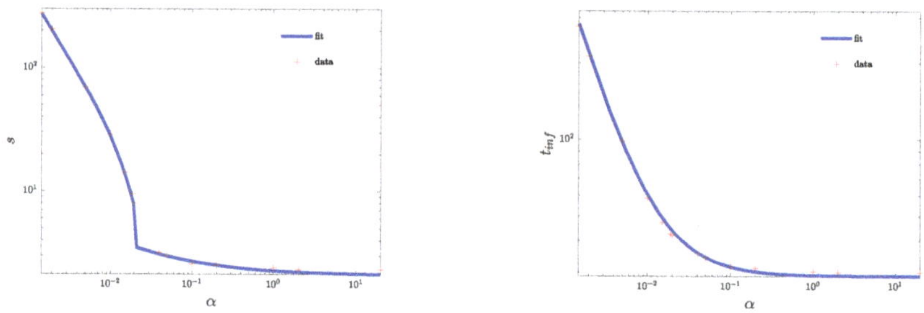

(a) (b)

Figure 10. Variation in the parameters t_{inf} (**a**) and s (**b**) as a function of the acceleration rate α in uniformly accelerated flows.

Similar conclusions can be drawn when these models are applied to characterize uniformly decelerated flow. The exponential model reasonably estimates the temporal response of Nu for high deceleration rates, but its accuracy decreases as the deceleration rate lowers. This is evident in the upper panels of Figure 11. In Figure 11a, which shows a high deceleration rate simulation, the model satisfactorily reproduces the instantaneous Nu values, except at the end of the recovery phase, where it overestimates the simulation results, and during the initial delay phase, where it predicts an average value and therefore fails to capture the oscillations observed during this phase.

For moderate decelerations (Figure 11b), the model not only overestimates Nu before the quasi-steady phase but also shows slight deviations during the early recovery phase. These deviations increase as the absolute value of α decreases as shown in Figure 11c.

Similar to the uniformly accelerated case, the hyperbolic tangent-based model proposed here satisfactorily estimates the temporal evolution of Nu across the entire range of α values. For high deceleration rates (Figure 11d), it is slightly less accurate than the exponential model, overestimating Nu during the final part of the recovery phase and slightly underestimating the average value during the delay phase. This underestimation persists for all α values. However, as the absolute value of α decreases, the proposed model captures the recovery phase much more accurately than the exponential model, significantly reducing the overestimation of the Nu values during the approach to the quasi-steady phase (Figure 11e,f).

The variation in the parameters t_{inf} and s with $|\alpha|$ follows a trend similar to that observed in uniformly accelerated flows. For t_{inf} (Figure 12a), a decrease is observed as $|\alpha|$ increases, which can be accurately fitted with a three-parameter exponential function:

$$t_{inf} = 0.51|\alpha|^{-1} + 14.91. \tag{32}$$

For parameter s (Figure 12b), two distinct phases are observed: a sharp decrease up to $|\alpha| \approx 0.15$, followed by a phase where s remains approximately constant, around 11.16. This behavior is well captured by the following expression:

$$s = 0.5(0.41|\alpha|^{-1} + 19.67) + 0.5(2.65 - 0.41|\alpha|^{-1}) \tanh\left(\frac{|\alpha| - t_{inf}}{s}\right). \tag{33}$$

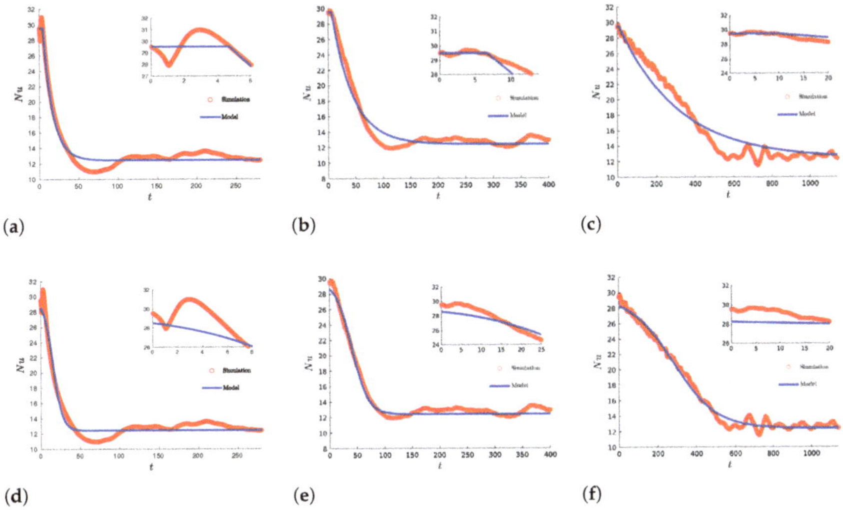

Figure 11. Characterization of the temporal response of the Nusselt number in uniformly decelerated flows. The top panels illustrate the performance of the model proposed by Nakamura et al. [12] when fitted to our data. (**a**) Results for $\alpha = -0.1$, representing rapid decelerations; (**b**) data for $\alpha = -0.02$, corresponding to moderate deceleration rates; and (**c**) data for $\alpha = -0.002$, corresponding to low deceleration rates. The bottom panels illustrate the performance of the model developed in this study, using the same α values as in the top panels: (**d**) $\alpha = -0.1$, (**e**) $\alpha = -0.02$, and (**f**) $\alpha = -0.002$. In all panels, the inset highlights the details of the initial delay phase.

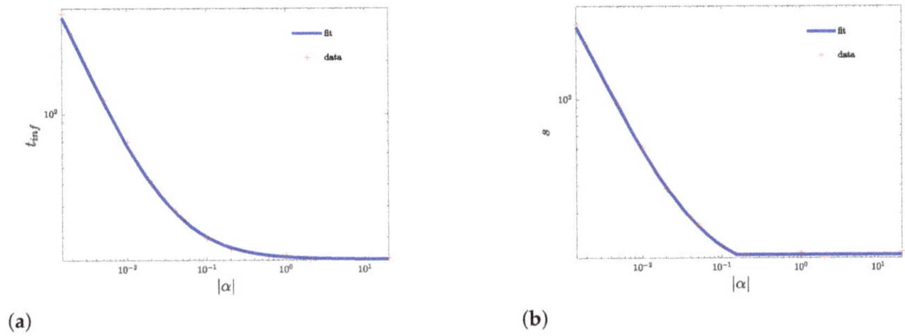

Figure 12. Variation in the parameters t_{inf} (**a**) and s (**b**) as a function of the absolute value of the deceleration rate $|\alpha|$ in uniformly decelerated flows.

3.4. Heat Transfer Gain or Loss Relative to Steady Flow

This section examines the heat transfer gain or loss in unsteady flows compared to steady flows with the same mean Re. As discussed in the introduction, unsteady flows can potentially enhance heat transfer in industrial processes compared to maintaining a constant flow rate. To investigate this possibility, it is essential to quantify how variations in the parameters governing unsteady flows affect Nu. This study specifically examines the impact of the acceleration (or deceleration) rate on Nu.

To quantify the heat transfer gain or loss compared to the steady case, the following parameter is defined:

$$\Delta Nu(\alpha) = \frac{Nu_m(\alpha) - Nu_{steady}}{Nu_{steady}} \times 100, \tag{34}$$

where $Nu_m(\alpha)$ represents the average Nusselt number during the period of acceleration or deceleration (excluding the steady period that follows these phases in the simulations), Nu_{steady} is the Nusselt number corresponding to the mean Reynolds number ($Re_m = 6400$) obtained from the Gnielinski correlation, which provides an accurate estimate of Nu in steady conditions for this Re. The values of ΔNu as a function of α for uniformly accelerated and decelerated flows are shown in Figure 13a,b, respectively.

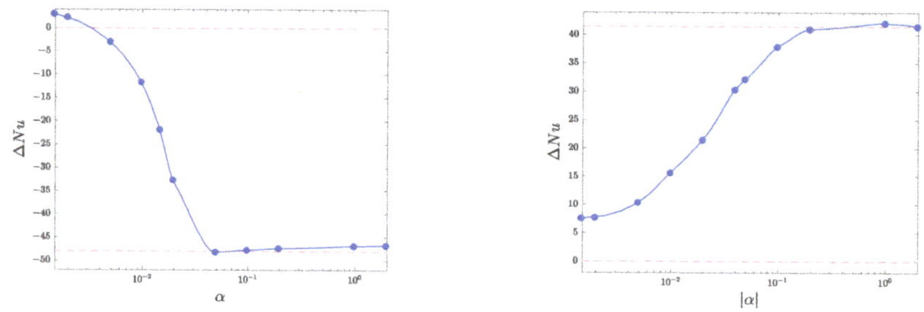

(**a**) (**b**)

Figure 13. Variation in the parameter ΔNu, representing the relative decrease or increase in Nu for uniformly accelerated (**a**) and decelerated (**b**) flows, as a function of the acceleration or deceleration rate, α. Each blue dot represents the result obtained for a specific value of α in our simulations. The brown dashed lines indicate the limits in each case. For accelerated flows, the upper limit corresponds to the maximum heat transfer loss, and the lower limit represents the quasi-steady condition. In decelerated flows, the upper limit corresponds to the maximum heat transfer gain, while the lower limit again represents the quasi-steady condition.

As explained in Section 3.1, the significant delay in the turbulence response to changes in the mean velocity results in a reduced heat transfer rate for uniformly accelerated flows compared to steady flows. It is worth noting that the average Nu in cases with quasi-steady behavior is slightly higher (by approximately 3%) than the steady Nu value. This deviation is, however, consistent with the expected errors in estimating this parameter using the Gnielinski correlation at $Re = 6400$, suggesting that heat transfer remains effectively unchanged from the steady case for these α values. For moderate α values, however, small changes in α can cause significant variations in the average Nu. The largest losses, approximately $\Delta Nu = -48\%$ relative to the steady flow, occur for α values, where the delay phase extends beyond the acceleration period.

In contrast, as discussed in Section 3.2, Nu values during deceleration remain consistently above the quasi-steady values. This is partly due to the presence of an instability that increases the intensity of turbulent fluctuations, resulting in a higher average Nu compared to the steady case. Even at the smallest values of $|\alpha|$, the average Nu shows an approximate 7.5% gain over steady conditions. However, the increase in Nu during deceleration is more gradual than the sharp decrease observed for accelerated flows, reaching maximum values of $\Delta Nu \approx 42\%$ in simulations with large $|\alpha|$, where the delay phase extends beyond the deceleration period.

These results suggest the potential for designing a periodic unsteady-flow cycle that includes a slow acceleration phase to minimize heat transfer losses, followed by a rapid deceleration phase to significantly enhance heat transfer compared to the steady case. The average Nusselt number for such a cycle would be higher than that of a steady flow, while maintaining the same mean Reynolds number in both cases.

4. Discussion

This paper presents the first study to use direct numerical simulations to systematically analyze the temporal evolution of the Nusselt number (Nu) in uniformly accelerated and decelerated turbulent pipe flows under constant heat flux. The findings confirm previous experimental results and provide new insights into how acceleration and deceleration rates affect heat transfer, a parameter not systematically explored in earlier research.

The results confirm the existence of three distinct phases, the delay, recovery, and quasi-steady phases, consistent with the previous experimental observations [11,12]. These phases are present at all acceleration rates (α), except when α is very low for accelerated flows, in which case Nu evolves quasi-steadily over time.

In accelerated flows, the delayed turbulence response reduces heat transfer by up to 48% compared with the steady case, while decelerated flows exhibit a maximum 42% increase due to a secondary instability that intensifies turbulence. Evidence of this instability is provided by the observed increase in turbulence intensity and convective transport, as well as changes in the topology of the flow structures. The typical elongated streaks seen in turbulent flows are replaced by more irregular structures with significant azimuthal extent, akin to the 'mottle structure' reported in [12]. While the exact mechanism driving the instability is unclear, it may be linked to inflection points in the velocity profile as suggested by recent studies [24,25]. Further research is needed to explore this phenomenon in detail.

Another important observation is the distinct temporal behavior of the friction coefficient (c_f) compared to Nu. It is observed that c_f responds more quickly to velocity changes, challenging the applicability of the Colburn analogy, which is commonly used in steady flows. This suggests that separate models are needed to accurately describe the dynamics of friction and heat transfer in unsteady turbulent flows.

This analysis also introduces a new model based on a hyperbolic tangent function that accurately characterizes the Nu response across various acceleration and deceleration rates. This model is more versatile than previous ones and may serve as a valuable tool in advancing both research and industrial practices related to optimizing heat transfer in unsteady-flow systems. However, it is valid only for the specific conditions investigated, as other parameters such as the initial and final Reynolds numbers, or non-linear acceleration profiles have not been considered. Future work will focus on extending the model to broader conditions.

One potential application of these findings is the design of flow cycles that enhance heat transfer in industrial processes. The results suggest that a periodic unsteady-flow cycle, comprising a slow acceleration phase to minimize heat transfer losses followed by a rapid deceleration phase to boost heat transfer, could outperform steady-state scenarios. Similar cycles have been recently proposed in the literature to reduce friction losses in turbulent pipes while producing net energy savings [26]. However, further research is required to investigate the behavior of Nu during direct transitions between acceleration and deceleration phases, as these may introduce new dynamics not captured in the present study.

Author Contributions: Conceptualization, I.E. and J.M.L.; methodology, I.E. and J.M.L.; software, J.M.L.; validation, I.E. and J.M.L.; formal analysis, I.E. and J.M.L.; investigation, I.E. and J.L; resources, J.M.L.; data curation, I.E. and J.L; writing—original draft preparation, J.M.L.; writing—review and editing, J.M.L. and I.E; supervision, J.M.L.; funding acquisition, J.M.L. All authors have read and agreed to the published version of the manuscript.

Funding: This research was funded by the grant PID2020-114043GB-I00 of the Spanish Ministry of Science and Innovation and the grant B1-2022_12 of the University of Malaga.

Data Availability Statement: The datasets generated and analyzed during the current study are available in the Zenodo repository [18]. The numerical simulations were conducted with the open source code nsPipeFlow, distributed under the terms of the GNU General Public License version 3. A detailed description of the code and user guide is provided in reference [17]. The code version used in this study, including the initial conditions employed in the simulations, is also openly available in [18].

Acknowledgments: The authors thank the Supercomputing and Bioinnovation Center (University of Málaga) for computational resources and technical support.

Conflicts of Interest: The authors declare no conflicts of interest. The funders had no role in the design of the study; in the collection, analyses, or interpretation of data; in the writing of the manuscript; or in the decision to publish the results.

References

1. Dec, J.E.; Keller, J.O.; Arpaci, V.S. Heat transfer enhancement in the oscillating turbulent flow of a pulse combustor tail pipe. *Int. J. Heat Mass Transfer* **1992**, *35*, 2311–2325. [CrossRef]
2. Habib, M.; Said, S.A.M.; Al-Farayedhi, A.; Al-Dini, S.; Asghar, A.; Gbadebo, S. Heat transfer characteristics of pulsated turbulent pipe flow. *Heat Mass Transf.* **1999**, *34*, 413–421. [CrossRef]
3. Barker, A.R.; Ffowcs Williams, J.E. Transient measurements of the heat transfer coefficient in unsteady, turbulent pipe flow. *Int. J. Heat Mass Transfer* **2000**, *43*, 3197–3207. [CrossRef]
4. Elshafei, E.A.; Safwat Mohamed, M.; Mansour, H.; Sakr, M. Experimental study of heat transfer in pulsating turbulent flow in a pipe. *Int. J. Heat Fluid Flow* **2008**, *29*, 1029–1038. [CrossRef]
5. Patel, J.T.; Attal, M.H. An Experimental Investigation of Heat Transfer Characteristics of Pulsating Flow in Pipe. *Int. J. Curr. Eng. Technol.* **2016**, *6*, 1515–1521.
6. Simonetti, M.; Caillol, C.; Higelin, P.; Dumand, C.; Revol, E. Experimental investigation and 1D analytical approach on convective heat transfers in engine exhaust-type turbulent pulsating flows. *Appl. Therm. Eng.* **2020**, *165*, 114548. [CrossRef]
7. Brahma, I.; Singh, S. Experimental, numerical and deep learning modeling study of heat transfer in turbulent pulsating pipe flow. *Appl. Therm. Eng.* **2024**, *244*, 122685. [CrossRef]
8. Wang, X.; Zhang, N. Numerical analysis of heat transfer in pulsating turbulent flow in a pipe. *Int. J. Heat Mass Transfer* **2005**, *48*, 3957–3970. [CrossRef]
9. Elshafei, E.A.M.; Mohamed, M.S.; Mansour, H.; Sakr, M. Numerical study of heat transfer in pulsating turbulent air flow. *J. Eng. Technol. Res.* **2012**, *4*, 89–97.
10. Nishandar, S.; Pise, A.; Bagade, P.; Gaikwad, M.; Singh, A. Computational modelling and analysis of heat transfer enhancement in straight circular pipe with pulsating flow. *Int. J. Interact. Des. Manuf.* **2024**. [CrossRef]
11. Shiibara, N.; Nakamura, H.; Yamada, S. Unsteady characteristics of turbulent heat transfer in a circular pipe upon sudden acceleration and deceleration of flow. *Int. J. Heat Mass Transfer* **2017**, *113*, 490–501. [CrossRef]
12. Nakamura, H.; Saito, R.; Yamada, S. Delay in response of turbulent heat transfer against acceleration or deceleration of flow in a pipe. *Int. J. Heat Fluid Flow* **2020**, *85*, 108661. [CrossRef]
13. Incropera, F.P.; DeWitt, D.P. *Fundamentals of Heat and Mass Transfer*, 4th ed.; John Wiley & Sons, Inc.: New York, NY, USA, 1996.
14. Piller, M. Direct numerical simulation of turbulent forced convection in a pipe. *Int. J. Num. Meth. Fluids* **2005**, *49*, 583–602. [CrossRef]
15. Redjem-Saad, L.; Ould-Rouiss, M.; Lauriat, G. Direct numerical simulation of turbulent heat transfer in pipe flows: Effect of Prandtl number. *Int. J. Heat Fluid Flow* **2007**, *28*, 847–861. [CrossRef]
16. Antoranz, A.; Gonzalo, A.; Flores, O.; García-Villalba, M. Numerical simulation of heat transfer in a pipe with non-homogeneous thermal boundary conditions. *Int. J. Heat Fluid Flow* **2015**, *55*, 45–51. [CrossRef]
17. López, J.M.; Feldmann, D.; Rampp, M.; Vela-Martín, A.; Shi, L.; Avila, M. nsCouette—A high-performance code for direct numerical simulations of turbulent Taylor–Couette flow. *SoftwareX* **2020**, *11*, 100395. [CrossRef]
18. López, J.M. Convective Heat Transfer in Uniformly Accelerated and Decelerated Turbulent Pipe Flows: Simulation data and numerical code. *Zenodo* **2024**. [CrossRef]
19. Willis, A.P. The Openpipeflow Navier–Stokes solver. *SoftwareX* **2017**, *6*, 124–127. [CrossRef]
20. He, S.; Jackson, J.D. A study of turbulence under conditions of transient flow in a pipe. *J. Fluid Mech.* **2000**, *408*, 1–38. [CrossRef]
21. Greenblatt, D.; Moss, E.A. Rapid temporal acceleration of a turbulent pipe flow. *J. Fluid Mech.* **2004**, *514*, 65–75. [CrossRef]
22. He, S.; Ariyaratne, C.; Vardy, A.E. Wall shear stress in accelerating turbulent pipe flow. *J. Fluid Mech.* **2011**, *685*, 440–460. [CrossRef]
23. Colburn, A.P. A method of correlating forced convection heat-transfer data and a comparison with fluid friction. *Int. J. Heat Mass Transfer* **1964**, *7*, 1359–1384. [CrossRef]
24. Kern, J.; Beneitez, M.; Hanifi, A.; Henningson, D. Transient linear stability of pulsating Poiseuille flow using optimally time-dependent modes. *J. Fluid Mech.* **2021**, *927*, A6. [CrossRef]

25. Moron, D.; Feldmann, D.; Avila, M. Effect of waveform on turbulence transition in pulsatile pipe flow. *J. Fluid Mech.* **2022**, *948*, A20. [CrossRef]
26. Scarselli, D.; Lopez, J.; Varshney, A.; Hof, B. Turbulence suppression by cardiac-cycle-inspired driving of pipe flow. *Nature* **2023**, *621*, 71–74. [CrossRef]

mathematics

MDPI

Article

Modelling the Transition from Shear-Driven Turbulence to Convective Turbulence in a Vertical Heated Pipe

Shijun Chu [1], Elena Marensi [2] and Ashley P. Willis [1,*]

[1] Applied Mathematics, School of Mathematical and Physical Sciences, University of Sheffield, Sheffield S3 7RH, UK; schu3@sheffield.ac.uk
[2] School of Mechanical, Aerospace and Civil Engineering, University of Sheffield, Sheffield S1 3JD, UK; e.marensi@sheffield.ac.uk
* Correspondence: a.p.willis@sheffield.ac.uk

Abstract: Heated pipe flow is widely used in thermal engineering applications, but the presence of buoyancy force can cause intermittency, or multiple flow states at the same parameter values. Such changes in the flow lead to substantial changes in its heat transfer properties and thereby significant changes in the axial temperature gradient. We therefore introduce a model that features a time-dependent background axial temperature gradient, and consider two temperature boundary conditions—fixed temperature difference and fixed boundary heat flux. Direct numerical simulations (DNSs) are based on the pseudo-spectral framework, and good agreement is achieved between present numerical results and experimental results. The code extends Openpipeflow and is available at the website. The effect of the axially periodic domain on flow dynamics and heat transfer is examined, using pipes of length $L = 5D$ and $L = 25D$. Provided that the flow is fully turbulent, results show close agreement for the mean flow and temperature profiles, and only slight differences in root-mean-square fluctuations. When the flow shows spatial intermittency, heat transfer tends to be overestimated using a short pipe, as shear turbulence fills the domain. This is particularly important when shear turbulence starts to be suppressed at intermediate buoyancy numbers. Finally, at such intermediate buoyancy numbers, we confirm that the decay of localised shear turbulence in the heated pipe flow follows a memoryless process, similar to that in isothermal flow. While isothermal flow then laminarises, convective turbulence in the heated flow can intermittently trigger bursts of shear-like turbulence.

Keywords: mixed convection; pipe flow; direct numerical simulation

MSC: 76F06; 76F10

1. Introduction

In the heated flow context, flow driven by an external pressure gradient is referred to as 'forced' flow, while buoyancy resulting from the expansivity of the fluid close to a heated wall can provide a force that partially or fully drives the flow, referred to as 'mixed' or 'natural convection', respectively. In a model, buoyancy may only need to counter drag forces in the vertical pipe. In practice, we are likely to encounter what could be called 'super-natural' convection, where the buoyancy must be larger than the local drag in order to drive flow in a wider circuit. In this case, flow in the vertical section of the circuit is subject to a reversed pressure gradient that limits the flow rate.

Turbulent mixed convection in a vertical pipe is a representative model for heat transfer that can be found in thermal engineering applications, e.g., heat exchangers, nuclear reactors, chemical plants and cooling systems for electronic components [1]. Despite the relatively simple geometry, the flow state and heat transfer can be difficult to predict in the presence of buoyancy. Buoyancy can enhance the heat transfer in a heated downward pipe flow but suppress heat transfer in upward heated pipe flow [1–5]. In an upward pipe flow, with the enhancement of heating, heat transfer first deteriorates slowly, then suddenly drops when shear-driven turbulence collapses, then recovers, and finally can approach as large values as for downward flow at large buoyancy parameters [1].

Heat transfer presents some complicated features in upward heated pipe flow, as well as the flow dynamics. Previous research has confirmed three flow states in different heating conditions and Reynolds numbers, i.e., shear turbulence, the laminar state, and convective turbulence [6,7]. The laminar state can persist up to Reynolds numbers of around 3000, versus approximately 2000 in isothermal flow. The addition of buoyancy suppresses and can laminarise shear turbulence. Research on the phenomenon of laminarisation in mixed convection can be traced at least as far back as that of Hall et al. [8], which provided a theoretical explanation of this phenomenon, suggesting that reduced shear stress in the buffer layer leads to a reduction in or even elimination of turbulence production. More recently, He et al. [9] modelled the buoyancy with a radially dependent axial body force added to isothermal flow, successfully reproducing the laminarisation phenomenon. They found that the body force makes little change to the key characteristics of turbulence, and proposed that laminarisation is caused by the reduction in the 'apparent Reynolds number', which is calculated based only on the pressure force of the flow (i.e., excluding the contribution of the body force). Similar laminarisation phenomena have also been observed for the isothermal case in the presence of a modified base flow [10,11]. It is conjectured that a flattened velocity profile reduces transient growth [12], thus suppressing shear turbulence. Chu et al. [13] examined the self-sustaining process [14] in this context and found that the flattened velocity profile can suppress the instability of streaks thereby disrupting the self-sustaining process of shear turbulence.

There is a developed history of numerical simulations of mixed convection in vertical pipe flow using various methods. In an early study, a modification of the Redichardt eddy diffusivity model was used to simulate mixed convection [15], but it proved that this approach did not adequately account for certain local features of the flow. Cotton et al. [16] used the low-Reynolds number $k-\epsilon$ turbulence model of Lauder et al. [17] to simulate the vertical heated pipe flow with some success. Behzademhr et al. [18] conducted a study of upward mixed convection in a longer pipe at two rather low Reynolds numbers ($Re = 1000$ and 1500) over a range of Grashof numbers, which measures the heat flux at the wall, using the Lauder–Sharma model. They identified two critical Grashof numbers for each Reynolds number, which correspond to laminar–turbulent transition and relaminarisation of the flow. More recently, direct numerical simulation (DNS) has been used in studies of mixed convection. Kasagi et al. [19] conducted a DNS study at $Re = 4300$ and several values of the Grashof number. The simulations show that buoyancy changes the distribution of Reynolds shear stress and shear production rate of turbulent kinetic energy, leading to heat transfer enhancement or suppression. You et al. [20] also performed the DNS for the mixed convection in vertical pipe flow, and compared the results of upward and downward flow. Kim et al. [21] presented an assessment of the performance of a variety of turbulence models in simulating buoyancy-aided, turbulent mixed convection in vertical pipes. They found the use of different methodologies for modelling the direct production of turbulence through the direct action of buoyancy has been shown to have little effect on predictions of mixed convection in vertical flows. Chu et al. [22] applied a well-resolved

DNS to investigate strongly heated airflow in a vertical pipe at $Re = 4240$ and 6020. The results showed excellent agreement in heat transfer and flow statistics. Recent calculations at larger flow rates include [23–25].

We wish to examine the detailed transient nature of transition, for which accurate DNS is necessary, and since the flow type ultimately affects the heat transfer and hence the heating of the fluid itself, we wish to explicitly include a time-dependent temperature gradient. The model developed by Marensi et al. [6] extends the pseudo-spectral code openpipeflow [26] to include a time-dependent spatially uniform heat sink. This form for the sink has the advantage of a simple analytic expression for the laminar state. Numerical results showed good agreement with the experimental results but were improved slightly by Chu et al. [7] by associating the heat sink with a time-dependent background temperature gradient along the axis of the pipe. In both Marensi et al.'s [6] and Chu et al.'s [7] works, fixed temperature conditions were used at the wall. In this work, we provide further details of the model of Chu et al. [7] and add a second case for the temperature boundary condition, that of fixed heat flux at the wall.

It should be noted that our model assumes axial periodicity, which implies that it should be applied to a straight section of pipe, downstream of the effects from an inlet or bend. This approximation is widely adopted for research in shear turbulence [27,28] and mixed convection [25] in pipe flows. Another potential limitation is the Boussinesq approximation [29,30] adopted in our model, which ignores the effect of heating on viscosity and assumes that changes of density only need be considered in the buoyancy force term in Navier–Stokes equations. Nevertheless, such modelling simplifies the simulation greatly and provides good results in many circumstances [29], and has been widely adopted in the simulations of mixed convection [20,25,31]. As we focus on flow and heating rates that are transitional with respect to flow regimes, we do not consider extreme parameter values here. When the Boussinesq approximation holds, there is mathematical equivalence between upward heated and downward cooled flow, i.e., the case modelled here could be experimentally examined by considering a hot fluid flowing down a pipe through a cold room. Although the temperature along the pipe will approach the room temperature exponentially under such circumstances, it can be modelled to be locally linear over a reasonable distance, and the temperature gradient along the pipe will depend on whether the flow is laminar or turbulent. Finally, it should also be noted that turbulence increases friction drag and hence pumping costs. The relative importance of this cost is very context specific, and therefore is not considered here. Our focus is on the enhanced heat transfer due to turbulence.

The plan of the paper is as follows. In Section 2, we present the model for the DNS of vertical heated pipe flow, including two types of temperature boundary conditions, i.e., fixed temperature difference and fixed boundary heat flux. In Section 3, we first show the results of DNS, then present the results of different lengths of pipe. Next, we show how the lifetime of shear turbulence changes with buoyancy force. Finally, the paper concludes with a summary in Section 4.

2. Model for Heated Pipe Flow

Let $\boldsymbol{x} = (r, \phi, z)$ denote cylindrical coordinates within a pipe of radius R. The total temperature satisfies

$$\frac{\partial T_{tot}}{\partial t} + (\boldsymbol{u}_{tot} \cdot \boldsymbol{\nabla}) T_{tot} = \kappa \boldsymbol{\nabla}^2 T_{tot} , \tag{1}$$

where κ is the thermal diffusivity. We decompose the total temperature as

$$T_{tot}(\boldsymbol{x}, t) = T_w(z, t) + T(\boldsymbol{x}, t) - T_0 , \tag{2}$$

$$T_w(z, t) = a(t)\, z + b , \tag{3}$$

where $a(t)$ is the time-dependent axial temperature gradient, b is a constant reference temperature, $T(\boldsymbol{x}, t)$ carries the temperature fluctuations, and T_0 is a constant that will be used as a temperature scale. The factor $-T_0$ is inserted in (2) so that the temperature fluctuations T are positive and largest at the hot wall. The bulk temperature, we write as

$$T_b = \langle T \rangle \,, \tag{4}$$

where the angle brackets denote the volume average. The important quantity that measures the heat flux is the Nusselt number

$$Nu = \frac{2R\, q_w}{\lambda\, (T|_{r=R} - T_b)} \,. \tag{5}$$

where λ is the thermal conductivity, and $q_w = \lambda\, \overline{(\partial T/\partial r)|_{r=R}}$ is the heat flux at the wall, where the overline denotes the time average. Note that Nu is an observed quantity, rather than a prescribed parameter, as it depends on the state of the flow.

For the fixed temperature boundary condition, T_w is the value of the temperature at the wall. Evaluating (2) at the wall gives $T|_{r=R} = T_0$. The wall temperature is locally isothermal (does not deviate from T_w), while the heat flux may exhibit variations. However, q_w can be measured and is expected to be statistically steady, except when interrupted by a change in state of the flow, such as from shear turbulence to convective turbulence.

For the fixed heat-flux boundary condition, q_w takes the same value everywhere. Local variations in the boundary temperature are possible, so that here, T_w represents an averaged wall temperature. Note that Nu will still vary through changes in T_b.

Throughout the rest of this work, dimensionless variables and equations are presented, except in the definition of the scales and dimensionless parameters. We use R as the length scale and twice the bulk flow speed $2U_b$ for the velocity scale, which for isothermal laminar flow coincides with the centreline speed. For the temperature scale, we use T_0, which will be linked to the boundary conditions in the following sections. Using these scales, we arrive at the dimensionless governing equation

$$\frac{\partial T}{\partial t} + (\boldsymbol{u}_{tot} \cdot \boldsymbol{\nabla}) T = \frac{1}{Re\, Pr} \boldsymbol{\nabla}^2 T - \boldsymbol{u}_{tot} \cdot \hat{\boldsymbol{z}}\, a(t), \tag{6}$$

where it is assumed that variations in the temperature gradient are much slower than variations in the local fluctuations, i.e., $\partial_t a(t) \ll \partial_t T(\boldsymbol{x}, t)$. The dimensionless parameters are the Reynolds and Prandtl numbers $Re = 2U_b R/\nu$ and $Pr = \nu/\kappa$, where ν and κ are the kinematic viscosity and thermal diffusivity. A Prandtl number of 0.7 is used in all calculations. The last term on the right-hand side is a sink term that withdraws the energy that enters through the boundary. The value for $a(t)$ at each instant is determined via the spatial average of (6) and depends on the boundary condition on the temperature as shown in the following sections. Axial periodicity over a dimensionless distance $L = 2\pi/\alpha$ is assumed for the temperature fluctuation field $T(\boldsymbol{x}, t)$.

Axial periodicity is also assumed for the velocity field $\boldsymbol{u}_{tot}(\boldsymbol{x}, t)$. Under the Boussinesq approximation [30], the dimensionless Navier–Stokes (NS) equations are

$$\frac{\partial \boldsymbol{u}_{tot}}{\partial t} + (\boldsymbol{u}_{tot} \cdot \boldsymbol{\nabla}) \boldsymbol{u}_{tot} = -\boldsymbol{\nabla} p + \frac{1}{Re} \boldsymbol{\nabla}^2 \boldsymbol{u}_{tot} + \frac{\gamma g R T_0}{(2U_b)^2} T \hat{\boldsymbol{z}} + \frac{4}{Re} (1 + \beta(t)) \hat{\boldsymbol{z}} \,, \tag{7}$$

with continuity equation

$$\boldsymbol{\nabla} \cdot \boldsymbol{u}_{tot} = 0 \,, \tag{8}$$

and no-slip condition $\boldsymbol{u}_{tot} = \boldsymbol{0}$ at the wall, where γ is the thermal expansivity and g is acceleration due to gravity. Here, $\langle \partial_z p \rangle = 0$, and the non-zero component of the axial pressure gradient appears in the final term of (7); $\beta(t)$ is the excess pressure fraction, relative to isothermal laminar flow, required to maintain the fixed dimensionless mass flux $\langle \boldsymbol{u}_{tot} \cdot \hat{\boldsymbol{z}} \rangle = 1/2$. Further decomposing the variables as

$$\begin{aligned} \boldsymbol{u}_{tot}(\boldsymbol{x}, t) &= u_0(r)\hat{\boldsymbol{z}} + \boldsymbol{u}(\boldsymbol{x}, t), \quad u_0 = 1 - r^2, &(9)\\ T(\boldsymbol{x}, t) &= \Theta_0(r) + \Theta(\boldsymbol{x}, t), \quad \Theta_0 = r^2, &(10) \end{aligned}$$

leads to governing equations for the deviation fields Θ and $\boldsymbol{u} = (u_r, u_\phi, u_z)$

$$\frac{\partial \Theta}{\partial t} + u_0 \frac{\partial \Theta}{\partial z} + u_r \frac{d\Theta_0}{dr} + (\boldsymbol{u} \cdot \boldsymbol{\nabla})\Theta = \frac{1}{RePr}\boldsymbol{\nabla}^2\Theta + \frac{4}{RePr} - (u_0 + u_z)a(t), \quad (11)$$

$$\frac{\partial \boldsymbol{u}}{\partial t} + u_0 \frac{\partial \boldsymbol{u}}{\partial z} + u_r \frac{du_0}{dr}\hat{\boldsymbol{z}} + (\boldsymbol{u} \cdot \boldsymbol{\nabla})\boldsymbol{u} = -\boldsymbol{\nabla} p + \frac{1}{Re}\boldsymbol{\nabla}^2\boldsymbol{u} + \frac{4}{Re}(C(\Theta + \Theta_0) + \beta(t))\hat{\boldsymbol{z}}, \quad (12)$$

with continuity condition $\nabla \cdot \boldsymbol{u} = 0$ and boundary condition $\boldsymbol{u} = \boldsymbol{0}$. The parameter C measures the buoyancy force relative to the pressure gradient for laminar flow. Equating buoyancy terms in (7) and (12), we have

$$\frac{4}{Re}C = \frac{\gamma g R T_0}{(2U_b)^2}, \quad (13)$$

where T_0 will be specified according to the boundary condition on Θ. To determine $\beta(t)$, we take the spatial average of the z-component of (12). By Gauss's theorem and the divergence-free condition, many terms drop. Noting also that $\langle u_0 \rangle = \langle \Theta_0 \rangle = 1/2$, the $\beta(t)$ that fixes $\langle u_z \rangle = 0$ is given by

$$\beta(t) = -C\left(\frac{1}{2} + \langle \Theta \rangle\right) - \frac{1}{2}\frac{\partial (u_z)_{00}}{\partial r}\bigg|_{r=1}, \quad (14)$$

where $(\cdot)_{00}$ denotes averaging over ϕ and z.

2.1. Fixed Temperature Difference Between Bulk and Boundary

We accompany the fixed temperature boundary condition with a fixed bulk temperature T_b in (4). Making the choice

$$T_0 = 2\,T_b \quad (15)$$

for the temperature scale, inserting in (13) and rearranging, we find

$$C_{\Delta T} = \frac{Gr_{\Delta T}}{16\,Re}, \qquad Gr_{\Delta T} = \frac{\gamma\, g\,(T|_{r=R} - T_b)(2R)^3}{\nu^2} \quad (16)$$

wherein we use the dimensional T of (2) and subscript the parameters to clarify that they are based on a temperature difference. $Gr_{\Delta T}$ is the Grashof number.

Using the scale $T_0 = 2T_b$ to non-dimensionalise (2) and (4), the dimensionless fluctuations satisfy $T|_{r=1} = 1$ and $\langle T \rangle = 1/2$. As a simple Θ_0 is chosen that satisfies these conditions, we have that (11) is accompanied by the boundary condition $\Theta|_{r=1} = 0$ and the condition $\langle \Theta \rangle = 0$. The latter condition is equivalent to saying that the energy within the domain is constant, and hence the energy entering the domain through the boundary must match the energy extracted by the sink term at each instant. This sets a value for $a(t)$. Taking the spatial average of (11) gives

$$a(t) = \frac{4}{RePr}\left(2 + \frac{\partial (\Theta)_{00}}{\partial r}\bigg|_{r=1}\right). \quad (17)$$

This model was applied in the simulations of Chu et al. [7].

2.2. Fixed Heat Flux at the Boundary

As we already have that $(\partial_r \Theta_0)|_{r=1} = 2$ in the decomposition (10), we suppose that this is the value of the temperature gradient everywhere, and accompany (11) with the boundary condition $(\partial_r \Theta)|_{r=1} = 0$. Using T_0 as the temperature scale, the dimensional flux at the wall is everywhere

$$q_w = 2\,\lambda \frac{T_0}{R}, \qquad \text{i.e., } T_0 = \frac{q_w\,R}{2\,\lambda}. \tag{18}$$

Inserting this T_0 in (13) and rearranging, we find

$$C_q = \frac{Gr_q}{128\,Re}, \qquad Gr_q = \frac{\gamma\, g\,(2R)^4 q_w}{\lambda\,\nu^2}, \tag{19}$$

where the subscripts are added to the parameters to indicate that they are based on the heat flux.

The fluctuations may be split into a spatial mean and varying component, $\Theta(\boldsymbol{x},t) = (\Theta)_{00}(r,t) + \Theta'(\boldsymbol{x},t)$, where $(\cdot)_{00}$ denotes averaging over ϕ and z. To the varying components, we apply the boundary condition $(\partial_r \Theta')|_{r=1} = 0$. The mean component evolves according to the spatial average of (11), which may be written

$$\frac{\partial(\Theta)_{00}}{\partial t} - \frac{1}{Re\,Pr}\nabla^2(\Theta)_{00} = (N)_{00} - (u_0 + (u_z)_{00})\,a(t). \tag{20}$$

We wish the mean component to be consistent with there being a constant background reference temperature in (3), and therefore apply the boundary condition $(\Theta)_{00}|_{r=1} = 0$. Note that the temperature can still vary at the boundary, as this condition only fixes the mean value. However, it still remains to apply the boundary condition $(\partial_r(\Theta)_{00})|_{r=1} = 0$, which is achieved through the variation in $a(t)$. Evaluating the radial derivative at the wall gives

$$a(t) = \left(\frac{\partial(N)_{00}}{\partial r} + \frac{1}{RePr}\frac{\partial\nabla^2(\Theta)_{00}}{\partial r}\right)\Bigg|_{r=1} \Bigg/ \left(-2 + \frac{\partial(u_z)_{00}}{\partial r}\right)\Bigg|_{r=1}. \tag{21}$$

It is worth mentioning that accompanying (11) with the condition $(\partial_r \Theta)|_{r=1} = 0$ alone, the problem is ill-posed; see [32,33]. The condition $(\Theta)_{00}|_{r=1} = 0$ removes non-uniqueness, but note that it cannot be trivially satisfied by evaluating (20) at the wall—$a(t)$ remains undetermined, as its coefficient is zero at the wall.

2.3. Time-Integration Code

The calculations are carried out by the open-source code openpipeflow.org (accessed on 15 March 2024) [26]. Variables are discretised on the domain $\{r,\phi,z\} = [0,1] \times [0,2\pi] \times [0,2\pi/\alpha]$, where $\alpha = 2\pi/L$, using Fourier decomposition in the azimuthal and streamwise directions and finite difference in the radial direction, with points clustered towards the wall. An arbitrary variable $f(\boldsymbol{x})$ is expanded in the form

$$f(r_s,\phi,z) = \sum_{k<|K|}\sum_{m<|M|}(f)_{km}(r_s)\,e^{i(\alpha k z + m\phi)}, \qquad s = 1,2,\ldots,S, \tag{22}$$

and the mode $(f)_{00}$ corresponds to the ϕ- and z-average. Temporal discretisation is via a second-order predictor-corrector scheme, with an Euler predictor and a Crank–Nicolson corrector applied to the nonlinear terms. The laminar solution is quickly calculated by eliminating azimuthal and axial variations using a resolution $S = 64, M = 1, K = 1$. For a periodic pipe of length $L = 5D$, the resolution is $S = 64, M = 76, K = 80$ at $Re = 5300$, and the resolution is $S = 64, M = 40, K = 44$ at $Re = 3000$. For a periodic pipe of length

$L = 25D$, the resolution is $S = 64, M = 76, K = 400$ at $Re = 5300$, and the resolution is $S = 64, M = 40, K = 220$ at $Re = 3000$. A time step of $\Delta t = 0.01$ is adopted. These resolutions ensure a drop-off of three to four orders of magnitude in the amplitude of the spectral coefficients, which experience has shown to be sufficient for accurately simulating shear-turbulence, matching the statistics from, for example, [27]. Within the parameter range considered here, the convective state is less computationally demanding to simulate.

3. Results

In this section, we compare the two different boundary conditions keeping $L = 5D$, then we consider the fixed temperature difference boundary condition and compare the flow in $L = 5D$ and $L = 25D$. Finally, we calculate the heat transfer and lifetimes for localised turbulence in the presence of the buoyancy force.

3.1. Laminar Flow, Shear Turbulence and Convective Turbulence

We first verify that the model produces the well-known properties of the laminar solution for both models and for increasing buoyancy parameter C [31,34], shown in Figure 1. The results in Figure 1 are calculated at $Re = 5300$, but laminar profiles are dependent on C and independent of Re [31]. The laminar velocity profile becomes flattened and even 'M' shaped with the enhancement of heating. Negative velocity near the centre of the pipe at $C_{\Delta T}, C_q = 20, 25$ indicates the occurrence of reversed flow. The laminar temperature profile becomes flattened as C increases. For the fixed temperature difference, an increased temperature gradient near the wall implies increased heat flux and increased Nusselt number Nu, defined in (5). For the fixed heat flux case, a reduced temperature difference between the wall and bulk results in increased Nu.

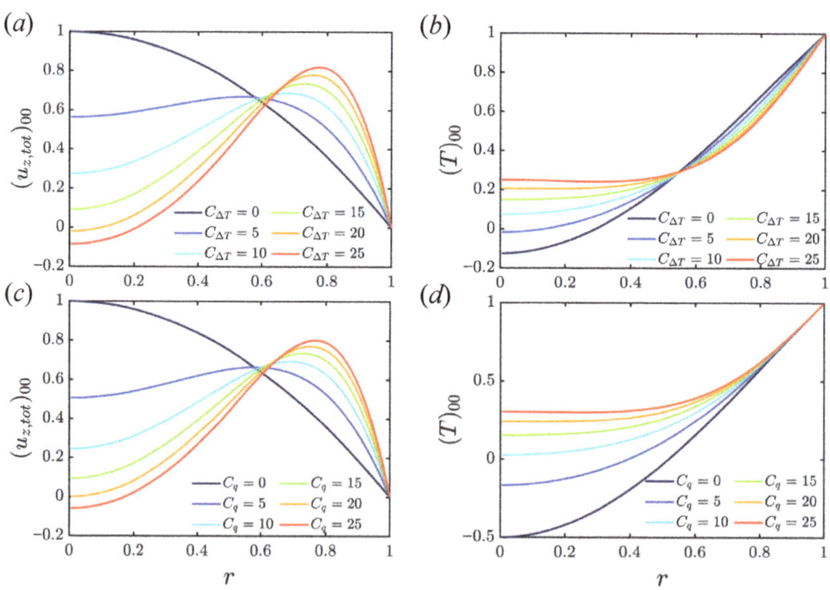

Figure 1. Laminar solution for (**a**,**b**) fixed temperature difference; (**c**,**d**) fixed boundary heat flux.

Turbulent mean profiles at $Re = 5300$ are shown in Figure 2. Two regimes are observed in both the velocity and temperature profiles, corresponding to shear-driven turbulence and convective turbulence. For the velocity profile, the former state has a flattened shape, while the latter has an 'M' shape due to the stronger influence of the buoyancy force. For these values of C, shear turbulence has much greater heat transfer than convective turbulence.

As C increases, it is observed that heat transfer first becomes weaker, then collapses, and finally, it gradually recovers. This trend is consistent with the results reported in the literature [1,20,35–37]. Both models capture a similar change in heat transfer but with different critical values of the C parameters.

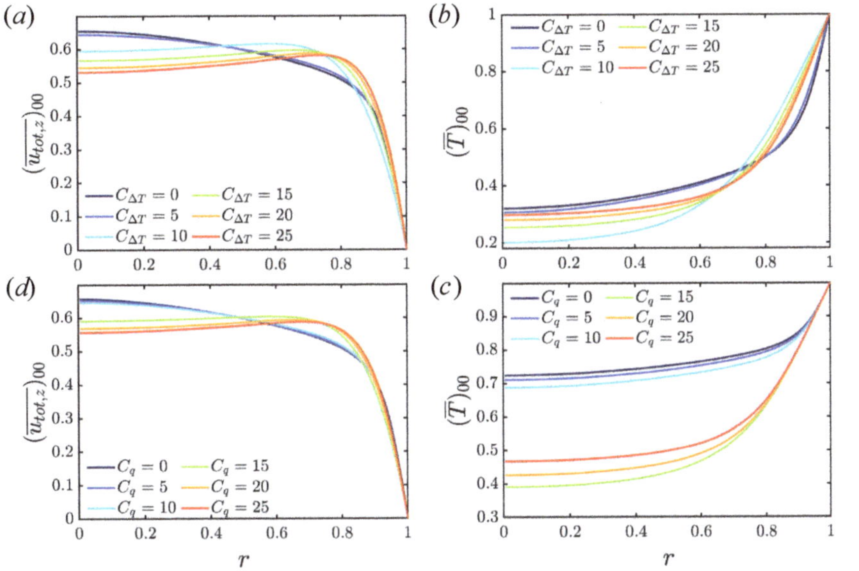

Figure 2. Turbulent mean velocity profiles $\overline{u_{tot,z}}$ and temperature profiles $\overline{T}$ at $Re = 5300, L = 5D$: (**a**,**b**) fixed temperature difference; (**c**,**d**) fixed boundary heat flux.

Numerical results for the present model are compared with the previous numerical results [6,20] and experimental results [35–37], shown in Figure 3 (Fixed temperature difference and uniform heat sink were adopted by Marensi et al. [6], while fixed heat flux was applied by You et al. [20]). Averages over at least 4000 time units are used in the calculation of Nu. Two regimes are clearly identified, i.e., the heat-transfer deterioration regime and the recovery regime, corresponding to shear turbulence and convective turbulence, respectively. Both temperature boundary conditions achieve good agreement with the experimental results and previous numerical results.

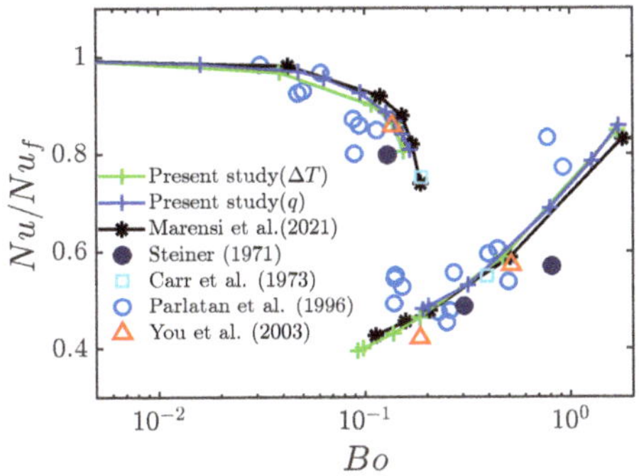

Figure 3. Change in heat flux, normalised by that for the isothermal state ($C \to 0$), as a function of $Bo = 8 \times 10^4(8\,Nu\,Gr_{\Delta T})/(Re^{3.425}Pr^{0.8})$ (fixed temperature difference) or $Bo = 8 \times 10^4(8Gr_q)/(Re^{3.425}Pr^{0.8})$ (fixed boundary heat flux). Present data from simulations at $Re = 5300$, $Pr = 0.7$. The upper and lower branches correspond to shear and convective turbulence, respectively. Data from [6,20,35–37].

At lower Reynolds numbers, there is a laminarisation regime, seen in Figure 4, which shows the approximate regions of the flow states for the two temperature boundary conditions. Although there is a difference between the values of $C_{\Delta T}$ and C_q at which transition between different flow regimes occurs, they are consistent in Figure 3.

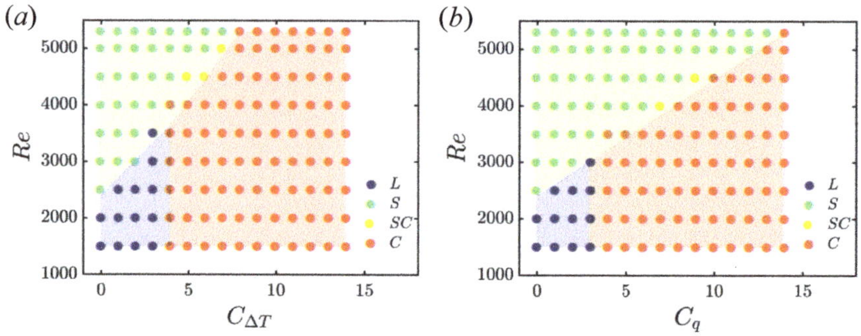

Figure 4. Approximate regions of laminar flow (L), shear turbulence (S), and convective turbulence (C); SC indicates that the flow may be in either of the two states. (**a**) Fixed temperature difference; (**b**) fixed boundary heat flux.

The time evolution of E_{3d} (energy of streamwise-dependent component of the flow) and instantaneous $Nu(t)$ at different $C_{\Delta T}$ and C_q are presented in Figure 5. Generally, as C is increased, E_{3d} first decreases gradually, then reduces to a much lower energy level at a critical value of C, indicating a flow state transition from shear turbulence to convective turbulence [7]. In the convective turbulence state, E_{3d} fluctuates with a much lower frequency. A clear gap between the shear turbulence regime and the convective turbulence regime (smaller E_{3d} and Nu) is observed. The critical C is not precise, since close to the border, both states can be observed. At $Re = 5300$, the critical values are $C_{\Delta T} \approx 7$ and $C_q \approx 15$. Interestingly, bistability is observed at $C_q = 15$, which switches between shear and convective turbulence. In particular, the convective state is capable of intermittently triggering bursts of shear-like turbulence, whereas at lower Re and in isothermal flow, it cannot switch back from the linearly stable laminar state.

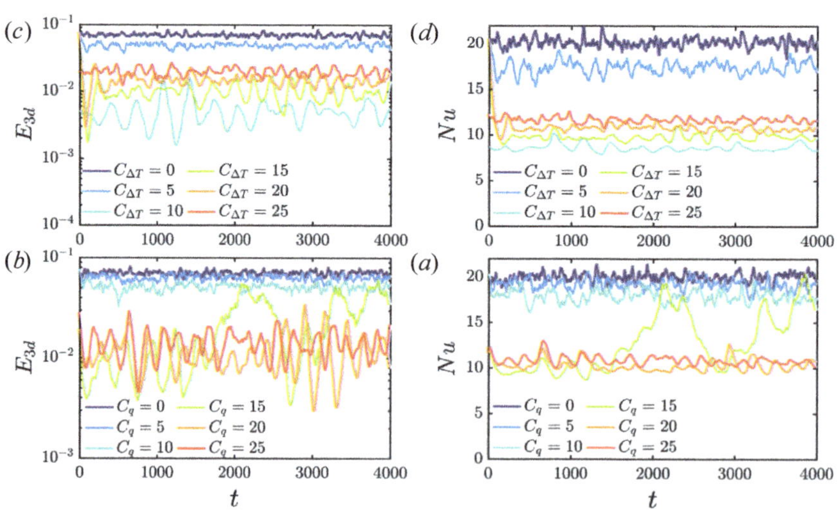

Figure 5. (**a**,**c**) Time series of E_{3d} (energy of the streamwise-dependent component of the flow) and (**b**,**d**) $Nu(t)$ at different $C_{\Delta T}$ and C_q for $Re = 5300$.

The time evolutions of the background temperature gradient $a(t)$ and of $Nu(t)$ are presented in Figure 6 during the transition from shear turbulence to the laminar state, and during the transition from shear turbulence to convective turbulence for the two types of boundary conditions. The transition from shear turbulence to either the laminar state or convective turbulence leads to a reduced Nusselt number. This is accompanied by a reduction in the gradient $a(t)$ for the fixed temperature difference model. As the heat transfer associated with the new flow is lower, the fluid is heated less, and the gradient reduces. For the fixed heat flux model, however, once the total temperature has adjusted (giving the change in Nu), the time average of $a(t)$ is forced to remain the same so that the heat flux out matches the fixed input flux. As the energy of the bulk is fixed for the fixed temperature difference, the input and output energies respond immediately to each other, so that $a(t)$ and $Nu(t)$ vary together. For the fixed flux condition, $Nu(t)$ varies due to differences in the bulk temperature, which responds in a time-integrated fashion relative to the heat flux out. Hence, fluctuations in $Nu(t)$ are less rapid than those in $a(t)$ for the fixed flux boundary condition.

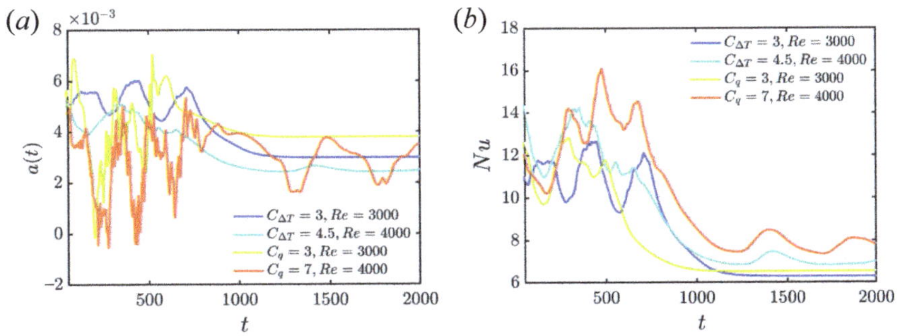

Figure 6. Time evolution of (**a**) $a(t)$ and (**b**) instantaneous Nusselt number when shear turbulence collapses to the laminar or convective state for the two boundary conditions.

Root-mean-square (RMS) deviations from $\overline{(u_{z,tot})_{00}}$ and $\overline{(T)_{00}}$ are shown in Figures 7 and 8 for the fixed temperature and fixed flux boundary conditions, respectively, using data from $t = 1000$ to $t = 4000$ for each simulation. Interestingly, there are two peaks of streamwise velocity fluctuation observed in convective turbulence when the fixed temperature difference is adopted; see Figure 7d. At $C_{\Delta T} = 10$, the peak near the wall dominates, while the peak far away from the wall is larger at $C_{\Delta T} = 25$. The two peaks are in good agreement with You et al. [20] in Figure 4 and Cruz et al. [25] in Figure 3. The main difference between the two models is in the temperature fluctuations T_{rms}. As only the mean temperature at the wall is fixed for the fixed flux model, fluctuations are possible even at the wall. T_{rms} for $C_q = 15$ is especially large, due to the bistability mentioned earlier (see Figure 5c,d). Otherwise, the results are similar, and differences between the shear and convective regimes are observed in the RMS fluctuations for both models. In the shear turbulence regime, the peak of temperature fluctuation is close to the wall and moves away from the wall with increased heating. In the convective turbulence regime, the peak of the temperature fluctuations is much further away from the wall, and moves closer to the wall again as the heating is increased. The peak fluctuations for all velocity components are close to the wall in the shear turbulence regime, and weaken as C increases. For the convective regime, fluctuations are spread more evenly across the domain and strengthen as C increases further. Results are consistent with other calculations of RMS quantities [20,25,38].

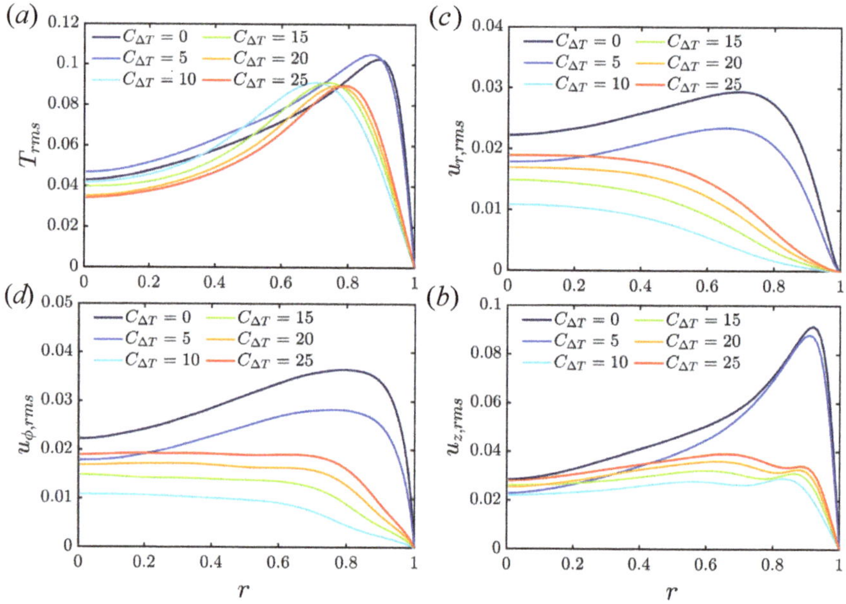

Figure 7. Profiles of RMS temperature and velocity fluctuations at $Re = 5300, L = 5D$: (**a**) T_{rms}; (**b**) $u_{r,rms}$; (**c**) $u_{\phi,rms}$; (**d**) $u_{z,rms}$. Fixed temperature difference.

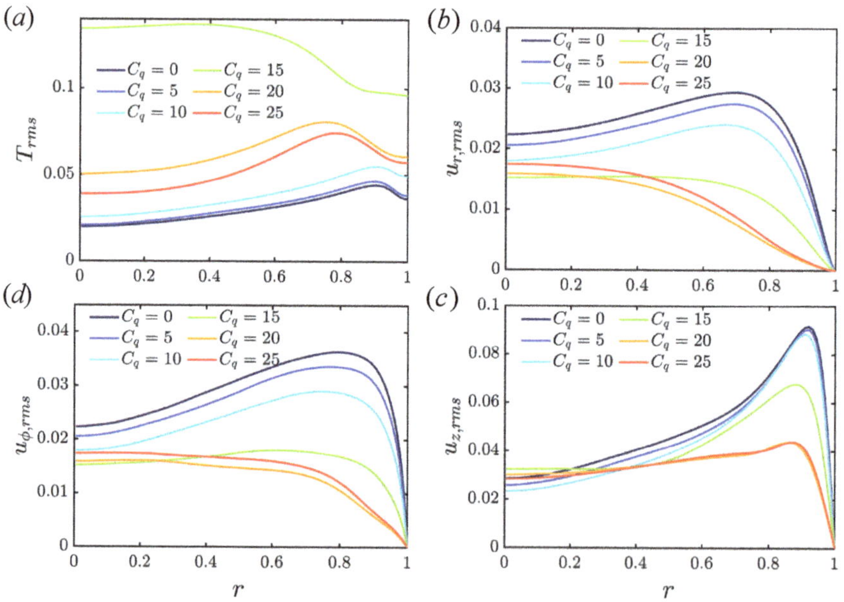

Figure 8. The profile of root mean square of temperature and velocity at $Re = 5300, L = 5D$: (**a**) T_{rms}; (**b**) $u_{r,rms}$; (**c**) $u_{\phi,rms}$; (**d**) $u_{z,rms}$. Fixed boundary heat flux.

3.2. Short vs. Long Periodic Pipes

As the two models give consistent results, only the fixed temperature difference model is considered here. The axially periodic boundary condition could impose some difference in the results compared to true flow. Thus, here we use a longer pipe, $L = 25D$, for comparison. Figure 9 shows the mean velocity and temperature profiles of a short pipe ($L = 5D$) and a longer pipe ($L = 25D$) in shear turbulence regime ($C_{\Delta T} = 5$) and strong convective turbulence ($C_{\Delta T} = 25$). The results for the two pipe lengths are in good agreement, suggesting that $L = 5D$ is enough for capturing the mean profiles. The distributions of the RMS of temperature and velocity for the short pipe and long pipes are shown in Figure 10. There are some small differences, but the agreement is still good. The differences are smaller for convective turbulence. For shear turbulence, there is a little deviation in the centre of the pipe for the cross-stream velocity components. The results in the near-wall region are well matched, suggesting that simulations in a short pipe are expected to capture the heat transfer processes accurately.

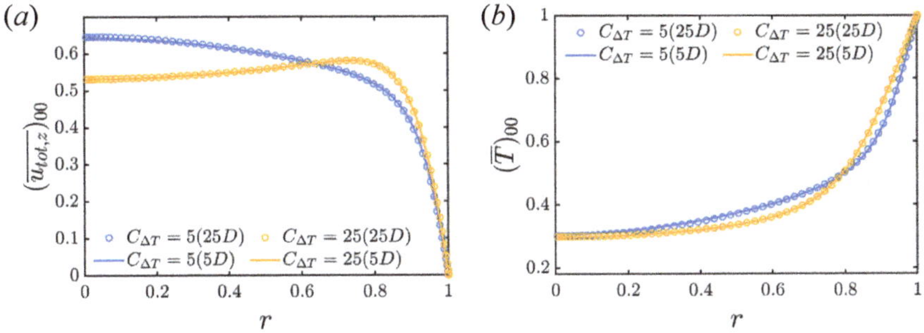

Figure 9. Comparison of mean (**a**) streamwise velocity and (**b**) temperature profile between short periodic pipe ($L = 5D$) and long periodic pipe ($L = 25D$). Two typical flow states are simulated, i.e., shear turbulence ($C_{\Delta T} = 5$) and convective turbulence ($C_{\Delta T} = 25$) at $Re = 5300$. The fixed temperature difference boundary condition is used.

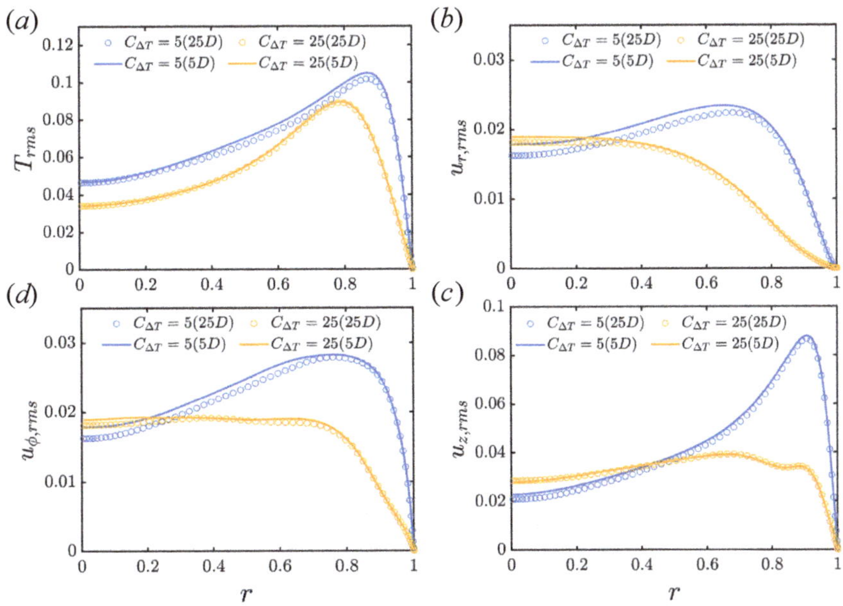

Figure 10. Comparison of (**a**) T_{rms}, (**b**) $u_{r,rms}$,(**c**) $u_{\phi,rms}$ and (**d**) $u_{z,rms}$ between short periodic pipe ($L = 5D$) and long periodic pipe ($L = 25D$). Two typical flow states are simulated, i.e., shear turbulence ($C_{\Delta T} = 5$) and convective turbulence ($C_{\Delta T} = 25$) at $Re = 5300$. Fixed temperature difference.

Contours of streamwise velocity and temperature in the rz cross section for the two pipe lengths are shown in Figure 11 and Figure 12, respectively. The difference in velocity between the shear turbulence (Figure 11a,c) and convective turbulence (Figure 11b,d) is clear: shear turbulence has strong low-speed regions near the wall (associated with streaks). These are essentially absent in convective turbulence, and are replaced with localised regions of fast flow near the wall, while the core flow moves more slowly. No obvious difference in the contour plots is observed between short and long pipes, for both velocity and temperature fields.

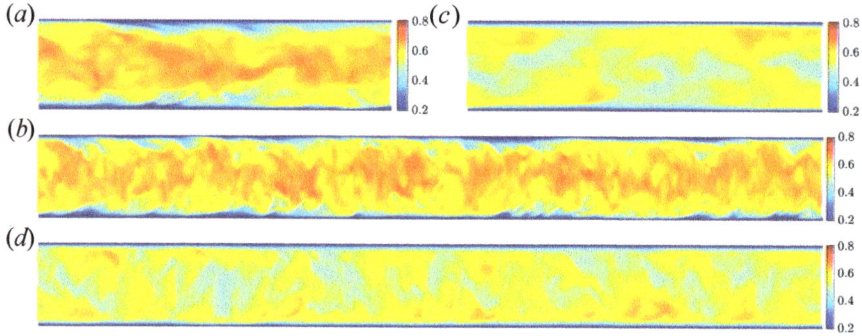

Figure 11. Contours of streamwise velocity in rz cross section for shear turbulence ($C_{\Delta T} = 5$) in (**a**) $L = 5D$, (**c**) $L = 25D$, and convective turbulence ($C_{\Delta T} = 25$) in (**b**) $L = 5D$, (**d**) $L = 25D$ at $Re = 5300$. For the long pipe, the z-axis is scaled to show the whole pipe.

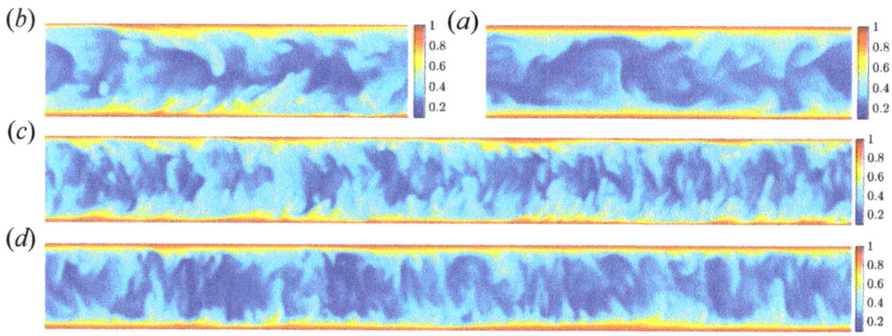

Figure 12. Contours of temperature in rz cross-section for shear turbulence ($C_{\Delta T} = 5$) in (**a**) $L = 5D$, (**c**) $L = 25D$, and convective turbulence ($C_{\Delta T} = 25$) in (**b**) $L = 5D$, (**d**) $L = 25D$ at $Re = 5300$. For the long pipe, the z-axis is scaled to show the whole pipe.

The time evolution of $a(t)$ for the two pipe lengths is shown in Figure 13a. The curves at matching $C_{\Delta T}$ are quite close, but smaller fluctuations in $a(t)$ are observed for the longer pipe. This is expected, as the larger domain gives more steady volume-averaged quantities used in the calculation of $a(t)$. Nusselt numbers for the short and long pipes at several $C_{\Delta T}$ are compared in Figure 13b. There is almost no difference in the Nusselt number over a wide range $C_{\Delta T}$ covering both shear turbulence and convective turbulence. Therefore, it is concluded that the simulation of a short periodic pipe ($L = 5D$) is enough to predict the heat transfer and flow dynamics for fully turbulent flow. For C close to critical, however, data from either one state or the other are used in the calculation of Nu so that intermittency is not fully accounted for. We consider this next.

In isothermal flow, localised turbulent patches are called puffs and slugs [39]. Puffs appear for $Re \approx 1800$ and are statistically steady in axial extent. From $Re \gtrsim 2250$, they start to expand and are called slugs. However, within the expanding turbulent region (that will eventually fill a periodic domain), laminar patches remain present for Re up to approximately 2800 [40]. Thus, there is a large range over which the intermittent nature of turbulence cannot be captured in a short periodic domain of length $L = 5D$. Puffs and slugs have frictional drag between the values extrapolated from the fully turbulent or laminar regimes, and are marked as a hatched area in the Moody diagram [41]. For a heated pipe, this will affect the estimations of *Nu*.

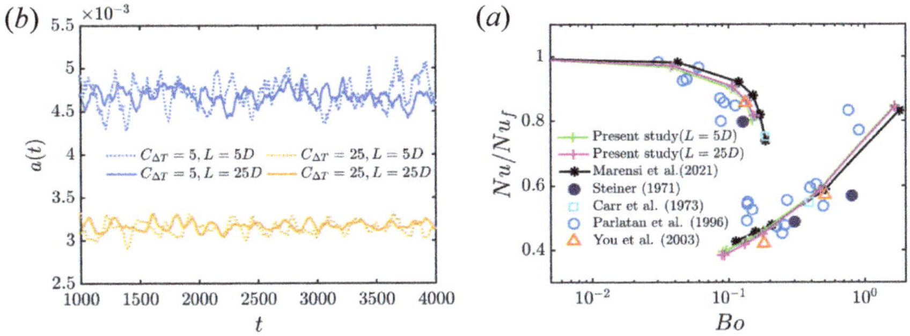

Figure 13. (**a**) Time evolution of $a(t)$ for short ($L = 5D$) and longer pipe ($L = 25D$). (**b**) Normalised Nusselt number for the short and longer pipe at $Re = 5300$. *Bo* defined as in Figure 3. Fixed temperature difference model. Data from [6,20,35–37].

In vertical heated pipe flow, intermittent turbulence exists around the boundary between laminar and shear turbulence at higher Reynolds numbers, at the meeting of the green and blue regions in Figure 4. Examples of puff and slug at $Re = 3000, C_{\Delta T} = 1.9$ are shown in Figure 14. Nusselt numbers for the short and long pipes at $Re = 3000$ are shown in Figure 15. At small $C_{\Delta T}$, there is almost no difference, as the turbulence fills the pipe. As $C_{\Delta T}$ increases, the difference in *Nu* between the short and long pipe becomes substantial, due to the appearance of localised turbulence. Eventually, laminarisation occurs, marked by the final two points.

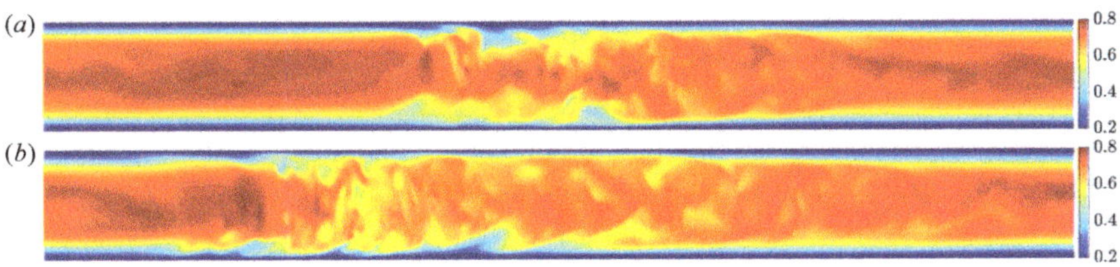

Figure 14. Contour of streamwise velocity in long pipe ($L = 25D$ at $Re = 3000, C_{\Delta T} = 1.9$): (**a**) puff and (**b**) slug.

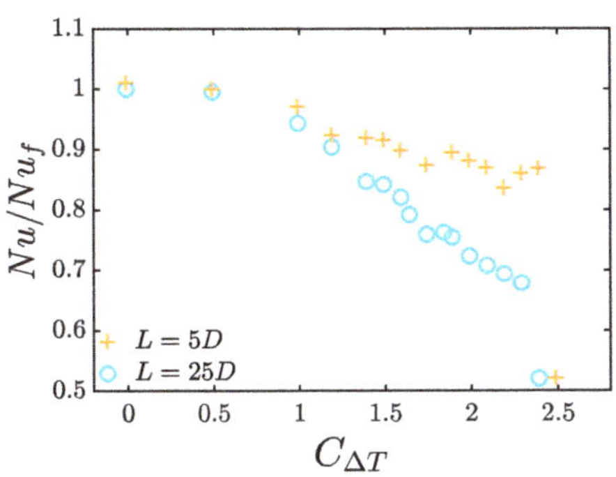

Figure 15. Comparison of Nusselt number for transitional $C_{\Delta T}$ for a short and long periodic domain ($L = 5D$, $25D$) at $Re = 3000$. Values for (intermittent) turbulence are shown, except for the final two laminar points.

3.3. The Lifetime of Localised Shear Turbulence

The mean lifetimes of turbulent puffs in isothermal flow, and its scaling with Reynolds number, have been closely investigated [28,42–44]. At each Re, the mean lifetime must be estimated from a series of simulations or experiments, and data are often truncated, due to the limited simulation time or the finite length of the pipe [28]. To examine whether the lifetime of puffs in heated pipes behave similarly, we calculate the survivor functions at $Re = 3000$ for several $C_{\Delta T}$. To generate the initial conditions for the simulations, a localised disturbance is applied to the laminar Poiseuille flow at $Re = 3000, C_{\Delta T} = 1.9$ and the resulting puff is evolved for $t \approx 5000$. Snapshots of the full velocity field are recorded every 20 time units, generating a large collection of initial conditions. Subsequently, simulations at larger $C_{\Delta T}$ are performed starting from these initial conditions and are monitored until the flow laminarises. The criterion for laminarisation is $E_{3d} < 10^{-3}$, below which turbulent motions are decayed beyond recovery.

The time evolution of E_{3d} of $n = 50$ arbitrary initial turbulent fields at $C_{\Delta T} = 2$ are shown in Figure 16a. Some cases decay to the laminar state, while others remain turbulent for the period of the simulation. The decay of turbulence leads to a large drop in the Nusselt number and an exponential decay of E_{3d} so that laminarisations are clearly identifiable. For a finite set of samples, the survivor function is approximated by

$$S(t) = \frac{r}{n}, \tag{23}$$

where r is the number of puffs that survive up to time t. For example, all initial conditions survive before $t = 10$, then $S(t) = 1$ when $t < 10$. In this way, we can calculate the lifetime of survivor probability from 1 to $\frac{1}{50}$. However, due to the finite time it takes for E_{3d} to drop to 10^{-3}, the data in Figure 16b are shifted to the left by the time of the earliest decay (≈ 250). As $C_{\Delta T}$ increases, the mean lifetime of puffs decreases. The distributions remain exponential in form for each $C_{\Delta T}$. This indicates that the puff decay induced by heating is also a memoryless process, corresponding to the escape from a strange saddle [28,42]. The enhancement of heating has a similar effect to that of the decrease in Reynolds number in isothermal flow.

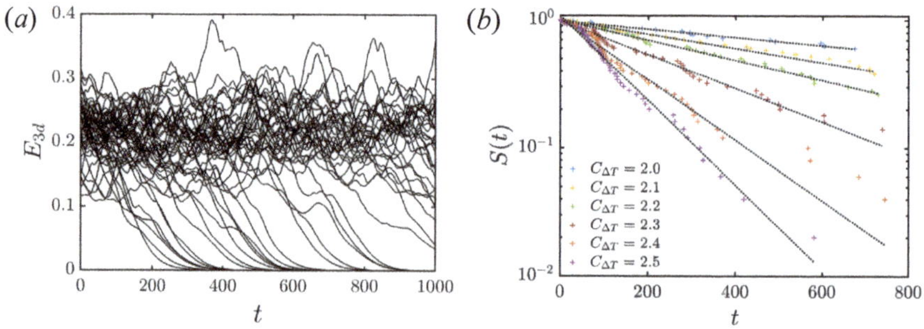

Figure 16. The time evolution of (**a**) E_{3d} of 50 arbitrary initial turbulent fields at $C_{\Delta T} = 2$. (**b**) Survivor function for several values of the buoyancy parameter. $n = 50$ samples for each case. $L = 25D$.

4. Conclusions

In this work, we have presented a derivation of a model for vertically heated pipe flow that includes a time-dependent axial temperature gradient. This gradient adjusts in response to the flow pattern. A transition from shear turbulence to convective turbulence is well known to lead to a drop in heat transfer. For the fixed temperature model, reduced heat transferred into the fluid leads to a reduction in the temperature gradient. With the fixed heat flux boundary condition, however, as the energy withdrawn from the domain is proportional to the gradient, the gradient is forced to remain the same on average to match the energy entering the domain.

Laminar solutions are calculated numerically for several values of the buoyancy parameter, and are consistent with previous reports [6,20,31]. For turbulent flow, the time-averaged velocity and temperature profiles, and their RMS fluctuations, are calculated for both boundary conditions. The two turbulent regimes, i.e., shear turbulence and convective turbulence, are easily distinguished in the mean profiles and RMS flucutations. The dependence of flow state over the space of Re and Nu is calculated for both boundary conditions along with various statistics. Statistics show minor differences between the boundary conditions, but both show good consistency with the previous calculations and experiments. Of particular interest are the RMS temperature fluctuations, as they can be non-zero at the wall for the fixed-flux case. Also of interest is that convective turbulence can trigger bursts of shear-like turbulence when close to the critical C between the two states (For isothermal flow, shear-turbulence cannot return from the linearly stable laminar state).

Further simulations are carried out to examine the effect of the periodic length of the pipe on the turbulent statistics and heat transfer. The short pipe $L = 5D$ and long pipe $L = 25D$ show almost no difference in the mean velocity and mean temperature profiles. However, there are some minor mismatches in the RMS of velocity and temperature. The length of the pipe is found to have more effect on shear turbulent state, possibly due to spatial intermittency. The mismatch mainly appears in the centre of the pipe, while there is always a good agreement in the near-wall regime. Hence, the short pipe still captures accurate Nusselt numbers, provided that the flow is not too intermittent. In that case, simulations with a short pipe are likely to overestimate heat transfer, as shear turbulence fills the domain.

Finally, we have recorded the lifetime of the localised turbulence with heating, confirming it also follows a memoryless process corresponding to the escape from a strange saddle. Using the previous model of [6] close to criticality at larger Re, strong fronts and puffs have been found to disappear [45].

The code used for these calculations is available at openpipeflow.org (accessed on 15 March 2024).

Author Contributions: Methodology, A.P.W.; Software, S.C., E.M. and A.P.W.; Investigation, S.C.; Writing—original draft, S.C.; Writing—review & editing, E.M. and A.P.W. All authors have read and agreed to the published version of the manuscript.

Funding: S.C. acknowledges funding from Sheffield–China Scholarships Council PhD Scholarship Programme (CSC no. 202106260029).

Informed Consent Statement: Informed consent was obtained from all subjects involved in the study.

Data Availability Statement: The original contributions presented in the study are included in the article, further inquiries can be directed to the corresponding author.

Conflicts of Interest: The authors declare no conflicts of interest.

Abbreviations

The following abbreviations are used in this manuscript:

RMS	Root Mean Square
DNS	Direct Numerical Simulation

References

1. Zhang, S.; Xu, X.; Liu, C.; Dang, C. A review on application and heat transfer enhancement of supercritical CO_2 in low-grade heat conversion. *Appl. Energy* **2020**, *269*, 114962. [CrossRef]
2. McEligot, D.; Coon, C.; Perkins, H. Relaminarization in tubes. *Int. J. Heat Mass Transf.* **1970**, *13*, 431–433. [CrossRef]
3. Ackerman, J. Pseudoboiling heat transfer to supercritical pressure water in smooth and ribbed tubes. *J. Heat Transf. Trans. ASME* **1970**, *92*, 490–498. [CrossRef]
4. Bae, J.H.; Yoo, J.Y.; Choi, H. Direct numerical simulation of turbulent supercritical flows with heat transfer. *Phys. Fluids* **2005**, *17*, 105104. [CrossRef]
5. Wibisono, A.F.; Addad, Y.; Lee, J.I. Numerical investigation on water deteriorated turbulent heat transfer regime in vertical upward heated flow in circular tube. *Int. J. Heat Mass Transf.* **2015**, *83*, 173–186. [CrossRef]
6. Marensi, E.; He, S.; Willis, A.P. Suppression of turbulence and travelling waves in a vertical heated pipe. *J. Fluid Mech.* **2021**, *919*, A17. [CrossRef]
7. Chu, S.; Willis, A.P.; Marensi, E. The minimal seed for transition to convective turbulence in heated pipe flow. *J. Fluid Mech.* **2024**, *997*, A46. [CrossRef]
8. Hall, W.B.; Jackson, J. Laminarization of a turbulent pipe flow by buoyancy forces. In *Proceedings of the Mechanical Engineering*; ASME—American Society of Mechanical Engineers: New York, NY, USA, 1969; Volume 91, p. 66.
9. He, S.; He, K.; Seddighi, M. Laminarisation of flow at low Reynolds number due to streamwise body force. *J. Fluid Mech.* **2016**, *809*, 31–71. [CrossRef]
10. Hof, B.; De Lozar, A.; Avila, M.; Tu, X.; Schneider, T.M. Eliminating turbulence in spatially intermittent flows. *Science* **2010**, *327*, 1491–1494. [CrossRef] [PubMed]
11. Kühnen, J.; Song, B.; Scarselli, D.; Budanur, N.B.; Riedl, M.; Willis, A.P.; Avila, M.; Hof, B. Destabilizing turbulence in pipe flow. *Nat. Phys.* **2018**, *14*, 386–390. [CrossRef]
12. Scheele, G.F.; Hanratty, T.J. Effect of natural convection on stability of flow in a vertical pipe. *J. Fluid Mech.* **1962**, *14*, 244–256. [CrossRef]
13. Chu, S.; Willis, A.P.; Marensi, E. Laminarising turbulent pipe flow by linear and nonlinear optimisation. *arXiv* **2024**, arXiv:2410.19699.
14. Hamilton, J.M.; Kim, J.; Waleffe, F. Regeneration mechanisms of near-wall turbulence structures. *J. Fluid Mech.* **1995**, *287*, 317–348. [CrossRef]
15. Hiroaki, T.; Ayao, T.; Masaru, H.; Nuchi, N. Effects of buoyancy and of acceleration owing to thermal expansion on forced turbulent convection in vertical circular tubes—criteria of the effects, velocity and temperature profiles, and reverse transition from turbulent to laminar flow. *Int. J. Heat Mass Transf.* **1973**, *16*, 1267–1288. [CrossRef]
16. Cotton, M.A. Theoretical Studies of Mixed Convection in Vertical Tubes. Ph.D. Thesis, University of Manchester, Manchester, UK, 1986.
17. Launder, B.E.; Sharma, B.I. Application of the energy-dissipation model of turbulence to the calculation of flow near a spinning disc. *Lett. Heat Mass Transf.* **1974**, *1*, 131–137. [CrossRef]
18. Behzadmehr, A.; Galanis, N.; Laneville, A. Low Reynolds number mixed convection in vertical tubes with uniform wall heat flux. *Int. J. Heat Mass Transf.* **2003**, *46*, 4823–4833. [CrossRef]
19. Kasagi, N.; Nishimura, M. Direct numerical simulation of combined forced and natural turbulent convection in a vertical plane channel. *Int. J. Heat Fluid Flow* **1997**, *18*, 88–99. [CrossRef]
20. You, J.; Yoo, J.Y.; Choi, H. Direct numerical simulation of heated vertical air flows in fully developed turbulent mixed convection. *Int. J. Heat Mass Transf.* **2003**, *46*, 1613–1627. [CrossRef]
21. Kim, W.; He, S.; Jackson, J. Assessment by comparison with DNS data of turbulence models used in simulations of mixed convection. *Int. J. Heat Mass Transf.* **2008**, *51*, 1293–1312. [CrossRef]
22. Chu, X.; Laurien, E.; McEligot, D.M. Direct numerical simulation of strongly heated air flow in a vertical pipe. *Int. J. Heat Mass Transf.* **2016**, *101*, 1163–1176. [CrossRef]
23. Antoranz, A.; Gonzalo, A.; Flores, O.; Garcia-Villalba, M. Numerical simulation of heat transfer in a pipe with non-homogeneous thermal boundary conditions. *Int. J. Heat Fluid Flow* **2015**, *55*, 45–51. [CrossRef]
24. Straub, S.; Forooghi, P.; Marocco, L.; Wetzel, T.; Vinuesa, R.; Schlatter, P.; Frohnapfel, B. The influence of thermal boundary conditions on turbulent forced convection pipe flow at two Prandtl numbers. *Int. J. Heat Mass Transf.* **2019**, *144*, 118601. [CrossRef]
25. Cruz, R.V.; Flageul, C.; Lamballais, E.; Duffal, V.; Le Coupanec, E.; Benhamadouche, S. High-fidelity simulation of turbulent mixed convection in pipe flow. *Int. J. Heat Fluid Flow* **2024**, *110*, 109640. [CrossRef]
26. Willis, A.P. The Openpipeflow Navier–Stokes solver. *SoftwareX* **2017**, *6*, 124–127. [CrossRef]
27. Eggels, J.G.; Unger, F.; Weiss, M.; Westerweel, J.; Adrian, R.J.; Friedrich, R.; Nieuwstadt, F.T. Fully developed turbulent pipe flow: A comparison between direct numerical simulation and experiment. *J. Fluid Mech.* **1994**, *268*, 175–210. [CrossRef]

28. Avila, M.; Willis, A.P.; Hof, B. On the transient nature of localized pipe flow turbulence. *J. Fluid Mech.* **2010**, *646*, 127–136. [CrossRef]
29. Gray, D.D.; Giorgini, A. The validity of the Boussinesq approximation for liquids and gases. *Int. J. Heat Mass Transf.* **1976**, *19*, 545–551. [CrossRef]
30. Turner, J.S.; Turner, J.S. *Buoyancy Effects in Fluids*; Cambridge University Press: Cambridge, UK, 1979.
31. Su, Y.C.; Chung, J.N. Linear stability analysis of mixed-convection flow in a vertical pipe. *J. Fluid Mech.* **2000**, *422*, 141–166. [CrossRef]
32. Piller, M. Direct numerical simulation of turbulent forced convection in a pipe. *Int. J. Numer. Methods Fluids* **2005**, *49*, 583–602. [CrossRef]
33. Baranovskii, E.S.; Domnich, A.A.; Artemov, M.A. Mathematical Analysis of the Poiseuille Flow of a Fluid with Temperature-Dependent Properties. *Mathematics* **2024**, *12*, 3337. [CrossRef]
34. Yoo, J.Y. The turbulent flows of supercritical fluids with heat transfer. *Annu. Rev. Fluid Mech.* **2013**, *45*, 495–525. [CrossRef]
35. Steiner, A. On the reverse transition of a turbulent flow under the action of buoyancy forces. *J. Fluid Mech.* **1971**, *47*, 503–512. [CrossRef]
36. Carr, A.; Connor, M.; Buhr, H. Velocity, Temperature, and Turbulence Measurements in Air for Pipe Flow with Combined Free and Forced Convection. *J. Heat Transf.* **1973**, *95*, 445–452. [CrossRef]
37. Parlatan, Y.; Todreas, N.; Driscoll, M. Buoyancy and property variation effects in turbulent mixed convection of water in vertical tubes. *J. Heat Transf.* **1996**, *118*, 381–387. [CrossRef]
38. Zhao, P.; Zhu, J.; Ge, Z.; Liu, J.; Li, Y. Direct numerical simulation of turbulent mixed convection of LBE in heated upward pipe flows. *Int. J. Heat Mass Transf.* **2018**, *126*, 1275–1288. [CrossRef]
39. Avila, M.; Barkley, D.; Hof, B. Transition to turbulence in pipe flow. *Annu. Rev. Fluid Mech.* **2023**, *55*, 575–602. [CrossRef]
40. Marensi, E.; Hof, B. The onset of fully turbulent pipe flow. In Proceedings of the APS Division of Fluid Dynamics Meeting Abstracts, Phoenix, AZ, USA, 21–23 November 2021; p. P31012M.
41. Moody, L.F. Friction Factors for Pipe Flow. *J. Fluids Eng.* **1944**, *66*, 671–678. [CrossRef]
42. Willis, A.; Kerswell, R. Critical behavior in the relaminarization of localized turbulence in pipe flow. *Phys. Rev. Lett.* **2007**, *98*, 014501. [CrossRef] [PubMed]
43. Willis, A.P.; Kerswell, R.R. Turbulent dynamics of pipe flow captured in a reduced model: Puff relaminarization and localized 'edge' states. *J. Fluid Mech.* **2009**, *619*, 213–233. [CrossRef]
44. Hof, B.; de Lozar, A.; Kuik, D.; Westerweel, J. Repeller or attractor? Selecting the dynamical model for the onset of turbulence in pipe flow. *Phys. Rev. Lett.* **2008**, *101*, 214501. [CrossRef] [PubMed]
45. Zhuang, Y.; Yang, B.; Mukund, V.; Marensi, E.; Hof, B. Discontinuous transition to shear flow turbulence. *arXiv* **2023**, arXiv:2311.11474.

mathematics

MDPI

Article

Geometrical Optics Stability Analysis of Rotating Visco-Diffusive Flows

Oleg Kirillov

Department of Mathematics, Physics and Electrical Engineering, Northumbria University, Newcastle upon Tyne NE1 8ST, UK; oleg.kirillov@northumbria.ac.uk

Abstract: Geometrical optics stability analysis has proven effective in deriving analytical instability criteria for 3D flows in ideal hydrodynamics and magnetohydrodynamics, encompassing both compressible and incompressible fluids. The method models perturbations as high-frequency wavelets, evolving along fluid trajectories. Detecting local instabilities reduces to solving ODEs for the wave vector and amplitude of the wavelet envelope along streamlines, with coefficients derived from the background flow. While viscosity and diffusivity were traditionally regarded as stabilizing factors, recent extensions of the geometrical optics framework have revealed their destabilizing potential in visco-diffusive and multi-diffusive flows. This review highlights these advancements, with a focus on their application to the azimuthal magnetorotational instability in magnetohydrodynamics and the McIntyre instability in lenticular vortices and swirling differentially heated flows. It introduces new analytical instability criteria, applicable across a wide range of Prandtl, Schmidt, and magnetic Prandtl numbers, which still remains beyond the reach of numerical methods in many important physical and industrial applications.

Keywords: rotating flows; swirling flows; magnetized flows; double diffusion; dissipation-induced instabilities; local stability analysis; magnetorotational instability; McIntyre instability

MSC: 76M45; 76E20; 76E25; 76U05; 35B35; 35Q35; 37J25; 47B50; 58K60; 58K45

1. Introduction

Consider a system of coupled nonlinear partial differential equations (PDEs) modeling a physical phenomenon in hydrodynamics or magnetohydrodynamics, incorporating additional factors such as fluid compressibility, rotation, density stratification, thermal gradients, and electromagnetic fields. Let the vector $\boldsymbol{L}(\boldsymbol{x},t) = (\boldsymbol{u}(\boldsymbol{x},t), p(\boldsymbol{x},t),\ldots)^T$ represent the unknown functions governed by the system. This vector includes the fluid velocity field $\boldsymbol{u}(\boldsymbol{x},t)$, pressure $p(\boldsymbol{x},t)$, and other quantities that may vary depending on the model, such as electromagnetic fields, temperature, or density, all of which depend on spatial coordinates $\boldsymbol{x}$ and time t.

Assume the base state of the system, described by the vector $\boldsymbol{L}_B(\boldsymbol{x},t) = (\boldsymbol{u}_B(\boldsymbol{x},t), p_B(\boldsymbol{x},t),\ldots)^T$, is known. To analyze its stability, we consider small perturbations such that $\boldsymbol{L}(\boldsymbol{x},t) = \boldsymbol{L}_B(\boldsymbol{x},t) + \boldsymbol{L}'(\boldsymbol{x},t)$, where $\boldsymbol{L}'(\boldsymbol{x},t) = (\boldsymbol{u}'(\boldsymbol{x},t), p'(\boldsymbol{x},t),\ldots)^T$. Linearizing the governing nonlinear equations about the base state produces a system of linear partial differential equations, enabling linear stability analysis and the application of the indirect Lyapunov method to establish instability criteria [1,2]. The validity of this approach is supported, e.g, by the studies [3,4], which demonstrate a connection between linear and nonlinear instability under specific conditions on the associated linear and nonlinear operators.

Introducing a small parameter $0 < \epsilon \ll 1$, we seek solutions to the linearized equations as asymptotic expansions in ϵ:

$$L'(x,t,\epsilon) = e^{\frac{i\Phi(x,t)}{\epsilon}}\left(L^{(0)}(x,t) + \epsilon L^{(1)}(x,t,\epsilon)\right) + \epsilon L^{(r)}(x,t,\epsilon), \tag{1}$$

where $i = \sqrt{-1}$, Φ is the wave phase (eikonal), and $L^{(j)} = (u^{(j)}, p^{(j)}, \ldots)^T$ $(j = 0, 1, r)$ are complex-valued amplitudes. The remainder $L^{(r)}$ is assumed to remain uniformly bounded in ϵ over any fixed time interval [5–12].

Substituting (1) into the linearized system and collecting terms at orders ϵ^{-1} and ϵ^0 yields a system of PDEs comprising the eikonal equation for $\Phi(x,t)$ and transport equations for the amplitude $L^{(0)}(x,t)$, with initial conditions $\Phi(x,0) = \Phi_0(x)$ and $L^{(0)}(x,0) = L_0^{(0)}(x)$.

Consider a fluid element following the trajectory

$$\frac{dx}{dt} = u_B, \quad x(0) = x_0. \tag{2}$$

Since the eikonal and transport equations involve only the advective derivative $d/dt = \partial_t + u_B \cdot \nabla$ along the base flow velocity u_B [9,10,13], the eikonal equation becomes an ODE describing the evolution of the wave vector $k(t) = \nabla\Phi(x(t), t)$ along the streamline (2), with initial condition $k(0) = k_0 = \nabla\Phi_0(x_0)$. Similarly, the transport equations become a system of ODEs along the streamlines for the amplitudes $L^{(0)}(x(t), t)$, forming the complete system of characteristic equations. These describe the motion of the perturbation envelope (viewed as a high-frequency wavelet [9]) initially localized at x_0, along with the fluid elements passing through x_0 at $t = 0$ [9,10,13].

For a sufficiently small ϵ, the leading-order terms dominate the solution (1) over an extended time [9,11]. This reduces the stability analysis to studying the growth rates of solutions of the transport ODEs, which are generally non-autonomous due to the time dependence of the wave vector. Stability conditions are determined by the boundedness of solutions: the existence of unbounded solutions implies instability [9,10]. This localized analysis provides sufficient instability and necessary stability conditions along the trajectories of the flow [9,10].

The geometrical optics stability analysis has proven highly effective in addressing stability problems in ideal hydrodynamics and magnetohydrodynamics for 3D flows, both compressible and incompressible, characterized by complex streamlines. Applications span a broad range of systems, including circular Couette–Taylor flow [14], flows with elliptical [15–18] and hyperbolic [16,19] streamlines; chaotic streamline systems like the ABC flow [14], helical (swirling) compressible [5,20] and incompressible [7,20] flows; vortex rings with swirl [21,22]; Kelvin–Helmholtz vortices [23]; Riemann ellipsoids in celestial mechanics [24–26]; geophysical flows [10]; and hydromagnetic systems [27–32]. For ideal flows with elliptical streamlines subject to elliptical parametric instability, the periodic amplitude transport equations are effectively addressed either numerically [26,33] or through perturbation methods [29,30], in combination with Floquet theory [15].

Maslov [34] noted that high-frequency oscillations of the form $\exp(i\epsilon^{-1}\Phi(x,t))$ rapidly decay due to viscosity, unless a quadratic dependence of viscosity on the small parameter ϵ is assumed: $\nu = \epsilon^2\tilde{\nu}$. This assumption allowed the extension of geometrical optics stability analysis to the Navier-=Stokes equations [11], where an integral transformation of the amplitude reduced the viscous transport equations to their inviscid form, revealing the stabilizing influence of viscosity [9,11,14,19]. Consequently, early applications of geometrical optics stability analysis were restricted to cases where viscosity or diffusivity had a purely stabilizing effect, even in visco-diffusive or multiple-diffusive settings [19,35].

For instance, to reduce mathematical complexity, early studies often assumed a Prandtl number $Pr = 1$ or a Schmidt number $Sc = 1$, corresponding to an equal ratio of viscosity to either heat conductivity or molecular diffusivity of the stratifying agent, respectively. Leblanc [36] highlighted the unique role of $Pr = 1$ ($Sc = 1$), stating: "The standard transformation used in non-stratified flows [19] is not valid here, except in the exceptional case where $Pr = 1$ ($Sc = 1$), which may be treated in closed form. In that case, introducing a change of variables reduces the amplitude equation to an inviscid homogeneous Hill's equation. With the wave vector being periodic and bounded in time, inviscid resonances are either damped or eventually suppressed by diffusion". For large Prandtl (Schmidt) numbers but small viscosity and diffusivity, particularly with vanishing thermal diffusivity, Leblanc further reduced the problem to a damped Mathieu equation, demonstrating that under certain conditions "viscosity suppresses parametric instability".

Similar observations have been made in magnetohydrodynamics, where both viscous dissipation and magnetic diffusion (their ratio is the magnetic Prandtl number, Pm) were considered [31]: "This shows first that if the diffusivities are equal, the only effect of dissipation is a reduction in growth rate. Second, assuming magnetic diffusivity is vanishingly small, the impact of dissipation primarily manifests as a decrease in the growth rate".

Building on the studies [37–39], which analyzed helical and azimuthal magnetorotational instabilities under the geometrical optics framework, it became clear that this method is effective even for systems with unequal diffusivities. In particular, it enabled the derivation of new analytical criteria for dissipation-induced instabilities, including the Goldreich–Schubert–Fricke instability [13], McIntyre instability [40–42], and salt-fingering double-diffusive instability [42].

Recently, Singh and Mathur [43] applied the geometrical optics approach to investigate the effect of the Schmidt number on elliptical instability under stable stratification. Their findings revealed that $Sc \neq 1$ significantly alters inviscid instability behavior and introduces a new branch of oscillatory instability, absent when $Sc = 1$. This observation aligns with earlier studies that demonstrated that damping broadens the region of combination parametric resonance in the context of solid mechanics and nonlinear dynamics [44,45].

These advancements have expanded the applicability of geometrical optics stability analysis to visco-diffusive and multi-diffusive rotating flows with circular and elliptical streamlines over a broad range of Prandtl, Schmidt, and magnetic Prandtl numbers; see, e.g., the recent studies [33,46–48].

In this review paper, we address three characteristic problems using the extended geometrical optics analysis. The first of these is the inductionless azimuthal magnetorotational instability (AMRI) in magnetohydrodynamics, important both in the astrophysical context of onset of turbulence in accretion disks and in the engineering context of liquid metal technology and related experiments [49]. The geometrical optics approach enabled us to identify conditions for the instability of quasi-Keplerian, differentially rotating, magnetized fluids subjected to azimuthal non-homogeneous magnetic fields, thereby overcoming the well-known "Liu limit" for the Rossby number, which quantifies the shear strength of the flow [37,38]. Building on the framework introduced in [1,39], we reinterpret AMRI within the broader theory of dissipation-induced instabilities [1,2,45]. Specifically, we analyze it as a Hamilton–Hopf bifurcation in the absence of diffusion and investigate the visco-diffusive AMRI as its dissipative unfolding. This analysis reveals a singular "Whitney umbrella" structure [45,50] on the neutral stability surface, elucidating the critical role of the magnetic Prandtl number $Pm = 1$. Furthermore, it establishes a connection between viscous or diffusive destabilization and the energy (or Krein) sign of the modes involved in the diffusionless Hamilton–Hopf bifurcation.

Next, following [40], we focus on the visco-diffusive instabilities of a "Gaussian lens" model representing a baroclinic lenticular vortex with the shape of an oblate ellipsoid, differentially rotating in a vertically stratified ambient fluid. This model facilitates the study of coherent lenticular vortices, which are ubiquitous in Earth's oceans (commonly known as "Meddies" in oceanographic contexts) [51] and were recently observed in Earth's stratosphere following wildfires in Canada and Australia [52]. Additionally, lenticular vortices represent long-lived coherent structures in the atmospheres of giant planets, such as Jupiter's Great Red Spot [53]. High temperature and concentration gradients often occur at the periphery of lenticular vortices due to their interaction with colder and more dilute ambient fluid. Both isolated and interacting lenticular vortices can emit internal gravity waves and exhibit fine-scale layering, driven by visco-diffusive and multi-diffusive mechanisms that may eventually lead to their disintegration. In this context, we present the analytical criteria of the McIntyre-like [41] visco-diffusive instability of Gaussian lenses and discuss the role of the Schmidt number in the onset of oscillatory and monotonic instabilities in these coherent structures.

Finally, using the ideas presented in [13,47], we examine the visco-thermodiffusive McIntyre instability of spiral Poiseuille flow (SPF) with a radial temperature gradient (SPFRT) using the generalized geometrical optics approach. The SPFRT combines a circular Couette flow and an annular Poiseuille flow driven by an axial pressure gradient, while the radial temperature gradient induces centrifugal buoyancy. Vertical Archimedean buoyancy is neglected [54] compared to the relevant recent study [47], a simplification that enables the derivation of analytical approximations for the thresholds of both oscillatory and monotonic McIntyre instability in these swirling flows. An important advancement in this study is based on the relationship between parametric optimization and the construction of envelopes of curve families [55]. This approach allows for the derivation of universal stability criteria by computing the envelopes of neutral stability curves, parameterized by the axial (or equivalently, azimuthal) wavenumber. By treating the equations for neutral stability curves as polynomials in the wavenumber, we identify their discriminant set, which includes the equation for the envelope and provides explicit instability criteria.

2. Singular Diffusionless Limit of Visco-Diffusive Instabilities in Magnetohydrodynamics

2.1. Governing Equations and Background Fields

Following [39], we consider azimuthal magnetorotational instability (AMRI) as a visco-diffusive oscillatory instability. The dynamics of a viscous, electrically conducting, incompressible Newtonian fluid interacting with a magnetic field are governed by the coupled Navier–Stokes and induction equations [1,37–39]:

$$\left.\begin{aligned}\frac{\partial \boldsymbol{u}}{\partial t}+\boldsymbol{u}\cdot\nabla\boldsymbol{u}-\frac{1}{\mu_0\rho}\boldsymbol{B}\cdot\nabla\boldsymbol{B}+\frac{1}{\rho}\nabla P-\nu\nabla^2\boldsymbol{u}=0,\\ \frac{\partial \boldsymbol{B}}{\partial t}+\boldsymbol{u}\cdot\nabla\boldsymbol{B}-\boldsymbol{B}\cdot\nabla\boldsymbol{u}-\eta\nabla^2\boldsymbol{B}=0,\end{aligned}\right\} \tag{3}$$

where $P = p + \frac{B^2}{2\mu_0}$ is the total pressure, p is the hydrodynamic pressure, ρ is the density, ν is the kinematic viscosity, $\eta = (\mu_0\sigma)^{-1}$ is the magnetic diffusivity, σ is the fluid's conductivity, and μ_0 is the magnetic permeability of free space. The flow velocity field $\boldsymbol{u}$ and magnetic field $\boldsymbol{B}$ are subject to the incompressibility and solenoidal field constraints:

$$\nabla\cdot\boldsymbol{u}=0,\quad \nabla\cdot\boldsymbol{B}=0. \tag{4}$$

For a differentially rotating flow in the gap between radii r_1 and $r_2 > r_1$ and purely azimuthal magnetic field, the steady solution to (3) and (4) has the following form:

$$\boldsymbol{u}_B(r) = r\,\Omega(r)\,\boldsymbol{e}_\phi, \quad p = p_B(r), \quad \boldsymbol{B}_B(r) = B_\phi^0(r)\boldsymbol{e}_\phi, \tag{5}$$

in cylindrical coordinates (r, ϕ, z).

In the magnetized circular Couette–Taylor flow (5), the angular velocity profile $\Omega(r)$ and the azimuthal magnetic field $B_\phi^0(r)$ are arbitrary functions of r subject to boundary conditions for an inviscid, non-resistive fluid. For viscous and resistive fluids, these profiles become $\Omega(r) = a + br^{-2}$ and $B_\phi^0(r) = cr + dr^{-1}$, with coefficients determined by boundary conditions. In the context of local linear stability analysis, boundary conditions are neglected, and the steady state of the visco-diffusive system coincides with that of the diffusionless system.

2.2. Transport Equations for Amplitudes and Their Dispersion Relation

Linearizing Equations (3) and (4) near the stationary solution (5), and seeking a solution in asymptotic form (1) under the assumptions $\nu = \epsilon^2\widetilde{\nu}$ and $\eta = \epsilon^2\widetilde{\eta}$ [34], we derive transport equations for the amplitudes $\boldsymbol{u}^{(0)}$ and $\boldsymbol{B}^{(0)}$ [28,37–39]:

$$\begin{aligned} \frac{d\boldsymbol{u}^{(0)}}{dt} &= \left[\frac{2\boldsymbol{k}\boldsymbol{k}^T}{|\boldsymbol{k}|^2} - \mathcal{I}\right]\mathcal{U}\boldsymbol{u}^{(0)} - \widetilde{\nu}|\boldsymbol{k}|^2\boldsymbol{u}^{(0)} + \frac{1}{\rho\mu_0}\left\{\left[\mathcal{I} - \frac{2\boldsymbol{k}\boldsymbol{k}^T}{|\boldsymbol{k}|^2}\right]\mathcal{B} + \boldsymbol{B}_B\cdot\boldsymbol{\nabla}\right\}\boldsymbol{B}^{(0)}, \\ \frac{d\boldsymbol{B}^{(0)}}{dt} &= \mathcal{U}\boldsymbol{B}^{(0)} - \widetilde{\eta}|\boldsymbol{k}|^2\boldsymbol{B}^{(0)} - (\mathcal{B} - \boldsymbol{B}_B\cdot\boldsymbol{\nabla})\boldsymbol{u}^{(0)}, \end{aligned} \tag{6}$$

where $\mathcal{I}$ is the 3×3 identity matrix, and the gradients of the background fields are

$$\mathcal{U} := \boldsymbol{\nabla}\boldsymbol{u}_B = \Omega\begin{pmatrix} 0 & -1 & 0 \\ 1+2Ro & 0 & 0 \\ 0 & 0 & 0 \end{pmatrix}, \quad \mathcal{B} := \boldsymbol{\nabla}\boldsymbol{B}_B = \frac{B_\phi^0}{r}\begin{pmatrix} 0 & -1 & 0 \\ 1+2Rb & 0 & 0 \\ 0 & 0 & 0 \end{pmatrix}, \tag{7}$$

with the time evolution of the wave vector $\boldsymbol{k} = (k_r, k_\phi, k_z)^T = \boldsymbol{\nabla}\Phi$ given by

$$\frac{d\boldsymbol{k}}{dt} = -\mathcal{U}^T\boldsymbol{k}, \tag{8}$$

where $d/dt = \partial_t + \boldsymbol{u}_B\cdot\nabla$. Equations (6) and (8) hold if $\boldsymbol{B}_B\cdot\boldsymbol{k} = 0$.

Defining $\alpha = k_z|\boldsymbol{k}|^{-1}$ and $|\boldsymbol{k}|^2 = k_r^2 + k_z^2$, we introduce the Alfvén angular velocity, viscous and resistive frequencies, and the hydrodynamic and magnetic Reynolds numbers [37,38]:

$$\omega_{A_\phi} = \frac{B_\phi^0}{r\sqrt{\rho\mu_0}}, \quad \omega_\nu = \widetilde{\nu}|\boldsymbol{k}|^2, \quad \omega_\eta = \widetilde{\eta}|\boldsymbol{k}|^2, \quad Re = \frac{\alpha\Omega}{\omega_\nu}, \quad Rm = \frac{\alpha\Omega}{\omega_\eta}, \tag{9}$$

and the fluid and magnetic Rossby numbers [37]:

$$Ro = \frac{rD\Omega}{2\Omega}, \quad Rb = \frac{rD\omega_{A_\phi}}{2\omega_{A_\phi}}, \tag{10}$$

where $D = \frac{d}{dr}$. Note that $Rm = RePm$ with $Pm = \frac{\nu}{\eta}$ as the magnetic Prandtl number.

Seeking solutions to Equations (6) in modal form [27,39], $\boldsymbol{u}^{(0)} = \widehat{\boldsymbol{u}}e^{\alpha\Omega\lambda t + im\phi}$ and $\boldsymbol{B}^{(0)} = \sqrt{\rho\mu_0}\widehat{\boldsymbol{B}}e^{\alpha\Omega\lambda t + im\phi}$, the amplitude equations yield

$$A\boldsymbol{z} = \lambda\boldsymbol{z}, \tag{11}$$

where $z = (\widehat{u}_R, \widehat{u}_\phi, \widehat{B}_R, \widehat{B}_\phi)^T \in \mathbb{C}^4$ and $A = A_0 + A_1 \in \mathbb{C}^{4\times 4}$ with

$$A_0 = \begin{pmatrix} -in & 2\alpha & inS & -2\alpha S \\ -\frac{2(1+Ro)}{\alpha} & -in & \frac{2(1+Rb)}{\alpha}S & inS \\ inS & 0 & -in & 0 \\ -\frac{2Rb}{\alpha}S & inS & \frac{2Ro}{\alpha} & -in \end{pmatrix}, \quad A_1 = \begin{pmatrix} \frac{-1}{Re} & 0 & 0 & 0 \\ 0 & \frac{-1}{Re} & 0 & 0 \\ 0 & 0 & \frac{-1}{Rm} & 0 \\ 0 & 0 & 0 & \frac{-1}{Rm} \end{pmatrix}. \tag{12}$$

Here, $n = m/\alpha$ is the modified azimuthal wavenumber, and $S = \omega_{A_\phi}/\Omega$ is the Alfvén angular velocity in units of Ω.

Defining a Hermitian matrix

$$G = \begin{pmatrix} 0 & -i & 0 & iS \\ i & 0 & -iS & 0 \\ 0 & iS & 4\frac{Ro-Rb}{\alpha n} & -i \\ -iS & 0 & i & 0 \end{pmatrix}, \tag{13}$$

the indefinite inner product in $\mathbb{C}^4$ becomes $[x, y] = \overline{y}^T G x$ [1,39], with the standard inner product $(x, y) = \overline{y}^T x$. The matrix $H_0 = -iGA_0$ is Hermitian:

$$H_0 = \begin{pmatrix} -\frac{2(S^2Rb-Ro-1)}{\alpha} & in(S^2+1) & -\frac{2S(1+Rb-Ro)}{\alpha} & -2inS \\ -in(S^2+1) & 2\alpha & 2inS & -2\alpha S \\ -\frac{2S(1+Rb-Ro)}{\alpha} & -2inS & \frac{2(S^2Rb+S^2+2Rb-3Ro)}{\alpha} & in(S^2+1) \\ 2inS & -2\alpha S & -in(S^2+1) & 2\alpha S^2 \end{pmatrix}. \tag{14}$$

The eigenvalue problem $A_0 z = \lambda z$ transforms to Hamiltonian form with H_0 [1,39]:

$$H_0 z = i^{-1} G \lambda z. \tag{15}$$

The symmetry $A_0 = -G^{-1}\overline{A_0}^T G$ ensures the spectrum of A_0 is symmetric about the imaginary axis.

The full eigenvalue problem (11) is a dissipative perturbation of the Hamiltonian problem (15):

$$(H_0 + H_1)z = i^{-1} G \lambda z, \tag{16}$$

where $H_1 = -iGA_1$ is complex and non-Hermitian:

$$H_1 = \begin{pmatrix} 0 & \frac{1}{Re} & 0 & -\frac{S}{Rm} \\ -\frac{1}{Re} & 0 & \frac{S}{Rm} & 0 \\ 0 & -\frac{S}{Re} & 4i\frac{Ro-Rb}{\alpha n Rm} & \frac{1}{Rm} \\ \frac{S}{Re} & 0 & -\frac{1}{Rm} & 0 \end{pmatrix}. \tag{17}$$

The dispersion relation for the visco-diffusive system (16) follows as

$$p(\lambda) := \det(H_0 + H_1 - i^{-1} G \lambda) = 0. \tag{18}$$

2.3. Krein Sign and Splitting of Double Eigenvalues with Jordan Block

A simple imaginary eigenvalue $\lambda = i\omega$ of the eigenvalue problem (15), with eigenvector z, has a positive Krein sign if $[z, z] > 0$ and a negative Krein sign if $[z, z] < 0$ [1,39].

Let p represent the parameters of the matrix H_0, i.e., $p = (S, Ro, Rb, n)^T \in \mathbb{R}^4$. Suppose that, at $p = p_0$, the matrix $H_0 = H(p_0)$ has a double imaginary eigenvalue $\lambda = i\omega_0$ ($\omega_0 \geq 0$), with a Jordan chain consisting of eigenvector z_0 and associated vector z_1, satisfying

$$H_0 z_0 = \omega_0 G z_0, \quad H_0 z_1 = \omega_0 G z_1 + i^{-1} G z_0. \tag{19}$$

Applying transposition and complex conjugation, we obtain

$$\overline{z}_0^T H_0 = \omega_0 \overline{z}_0^T G, \quad \overline{z}_1^T H_0 = \omega_0 \overline{z}_1^T G - i^{-1} \overline{z}_0^T G. \tag{20}$$

From these, it follows that $[z_0, z_0] = 0$ and $[z_0, z_1] = -[z_1, z_0]$.

Varying the parameters along a curve $p = p(\varepsilon)$ ($p(0) = p_0$), where ε is a real parameter, yields:

$$\lambda_\pm = i\omega_0 \pm i\omega_1 \varepsilon^{1/2} + o(\varepsilon^{1/2}), \quad z_\pm = z_0 \pm i\omega_1 z_1 \varepsilon^{1/2} + o(\varepsilon^{1/2}), \tag{21}$$

with

$$\omega_1 = \sqrt{i \frac{\overline{z}_0^T \Delta H z_0}{\overline{z}_1^T G z_0}}, \quad \Delta H = \sum_{s=1}^{4} \frac{\partial H}{\partial p_s} \frac{dp_s}{d\varepsilon}\bigg|_{\varepsilon=0} = \overline{(\Delta H)}^T. \tag{22}$$

Given that $\overline{z}_0^T \Delta H z_0$ is real and $\overline{z}_1^T G z_0$ is imaginary, we assume $\omega_1 > 0$. For $\varepsilon > 0$, the eigenvalue $i\omega_0$ splits into $\lambda_\pm = i\omega_0 \pm i\omega_1\sqrt{\varepsilon}$ (stability). For $\varepsilon < 0$, the split produces a pair of complex eigenvalues with real parts of opposite signs (instability). Thus, the system exhibits a linear Hamilton–Hopf bifurcation at p_0, which is a regular point on the stability boundary.

For $\varepsilon > 0$, the indefinite inner product of perturbed eigenvectors gives [1,39]

$$[z_+, z_+] = +2i\omega_1 \overline{z}_0^T G z_1 \varepsilon^{1/2} + o(\varepsilon^{1/2}), \quad [z_-, z_-] = -2i\omega_1 \overline{z}_0^T G z_1 \varepsilon^{1/2} + o(\varepsilon^{1/2}). \tag{23}$$

Hence, λ_+ and λ_- have opposite Krein signs. As ε decreases towards zero, these eigenvalues merge at $i\omega_0$ and then split into complex eigenvalues for $\varepsilon < 0$. The presence of opposite Krein signs is both a necessary and sufficient condition for the imaginary eigenvalues to leave the imaginary axis.

Below, we demonstrate the Krein collision at the onset of the diffusionless azimuthal magnetorotational instability (AMRI) by calculating the roots of the dispersion relation both analytically and numerically.

2.4. Threshold of Oscillatory Instability in the Diffusionless Case

In the Hamiltonian case ($\frac{1}{Re} = 0$, $\frac{1}{Rm} = 0$), the dispersion relation $p_0(\lambda) = \det(H_0 - i^{-1}G\lambda) = 0$ has a compact form [1,27,39]:

$$p_0(\lambda) = 4\delta^2 + 4\left(i\lambda - n + nS^2\right)^2 - \left(2\delta - (i\lambda - n)^2 + n^2S^2\right)^2 = 0, \tag{24}$$

where $\delta = Ro - RbS^2$. For $S = 1$, this factorizes into

$$p_0(\lambda)|_{S=1} = [\lambda^3 + 4in\lambda^2 + 4(1 - n^2 + Ro - Rb)\lambda + 8in(Ro - Rb)]\lambda = 0. \tag{25}$$

The negative discriminant of the cubic polynomial factor provides the criterion for oscillatory instability [1,39]:

$$4n^4 + ((Ro - Rb)^2 + 20(Ro - Rb) - 8)n^2 + 4(Ro - Rb + 1)^3 < 0. \tag{26}$$

Equality in (26) marks the transition from marginal stability to oscillatory instability via a linear Hamilton–Hopf bifurcation (see Figure 1). Marginal stability corresponds to one eigenvalue λ being zero and simple, another simple and imaginary, and the last two forming a double imaginary eigenvalue with a Jordan block. At $Rb = -1$, the critical fluid Rossby number is derived from (26)

$$Ro_c(n) = \frac{\beta^{\frac{1}{3}} - n^2}{12} - \frac{n^2}{\beta^{\frac{1}{3}}}\left(18 - \frac{n^2}{12}\right) - 2, \quad \beta(n) = -n^2\left(n^4 + 540n^2 - 5832 - 24\sqrt{3(n^2+27)^3}\right). \tag{27}$$

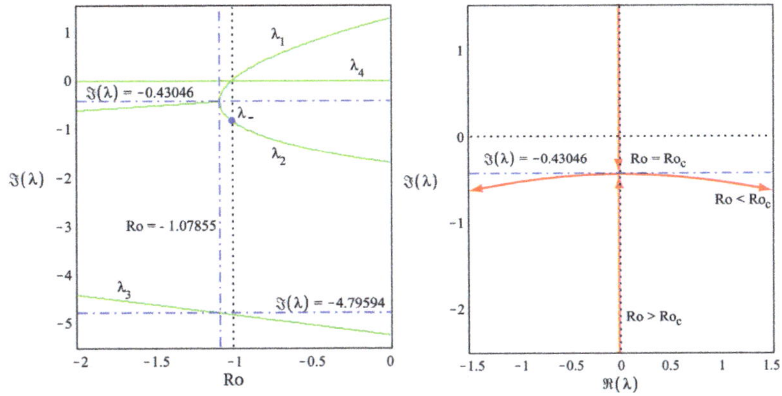

Figure 1. (**Left**) Evolution of the root frequencies of the dispersion relation (25) as Ro varies for $S = 1$, $Rb = -1$, and $n = \sqrt{2}$, highlighting the Hamilton–Hopf bifurcation at $Ro = Ro_c \approx -1.07855$ as determined by (27). (**Right**) The corresponding linear Hamilton–Hopf bifurcation in the complex plane. As Ro decreases, two simple imaginary eigenvalues collide to form a double imaginary eigenvalue with a Jordan block (an exceptional point [1,39]). This eigenvalue then splits into two complex ones, signaling the onset of oscillatory instability.

Although Krein signs of the imaginary eigenvalues in Figure 1 can be evaluated numerically, it is instructive to analyze the case $Ro = Rb = -1$ and $S = 1$. Here, Equation (25) yields a double semi-simple zero eigenvalue $\lambda_0 = 0$ with eigenvectors $z_1 = (0,1,0,1)^T$ and $z_2 = (1,0,1,0)^T$, and two imaginary eigenvalues $\lambda_\pm = -2i(n \pm 1)$ with eigenvectors $z_+ = \left(-i\alpha, \frac{-n}{2+n}, \frac{in\alpha}{2+n}, 1\right)^T$ and $z_- = \left(i\alpha, \frac{n}{2-n}, \frac{in\alpha}{2-n}, 1\right)^T$. See Figure 1 (left). These eigenvalues have opposite Krein signs [1,39]:

$$\frac{[z_+, z_+]}{(z_+, z_+)} = -\frac{2\alpha}{1+\alpha^2}\frac{2(n+1)^2}{1+(n+1)^2} < 0, \quad \frac{[z_-, z_-]}{(z_-, z_-)} = \frac{2\alpha}{1+\alpha^2}\frac{2(n-1)^2}{1+(n-1)^2} > 0. \tag{28}$$

For instance, at $n = \sqrt{2}$, $\frac{1+\alpha^2}{2\alpha}\frac{[z_-,z_-]}{(z_-,z_-)} = 1 - \frac{\sqrt{2}}{2} \approx 0.2929$, implying that λ_- has a positive Krein sign. The solid circle representing λ_- belongs to the branch labeled λ_2 in Figure 1 (left), where all λ_2 eigenvalues for $Ro_c < Ro < -1$ have positive Krein signs. Conversely, according to (23), the λ_1 branch eigenvalues in Figure 1 (left) have negative Krein signs in the same range.

Thus, the onset of nonaxisymmetric oscillatory instability (diffusionless AMRI) involves a Krein collision between modes of positive and negative Krein signs. Krein signs directly relate to the energy sign of a mode, and the linear Hamilton–Hopf bifurcation represents a collision of imaginary eigenvalues with opposite Krein (energy) signs [1,2,39].

2.5. Dissipative Perturbation of Simple Imaginary Eigenvalues

The complex non-Hermitian matrix of the dissipative perturbation, $\boldsymbol{H}_1$, can be decomposed into Hermitian and anti-Hermitian components: $\boldsymbol{H}_1 = \boldsymbol{H}_1^H + \boldsymbol{H}_1^A$, where [1,39]

$$\boldsymbol{H}_1^H = \frac{S(Pm-1)}{2Rm}\begin{pmatrix} 0 & 0 & 0 & 1 \\ 0 & 0 & -1 & 0 \\ 0 & -1 & 0 & 0 \\ 1 & 0 & 0 & 0 \end{pmatrix}, \quad \boldsymbol{H}_1^A = \frac{1}{Rm}\begin{pmatrix} 0 & Pm & 0 & -\frac{S(Pm+1)}{2} \\ -Pm & 0 & \frac{S(Pm+1)}{2} & 0 \\ 0 & -\frac{S(Pm+1)}{2} & 4i\frac{Ro-Rb}{\alpha n} & 1 \\ \frac{S(Pm+1)}{2} & 0 & -1 & 0 \end{pmatrix}.$$

At a large Rm, the increment $\delta\lambda$ to a simple imaginary eigenvalue λ with eigenvector z is determined using standard perturbation theory [1,39]:

$$\delta\lambda = i\frac{\overline{z}^T \boldsymbol{H}_1 z}{\overline{z}^T \boldsymbol{G} z} = i\frac{(\boldsymbol{H}_1 z, z)}{[z, z]}. \tag{29}$$

The increment due to the Hermitian component, $\delta\lambda^H = i\frac{(\boldsymbol{H}_1^H z, z)}{[z,z]}$, is purely imaginary. Notably, $\boldsymbol{H}_1^H = 0$ when $Pm = 1$, implying that frequencies are unaffected by the Hermitian component of the dissipative perturbation when the contributions of viscosity and resistivity are equal.

In contrast, the increment due to the anti-Hermitian component, $\delta\lambda^A = i\frac{(\boldsymbol{H}_1^A z, z)}{[z,z]}$, is real. For example, the eigenvalues λ_+ and λ_- in Figure 1 (left) acquire the following increments:

$$\delta\lambda_\pm^A = -\frac{Pm+1}{2Rm} = -\frac{1}{h} = -\frac{1}{2}\left(\frac{1}{Re} + \frac{1}{Rm}\right), \quad \delta\lambda_\pm^H = 0, \tag{30}$$

where h is the harmonic mean of the two Reynolds numbers.

In the vicinity of the critical Rossby number for the Hamilton–Hopf bifurcation, $Ro_c \approx -1.07855$, the real increment $\delta\lambda^A$ to the imaginary eigenvalues λ_1 (with a negative Krein sign) and λ_2 (with a positive Krein sign) is shown in Figure 2 (left) for fixed $Rm = 10^3$ and varying Pm (where the fluid Reynolds number is calculated as $Re = Rm/Pm$).

Eigenvalues with a negative Krein sign become dissipatively destabilized when $Pm > 1$, i.e., when fluid viscosity dominates over ohmic losses. Interestingly, eigenvalues with a positive Krein sign can also develop positive growth rates. This occurs for $Pm < 1$, where electrical resistivity outweighs kinematic viscosity.

The interval of negative real increments in Figure 2 (left) shrinks as the deviation from the critical Rossby number, $\Delta Ro = Ro - Ro_c$, approaches zero. At $\Delta Ro = 0$, the stable interval reduces to a single point: $Pm = 1$. Thus, weak ohmic diffusion ($Pm < 1$) destabilizes positive-energy waves, while weak kinematic viscosity ($Pm > 1$) destabilizes negative-energy waves, provided $|Ro - Ro_c|$ is sufficiently small.

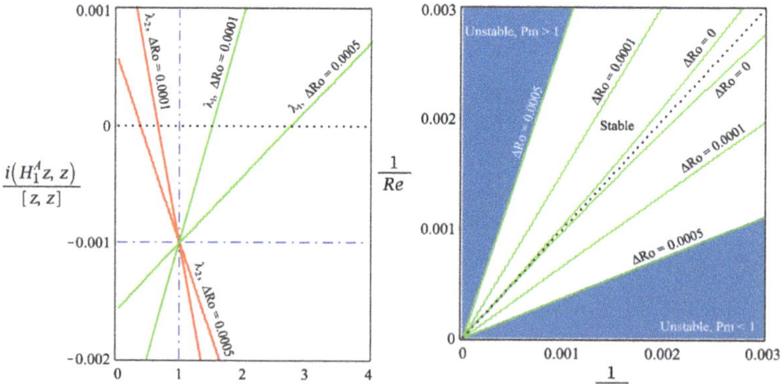

Figure 2. (**Left**) Real increments $\delta\lambda^A$ for eigenvalues λ_1 (negative Krein sign) and λ_2 (positive Krein sign) as computed from Equation (29), with $Rm = 1000$. The stability interval (negative increments) around $Pm = 1$ narrows as $\Delta Ro := Ro - Ro_c$ approaches zero. (**Right**) Neutral stability curves in the (Rm^{-1}, Re^{-1}) plane, corresponding to inverse magnetic and fluid Reynolds numbers, for $S = 1$, $Rb = -1$, and $n = \sqrt{2}$, at various values of ΔRo. For $\Delta Ro > 0$, the stability domain forms an angular sector, while at $\Delta Ro = 0$, it exhibits a cusp with a single tangent line at $Pm = 1$ [1,39].

2.6. *Diffusionless and Visco-Diffusive Criteria Meet at Pm* = 1

We extend the sensitivity analysis of eigenvalues for the diffusionless Hamiltonian eigenvalue problem under visco-diffusive perturbation by directly computing the stability boundaries using the algebraic Bilharz stability criterion. This criterion ensures that all roots of a complex polynomial of degree n lie to the left of the imaginary axis in the complex plane if all even-order principal minors of the $2n \times 2n$ Bilharz matrix, constructed from the real and imaginary parts of the polynomial coefficients, are positive [1].

Applying the Bilharz criterion to (18), we plot the neutral stability curves in the plane of inverse Reynolds numbers, Rm^{-1} and Re^{-1}, for various values of $\Delta Ro = Ro - Ro_c$, where Ro_c is defined in (27). These plots, shown in Figure 2 (right), correspond to $S = 1$, $Rb = -1$, and $n = \sqrt{2}$. Notably, the diagonal line corresponding to $Pm = 1$ remains within the stability domain for $\Delta Ro \geq 0$ and is the only tangent to the stability boundary at the cuspidal origin when $Ro = Ro_c$.

Furthermore, at $Ro = Ro_c$ and $Re = Rm$, the spectrum of the double-diffusive system with $S = 1$ and $Rb = -1$ includes double complex eigenvalues, also known as exceptional points [1]:

$$\lambda_d = \lambda_c(n) - Rm^{-1}. \tag{31}$$

Here, the imaginary eigenvalue $\lambda_c(n)$ is determined by (25) for $Ro = Ro_c(n)$, as specified in (27).

2.7. *Visco-Diffusive Instability at Pm* ≠ 1

As $Re = Rm > 0$, varying Ro at fixed $Rb = -1$, $S = 1$, and n leads to a bifurcation at $Ro = Ro_c$ of the double complex eigenvalue (31) with a negative real part of $-Rm^{-1}$, as shown in Figure 3 (left). At $Pm = 1$, dissipation shifts the Hamilton–Hopf bifurcation to the left in the complex plane, so the oscillatory instability in the visco-diffusive system with equal viscosity and resistivity occurs through the classical Hopf bifurcation at $Ro(Rm) < Ro_c$, with $Ro(Rm)$ approaching Ro_c as $Rm \to \infty$.

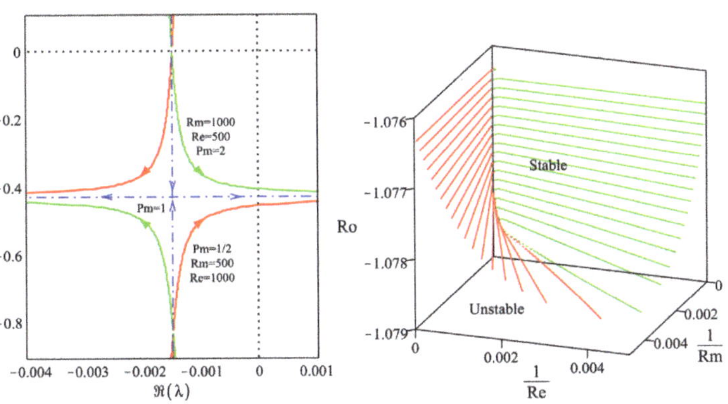

Figure 3. (**Left**) At $Rb = -1$, $S = 1$, and $n = \sqrt{2}$, the dot-dashed lines illustrate the interaction of complex eigenvalues with negative real parts in the complex λ-plane as Ro decreases, with $Re = Rm = h = \frac{2}{\frac{1}{500}+\frac{1}{1000}}$, i.e., $Pm = 1$. At $Ro = Ro_c$, the eigenvalues merge into the double complex eigenvalue (31). The quasi-hyperbolic curves show the imperfect merging of modes (avoided crossing), where the mode with positive Krein (energy) sign becomes unstable for $Pm < 1$ and the mode with negative Krein (energy) sign becomes unstable for $Pm > 1$. (**Right**) The neutral stability surface, represented by contours of Ro = const. in the (Re^{-1}, Rm^{-1}, Ro)-space, has a "Whitney umbrella" singular point at $(0, 0, Ro_c)$, yielding a cusp in the cross-section $Ro = Ro_c$ with a single tangent line at $Pm = 1$ [1,39].

When the magnetic Prandtl number deviates slightly from $Pm = 1$, the shifted Hamilton–Hopf bifurcation unfolds into two quasi-hyperbolic eigenvalue branches, passing close in an avoided crossing [56] centered at the exceptional point λ_d of (31) with a real part, $-h^{-1}$, where $h = \frac{2}{\frac{1}{Re}+\frac{1}{Rm}}$ is the harmonic mean of the fluid and magnetic Reynolds numbers ($Re \neq Rm$), as seen in Figure 3 (left).

The unfolding of the eigenvalue crossing into an avoided crossing depends on the sign of $Pm - 1$. For $Pm < 1$ ($Pm > 1$), the complex eigenvalues, originating from the imaginary eigenvalues of the diffusionless system with positive (negative) Krein sign, form a branch that bends rightward and crosses the imaginary axis at some $Ro(Re, Rm) \neq Ro_c$, as shown in Figure 3 (left), cf. [56]. The critical values $Ro(Re, Rm)$ of the visco-diffusive system lie on a surface in the (Re^{-1}, Rm^{-1}, Ro)-space, with a self-intersection along the Ro-axis, as depicted in Figure 3 (right). The angle of the self-intersection tends to zero as $Ro \to Ro_c$, and at the point $(0, 0, Ro_c)$, the surface has a singularity, known as the Whitney umbrella [1,45,50].

Near the Ro-axis, the instability threshold forms a ruled surface [50], with each ruler's slope determined by Pm. As the Reynolds numbers approach infinity while Pm remains fixed, the Ro-axis is approached along a ruler corresponding to that value of Pm. For all values of Pm except $Pm = 1$, a ruler leads to a limiting value of Ro greater than Ro_c, extending the instability interval compared to the diffusionless system, as seen in Figure 3 (right). The plane $Pm = 1$ divides the neutral stability surface near $Ro = Ro_c$ into two regions, one for positive-energy modes destabilized by dominant ohmic diffusion at $Pm < 1$ and one for negative-energy modes destabilized by dominant fluid viscosity at $Pm > 1$, as shown in Figure 3 (right). The ray defined by $Re = Rm > 0$, $Ro = Ro_c$ lies within the stability domain and contains exceptional points (31) that govern the eigenvalue behavior shown in Figure 3 (left). The Whitney umbrella singularity of the neutral stability surface is the reason for persistence of diffusive destabilization even in the limit of vanishing dissipation [1,41,45,50].

3. Diffusive Instabilities of Baroclinic Lenticular Vortices

3.1. Nonlinear Equations of Motion and the Base State

Following [40], we consider a model of a circular lenticular vortex immersed in a deep, vertically stratified viscous incompressible Newtonian fluid under gravity and rotation. The coordinate system $(\tilde{r}, \tilde{\theta}, \tilde{z})$ rotates with angular velocity $(0, 0, f/2)$, where f (the Coriolis parameter) can be positive or negative. Gravity $(0, 0, -g)$ is antiparallel to the $\tilde{z}$-axis, and the centrifugal force is negligible [40,41]. The ambient fluid is linearly stratified along the direction of gravity, incorporating viscosity (ν) and diffusion (κ) of the stratifying agent, unlike McIntyre's study [41], which considered viscosity and thermal diffusion.

The baroclinic vortex, modeled as an ellipsoid with angular velocity $(0, 0, \tilde{\Omega}(\tilde{r}, \tilde{z}))$, is embedded in a motionless (in the rotating frame), stratified fluid far from the vortex core, with boundaries assumed non-influential. Adopting the Boussinesq–Oberbeck approximation, we describe the stable background density gradient as $-\frac{\rho_0 N^2}{g}$, where $N = \sqrt{-\frac{g}{\rho_0}\frac{d\tilde{\rho}}{d\tilde{z}}}$ is the Brunt–Väisälä frequency. The total density is then presented as [40]

$$\tilde{\rho}(\tilde{r}, \tilde{z}) = \rho_0 - \rho_0 \frac{N^2}{g}\tilde{z} + \tilde{\rho}_A(\tilde{r}, \tilde{z}), \tag{32}$$

where the density anomaly $\tilde{\rho}_A$ captures the vortex's internal stratification.

Introducing characteristic scales R, Z, U, W, with $W = \alpha U$ and $\alpha = Z/R$, and the time scale R/U yields the scales $\rho_0 f R U$ for pressure and $\rho_0 f U/(g\alpha)$ for density [40]. The horizontal Froude number F_h, vortex Rossby number Ro, and Burger number Bu are defined as

$$F_h = \frac{U}{RN}, \quad Ro = \frac{U}{fR}, \quad Bu = \frac{\alpha^2 Ro^2}{F_h^2}. \tag{33}$$

Anticyclonic (cyclonic) eddies correspond to $Ro < 0$ ($Ro > 0$) for $U > 0$. The Schmidt and Ekman numbers are given by:

$$Sc = \frac{\nu}{\kappa}, \quad Ek = \frac{\nu}{fR^2} = \frac{Ro}{Re}, \tag{34}$$

where $Re = UR/\nu > 0$ is the Reynolds number. Both Ek and Ro can be positive or negative but share the same sign.

The background flow is assumed to be purely azimuthal:

$$\boldsymbol{u}_B = (0, r\Omega(r,z), 0), \tag{35}$$

where $\Omega(r,z) = (R/U)\tilde{\Omega} = e^{-r^2-z^2} > 0$ is the dimensionless angular velocity. Then, from (32), the dimensionless density is [40]

$$\rho(r,z) = \frac{g\alpha}{fU} - z\frac{Bu}{Ro} + \rho_A(r,z), \tag{36}$$

with the density anomaly

$$\rho_A(r,z) = -z\Omega(1 + Ro\Omega), \tag{37}$$

and $r = \tilde{r}/R$, $\theta = \tilde{\theta}$, $z = \tilde{z}/Z$.

With the scaling adopted, the dimensionless equations of motion are

$$\nabla \cdot \boldsymbol{u} = 0, \tag{38a}$$

$$Ro\frac{d\boldsymbol{u}}{dt} + \boldsymbol{e}_z \times \boldsymbol{u} = -\nabla_\alpha P - \frac{\rho}{\alpha^2}\boldsymbol{e}_z + Ek\mathcal{D}\boldsymbol{u}, \tag{38b}$$

$$Ro\frac{d\rho}{dt} = \frac{Ek}{Sc}\mathcal{D}\rho, \tag{38c}$$

where $t = \tilde{t}U/R$, $\boldsymbol{u} = (u_r, u_\theta, u_z)^T$ is the velocity field, P is the pressure, $d/dt = \partial_t + \boldsymbol{u}\cdot\nabla$, $\mathcal{D} = \nabla_h^2 + \alpha^{-2}\partial_z^2$, ∇_h^2 is the horizontal Laplacian, and $\nabla_\alpha = (\partial_r, r^{-1}\partial_\theta, \alpha^{-2}\partial_z)^T$ is the modified gradient operator [40].

3.2. Linearization and Geometrical Optics Equations

Linearizing (38) about the base state (35), assuming $Ek = \epsilon^2\widetilde{Ek}$ [34,40], and seeking solutions in the asymptotic form (1), we derive transport equations for the leading-order amplitudes $\boldsymbol{u}^{(0)}$ and $\rho^{(0)}$ of a localized wave packet moving along the base flow streamlines [40]:

$$\begin{aligned} Ro\frac{d\boldsymbol{u}^{(0)}}{dt} &= -Ek\boldsymbol{u}^{(0)} - Ro\left(\mathcal{I} - 2\frac{\mathcal{K}}{\beta^2}\right)\mathcal{U}\boldsymbol{u}^{(0)} - \left(\mathcal{I} - \frac{\mathcal{K}}{\beta^2}\right)\boldsymbol{e}_z \times \boldsymbol{u}^{(0)} - \left(\mathcal{I} - \frac{\mathcal{K}}{\beta^2}\right)\boldsymbol{e}_z\frac{\rho^{(0)}}{\alpha^2}, \\ Ro\frac{d\rho^{(0)}}{dt} &= -\frac{Ek}{Sc}\rho^{(0)} - \left(\mathcal{B}^T Ro - \boldsymbol{e}_z^T Bu\right)\boldsymbol{u}^{(0)}, \end{aligned} \tag{39}$$

where $Ek = \widetilde{Ek}|\boldsymbol{k}_\alpha^T\boldsymbol{k}|$, $d/dt = \partial_t + \boldsymbol{u}_B\cdot\nabla$, $\mathcal{I}$ is the 3×3 identity matrix, $\mathcal{U} = \nabla\boldsymbol{u}_B$, and $\mathcal{B} = \nabla\rho_A$, given by

$$\mathcal{U} = \begin{pmatrix} 0 & -\Omega & 0 \\ \Omega + r\partial_r\Omega & 0 & r\partial_z\Omega \\ 0 & 0 & 0 \end{pmatrix}, \quad \mathcal{B} = \begin{pmatrix} -z\frac{\partial\Omega}{\partial r}(1 + 2Ro\Omega) \\ 0 \\ -z\frac{\partial\Omega}{\partial z}(1 + 2Ro\Omega) - \Omega(1 + Ro\Omega) \end{pmatrix}. \tag{40}$$

The matrix $\mathcal{K} = \boldsymbol{k}_\alpha \boldsymbol{k}^T$ in (39) is defined by the wavevector $\boldsymbol{k} = \nabla\Phi = (k_r, k_\theta, k_z)^T$ and its scaled counterpart $\boldsymbol{k}_\alpha = \nabla_\alpha \Phi = (k_r, k_\theta, k_z/\alpha^2)^T$, where $\boldsymbol{k}$ satisfies the eikonal equation

$$\frac{d\boldsymbol{k}}{dt} = -\mathcal{U}^T \boldsymbol{k}. \tag{41}$$

From (41), we find k_r and k_z to be constants, while $k_\theta = 0$. Introducing scaled wavenumbers $q_r = k_r/\beta$ and $q_z = k_z/\beta$, where $\beta^2 = \boldsymbol{k}^T\boldsymbol{k}_\alpha = k_r^2 + k_\theta^2 + k_z^2/\alpha^2$, we have $q_r = \sqrt{1 - q_z^2/\alpha^2}$. The matrix $\mathcal{K}$ can then be expressed as

$$\mathcal{K} = \boldsymbol{q}_\alpha \boldsymbol{q}^T, \quad \boldsymbol{q} = (q_r, 0, q_z)^T, \quad \boldsymbol{q}_\alpha = (q_r, 0, q_z/\alpha^2)^T.$$

3.3. Dispersion Relation

As shown in [13,40], eliminating $u_z^{(0)}$ from (39) reduces the system to three equations for $u_r^{(0)}$, $u_\theta^{(0)}$, and $\rho^{(0)}$. Introducing the complex growth rate λ and azimuthal wavenumber m via the ansatz,

$$\left(u_r^{(0)}, u_\theta^{(0)}, \rho^{(0)}\right) = \left(\hat{u}_r^{(0)}, \hat{u}_\theta^{(0)}, \hat{\rho}^{(0)}\right) \exp(\lambda t + im\theta),$$

yields the eigenvalue problem $\mathcal{H}\xi = \hat{\lambda}\xi$, where $\xi = \left(\hat{u}_r^{(0)}, \hat{u}_\theta^{(0)}, \hat{\rho}^{(0)}\right)^T$, $\hat{\lambda} = Ro(\lambda + im\Omega) + Ek$, and $\mathcal{H}$ is a 3×3 matrix:

$$\mathcal{H} = \begin{pmatrix} 0 & \dfrac{q_z^2}{\alpha^2}\dfrac{2j}{r^2} & \dfrac{q_r q_z}{\alpha^2} \\ -\dfrac{r^2(q_z\kappa_r^2 - q_r\kappa_z^2)}{2q_z j} & 0 & 0 \\ -\dfrac{Ro(q_z\partial_r\rho_A - q_r\partial_z\rho_A) + q_r Bu}{q_z} & 0 & Ek\dfrac{Sc-1}{Sc} \end{pmatrix},$$

where $j(r,z)$ is the angular momentum per unit mass, κ_r is the epicyclic frequency, and κ_z is the vertical oscillation frequency, given by

$$j = \frac{r^2}{2}(1 + 2Ro\Omega), \quad \kappa_r^2 = r^{-3}\frac{\partial j^2}{\partial r}, \quad \kappa_z^2 = r^{-3}\frac{\partial j^2}{\partial z}.$$

The dispersion relation $p(\hat{\lambda}) = \det(\mathcal{H} - \hat{\lambda}I)$ is a cubic polynomial [40]:

$$p(\hat{\lambda}) = \hat{\lambda}^3 + Ek\frac{1-Sc}{Sc}\hat{\lambda}^2 + (\gamma_1 + \gamma_2)\hat{\lambda} + Ek\frac{1-Sc}{Sc}\gamma_1, \tag{42}$$

where

$$\gamma_1 = \frac{q_z}{\alpha^2}\left(q_z\kappa_r^2 - q_r\kappa_z^2\right), \quad \gamma_2 = \frac{q_r}{\alpha^2}\left[Ro\left(q_z\frac{\partial\rho_A}{\partial r} - q_r\frac{\partial\rho_A}{\partial z}\right) + q_r Bu\right] \tag{43}$$

and $\partial_r\rho_A$ and $\partial_z\rho_A$ are given by (40). The parameters γ_1 and γ_2 represent shear effects from differential rotation and buoyancy effects from ambient density stratification, respectively. Both can take positive or negative values depending on the vortex and stratification properties.

3.4. Stability Analysis

3.4.1. Diffusionless and $Sc = 1$ Cases

When $Ek = 0$ or $Sc = 1$, the dispersion relation (42) simplifies, factorizing into a product of quadratic and linear polynomials in $\hat{\lambda}$, allowing explicit solutions.

In these cases, the eigenvalues associated with centrifugal instability are given by [40]

$$\lambda^\pm = -\frac{im\Omega}{Ro} \pm \frac{1}{Ro}\sqrt{-(\gamma_1 + \gamma_2)}, \tag{44}$$

leading to the instability criterion:

$$\gamma_1 + \gamma_2 < 0. \tag{45}$$

3.4.2. Criteria for Visco-Diffusive Monotonic and Oscillatory Instabilities

Applying the Bilharz criterion to (42) with $Ek/Ro = 1/Re > 0$, the base flow is stable for $Sc > 0$ and $m = 0$ if and only if the following three inequalities are satisfied simultaneously [40]:

$$2(Sc+1)^2Ek^2 + Sc(2Sc\gamma_1 + \gamma_2(Sc+1)) > 0, \tag{46a}$$

$$(Sc+2)Ek^2 + Sc(\gamma_1+\gamma_2) > 0, \tag{46b}$$

$$Ek^2 + Sc\gamma_2 + \gamma_1 > 0. \tag{46c}$$

Conditions (46) are linear in γ_1 and γ_2, allowing the stability domain to be represented in the (γ_1, γ_2) plane [40,43]. The stability region is the intersection of the half-planes defined by (46a)–(46c), as shown in Figure 4.

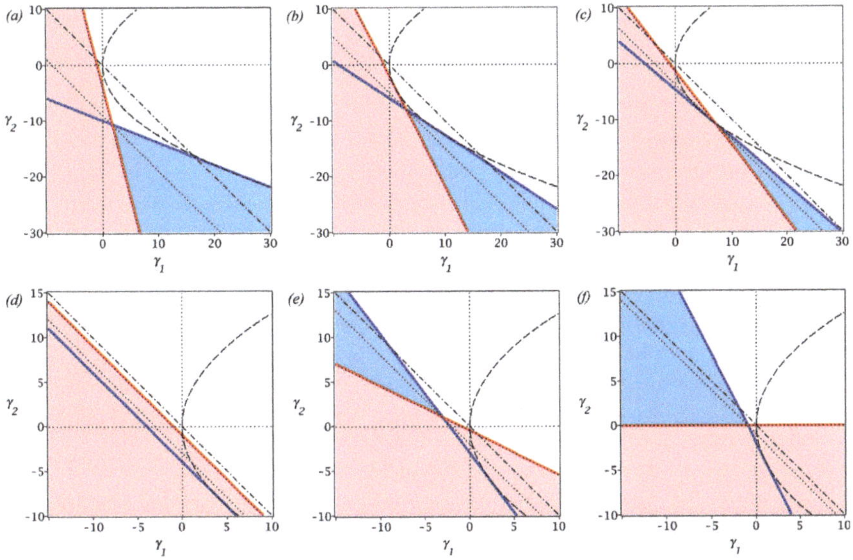

Figure 4. Stability maps showing codimension-2 points (47) on the neutral stability curve for $Ek = 1$ and (**a**) $Sc = 0.25$, (**b**) $Sc = 0.5$, (**c**) $Sc = 0.75$, (**d**) $Sc = 1$, (**e**) $Sc = 2$, (**f**) $Sc \to +\infty$. The red solid line marks the boundary of the monotonic axisymmetric (MA) instability domain (46c) (pink, light-shaded), while the blue solid line represents the boundary of the oscillatory axisymmetric (OA) instability domain (46a) (blue, dark-shaded). The stability domain is indicated in white. The dashed line corresponds to the envelope $\gamma_1 = \frac{\gamma_2^2}{16Ek^2}$ of the OA instability boundaries parametrized by Sc, and the dot-dashed line indicates the neutral stability boundary for the diffusionless system (45). The oblique dotted line represents the condition (46b) [40].

The intersection of the neutral stability lines corresponding to the criteria (46) defines a codimension-2 point with the following coordinates [40,43]:

$$\gamma_1 = Ek^2\frac{1+Sc}{1-Sc}, \quad \gamma_2 = \frac{2Ek^2}{Sc(Sc-1)}. \tag{47}$$

At this point, the slopes of the lines defining the inequalities (46a)–(46c) are

$$\sigma_1 = -\frac{2Sc}{Sc+1}, \quad \sigma_2 = -1, \quad \sigma_3 = -\frac{1}{Sc}. \tag{48}$$

The relationships between the slopes depend on Sc [40]:

$$\left.\begin{array}{r}-1 \geq \sigma_1 > -2 \\ \sigma_2 = -1 \\ -1 \leq \sigma_3 < 0\end{array}\right\} \quad \text{if} \quad 1 \leq Sc < +\infty,$$
$$\left.\begin{array}{r}0 > \sigma_1 > -1 \\ \sigma_2 = -1 \\ -\infty < \sigma_3 < -1\end{array}\right\} \quad \text{if} \quad 0 < Sc < 1. \tag{49}$$

Actually, reversed inequality (46c) determines monotonic axisymmetric (MA) instability, corresponding to a monotonically growing perturbation, while the reversed inequality (46a) stands for oscillatory axisymmetric (OA) instability, i.e., growing oscillation.

For $0 < Sc < 1$, the slope of the neutral stability line defining (46c) is steeper than that defining (46a) (Figure 4a–c). This causes the stability domain to be convex, with a wedge extending into the region of centrifugal instability. The codimension-2 point, a well-known phenomenon in hydrodynamics [13], existing for $\gamma_2 < 0$, separates OA and MA instability regions. Diffusion destabilizes centrifugally stable vortices due to difference in the slopes σ_1 and σ_3 from $\sigma_2 = -1$, if the absolute values of γ_1 and γ_2 are large enough, as shown in Figure 4a–c.

At $Sc = 1$, the slopes (48) converge ($\sigma_1 = \sigma_2 = \sigma_3 = -1$), and the stability boundaries of the diffusionless and visco-diffusive systems coincide for $Ek \to 0$. However, for $Ek \neq 0$, viscosity and diffusion can stabilize centrifugally unstable diffusionless vortices (Figure 4d).

For $Sc > 1$, the codimension-2 point reappears at infinity for $\gamma_2 > 0$ and moves along an asymptotic direction until it reaches the final location at $\gamma_1 = -Ek^2$ and $\gamma_2 = 0$ as $Sc \to \infty$ (Figure 4f). This qualitative change in location of the codimension-2 point is accompanied by the exchange of the stability criteria: the condition (46c) becomes dominating over (46a) and vice versa (Figure 4e,f).

Figure 4 provides evidence that stability boundary consisting of two straight lines that intersect at a codimension-2 point in the (γ_1, γ_2) plane exhibit a qualitative change at $Sc = 1$ such that, for $Sc < 1$ ($Sc > 1$), the upper (lower) line corresponds to the onset of MA instability and the lower (upper) line to the onset of OA instability.

Even as $Ek \to 0$, these qualitative phenomena persist, aligning with the properties of McIntyre instability [41] and other dissipation-induced instabilities [1,45,50]. The existence of the codimension-2 point qualitatively distinguishes the diffusive case from the diffusionless one, where the onset of instability corresponds to the monotonic axisymmetric centrifugal instability only, Figure 4d. Hence, the oscillatory axisymmetric instability is a genuine dissipation-induced instability [1] which is as important as the monotonic axisymmetric one despite its relatively low growth rate, because in a large set of parameters, the oscillatory axissymmetric modes are the first to be destabilized by the differential diffusion of mass and momentum.

4. Spiral Poiseuille Flow with Radial Temperature Gradient

4.1. Nonlinear Equations of Motion

Following [13,47,54], we consider an incompressible Newtonian fluid with constant reference density ρ and constant thermal expansion coefficient α, kinematic viscosity ν, and thermal diffusivity κ within an infinitely long cylindrical annulus with a gap width $d = R_2 - R_1$, where R_1 is the radius of the inner cylinder at temperature T_1, rotating with angular velocity Ω_1, and R_2 is the radius of the outer cylinder at temperature $T_2 = T_1 - \Delta T$, rotating with angular velocity Ω_2. The Z-axis of the cylindrical coordinates (R, φ, Z) aligns with the common rotation axis of the cylinders. We assume the inner cylinder velocity, $V_0 = \Omega_1 R_1$, to be the velocity scale,

d the length scale, d/V_0 the time scale, and ρV_0^2 the pressure scale to write the dimensionless governing equations in the Boussinesq–Oberbeck approximation:

$$\nabla \cdot \boldsymbol{u} = 0, \tag{50a}$$

$$\frac{d\boldsymbol{u}}{dt} + \nabla p - \frac{1}{Re}\nabla^2 \boldsymbol{u} + \gamma \frac{v^2}{r}\boldsymbol{e}_r \theta = 0, \tag{50b}$$

$$\frac{d\theta}{dt} - \frac{1}{RePr}\nabla^2 \theta = 0. \tag{50c}$$

Here, p is pressure, $\boldsymbol{u} = (u, v, w)$ represents the velocity field, $\theta = \frac{T-T_2}{\Delta T}$ is the temperature deviation, $\Delta T = T_1 - T_2$, $\frac{d}{dt} = \frac{\partial}{\partial t} + \boldsymbol{u} \cdot \nabla$, $r = \frac{R}{d}$, and $z = \frac{Z}{d}$. The dimensionless control parameter $Re = \frac{V_0 d}{\nu}$ in Equation (50) is the Reynolds number associated with the rotation of the inner cylinder, $Pr = \frac{\nu}{\kappa}$ is the Prandtl number, and $\gamma = \alpha \Delta T$, with $\gamma < 0$ for inward heating ($T_1 < T_2$) [13,47].

4.2. Base State

We assume the base flow to be the spiral Poiseuille flow (SPF), which combines the annular Poiseuille flow, characterized by an axial velocity driven by an external pressure gradient, and the circular Couette flow, defined by the azimuthal velocity profile induced by the differential rotation of the cylinders. The two-component dimensionless velocity field of SPF and the base temperature distribution are expressed as

$$\boldsymbol{u}_B(r) = \left(0, V(r), S^{-1}W(r)\right), \quad \theta_B(r) = \Theta(r), \tag{51}$$

where $S = \frac{V_0}{W_m}$ is the swirl parameter, W_m is the mean velocity of the annular Poiseuille flow, and $W(r)$, $V(r)$, and $\Theta(r)$ are the dimensionless axial, azimuthal, and temperature profiles, respectively. Defining the axial Reynolds number as $Re_z = \frac{W_m d}{\nu}$, we can write $S = \frac{Re}{Re_z}$.

The axial velocity profile $W(r)$ of SPF is given by [54]

$$W(r) = \frac{2(1-\eta)^2 \ln \eta}{\eta^2 - (\eta^2+1)\ln \eta - 1}\left[r^2 - r_2^2 + \frac{1}{\ln \eta}\frac{1+\eta}{1-\eta}\ln\left(\frac{r}{r_2}\right)\right]. \tag{52}$$

The azimuthal velocity profile $V(r)$ in (51) corresponds to the circular Couette flow [13,54]:

$$V(r) = \frac{\eta}{1+\eta}\left(\frac{1-\mu}{(1-\eta)^2}\frac{1}{r} - \frac{\eta^2-\mu}{\eta^2}r\right). \tag{53}$$

The temperature profile $\Theta(r)$ in (51) is expressed as [13,54]

$$\Theta(r) = \frac{\ln[r(1-\eta)]}{\ln \eta}. \tag{54}$$

Here, the geometric and rotational parameters are defined as follows:

- $\eta = R_1/R_2$, the ratio of the inner (R_1) to outer (R_2) cylinder radii;
- $\mu = \Omega_2/\Omega_1$, the ratio of the angular velocities of the outer (Ω_2) to inner (Ω_1) cylinders;
- $r_1 = \frac{\eta}{1-\eta}$, the inner radius in dimensionless form;
- $r_2 = \frac{1}{1-\eta}$, the outer radius in dimensionless form;
- $r_g = \sqrt{r_1 r_2} = \frac{\sqrt{\eta}}{1-\eta}$, the geometric mean radius, at which we will evaluate all parameters in subsequent analyses.

4.3. Geometrical Optics Equations

After linearization of the governing equations (50) about the base SPF flow (51), assuming $Re \sim \epsilon^{-2}$ in the linearized equations [34] and seeking a solution in the asymptotic form (1), we find the transport equations for the leading-order amplitudes $\boldsymbol{u}^{(0)}$ and $\theta^{(0)}$

of the localized wave packet moving along the streamlines of the base flow written in the stationary frame [13,47]:

$$\begin{aligned} \frac{d\boldsymbol{u}^{(0)}}{dt}+\frac{|\boldsymbol{k}|^2}{Re}\boldsymbol{u}^{(0)} &= -\left(\mathcal{I}-\frac{\boldsymbol{k}\boldsymbol{k}^T}{|\boldsymbol{k}|^2}\right)\gamma\frac{V^2}{r}\boldsymbol{e}_r\theta^{(0)} \\ &\quad -\left(\mathcal{I}-2\frac{\boldsymbol{k}\boldsymbol{k}^T}{|\boldsymbol{k}|^2}\right)\mathcal{U}\boldsymbol{u}^{(0)}-2\gamma\Theta\Omega\left(\mathcal{I}-\frac{\boldsymbol{k}\boldsymbol{k}^T}{|\boldsymbol{k}|^2}\right)\boldsymbol{e}_r\boldsymbol{e}_\varphi^T\boldsymbol{u}^{(0)}, \\ \frac{d\theta^{(0)}}{dt}+\frac{|\boldsymbol{k}|^2}{RePr}\theta^{(0)} &= -(\nabla\Theta)^T\boldsymbol{u}^{(0)}, \end{aligned} \tag{55}$$

where $\mathcal{I}$ is the 3×3 identity matrix, and the eikonal equation determining the evolution of the wavevector $\boldsymbol{k}=(k_r,k_\varphi,k_z)^T=\epsilon^{-1}\nabla\Phi$, $\boldsymbol{k}\cdot\boldsymbol{u}^{(0)}=0$; in the stationary frame,

$$\frac{d\boldsymbol{k}}{dt}=-\mathcal{U}^T\boldsymbol{k}. \tag{56}$$

The gradients of the base state are given by

$$\mathcal{U}=\nabla\boldsymbol{u}_B=\begin{pmatrix} 0 & -\Omega & 0 \\ (1+2Ro)\Omega & 0 & 0 \\ \frac{1}{S}DW & 0 & 0 \end{pmatrix},\quad \nabla\Theta=\begin{pmatrix} D\Theta \\ 0 \\ 0 \end{pmatrix} \tag{57}$$

with $D=\frac{d}{dr}$, $\Omega=\frac{V}{r}$, and the Rossby number is defined in (10).

4.4. Dispersion Relation

From Equation (56), it follows that, under the condition [5,7,47],

$$k_\varphi=-\overline{DW}k_z,\quad \text{with}\quad \overline{DW}=\frac{DW}{2\Omega RoS}, \tag{58}$$

the components of the wave vector $\boldsymbol{k}$ remain time-independent in the rotating frame: k_r = const., k_φ = const., k_z = const.. This condition describes the most unstable and exponentially growing 3D perturbations in swirling flows that exhibit helical symmetry, i.e., remain invariant along circular helices with a pitch of $2\pi r\overline{DW}$ [5,7,47]. Additionally, under the constraint (58), the amplitude equations (55) are autonomous in the rotating frame [5,7,47].

Writing explicitly the material derivative in the left side of the amplitude equations, explicitly computing its right hand side, exploiting the relation

$$|\boldsymbol{k}|^2=k_r^2+k_z^2\left[1+\overline{DW}^2\right], \tag{59}$$

and assuming $\boldsymbol{u}^{(0)},\theta^{(0)}\sim e^{st+\mathrm{i}m\varphi+\mathrm{i}k_z z}$, where $s=\sigma+\mathrm{i}\omega$, $\sigma,\omega\in\mathbb{R}$ is the complex growth rate, and $m=k_\varphi r$ and k_z are the integer azimuthal and real axial wavenumbers, we find the dispersion relation as the characteristic polynomial

$$p(\lambda)=-\det(\mathcal{H}-\lambda\mathcal{I})=a_3\lambda^3+a_2\lambda^2+a_1\lambda+a_0 \tag{60}$$

of the matrix $\mathcal{H}$, where $\lambda=\sigma+\mathrm{i}(\omega+m\Omega+k_zW/S)$ and

$$\mathcal{H}=\begin{pmatrix} -2\Omega\overline{DW}\frac{k_rk_z}{|\boldsymbol{k}|^2}-\frac{|\boldsymbol{k}|^2}{Re} & 2\Omega(1-\gamma\Theta)\left(1-\frac{k_r^2}{|\boldsymbol{k}|^2}\right) & -r\gamma\Omega^2\left(1-\frac{k_r^2}{|\boldsymbol{k}|^2}\right) \\ -2\Omega\left(Ro+\frac{k_r^2+k_z^2}{|\boldsymbol{k}|^2}\right) & 2\Omega(1-\gamma\Theta)\overline{DW}\frac{k_rk_z}{|\boldsymbol{k}|^2}-\frac{|\boldsymbol{k}|^2}{Re} & -r\gamma\Omega^2\overline{DW}\frac{k_rk_z}{|\boldsymbol{k}|^2} \\ -D\Theta & 0 & \frac{|\boldsymbol{k}|^2}{Re}\frac{Pr-1}{Pr}-\frac{|\boldsymbol{k}|^2}{Re} \end{pmatrix}. \tag{61}$$

4.5. Stability Analysis

The dispersion relation (60) has real coefficients. Consequently, the stability conditions of the base flow ($\sigma < 0$) are determined by the Liénard–Chipart stability criterion: $a_0 > 0$, $a_2 > 0$, and $a_1 a_2 - a_0 > 0$ [1]. Note that $a_2 = \frac{k_r k_z}{|k|^2}\frac{DW}{SRo}\gamma\Theta + \frac{2Pr+1}{Pr}\frac{|k|^2}{Re}$ is positive in both the isothermal case ($\gamma = 0$) and the pure azimuthal circular Couette flow with a radial temperature gradient ($DW = 0$). In these cases, the inequality $a_0 < 0$ extends the Rayleigh centrifugal instability criterion, while the inequality $a_1 a_2 - a_0 < 0$ characterizes oscillatory instability [13,40,41].

4.5.1. Pure Azimuthal Circular Couette Flow with Radial Temperature Gradient

The condition $a_0 = 0$ defines the neutral stability boundary in the (Pr, Re) plane for the non-oscillatory (stationary) Goldreich–Schubert–Fricke (GSF) instability [13,46]. The neutral stability curves are parameterized by the axial wavenumber k_z, with $a_0 = 0$ leading to a polynomial equation in k_z. The envelope of this family of curves can be determined through three equivalent approaches: (1) computing the discriminant of the polynomial; (2) solving the equations $a_0(k_z) = 0$ and $\frac{da_0(k_z)}{dk_z} = 0$ simultaneously; or (3) expressing Re as a function of k_z from $a_0 = 0$ and minimizing Re with respect to k_z [55]. All approaches yield the same expression for the envelope:

$$Re_0^S = \frac{3\sqrt{3}k_r^2}{2\Omega}\frac{1}{\sqrt{4(Ro_R^S - Ro)(1-\gamma\Theta)}}, \tag{62}$$

where Ro_R^S is the modified Rayleigh line for non-isothermal flows [47]:

$$Ro_R^S = -1 + \frac{rD\Theta\gamma Pr}{4(1-\gamma\Theta)}. \tag{63}$$

The same procedure applied to the equation $a_1 a_2 = a_0$ yields the envelope of the neutral stability curves for the oscillatory instability:

$$Re_0^O = \frac{3\sqrt{3}k_r^2}{2\Omega}\frac{Pr+1}{Pr\sqrt{4(Ro_R^O - Ro)(1-\gamma\Theta)}}, \tag{64}$$

where

$$Ro_R^O = -1 + (Ro_R^S + 1)\frac{Pr+1}{2Pr^2}. \tag{65}$$

Note that $Ro_R^O = Ro_R^S$ and $Re_0^O = 2Re_0^S$ at $Pr = 1$. Moreover, rewriting Equation (62) and Equation (64) in terms of the Taylor number $Ta = \frac{2Re\Omega}{3\sqrt{3}k_r^2}$ exactly reproduces the result of [13].

The criterion for the stationary GSF instability given by the inequality $Re > Re_0^S$ can be written in terms of the Rayleigh discriminant $N_\Omega^2 = 4(1+Ro)\Omega^2$ and the square of the centrifugal Brunt–Väissälä frequency $N^2 = -\gamma\Omega^2 rD\Theta$ as follows:

$$N_\Omega^2(1-\gamma\Theta) + PrN^2 + \frac{27k_r^4}{4Re^2} < 0, \tag{66}$$

while the criterion for oscillatory instability $Re > Re_0^O$ takes the form of

$$N_\Omega^2(1-\gamma\Theta) + \frac{Pr+1}{2Pr}N^2 + \frac{(Pr+1)^2}{4Pr^2}\frac{27k_r^4}{Re^2} < 0. \tag{67}$$

Setting $\gamma = 0$ and $N = 0$ in (66) exactly reproduces the centrifugal instability criterion for isothermal viscous Couette–Taylor flow found in [14] through a local geometrical optics approach.

In Figure 5, the envelopes (62) and (64) are depicted in the (Pr, Re) plane by red and blue curves, respectively, with the instability domain located above these curves. In the Rayleigh-unstable case ($\mu < \eta^2$) shown in Figure 5a, for outward heating ($\gamma > 0$), the envelopes intersect, forming a codimension-2 point at a specific value of Pr, which is detailed in [13]. In this scenario, the GSF instability dominates for $Pr < 1$, while the oscillatory instability becomes critical for $Pr > 1$.

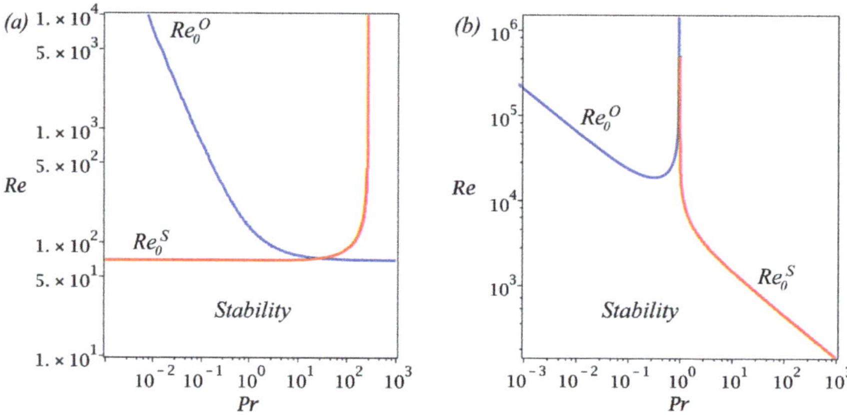

Figure 5. The envelope (red) $Re_0^S(Pr)$ of the neutral stability curves $a_0 = 0$ (62) and (blue) $Re_0^O(Pr)$ of the neutral stability curves $a_1a_2 = a_0$ (64) in the (Pr, Re) plane for pure azimuthal circular Couette flow with a radial temperature gradient. The parameters are $k_r = 3\sqrt{2}$, with (**a**) $\eta = 0.5$, $\mu = 0$, $\gamma = 0.01$ (Rayleigh-unstable, outward heating), and (**b**) $\eta = 0.99$, $\mu = \eta^{3/2}$, $\gamma = -0.01$ (Rayleigh-stable, quasi-Keplerian, inward heating). All computations were performed at the mean geometric radius $r = \sqrt{r_1 r_2}$. Instability is above the curves [13,57].

Conversely, for Rayleigh-stable flow ($\mu > \eta^2$), inward heating destabilizes the system through an oscillatory instability mechanism when $Pr \lesssim 1$ and through GSF when $Pr \gtrsim 1$, as illustrated in Figure 5b. This behavior was first identified using the local geometrical optics approach in [13] and later confirmed by numerical global stability analysis in [57]. The parameters characterized by low Prandtl numbers and high Reynolds numbers, corresponding to oscillatory instability as shown in Figure 5b, are particularly relevant to the dynamics of accretion disks in astrophysics [49,58,59].

4.5.2. Isothermal Spiral Poiseuille Flow (SPF)

Setting $\Theta \equiv 0$ and $\gamma = 0$ in the matrix (61) corresponds to the isothermal spiral Poiseuille flow. Under these conditions, the dispersion relation simplifies, separating into a linear equation with no physical significance and a quadratic polynomial. The quadratic polynomial determines centrifugal instability via the sole relevant condition of the Liénard–Chipart criterion: $a_0 < 0$. Computing the discriminant of $a_0 = 0$, considered a polynomial in k_z, yields the envelope of the neutral stability curves in the (Re_z, Re) plane [47]:

$$E(Re_z, Re) = \frac{N_\Omega^2}{\Omega^2} - \frac{4\overline{DW}^2}{1+\overline{DW}^2} + \frac{27}{4\Omega^2}\frac{k_r^4}{Re^2} = 0. \tag{68}$$

The centrifugal instability of the isothermal viscous swirling flow is then determined by the condition $E(Re_z, Re) < 0$ [47] that for isothermal inviscid swirling flows ($Re \to \infty$) reduces to the result

$$\frac{N_\Omega^2}{\Omega^2} - \frac{4\overline{DW}^2}{1+\overline{DW}^2} < 0, \tag{69}$$

previously obtained in [5,7] using the local geometrical optics approach, and in [60,61] via the global stability analysis. The equality in (69) determines asymptotes to the envelope (68) shown in Figure 6b by oblique straight lines for the Rayleigh-stable flow. The envelope (68) also has a horizontal asymptote [47]

$$Re_\infty = \frac{3\sqrt{3}k_r^2}{4\Omega\sqrt{-Ro}} \quad \text{as} \quad |Re_z| \to \infty \tag{70}$$

as shown in Figure 6a,b by the dot-dashed line.

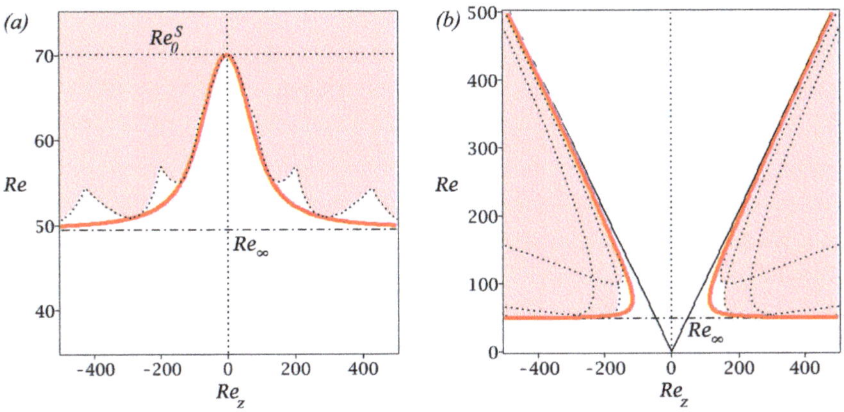

Figure 6. For isothermal SPF with $k_r = 3\sqrt{2}$, the thick red line represents the envelope (68) of the neutral stability curves ($a_0 = 0$) that bounds the union (shaded area) of individual instability domains. These domains are shown for (**a**) $k_z = 0.5, 1, 2, 3$ for the Rayleigh-unstable flow ($\eta = 0.5$, $\mu = 0$) and (**b**) $k_z = 0.4, 0.7, 3$ for the Rayleigh-stable flow ($\eta = 0.5$, $\mu = 0.5$). The dot-dashed horizontal asymptotes of the envelope correspond to $Re_\infty \approx 49.60$, from Equation (70). The envelope's maximum value for the Rayleigh-unstable flow at $Re_z = 0$ is $Re_0^S \approx 70.15$, derived from Equation (62) for $\gamma = 0$. The solid oblique lines in (**b**) represent the inviscid criterion (69).

4.5.3. Spiral Poiseuille Flow with Radial Temperature Gradient (SPFRT)

The radial temperature gradient induces a splitting of the envelope bounding the domain of centrifugal instability in swirling flows [47].

For Rayleigh-unstable, non-isothermal swirling flows, the envelope comprises two branches that intersect at $Re_z = 0$ and $Re = Re_0^S$, where Re_0^S is defined in (62). A linear approximation for the branches of the envelope near the intersection is given by the following formula [47]:

$$\frac{Re(Re_z)}{Re_0^S} = 1 \pm \gamma\Theta\frac{\sqrt{2}}{9k_r^2}\frac{DW}{Ro}Re_z + o(Re_z). \tag{71}$$

The horizontal asymptote (70) also splits, with the new values of Re_∞ determined as the roots of the following bicubic equation:

$$b_3(\Omega Re)^6 + b_2(\Omega Re)^4 + b_1(\Omega Re)^2 + b_0 = 0, \tag{72}$$

where the coefficients are defined as

$$
\begin{aligned}
b_3 &= 16[(\gamma\Theta)^2 + A]A^5, \\
b_2 &= k_r^4[27(\gamma\Theta)^6 - 265A(\gamma\Theta)^4 - 492A^2(\gamma\Theta)^2 - 216A^3]A^2, \\
b_1 &= 3k_r^8[-144(\gamma\Theta)^8 - 96A(\gamma\Theta)^6 - 8A^2(\gamma\Theta)^4 + 216A^3(\gamma\Theta)^2 + 243A^4], \\
b_0 &= 1024k_r^{12}(\gamma\Theta)^6, \\
A &= 4(1-\gamma\Theta)(1 + Ro_R^S - Ro),
\end{aligned}
\tag{73}
$$

and where Ro_R^S is the modified Rayleigh line (63).

Using perturbation theory for $|\gamma| \ll 1$, an approximate expression for the splitting of the horizontal asymptote can be derived from (72)

$$
\frac{Re_\infty(\gamma)}{Re_\infty} = 1 + \gamma\Theta\left[\frac{1}{2} + \frac{Pr}{4}\frac{Rt}{Ro} \pm \frac{1}{\sqrt{-6Ro}}\right] + o(\gamma), \tag{74}
$$

where Re_∞ is defined in (70), and $Rt = \frac{rD\Theta}{2\Theta}$ [13].

In Figure 7a, the envelope of the centrifugal instability domains of the Rayleigh-unstable SPF with a radial temperature gradient (SPFRT) is split, exhibiting two horizontal asymptotes at $Re_\infty \approx 49.66$ and $Re_\infty \approx 49.80$. These values, derived from (74), are indistinguishable from the exact results given by (72). Furthermore, as predicted by (74), these values demonstrate that the temperature gradient not only splits the isothermal horizontal asymptote $Re_\infty \approx 49.60$ shown in Figure 6a for the same parameter values as in Figure 7a, but also shifts it vertically. Note that the splitting of the envelope introduces asymmetry in the instability domains with respect to the sign of k_z: for $Re_z > 0$, the critical Re corresponding to the lower branch of the envelope has $k_z > 0$, whereas for $Re_z < 0$, the critical Re corresponding to the lower branch has $k_z < 0$ (Figure 7a).

Figure 7b illustrates that the splitting of the envelope of the centrifugal instability domains for the Rayleigh-stable SPFRT results in not only the two horizontal asymptotes from (74) as $|Re_z| \to \infty$, but also two oblique asymptotic lines as $Re \to \infty$. The outer branch of the envelope follows the asymptotic line given by the following expression:

$$
\frac{N_\Omega^2}{\Omega^2}(1-\gamma\Theta) + Pr\frac{N^2}{\Omega^2} = \frac{\overline{DW}^2}{1+\overline{DW}^2}(2-\gamma\Theta)^2 \tag{75}
$$

If the left-hand side of (75) exceeds its right-hand side, this inequality defines the centrifugal stability of the SPFRT. The inner branch of the envelope lies within the centrifugal instability domain and has the asymptote

$$
\frac{N_\Omega^2}{\Omega^2}(1-\gamma\Theta) + Pr\frac{N^2}{\Omega^2} = \frac{4\overline{DW}^2}{1+\overline{DW}^2}(1-\gamma\Theta). \tag{76}
$$

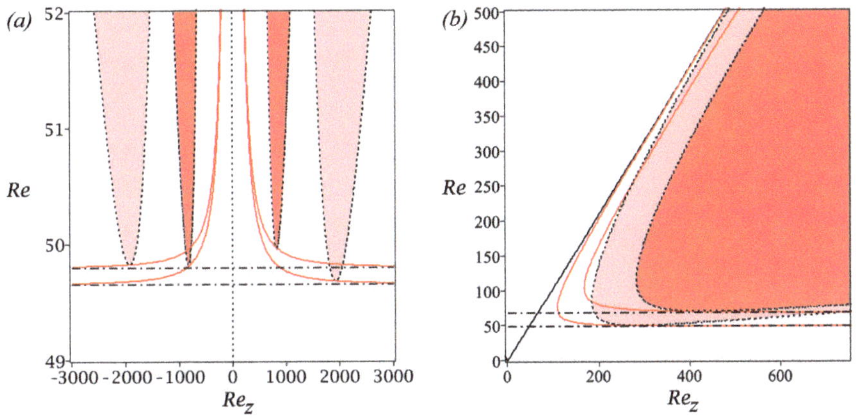

Figure 7. (**a**) The outward radial temperature gradient with $\gamma = 0.01$ and $Pr = 0.01$ causes a splitting of the envelope (red lines) of the neutral stability curves bounding the GSF instability domains $a_0 = 0$ (shown light-shaded for $k_z = 0.15$ and dark-shaded for $k_z = -0.35$) for non-isothermal Rayleigh-unstable SPFRT with $\eta = 0.5$, $\mu = 0$, and $k_r = 3\sqrt{2}$. The maximum value of the envelope ($Re_0^S \approx 70.33$, not shown) is given by (62), while (dot-dashed) the two horizontal asymptotes at $Re_\infty \approx 49.66$ and $Re_\infty \approx 49.80$ are provided by (74), in excellent agreement with (72). (**b**) For the Rayleigh-stable SPFRT with $\eta = 0.5$, $\mu = 0.5$, $Pr = 0.01$, $\gamma = 0.5$, and $k_r = 3\sqrt{2}$, the (red) envelope of the neutral stability curves splits into two branches. The outer branch touches the GSF instability domains with $k_z > 0$ (light-shaded, $k_z = 0.5$), while the inner branch touches the GSF instability domains with $k_z < 0$ (dark-shaded, $k_z = -0.5$). The oblique straight line represents the asymptote (75). The dot-dashed lines correspond to $Re_\infty \approx 48.56$ and $Re_\infty \approx 67.72$, as provided by (72).

Since the splitting of the envelope of the centrifugal instability domains is small for $|\gamma| \ll 1$, we can derive a simple approximation by substituting $D\Theta = -\frac{N^2}{\gamma\Omega^2 r}$ into the equation $a_0 = 0$, taking the limit as $\gamma \to 0$ while keeping the centrifugal Brunt–Väissälä frequency N fixed, and then calculating the discriminant of the resulting equation (treated as a polynomial in k_z). This procedure yields the following approximate expression for the envelope:

$$\frac{N_\Omega^2}{\Omega^2} + Pr\frac{N^2}{\Omega^2(1-\gamma\Theta)} - \frac{4\overline{DW}^2}{1+\overline{DW}^2} + \frac{27k_r^4}{4\Omega^2 Re^2} = 0. \tag{77}$$

As $|Re_z| \to \infty$, the approximation (79) to the envelope has a horizontal asymptote:

$$Re_\infty^S = \frac{3\sqrt{3}k_r^2}{4\Omega\sqrt{1+Ro_R^S - Ro}}. \tag{78}$$

The approximation (77) represents a non-isothermal extension of the envelope (68) for the centrifugal instability domains of viscous swirling flows and is valid when $|\gamma| \ll Pr$. It forms a single smooth curve (see Figure 8) that aligns closely with the minimal splitting of individual neutral stability curves for specific k_z. This splitting is so subtle that it is imperceptible to the naked eye in Figure 8.

Applying the above procedure to the equation $a_1 a_2 = a_0$, we derive a similar approximation for the envelope of the oscillatory instability domains of SPFRT in the (Re_z, Re)-plane, shown as thick blue lines in Figure 8:

$$\frac{N_\Omega^2}{\Omega^2} + \frac{N^2}{\Omega^2(1-\gamma\Theta)}\frac{Pr+1}{2Pr} - \frac{4\overline{DW}^2}{1+\overline{DW}^2} + \frac{(Pr+1)^2}{Pr^2}\frac{27k_r^4}{4\Omega^2 Re^2} = 0 \tag{79}$$

The approximation (79) is valid when $|\gamma| \ll Pr$. Requiring the left-hand side of (79) to be negative extends the criterion (67) to swirling flows with a radial temperature gradient. As $|Re_z| \to \infty$, the approximation (79) to the envelope has a horizontal asymptote:

$$Re_\infty^O = \frac{3\sqrt{3}k_r^2}{4\Omega\sqrt{1 + Ro_R^O - Ro}} \frac{Pr + 1}{Pr}. \tag{80}$$

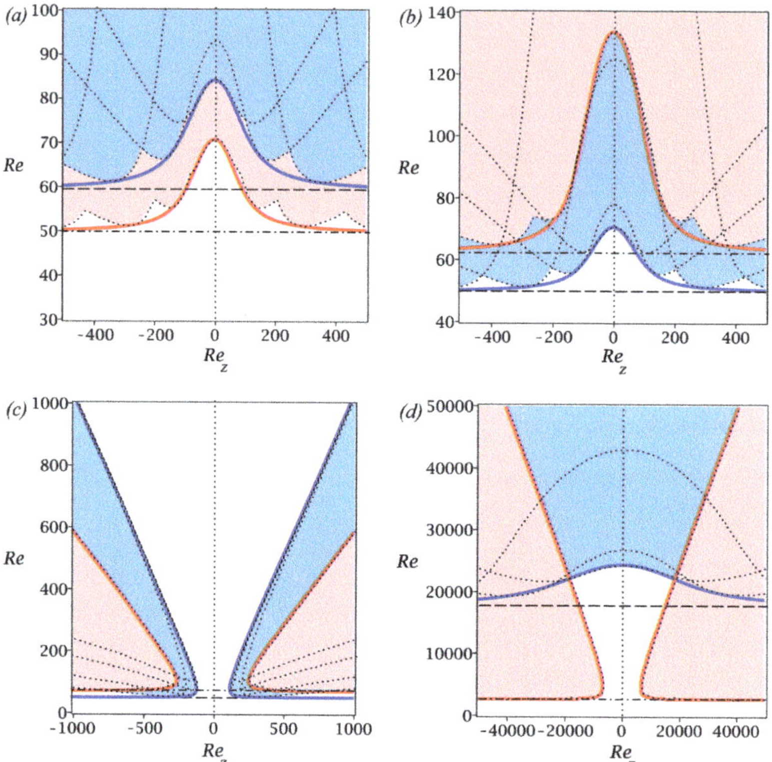

Figure 8. (**a**,**b**) Rayleigh -unstable SPFRT with $\eta = 0.5$, $\mu = 0$, $\gamma = 0.01$, $k_r = 3\sqrt{2}$, and (**a**) $Pr = 5$ and (**b**) $Pr = 200$, cf. Figure 5a. Pink (light-shaded) and blue (dark-shaded) areas represent the domains of centrifugal and oscillatory instability, respectively, for $k_z = 0.5, 1, 2, 3$. The thick red and blue lines denote approximations to the envelopes (77) and (79), respectively. The maximal Reynolds numbers are (**a**) $Re_0^S \approx 70.97$ and (**b**) $Re_0^S \approx 134.10$ from (62), and $Re_0^O \approx 84.48$ in (**a**) and $Re_0^O \approx 70.74$ in (**b**) from (64). The dot-dashed line corresponds to $Re_\infty^S \approx 49.88$ in (**a**) and $Re_\infty^S \approx 62.17$ in (**b**), as given by (78). The dashed line corresponds to $Re_\infty^O \approx 59.55$ in (**a**) and $Re_\infty^O \approx 49.87$ in (**b**), as given by (80). (**c**,**d**) Rayleigh-stable SPFRT with $k_z = 0.5, 1, 2, 3$, $k_r = 3\sqrt{2}$: (**c**) $\eta = 0.5$, $\mu = 0.5$, $Pr = 70$, $\gamma = 0.01$, $Re_\infty^S \approx 70.56$, and $Re_\infty^O \approx 50.40$; (**d**) $\eta = 0.99$, $\mu = \eta^{3/2}$, $Pr = 0.1$, $\gamma = -0.01$, $Re_\infty^S \approx 2637.17$, $Re_\infty^O \approx 17{,}657.29$, and $Re_0^O \approx 24{,}277.26$.

A comparison of Figure 8a,b and Figure 5a reveals that the Rayleigh-unstable SPFRT with an outward temperature gradient ($\gamma > 0$) can exhibit either centrifugal instability (at small Pr) or oscillatory instability (at large Pr). The transition between these regimes occurs at a critical Pr, corresponding to a codimension-2 point in the (Pr, Re)-plane at $Re_z = 0$, as shown in Figure 5a.

The Rayleigh-stable SPFRT depicted in Figure 8c,d can exhibit oscillatory instability in the presence of an outward temperature gradient ($\gamma > 0$) at large Pr, as shown in Figure 8c, when $|Re_z|$ exceeds a critical value. For an inward temperature gradient ($\gamma < 0$), Figure 8d indicates that stability is lost via oscillatory instability at small $|Re_z|$ and via centrifugal instability at large axial Reynolds numbers when $Pr < 1$, consistent with the numerical results of [54]. For $Pr > 1$, this behavior is reversed.

5. Conclusions

The geometrical optics local stability analysis, initially developed for the hydrodynamics of ideal fluids, was revisited and extended to visco-diffusive rotating flows. This approach was applied to three cases: the azimuthal magnetorotational instability (AMRI) in magnetized differentially rotating flows, the McIntyre instability in baroclinic lenticular vortices and the spiral Poiseuille flow with a radial temperature gradient (SPFRT).

The influence of the hydrodynamic (Pr) and magnetic (Pm) Prandtl numbers, and Schmidt (Sc) number on the onset of stationary and oscillatory instabilities was explored, with a focus on the exchange of instabilities near the critical value where the ratio of viscosity to diffusivity equals a finite value, which, in many applications, is simply one.

It was demonstrated that AMRI can be interpreted as a dissipative unfolding of the linear Hamilton–Hopf bifurcation, represented by the Whitney umbrella singularity on the neutral stability surface. This singularity explains the persistence of diffusive destabilization even in the limit of vanishing dissipation, provided $Pm \neq 1$. The thresholds for diffusive and diffusionless AMRI coincide only at $Pm = 1$.

A special role of $Sc = 1$ was observed in the visco-diffusive McIntyre-like instability of lenticular vortices, where it acts as the trigger between oscillatory and stationary instabilities, determining the transition between these regimes. This method also proved effective in deriving instability criteria for swirling flows with radial temperature gradients, highlighting the role of Pr in the exchange between centrifugal and oscillatory instabilities.

This analysis offers a robust framework for deriving instability criteria analytically, even for parameter values inaccessible in numerical or physical experiments, providing valuable insights and guidance for future studies.

Funding: This research received no external funding.

Data Availability Statement: The original contributions presented in this study are included in the article. Further inquiries can be directed to the corresponding author.

Conflicts of Interest: The author declares no conflicts of interest.

References

1. Kirillov, O.N. *Nonconservative Stability Problems of Modern Physics*, 2nd ed.; De Gruyter: Berlin, Germany, 2021; pp. 1–548.
2. Krechetnikov, R.; Marsden, J.E. Dissipation-induced instabilities in finite dimensions. *Rev. Mod. Phys.* **2007**, *79*, 519–553. [CrossRef]
3. Daleckii, J.L.; Krein, M.G. *Stability of Solutions of Differential Equations in Banach Space*; AMS: Providence, RI, USA, 1974.
4. Yudovich, V.I. *The Linearization Method in Hydrodynamic Stability Theory*; AMS: Providence, RI, USA, 1989.
5. Eckhoff, K.S.; Storesletten, L. A note on the stability of steady inviscid helical gas flows. *J. Fluid Mech.* **1978**, *89*, 401–411. [CrossRef]
6. Eckhoff, K.S. On stability for symmetric hyperbolic systems, I. *J. Diff. Eq.* **1981**, *40*, 94–115. [CrossRef]
7. Eckhoff, K.S. A note on the instability of columnar vortices. *J. Fluid Mech.* **1984**, *145*, 417–421. [CrossRef]
8. Friedlander, S.; Vishik, M.M. Instability criteria for the flow of an inviscid incompressible fluid. *Phys. Rev. Lett.* **1991**, *66*, 2204–2206. [CrossRef]
9. Friedlander, S.; Lipton-Lifschitz, A. Localized instabilities in fluids. In *Handbook of Mathematical Fluid Dynamics 2*; Friedlander, S.J., Serre, D., Eds.; North-Holland: Amsterdam, The Netherlands, 2003; pp. 289–354.
10. Ionescu-Kruse, D. On the short-wavelength stabilities of some geophysical flows. *Philos. Trans. R. Soc. A* **2017**, *376*, 20170090. [CrossRef]
11. Lifschitz, A. Short wavelength instabilities of incompressible threedimensional flows and generation of vorticity. *Phys. Lett. A* **1991**, *157*, 481–487. [CrossRef]
12. Lifschitz, A.; Hameiri, E. Local stability conditions in fluid dynamics. *Phys. Fluids A Fluid Dyn.* **1991**, *3*, 2644–2651. [CrossRef]

13. Kirillov, O.N.; Mutabazi, I. Short wavelength local instabilities of a circular Couette flow with radial temperature gradient. *J. Fluid Mech.* **2017**, *818*, 319–343. [CrossRef]
14. Eckhardt, B.; Yao, D. Local stability snalysis along Lagrangian paths. *Chaos Solit. Fract.* **1995**, *5*, 2073–2088. [CrossRef]
15. Bayly, B.J. Three-dimensional instability of elliptical flow. *Phys. Rev. Lett.* **1986**, *57*, 2160–2163. [CrossRef] [PubMed]
16. Mathur, M.; Ortiz, S.; Dubos, T.; Chomaz, J.-M. Effects of an axial flow on the centrifugal, elliptic and hyperbolic instabilities in Stuart vortices. *J. Fluid Mech.* **2014**, *758*, 565–585. [CrossRef]
17. Nagarathinam, D.; Sameen, A.; Mathur, M. Centrifugal instability in non-axisymmetric vortices. *J. Fluid Mech.* **2015**, *769*, 26–45. [CrossRef]
18. Pierrehumbert, R.T. Universal short-wave instability of two-dimensional eddies in an inviscid fluid. *Phys. Rev. Lett.* **1986**, *57*, 2157–2159. [CrossRef]
19. Lagnado, R.R.; Phan-Thien, N.; Leal, L.G. The stability of two-dimensional linear flows. *Phys. Fluids* **1984**, *27*, 1094–1101. [CrossRef]
20. Leblanc, S.; Le Duc, A. The unstable spectrum of swirling gas flows. *J. Fluid Mech.* **2005**, *537*, 433–442. [CrossRef]
21. Hattori, Y.; Hijiya, K. Short-wavelength stability analysis of Hill's vortex with/without swirl. *Phys. Fluids* **2010**, *22*, 074104. [CrossRef]
22. Lifschitz, A.; Hameiri, E. Localized instabilities of vortex rings with swirl. *Comm. Pure Appl. Math.* **1993**, *46*, 1379–1408. [CrossRef]
23. Aravind, H.M.; Dubos, T.; Mathur, M. Local stability analysis of homogeneous and stratified Kelvin–Helmholtz vortices. *J. Fluid Mech.* **2022**, *943*, A18. [CrossRef]
24. Lebovitz, N.R.; Lifschitz, A. Short-wavelength instabilities of Riemann ellipsoids. *Philos. Trans. R. Soc. A* **1996**, *354*, 927–950.
25. Mizerski, K.A.; Bajer, K. The influence of magnetic field on short-wavelength instability of Riemann ellipsoids. *Phys. D Nonlin. Phen.* **2011**, *240*, 1629–1635. [CrossRef]
26. Vidal, J.; Cébron, D. Inviscid instabilities in rotating ellipsoids on eccentric Kepler orbits. *J. Fluid Mech.* **2017**, *833*, 469–511. [CrossRef]
27. Friedlander, S.; Vishik, M.M. On stability and instability criteria for magnetohydrodynamics. *Chaos* **1995**, *5*, 416–423. [CrossRef]
28. Kucherenko, V.V.; Kryvko, A. Interaction of Alfvèn waves in the linearized system of magnetohydrodynamics for an incompressible ideal fluid. *Russ. J. Math. Phys.* **2013**, *20*, 56–67. [CrossRef]
29. Lebovitz, N.R.; Zweibel, E. Magnetoelliptic instabilities. *Astrophys. J.* **2004**, *609*, 301–312. [CrossRef]
30. Mizerski, K.A.; Bajer, K. The magnetoelliptic instability of rotating systems. *J. Fluid Mech.* **2009**, *632*, 401–430. [CrossRef]
31. Mizerski, K.A.; Bajer, K.; Moffatt, H.K. The mean electromotive force generated by elliptic instability. *J. Fluid Mech.* **2012**, *707*, 111–128. [CrossRef]
32. Salhi, A.; Cambon, C. Magneto-gravity-elliptic instability. *J. Fluid Mech.* **2023**, *963*, A9. [CrossRef]
33. Vidal, J.; Cébron, D.; ud-Doula, A.; Alecian, E. Fossil field decay due to nonlinear tides in massive binaries. *A&A* **2019**, *629*, A142.
34. Maslov, V.P. Coherent structures, resonances, and asymptotic non-uniqueness for Navier-Stokes equations with large Reynolds numbers. *Russ. Math. Surv.* **1986**, *41*, 23–42. [CrossRef]
35. Craik, A.D.D.; Criminale, W.O. Evolution of wavelike disturbances in shear flows: A class of exact solutions of the Navier-Stokes equations. *Proc. R. Soc. London. A* **1986**, *406*, 13–26.
36. Leblanc, S. Internal wave resonances in strain flows. *J. Fluid. Mech.* **2003**, *477*, 259–283. [CrossRef]
37. Kirillov, O.N.; Stefani, F. Extending the range of the inductionless magnetorotational instability. *Phys. Rev. Lett.* **2013**, *111*, 061103. [CrossRef] [PubMed]
38. Kirillov, O.N.; Stefani, F.; Fukumoto, Y. Local instabilities in magnetized rotational flows: A short-wavelength approach. *J. Fluid Mech.* **2014**, *760*, 591–633. [CrossRef]
39. Kirillov, O.N. Singular diffusionless limits of double-diffusive instabilities in magnetohydrodynamics. *Proc. R. Soc. A* **2017**, *473*, 20170344. [CrossRef]
40. Labarbe, J.; Kirillov, O.N. Diffusive instabilities of baroclinic lenticular vortices. *Phys. Fluids* **2021**, *33*, 104108. [CrossRef]
41. McIntyre, M.E. Diffusive destabilisation of the baroclinic circular vortex. *Geophys. Fluid Dyn.* **1970**, *1*, 19–57. [CrossRef]
42. Singh, S.; Mathur, M. Diffusive effects in local instabilities of a baroclinic axisymmetric vortex. *J. Fluid Mech.* **2021**, *928*, A14. [CrossRef]
43. Singh, S.; Mathur, M. Effects of Schmidt number on the short-wavelength instabilities in stratified vortices. *J. Fluid Mech.* **2019**, *867*, 765–803. [CrossRef]
44. Hoveijn, I.; Ruijgrok, M. The stability of parametrically forced coupled oscillators in sum resonance. *Z. Angew. Math. Phys.* **1995**, *46*, 384–392. [CrossRef]
45. Kirillov, O.N.; Verhulst, F. Paradoxes of dissipation-induced destabilization or who opened Whitney's umbrella? *Z. Angew. Math. Mech.* **2010**, *90*, 462–488. [CrossRef]

46. Dymott, R.W.; Barker, A.J.; Jones, C.A.; Tobias, S.M. Linear and non-linear properties of the Goldreich–Schubert–Fricke instability in stellar interiors with arbitrary local radial and latitudinal differential rotation. *Mon. Not. R. Astron. Soc.* **2023**, *524*, 2857–2882. [CrossRef]
47. Kirillov, O.N.; Mutabazi, I. Unification theory of instabilities of visco-diffusive swirling flows. *Phys. Rev. Fluids* **2024**, *9*, 124802. [CrossRef]
48. Petitdemange, L.; Marcotte, F.; Gissinger, C.; Daniel, F. Tayler–Spruit dynamo simulations for the modeling of radiative stellar layers. *A&A* **2024**, *681*, A75.
49. Stefani, F. Liquid-metal experiments on geophysical and astrophysical phenomena. *Nat. Rev. Phys.* **2024** *6*, 409–425. [CrossRef]
50. Bottema, O. The Routh-Hurwitz condition for the biquadratic equation. *Indag. Math.* **1956**, *59*, 403–406. [CrossRef]
51. Chen, G.; Han, G.G.; Yang, X. On the intrinsic shape of oceanic eddies derived from satellite altimetry. *Remote Sens. Environ.* **2019**, *228*, 75–89. [CrossRef]
52. Lestrelin, H.; Legras, B.; Podglajen, A.; Salihoglu, M. Smoke-charged vortices in the stratosphere generated by wildfires and their behaviour in both hemispheres: Comparing Australia 2020 to Canada 2017. *Atmos. Chem. Phys.* **2021**, *21*, 7113–7134. [CrossRef]
53. Lemasquerier, D.; Facchini, G.; Favier, B.; Le Bars, M. Remote determination of the shape of Jupiter's vortices from laboratory experiments. *Nat. Phys.* **2020**, *16*, 695–700. [CrossRef]
54. Cotrell, D.L.; McFadden, G.B. Linear stability of spiral Poiseuille flow with a radial temperature gradient: Centrifugal buoyancy effects. *Phys. Fluids* **2005**, *17*, 114102. [CrossRef]
55. Hull, D. Finding envelope is an optimization problem. *J. Optim. Theory Appl.* **2020**, *186*, 453–458. [CrossRef]
56. Jones, C.A. Multiple eigenvalues and mode classification in plane Poiseuille flow. *Q. J. Mech. Appl. Math.* **1988**, *41*, 363–382. [CrossRef]
57. Meyer, A.; Mutabazi, I.; Yoshikawa, H.N. Stability of Rayleigh-stable Couette flow between two differentially heated cylinders. *Phys. Rev. Fluids* **2021**, *6*, 033905. [CrossRef]
58. Garaud, P. Double diffusive convection at low Prandtl number. *Annu. Rev. Fluid Mech.* **2018**, *50*, 275–298. [CrossRef]
59. Garaud, P. Journey to the center of stars: The realm of low Prandtl number fluid dynamics. *Phys. Rev. Fluids* **2021**, *6*, 030501. [CrossRef]
60. Leibovich, S.; Stewartson, K. A sufficient condition for the instability of columnar vortices. *J. Fluid Mech.* **1983**, *126*, 335–356. [CrossRef]
61. Ludwieg, H. Stabilität der Strömung in einem zylindrischen Ringraum. *Z. Flugwiss.* **1960**, *5*, 135–140.

mathematics

MDPI

Article

Buoyant Flow and Thermal Analysis in a Nanofluid-Filled Cylindrical Porous Annulus with a Circular Baffle: A Computational and Machine Learning-Based Approach

Pushpa Gowda [1], Sankar Mani [2,†], Ahmad Salah [2,†] and Sebastian A. Altmeyer [3,*]

[1] College of Computing and Information Sciences, University of Technology and Applied Sciences, Nizwa 611, Oman; pushpa.gowda@utas.edu.om
[2] College of Computing and Information Sciences, University of Technology and Applied Sciences, Ibri P.O. Box 466, Oman; sankar.mani@utas.edu.om (S.M.); ahmad.salah@utas.edu.om (A.S.)
[3] Department of Physics—Aerospace Division, Universitat Politècnica de Catalunya—Barcelona Tech, 08034 Barcelona, Spain
* Correspondence: sebastian.andreas.altmeyer@upc.edu
† These authors contributed equally to this work.

Abstract: Control of buoyancy-assisted convective flow and the associated thermal behavior of nanofluids in finite-sized conduits has become a great challenge for the design of many types of thermal equipment, particularly for heat exchangers. This investigation discusses the numerical simulation of the buoyancy-driven convection (BDC) of a nanofluid (NF) in a differently heated cylindrical annular domain with an interior cylinder attached with a thin baffle. The annular region is filled with non-Darcy porous material saturated-nanofluid and both NF and the porous structure are in local thermal equilibrium (LTE). Higher thermal conditions are imposed along the interior cylinder as well as the baffle, while the exterior cylinder is maintained with lower or cold thermal conditions. The Darcy–Brinkman–Forchheimer model, which accounts for inertial, viscous, and non-linear drag forces was adopted to model the momentum equations. An implicit finite difference methodology by considering time-splitting methods for transient equations and relaxation-based techniques is chosen for the steady-state model equations. The impacts of various pertinent parameters, such as the Rayleigh and Darcy numbers, baffle dimensions, like length and position, on flow, thermal distributions, as well as thermal dissipation rates are systematically estimated through accurate numerical predictions. It was found that the baffle dimensions are very crucial parameters to effectively control the flow and associated thermal dissipation rates in the domain. In addition, machine learning techniques were adopted for the chosen analysis and an appropriate model developed to predict the outcome accurately among the different models considered.

Keywords: annulus; baffle; porosity; machine learning; numerical technique

MSC: 37M05; 37M10; 37M20

1. Introduction

Buoyancy-induced convection in finite, closed conduits of different shapes has been investigated experimentally as well as theoretically for the last several decades. This interest among researchers mainly reflects the advantage of the use of cooling processes without any aiding external mechanisms in these processes. Further, due to the lower thermal conductivity of traditional or conventional fluids, a significant challenge is posed for cooling the model electronic equipment. The invention of NFs or nanoliquids, which involve a base-fluid and nano-sized particles of oxides or metals, provides a very effective means of replaceing these conventional fluids [1] to achieve comparatively higher cooling rates. The superior thermal conductivity of NFs has led to many important investigations and produced qualitative as well as quantitative information about the choice of nanoparticle (NP) and the optimal concentration to yield higher thermal transport rates [2,3]. Among the various finite-sized conduits, an annular space formed between two co-axial cylindrical-shaped tubes is applied in many important thermal applications, from nuclear reactors to crystal growth design equipment [4–6]. Augmentation of the thermal dissipation rate (TDR) by the inclusion of NFs is the major driver behind these investigations.

The thermal management of electronic equipment is one of the fundamental requirements of the electronics industry, the application of which has increased in recent times. To cater to the needs of modern electronic industries, among the several strategies tried by numerous researchers and scientists, attaching a baffle in one or more of the thermally active walls of the enclosure has been found to provide a better way to enhance the thermal transport rates. In this direction, one of the pioneering studies to analyze the impacts of a baffle in a tall tiled rectangular conduit is that of Scozia and Frederick [7]. The numerical prediction was carried out by considering up to 20 conducting baffles and it was concluded that decreasing the spacing between the baffles or increasing the baffles tends to produce a multi-cellular flow structure and reduction in the overall TDR. For a similar geometrical structure, Facas [8] reported the impacts of three baffles attached alongside hot and cold boundaries considering three different lengths, and concluded that a longer baffle induces a multi-cellular structure and produces higher TDRs compared to other baffle dimensions. Later, a full-blown analysis of the size and positional influences of a thin baffle on BDC and TDR in a square conduit was performed and it was concluded that an optimum dimension of baffle could be found at which the thermal transport rate could be significantly enhanced compared to non-baffle situations [9,10].

Further to the enhancement of TDR shown by fixing baffles to the active boundaries of the conduits, replacing the traditional working fluids by novel NFs was suggested to further improve the heat transfer, with an enhancement in TDR by as much as 10–20 percent demonstrated with use of NFs in [11]. The impacts of the fin height and NP concentration on the enhancement of TDR were examined by considering two different NPs in a rectangular conduit with longer fins predicted to induce heat transport in [12]. A 3D mixed convective flow in a perforated heat sink with several cylindrical-shaped fins was quantiatively analyzed by Bakhti and Si-Ameur [13] considering three NFs. A detailed combined conduction-convection analysis identified that use of Cu NPs induced higher TDR compared to other NPs, and predicted an enhanced frictional effect as well as NF movement with an increase in the Reynolds number. In a 3D triangular conduit, having a stationary as well as a rotating fin, Kolsi et al. [14] numerically predicted the fin conditions as well as the NP concentration to enhance the TDR. The combined influences of a moving boundary, adiabatic projection at the lower boundary, and an adiabatic baffle on the NF buoyant-flow and associated TDR in a square conduit showed that the energy transport in the chamber could be effectively determined by the dimensions of the adiabatic block as well as the position of the baffle [15]. Hussein et al. [16] presented a numerical examination of BDC in a slanted rectangular conduit with a baffle which was filled with two different nanofluids to predict the thermal behavior relative to the baffle dimensions. In many situations, the combined influences of magnetic fields and baffle(s) provide an effective method for controlling convective heat transfer in NF-filled finite geometries, as demonstrated by numerous research studies [17,18]. The optimal control of buoyant-assisted convection by utilizing single or multiple baffle(s) in various geometrical shapes, such as cylinders

[19], wavy conduits [20], and vented domains [21] has been examined. The choice of the different geometrical configurations in the above studies stems from the necessity to achieve enhanced heat transfer rates, maintain economic viability in production, ensure ease of manufacture, and optimize operational performance.

The utilization of one or multiple baffles in confined NF-filled porous geometries has emerged as a prominent research arena, motivated by the extensive potential engineering applications to improve the thermal efficiency. The porous materials, characterized by their unique structural properties and enhanced thermal transport capabilities, are present in many critical systems, including shell-and-tube heat exchangers, flat-plate solar collectors, and nuclear reactor cooling channels. Recognizing these advantages, researchers have systematically investigated various aspects of porous media and their integration with conductive or non-conductive baffle(s) to achieve optimum heat transfer intensification [22–24]. Mahalakshmi et al. [25] examined the characteristics of MHD mixed convection in a lid-driven porous conduit with a center heater to demonstrate the collective effects of the magnetic force strength, heater orientation, and nanofluid properties on thermal transport performance. The investigation predicted that a horizontal heater arrangement would achieve maximum heat transfer enhancement, and that the magnetic force effectively controls the convective movements within the porous medium. Aly et al. [26] numerically investigated BDC in a nanofluid-filled porous cavity with different heated fin shapes using a modified ISPH technique. Their analysis revealed that an H-fin shape maximizes the flow circulation rate while a Z-fin shape achieved the highest heat transfer rate. Subsequently, a CFD analysis conducted on magneto-convection in a slanted porous conduit with two conducting fins showed enhanced heat transfer with optimal fin configurations, such as fin space and dimensions, and cavity inclination of 30°, demonstrating superior performance compared to no-fin configurations [27].

Recently, porous fins have often been utilized in place of metal fins in thermal applications due to several key advantages, including the enhanced surface area provided by the internal pores, improved fluid mixing through tortuous flow paths, and reduced weight and material costs, among many other advantages [28,29]. Further, the incorporation of porous substance within irregular geometric configurations for analyzing buoyancy-driven NF convection represents a significant research domain with multidisciplinary implications, including enhanced geothermal systems, advanced heat exchangers, and microfluidic devices [30–32]. The detailed utilization of baffle(s) in controlling BDC flow and associated thermal transport in a variety of geometries filled with diverse NFs, and by considering different constraints, has been reported in comprehensive reviews [33,34]. An exhaustive, systematic review of the literature on the implications of various shaped baffle(s) across diverse porous and non-porous NF-filled geometrical configurations reveals a significant research gap. Specifically, the analysis of BDC within baffled porous annular geometries, particularly when integrated with a generalized porous media model and machine learning approaches, remains largely unexplored. Despite the significant industrial and engineering relevance of this configuration, the critical intersection of porous media dynamics, baffle design, and computational methodologies has received insufficient scholarly attention. The current examination addresses this substantial knowledge gap by presenting a comprehensive analysis that bridges traditional fluid dynamics with modern machine learning techniques in the context of baffled NF-saturated porous annular systems.

Despite high-quality outputs from CFD simulations for an individual set of parameters, their inherently high computational cost (which can typically process each simulation case in hours) is often a major obstacle. Running CFD simulations for each new operating condition or design iteration is usually prohibitively expensive in computational time, so a full exploration or fast decision-making becomes out of reach. This is where ML can provide significant potential improvements, taking the shape of powerful surrogate models. Once they have been trained on a representative dataset created by high-fidelity CFD simulations, the ML models can predict the overall performance metrics (e.g., Average Nusselt Number) in a fraction of the time (in many cases, orders of magnitude faster, <0.1 s/prediction). This fast prediction time, even though for an individual point it is less accurate than a full CFD approach, allows for tasks which seemed impossible, such as performing a full exploration of design space to identify new relationships or optimal space, the rapid screening of many design candidates to identify promising designs for more in-depth CFD analysis, or even for use in real-time processes where an instant response is needed. Thus, the ML approach is not meant to replace the ability of CFD for accurate, final validation of some chosen designs; it is instead intended to complement the capabilities of CFD by allowing efficient, large-scale investigation or dynamic applications that are beyond the practical application possibility of direct, iterative CFD simulations.

2. Mathematical Formulation of the Problem

2.1. Governing Model Equations

The present study examines BDC flow and thermal transfer in an annular configuration consisting of two upright cylinders arranged concentrically, with inner and outer radii represented as r_i and r_o, as illustrated in Figure 1. The configuration also includes a thin circular baffle attached to the inner cylinder, whose dimension and location can be adjusted to study their impacts on the fluid flow and heat transport characteristics. The thermal boundary conditions are established such that the inner cylinder and baffle are maintained at an elevated temperature, while the outer cylinder is kept at a lower temperature. However, the top and bottom cylindrical surfaces are considered to be both thermally insulated and rigid.

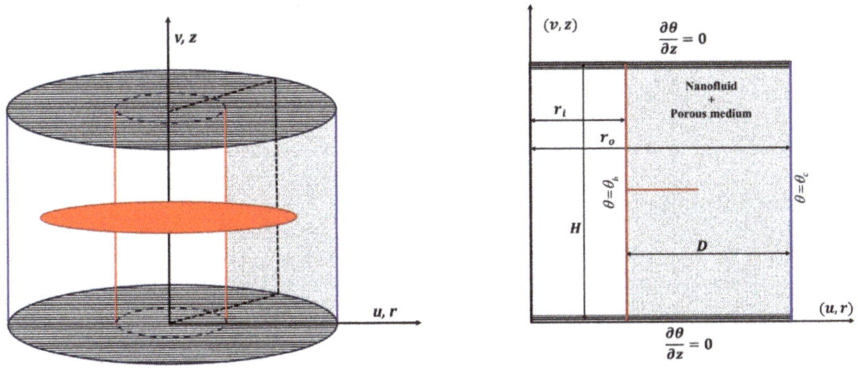

(**a**) 3D Annular baffled-geometry (**b**) Axi-symmetric view

Figure 1. Schematic representation of the baffled annular geometry: (**a**) three-dimensional view depicting the physical domain, and (**b**) axisymmetric cross-sectional view with thermal boundary conditions and characteristic dimensions.

The annular portion is filled with an NF-saturated porous material, where silver (Ag) NPs are dispersed in H_2O as the base-fluid. The analysis assumes local thermal equilibrium between the NPs and the base-fluid. The flow is considered to be two-dimensional and laminar, with constant thermophysical properties except for density variabilities, which are accounted for using the Boussinesq approximation. The relevant thermophysical properties of both the NPs and H_2O are provided in Table 1. The thermophysical properties of NFs depend on the volume fraction of NPs (ϕ) and the properties of both the base-fluid (f) and the NPs (p). Table 2 summarizes these properties with the corresponding mathematical models adopted in the current analysis, with the subscripts nf, f, and p denoting nanofluid, base-fluid, and nanoparticle, respectively.

Table 1. Physical properties of H_2O and Ag.

Physical Properties	H_2O	Ag
C_p (J/Kg K)	4179	235
ρ (Kg/m^3)	997.1	10,500
k (W/mK)	0.613	429
β (1/K)	21×10^{-5}	1.89×10^{-5}

Table 2. Thermophysical properties of NFs and the adopted models.

Properties of NFs	Volume Averaged Models
Density	$\rho_{nf} = (1-\phi)\rho_f + \phi\rho_p$
Thermal expansion coefficient	$(\rho\beta)_{nf} = (1-\phi)(\rho\beta)_f + \phi(\rho\beta)_p$
Heat capacitance	$(\rho C_p)_{nf} = (1-\phi)(\rho C_p)_f + \phi(\rho C_p)_p$
Thermal conductivity	$\frac{k_{nf}}{k_f} = \frac{k_p+2k_f-2\phi(k_f-k_p)}{k_p+2k_f+\phi(k_f-k_p)}$
Viscosity	$\mu_{nf} = \frac{\mu_f}{(1-\phi)^{2.5}}$
Thermal diffusivity	$\alpha_{nf} = \frac{k_{nf}}{(\rho C_p)_{nf}}$

To describe the flow through the porous medium, we employ the Darcy–Brinkman–Forchheimer model, which comprehensively accounts for viscous, inertial, and non-linear drag forces. Based on these assumptions and physical considerations, we develop the governing equations following similar approaches to those found in the contemporary literature on porous media flow and heat transfer [2,35]. The dimensional form of the model equations for the present analysis are as follows:

$$\nabla \cdot \vec{q} = 0 \tag{1}$$

$$\begin{aligned} \frac{\rho_{nf}}{\epsilon}\left[\frac{\partial \vec{q}}{\partial t^*} + \frac{1}{\epsilon}(\vec{q}\cdot\nabla)\vec{q}\right] &= -\nabla p + \frac{\mu_{nf}}{\epsilon}\nabla_1^2\vec{q} - \frac{\mu_{nf}}{K}\vec{q} \\ &- \frac{\rho_{nf}F\vec{q}\,|\vec{q}\,|}{\sqrt{K}} + (\rho\beta)_{nf}\vec{g}\,(\theta-\theta_c) \end{aligned} \tag{2}$$

$$\sigma\frac{\partial\theta}{\partial t^*} + (\vec{q}\cdot\nabla)\theta = \alpha_{nf}\nabla_1^2\theta \tag{3}$$

where ϵ and K are, respectively, the porosity and permeability, $\sigma = \frac{(\rho c_p)_{eff}}{(\rho c_p)_{nf}}$ is assumed to be unity by considering the thermal properties of NF and solid matrix to be identical, and F is the Forchheimer coefficient and is given by $F = \frac{1}{\sqrt{150}\epsilon^{3/2}}$. Also, $\nabla_1^2 = \frac{\partial^2}{\partial r^2} + \frac{1}{r}\frac{\partial}{\partial r} + \frac{\partial^2}{\partial z^2}$

The following dimensionless transformations are utilized to transform the Equations (1)–(3) to recast to dimensionless form.

$$(R,Z) = \frac{(r,z)}{D}, \quad (U,V) = \frac{(u,v)D}{\alpha_f}, \quad t = \frac{t^*\alpha_f}{D^2}, \quad T = \frac{(\theta-\theta_c)}{(\theta_h-\theta_c)}, \quad P = \frac{pD^2}{\rho_{nf}\alpha_f^2} \tag{4}$$

Using the transformations (4), the dimensionless model equations assume the following form:

$$\frac{\partial U}{\partial R}+\frac{\partial V}{\partial Z}+\frac{U}{R} = 0 \tag{5}$$

$$\frac{1}{\epsilon}\left[\frac{\partial U}{\partial t}+\frac{1}{\epsilon}\left(U\frac{\partial U}{\partial R}+V\frac{\partial U}{\partial Z}\right)\right] = -\frac{\partial P}{\partial R}+\frac{\mu_{nf}}{\rho_{nf}\alpha_f\epsilon}\left(\nabla^2 U-\frac{U}{R^2}\right)-\frac{\mu_{nf}}{\rho_{nf}\alpha_f Da}U - \left(\frac{1.75\sqrt{U^2+V^2}}{\sqrt{Da}\sqrt{150\epsilon^3}}\right)U \tag{6}$$

$$\frac{1}{\epsilon}\left[\frac{\partial V}{\partial t}+\frac{1}{\epsilon}\left(U\frac{\partial V}{\partial R}+V\frac{\partial V}{\partial Z}\right)\right] = -\frac{\partial P}{\partial Z}+\frac{\mu_{nf}}{\rho_{nf}\alpha_f\epsilon}\nabla^2 V-\frac{\mu_{nf}}{\rho_{nf}\alpha_f Da}V - \left(\frac{1.75\sqrt{U^2+V^2}}{\sqrt{Da}\sqrt{150\epsilon^3}}\right)V+\frac{(\rho\beta)_{nf}}{\rho_{nf}\beta_f}Ra\cdot Pr\frac{\partial T}{\partial R} \tag{7}$$

$$\frac{\partial T}{\partial t}+U\frac{\partial T}{\partial R}+V\frac{\partial T}{\partial Z} = \frac{\alpha_{nf}}{\alpha_f}\nabla^2 T \tag{8}$$

For BDC modeling, generally, the pressure terms are eliminated through cross-differentiation, and a new physical quantity known as vorticity is introduced. Vorticity is physically introduced at the walls and diffused into NF stream. Also, introducing a two-dimensional stream function in the cylindrical polar co-ordinates, the non-dimensional vorticity-stream function equations are as follows:

$$\frac{1}{\epsilon}\left[\frac{\partial \zeta}{\partial t}+\frac{1}{\epsilon}\left(U\frac{\partial \zeta}{\partial R}+V\frac{\partial \zeta}{\partial Z}-\frac{U\zeta}{R}\right)\right] = \frac{\mu_{nf}}{\rho_{nf}\alpha_f\epsilon}\left[\nabla^2\zeta-\frac{\zeta}{R^2}\right]-\frac{\mu_{nf}}{\rho_{nf}\alpha_f Da}\zeta - \left(\frac{1.75\sqrt{U^2+V^2}}{\sqrt{Da}\sqrt{150\epsilon^3}}\right)\zeta-\frac{(\rho\beta)_{nf}}{\rho_{nf}\beta_f}Ra\cdot Pr\frac{\partial T}{\partial R} \tag{9}$$

$$\zeta = \frac{1}{R}\left[\frac{\partial^2\psi}{\partial R^2}-\frac{1}{R}\frac{\partial\psi}{\partial R}+\frac{\partial^2\psi}{\partial Z^2}\right]. \tag{10}$$

$$U=\frac{1}{R}\frac{\partial\psi}{\partial Z},\quad V = -\frac{1}{R}\frac{\partial\psi}{\partial R} \tag{11}$$

In the above equations, $\nabla^2=\frac{\partial^2}{\partial R^2}+\frac{1}{R}\frac{\partial}{\partial R}+\frac{\partial^2}{\partial Z^2}$, $Ra=\frac{g\beta_f\Delta\theta D^3}{\nu_f\alpha_f}$, $Da=\frac{K}{D^2}$ and $Pr=\frac{\nu_f}{\alpha_f}$.

2.2. The Dimensionless Auxiliary Conditions

(i) Initial and hydrodynamic boundary conditions

$$\text{At } t=0, U=V=T=0, \psi=\zeta=0;\quad \frac{1}{\lambda-1}\le R\le\frac{\lambda}{\lambda-1},\quad 0\le Z\le A$$

$$\text{At } t>0, \psi=\frac{\partial\psi}{\partial R}=0,\ \text{at } R=\frac{1}{\lambda-1} \text{ and } \frac{\lambda}{\lambda-1}, 0\le Z\le A \text{ and at baffle boundaries}$$

$$\psi=\frac{\partial\psi}{\partial Z}=0,\ \text{at } Z=0 \text{ and } Z=A$$

(ii) Thermal boundary conditions at $t>0$

$R=\frac{1}{\lambda-1}$	$R=\frac{\lambda}{\lambda-1}$	On the baffle	$Z=0$ and A
$T=1$	$T=0$	$T=1$	$\frac{\partial T}{\partial Z}=0$

2.3. Thermal Transport Rates

In any thermal system, the quantitative measure to evaluate the thermal efficiency as well as the heat transport rate is predicted by estimating the local (Nu) and overall $\overline{Nu}$ numbers. These quantities are defined as follows:

$$\overline{Nu} = \frac{1}{A}\int_0^A Nu\, dZ, \quad \text{where} \quad Nu = -\frac{k_{nf}}{k_f}\left(\frac{\partial T}{\partial R}\right) \tag{12}$$

3. Description of Numerical Methodology

3.1. Finite Difference Methodology

The mathematical modeling of BDC phenomena within the complex nanofluid-saturated porous baffled annular domain poses significant computational difficulties. To address these challenges, our investigation adopts a robust hybrid numerical methodology that combines different finite difference (FD) techniques for a stable and accurate solution. The governing partial differential equations (PDEs) consist of non-linear and coupled vorticity transport, energy balance, and stream function equations. In particular, the vorticity-transport equation incorporates Darcy–Forchheimer–Brinkman terms to account for porous media effects, and additional terms to model the modified thermophysical properties of NF. Further, the baffled annular configuration also introduces additional complexities through the boundary conditions at the baffle interfaces.

Our solution methodology employs a domain discretization using a uniform grid across the entire annular region and special care has been taken while assigning grids along the baffle. For the temporal and spatial discretization, we adopt the following FD approximations:

1. Temporal Derivative: Forward difference quotients are implemented for all time-dependent terms, resulting in first-order accuracy in time (Δt).
2. Spatial Derivatives: Central difference schemes are utilized for spatial derivatives, providing second-order accuracy $(\Delta R^2$ and $\Delta Z^2)$ in the computational domain.

The solution methodology strategically integrates two different numerical techniques:

1. Alternating-Direction Implicit (ADI) Procedure: The parabolic nature of the vorticity and energy transport equations has been integrated by a two-step ADI scheme. In the first half-time step, the FD equations are solved implicitly in the R-direction while treating the Z-direction terms explicitly. In the second half-time step, the process is reversed, ensuring unconditional stability while maintaining computational efficiency.
2. Successive Line Over-Relaxation (SLOR): The elliptic stream function equation is solved using SLOR, where each grid line is solved implicitly while sweeping through the domain. An optimal over-relaxation parameter (ω) between 1.0 and 2.0 was dynamically adjusted to accelerate convergence based on the control parameters of the chosen problem.

The FD discretization process transforms the PDEs into systems of linear algebraic equations with tri-diagonal coefficient matrices. These systems are efficiently solved using the popular Thomas algorithm (tri-diagonal matrix algorithm or TDMA), which provides direct solutions.

The iterative solution process employs dual convergence criteria for transient as well as stationary cases:

1. For transient PDEs, iterations are carried out until: $\max|\Phi_{i,j}^{n+1} - \Phi_{i,j}^{n}| < \Gamma_1$, where Φ represents either vorticity or temperature, and Γ_1 is a predefined temporal tolerance, typically set at 10^{-6}.

2. For the stream-function equation, spatial convergence is achieved when: max $|\psi_{i,j}^{k+1} - \psi_{i,j}^{k}| < \Gamma_2$, where k denotes the special iteration level and Γ_2 is the spatial tolerance, typically set at 10^{-8}.

An in-house code in ForTran was developed to systematically invert the system of equations arising from the different model equations. The algorithm implementation follows a sequential approach where the energy and vorticity equations are advanced in time, followed by stream function updates and velocity-stream function relations at each time step, ensuring proper coupling between the momentum and energy transport mechanisms in the complex NF-saturated porous annular domain. Before the simulations, a systematic and proper grid independence trial was conducted by choosing coarse to fine grids from 51×51 to 201×201 and an optimum grid structure was chosen based on the solution accuracy and computational time. For choosing the optimal grid size, we identified the average Nu and $|psi_{max}|$ as the sensitive measure to decide the appropriate grid size. Based on these careful experiments, we found a grid size of 161×161 satisfactorily provided the accurate predictions as compared to the other grid sizes. However, the details pertaining to the grid independence tests are not provided here for brevity, but can be found in our recent studies [5,35,36].

3.2. Validation

To validate the current simulation outcomes, in this section, we report several important trial simulations to compare, qualitatively as well as quantitatively, with standard benchmark predictions existing in the literature, which are illustrated through Table 3 and contour illustrations (Figure 2), to support the credibility of the in-house developed code. In this regard, first, we modified our code with uniform heating and cooling, without the presence of a baffle ($\delta = 0$), for a uniformly heated-cooled non-baffled annulus and square geometry. We performed simulations for a thermal-buoyancy-assisted convection and obtained the thermal transport rates for an annular geometry without baffle ($\delta = 0$) to compare with the quantitative predictions of Abouali and Falahatpishesh [4]. Our predictions in the annular conduit for different magnitudes of Ra and ϕ are found to be in fair agreement with the numerical outcomes of Abouali and Falahatpishesh [4], as displayed in Table 3, with minimum allowable deviations.

Furthermore, in another comparison with a square geometry, we performed additional simulations, by putting $\lambda = 0$, to mimic the contour simulations of Nguyen et al. [2] for a square geometry containing Cu-H_2O NF, and present the same in Figure 2. The comparative predictions of the streamlines and isotherms vividly reveal the excellent similarity between our simulations and the predictions of Nguyen et al. [2] for two different NP concentrations. These qualitative and quantitative validations with systematic grid independence tests ensure the authenticity of our in-house code and provide confidence to perform further simulations in this investigation.

Table 3. Validation of average Nu with Abouali and Falahatpishesh [4] for different magnitudes of Ra and ϕ.

Ra ($Gr \times Pr$)	Average Nusselt Number ($\overline{Nu}$) Abouali and Falahatpishesh [4]	Present Study	Relative Difference (%)	
6×10^3	2.867	2.884	0.59	$\phi = 0.00$
	2.729	2.740	0.40	$\phi = 0.02$
6×10^4	5.439	5.480	0.75	$\phi = 0.00$
	5.176	5.184	0.14	$\phi = 0.02$
6×10^5	10.315	10.402	0.83	$\phi = 0.00$
	9.818	9.913	0.96	$\phi = 0.02$

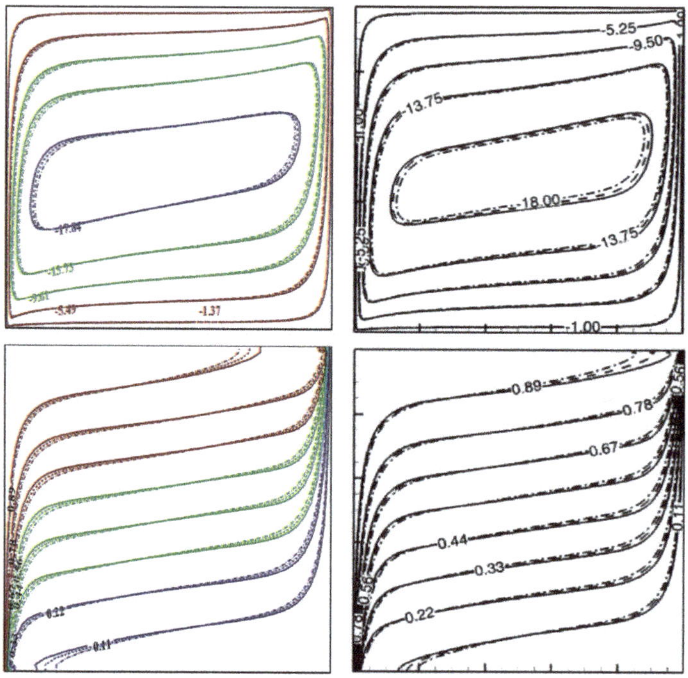

Figure 2. Streamlines (**top**) and isotherms (**bottom**) at $Ra = 10^9$, $Da = 10^{-6}$ and $\epsilon = 0.4$ of present study (**left**) with Nguyen et al. [2] (**right**) for base-fluid (solid curve) and Cu-H_2O NF with $\phi = 0.025$ (dashed curve) and $\phi = 0.05$ (dash-dotted curve).

3.3. Proposed Machine Learning Methodology

The proposed methodology outlined in this study investigates whether machine learning techniques can be used to predict the mean Nusselt number, a critical indicator of heat transfer performance, within a cylindrical annular domain. This approach employs a thorough data-driven pipeline consisting of data analysis and preprocessing, model training, hyperparameter tuning, and model validation. We use a conventional machine-learning algorithms in addition to a deep learner that relates the dependent variables (e.g., Rayleigh number, baffle length, etc.) to the predictee. The primary motivation for this is to develop reliable and accurate predictive models to support thermal equipment designers.

The preprocessing step is essential for maintaining the quality of data and readiness for model training. Our first step is exploratory data analysis to develop an understanding of individual feature distributions, potential outliers, and correlations across features. The dataset also contains missing values, and therefore, we impute for missing values. Next, we standardize the data to have a mean of zero and a variance of one. This step is important because it helps ensure that features with larger magnitudes do not dominate the learning process, especially with distance-based algorithms and neural networks. Lastly, a train–test split is completed to separate the dataset into independent train and test datasets which is crucial to create an unbiased evaluation of model generalization performance.

We utilized a range of machine learning models to predict the mean Nusselt number. This list of models includes ensemble models such as Random Forest and Gradient Boosting, known for their robustness to complexities and ability to capture non-linearities. A Support Vector Regressor (SVR) is also considered as it allows flexibility in modeling different kinds of relationships through kernel functions. Additionally, we implement a Ridge Regression model as a baseline linear model to compare against the more complex models. Finally, we developed an Artificial Neural Network (ANN) to test the capabilities of deep learning.

Hyperparameter optimization is conducted for each model to maximize performance. Instead of an exhaustive grid search, we opted for a randomized search. This method still allows for exploration of the hyperparameter space by choosing a fixed number of hyperparameter combinations to sample. This method represents a good trade-off of computational cost and probability of finding near-optimal hyperparameters. A repeated k-fold cross-validation is also used for model hyper-parameter tuning to provide a robust estimate of model performance and counteract overfitting to the training data.

Model performance is evaluated using a comprehensive suite of metrics, including R-squared (R^2), Root Mean Squared Error (RMSE), Mean Absolute Error (MAE), and Mean Absolute Percentage Error (MAPE). These metrics are defined as follows, where y_i represents the true value, $\hat{y}_i$ represents the predicted value, and n is the number of samples:

- **R-squared (R^2):** Measures the proportion of variance in the dependent variable that is predictable from the independent variables. A value of 1 indicates a perfect fit.

$$R^2 = 1 - \frac{\sum_{i=1}^{n}(y_i - \hat{y}_i)^2}{\sum_{i=1}^{n}(y_i - \bar{y})^2} \quad (13)$$

  where $\bar{y}$ is the mean of the true values.
- **Root Mean Squared Error (RMSE):** Represents the square root of the average squared difference between the predicted and actual values. Lower values indicate better fit.

$$RMSE = \sqrt{\frac{1}{n}\sum_{i=1}^{n}(y_i - \hat{y}_i)^2} \quad (14)$$

- **Mean Absolute Error (MAE):** Represents the average absolute difference between the predicted and actual values. Lower values indicate better fit.

$$MAE = \frac{1}{n}\sum_{i=1}^{n}|y_i - \hat{y}_i| \quad (15)$$

- **Mean Absolute Percentage Error (MAPE):** Represents the average absolute percentage difference between the predicted and actual values. Lower values are better, with 0% indicating a perfect fit.

$$MAPE = \frac{1}{n}\sum_{i=1}^{n}\left|\frac{y_i - \hat{y}_i}{y_i}\right| \times 100\% \quad (16)$$

These evaluation metrics each provide different insights about different aspects of model accuracy. In addition to these metrics, we also look at the residuals in order to evaluate the stated assumptions of the model and examine any systematic biases. The best overall model is determined by sufficient overall performance against these metrics, with emphasis on generalization ability on the hold-out test set.

The proposed methodology is summarized in Algorithm 1, PREDICT NUSSELT NUMBER, which outlines the complete workflow for predicting the average Nusselt number. It begins with data analysis and preprocessing, including splitting the data into training and testing sets and applying a preprocessing pipeline for imputation and scaling. The core of the algorithm involves iterating through a set of predefined models, including both traditional machine learning algorithms and an Artificial Neural Network (ANN). For each model, hyperparameter optimization is performed using randomized search with cross-validation, except for the ANN, which is trained with techniques like early stopping.

Algorithm 1 Predicting average Nusselt number

Input: Dataset $D = \{(x_i, y_i)\}_{i=1}^{N}$, where x_i is a feature vector and y_i is the Nusselt number.
Output: Best predictive model M^*, evaluation metrics.
procedure PREDICTNUSSELTNUMBER(D)
    $D_{analysis} \leftarrow D$ ▷ Copy for analysis
    Perform data analysis on $D_{analysis}$ (histograms, correlation matrix, etc.)
    $X, Y \leftarrow$ Separate features (X) and target (Y) from D
    $X_{train}, X_{test}, Y_{train}, Y_{test} \leftarrow$ Split X, Y into training and testing sets (e.g., 80/20 split)
    $Preprocessor \leftarrow$ Create preprocessing pipeline (imputation, scaling)
    $X_{train}^{scaled} \leftarrow Preprocessor.fit\_transform(X_{train})$
    $X_{test}^{scaled} \leftarrow Preprocessor.transform(X_{test})$
    $Models \leftarrow$ {RandomForest, GradientBoosting, SVR, Ridge, ANN}
    $BestModels \leftarrow \{\}$
    $Results \leftarrow \{\}$
    for $M \in Models$ **do**
        if M is ANN **then**
            Define ANN architecture (layers, activation functions, etc.)
            Compile ANN model (optimizer, loss function)
            Train ANN with cross-validation, early stopping, and learning rate scheduling
            $BestModels[M] \leftarrow$ Trained ANN
        else
            Define hyperparameter search space for M
            Perform randomized search with cross-validation to find best hyperparameters
            $BestModels[M] \leftarrow$ Model M with best hyperparameters
        end if
        Evaluate $BestModels[M]$ on $X_{train}^{scaled}, Y_{train}$ and $X_{test}^{scaled}, Y_{test}$
        Store evaluation metrics (R^2, RMSE, MAE, MAPE) in $Results[M]$
    end for
    $M^* \leftarrow$ Select best model based on evaluation metrics (e.g., lowest MAE on test set)
    return M^*, $Results$
end procedure

Algorithm 1 then evaluates each trained model on both the training and testing sets, storing the results. Finally, it selects the best-performing model based on a chosen evaluation metric (e.g., MAE on the test set) and returns this model along with the comprehensive evaluation results for all models. This structured approach ensures a rigorous and reproducible methodology for model development and selection.

3.4. Implementation Details

The developed ML models are proposed to predict the Average Nusselt Number ($\overline{Nu}$). The used dataset was split into a training set, 80% of the samples, and a test set, 20% of the samples. The splitting of the data was completed using the scikit-learn `train_test_split` function. Then, a preprocessing stage was executed, where all input features were standardized using scikit-learn's `StandardScaler`. For those models that were developed rather than the neural network-based model, namely, Random Forest, Gradient Boosting, SVR, and Ridge Regression, a hyperparameter search was conducted using `RandomizedSearchCV` provided by scikit-learn. `RandomizedSearchCV` evaluates a prespecified set of hyperparameter values for each model, on the training dataset (employing a 5-fold cross-validation). The goal was to determine a set of hyperparameter values that maximized the R^2 score. The key hyperparameters that were tuned included `n_estimators`, `max_depth` for the various ensemble-based models, `learning_rate` for GradientBoosting, C, γ and kernel type for SVR, and α for the regularization strength in the Ridge Regression.

The proposed ANN architecture was constructed as a sequential multi-layer perceptron model with the TensorFlow Keras API. The architecture consisted of an input layer with three hidden dense layers (e.g., consisting of 128, 64, and 32 neurons, respectively) with 1 dense output layer with a linear activation function for the regression problem. The activation function in the hidden layers was the ReLU (Rectified Linear Unit). To reduce overfitting, the model had L_2 regularization applied to the weights of the hidden layers, batch normalization following the hidden dense model, and dropouts (e.g., with 0.2 probability rate) between the hidden dense layers. The ANN model was compiled with an initial learning rate of the Adam optimizer, with the goal of minimizing the mean squared error. Training had a predetermined upper limit for the epoch (i.e., 500 maximum epochs) and employed a count to the batch size of the training samples.

4. Results and Discussion

The current analysis involves nine dimensionless parameters, namely, the Rayleigh (Ra), Darcy (Da), and Prandtl (Pr) numbers, the baffle length (δ) and location (L), porosity (ϵ), NP concentration (ϕ), aspect (A) and radii (λ) ratios, and a full-blown parametric study along with ANN modeling, which would be a formidable task. Hence, in our analysis, the parameters, A, Pr and λ are fixed at $1, 6.2$, and 2, respectively. However, the ranges of the other parameters are as follows: $10^3 \leq Ra \leq 10^6$, $10^{-5} \leq Da \leq 10^{-1}$, $0 \leq \phi \leq 0.05$, $0.2 \leq L, \delta \leq 0.8$, $0.1 \leq \epsilon \leq 0.9$. These parametric ranges would highlight the weaker, meager, and stronger impacts of all pertinent parameters on the qualitative as well as quantitative predictions.

4.1. CFD Simulation Results

4.1.1. Impact of Control Parameters on Flow and Thermal Contours

In the streamline contour graphs, the positive and negative values have important physical meanings. The positive streamlines indicate counterclockwise rotation of fluid, representing the fluid motion in the counterclockwise direction. However, the negative streamlines refer to clockwise circulation of fluid, indicating fluid movement along the clockwise direction.

The flow and thermal contours depicted in Figure 3 illustrate the significant influence of Ra on the flow and thermal characteristics within the annular domain (the arrows in the streamline plots highlight the direction of the vortex rotation in the annulus). At $Ra = 10^3$, the flow exhibits a single primary circulation vortex with relatively symmetric and organized patterns, suggesting a conduction-dominated thermal transport regime. The isotherms at this lower Ra appear nearly vertical with minimal distortion, further confirming the dominance of conductive heat transfer. The presence of a baffle introduces only minor perturbations in both flow and thermal distributions, while maintaining the overall stability of the system. In contrast, at $Ra = 10^6$, the flow structure undergoes a substantial transformation. The streamlines reveal the formation of multiple circulation cells with significantly higher flow intensities, evidenced by the densely packed streamline contours. The flow field exhibits pronounced distortion near the baffle, indicating strong convective currents. The corresponding isotherms at this higher Ra display substantial distortion and clustering, particularly near the walls and baffle, resulting in the formation of distinct thermal boundary layers and enhanced temperature stratification in the core region. This behavior clearly signifies the transition to a convection-dominated heat transfer regime. The comparison between base-fluid ($\phi = 0$, continuous curves) and NF ($\phi = 0.05$, dotted curves) reveals subtle yet important differences in both flow and thermal characteristics. Although the overall flow structure basically remains similar, the presence of NPs modifies the flow patterns and enhances the heat transfer characteristics. This enhancement is particularly evident in the high Ra case, where the NF demonstrates improved thermal mixing and heat transfer capabilities.

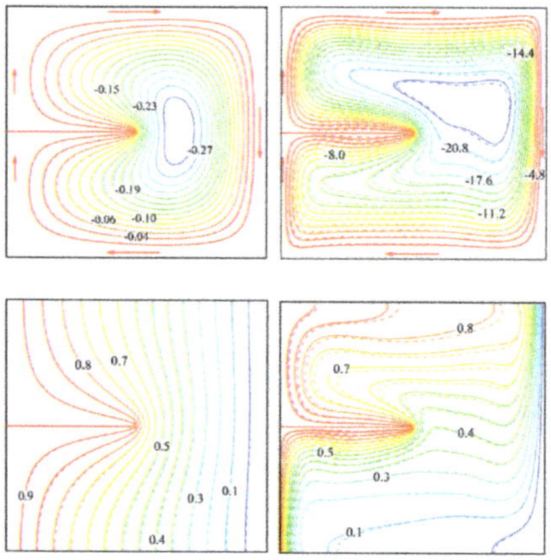

(**a**) $Ra = 10^3$ (**b**) $Ra = 10^6$

Figure 3. Effect of Rayleigh number on streamlines and isotherms at $L = \delta = 0.5$, $\epsilon = 0.4$, $Da = 10^{-2}$. Continuous and dotted curves, respectively, represent $\phi = 0$ and $\phi = 0.05$ (the arrows in the upper figures highlight the direction of the vortex rotation in the annulus).

The analysis of the Da influence on the flow features and thermal patterns reveals compelling insights into porous material behavior, as illustrated in Figure 4. At a higher Darcy number $(Da = 10^{-1})$, manifesting enhanced permeability, the NF flow exhibits complex patterns characterized by dual circulation cells and pronounced flow distortions, particularly near the boundary regions. The corresponding isotherm contours exhibit strong clustering, indicating the presence of steep thermal gradients across the domain. The impact of different porosities ($\epsilon = 0.4$ and $\epsilon = 0.9$) becomes significant at this higher Darcy number, with higher porosity resulting in more intense circulation patterns. In contrast, at a lower Darcy number $(Da = 10^{-5})$, indicating reduced permeability, the flow structure shows simpler patterns, characterized by a single primary circulation vortex, and the thermal distribution shows a higher uniform spacing and smoother transitions. The influence of porosity variation becomes less pronounced at this lower Darcy number, indicating that permeability effects play a dominant role over porosity impacts. The influence of the baffle dimensions (δ) and locations (L) on the flow and thermal patterns within the porous annular region is reported in Figure 5. Four distinct baffle configurations are analyzed, characterized by varying different combinations of L and δ dimensions. For the case of $L = 0.2, \delta = 0.2$, denoting a shorter baffle positioned closer to the bottom, the flow field exhibits a primary circulation pattern with densely positioned streamlines, while the isotherms show moderate thermal stratification. However, for $\delta = 0.2$ but increasing $L = 0.2$ to 0.8 (shifting the baffle to a higher location), a notable alteration in the flow structure occurs with a more pronounced distortion in the streamlines adjacent to the baffle region, accompanied by enhanced thermal mixing, as evidenced by the isothermal patterns. For configurations with longer baffles $(\delta = 0.8)$, the flow and thermal characteristics exhibit larger significant variations. At $L = 0.2$, the extended baffle creates a more restricted flow passage, causing strong flow circulation rates in the restricted region and more pronounced thermal gradients. The case of $L = 0.8, \delta = 0.8$ shows intense flow modification, with different flow separation and recirculation zones, along with sharp thermal gradients, particularly near the baffle edge.

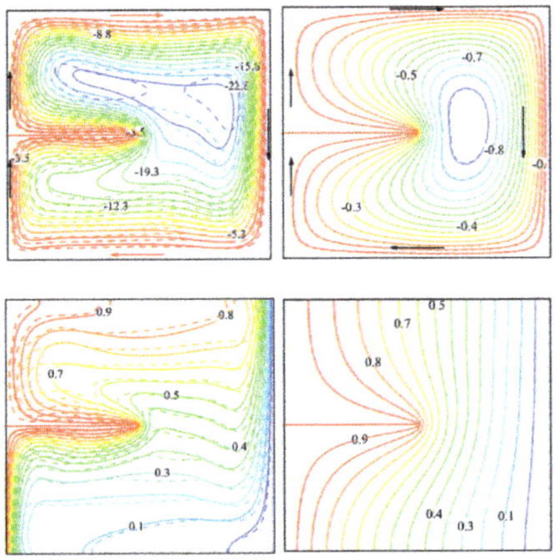

(**a**) $Da = 10^{-1}$ (**b**) $Da = 10^{-5}$

Figure 4. Darcy number influence on streamlines and isotherms for $L = \delta = 0.5, \epsilon = 0.4, \phi = 0.04$, $Ra = 10^6$. Continuous and dotted curves, respectively, represent $\epsilon = 0.4$ and $\epsilon = 0.9$ (the arrows in the upper figures highlight the direction of the vortex rotation in the annulus).

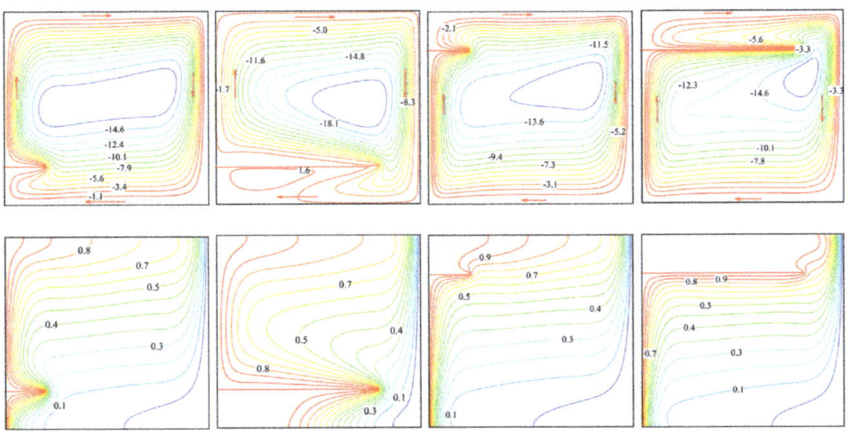

(**a**) $L = 0.2, \delta = 0.2$ (**b**) $L = 0.2, \delta = 0.8$ (**c**) $L = 0.8, \delta = 0.2$ (**d**) $L = 0.8, \delta = 0.8$

Figure 5. Impact of baffle dimension and location on flow and thermal distributions for $\phi = 0.04$, $Ra = 10^6$, $\epsilon = 0.4$, $Da = 10^{-3}$ (the arrows in the upper figures highlight the direction of the vortex rotation in the annulus).

4.1.2. Impact of Control Parameters on Thermal Transport Rates

Figure 6 illustrates the thermal efficiency relationship between the average Nu and the Darcy number for various fin positions (L). The thermal performance predicts a clear physical trend, indicating at low Darcy numbers (10^{-5}) that the flow drag is severe, and the heat transfer is primarily conduction-dominated, resulting in low $\overline{Nu}$ across all fin positions. As the Da increases, particularly between 10^{-4} and 10^{-2}, a drastic enhancement in heat transfer due to stronger convective effects occurs. The fin position closer to the bottom $(L = 0.2)$ consistently records superior thermal performance, achieving a maximum Nusselt number. This superiority can be attributed to better utilization of the buoyancy-driven flow, as the lower fin position allows for more effective development of thermal boundary layers and convective currents. Conversely, higher fin positions $(L = 0.8)$ show reduced thermal efficiency, suggesting that placing the fin at higher locations impedes the BDC flow pattern. The variation in the average Nu curves indicates that further increase in permeability beyond $Da = 10^{-2}$ produces minor variations in heat transfer enhancement. The interplay between the baffle dimension (δ) and Darcy number (Da) on heat transfer effectiveness is reported in Figure 7. An overview of the predictions suggests that shorter fins ($\delta = 0.2$) consistently outperform longer ones, achieving the highest thermal transfer ($\overline{Nu}$). This superior performance of shorter fins could be attributed to reduced flow blockage, as seen in a longer baffle, permitting better fluid circulation and hence enhanced convective thermal transport. As the baffle dimension increases to $\delta = 0.8$, the thermal performance deteriorates due to higher flow resistance, which leads to reduced convective mixing. The influence of permeability (Da) follows a characteristic pattern. At low Da (10^{-5}), conduction dominates and heat transfer is minimal across all fin lengths. A sharp enhancement in thermal transport occurs between $Da = 10^{-4}$ and 10^{-2}, marking the transition from conduction- to convection-dominated regimes. Beyond $Da = 10^{-2}$, the variation in the curves stabilizes, suggesting that further increases in permeability provide minimal thermal benefits.

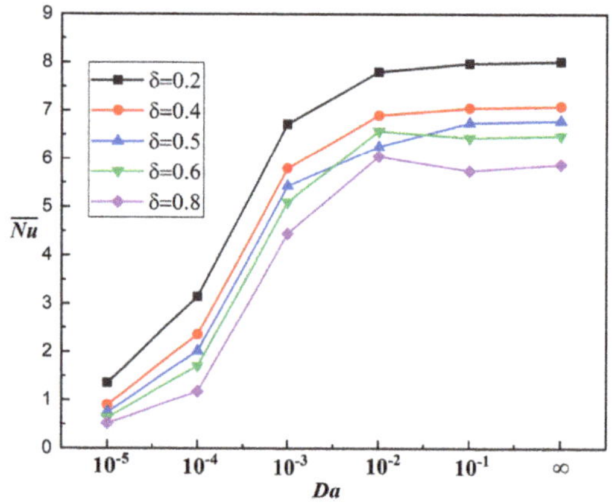

Figure 6. Examination of $\overline{Nu}$ sensitivity to variations of Da and L for $Ra = 10^6, \epsilon = 0.4$, $\phi = 0.04$, $\delta = 0.5$.

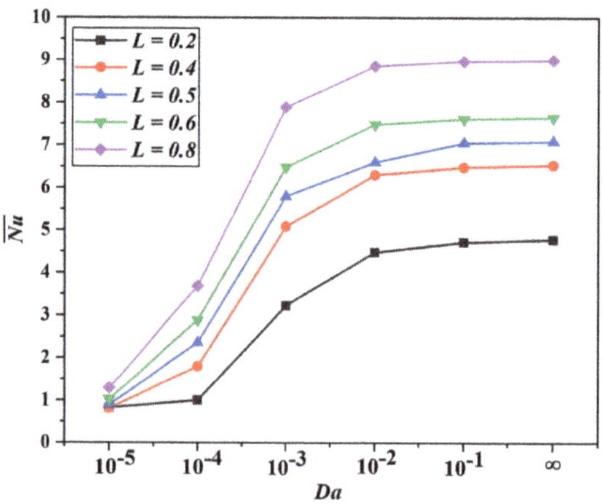

Figure 7. Thermal efficiency variations with Darcy number and fin dimension at $Ra = 10^6, \epsilon = 0.4$, $\phi = 0.04, L = 0.5$.

Figure 8 demonstrates the collective impacts of the fin length (δ) and position (L) on the thermal efficiency for the fixed parameters ($Ra = 10^6$, $\epsilon = 0.4$, $\phi = 0.04$, $Da = 10^{-2}$). For the combinations of shorter fins ($\delta = 0.2$) and lowered positions ($L = 0.2$), the heat transfer performance is predicted to be superior, with $\overline{Nu}$ around 6.5. However, as the baffle position increases to $L = 0.8$, an increase of 38% in the average Nu could be achieved. In addition, it could be observed that the performance differences between various fin dimensions become less pronounced, with all curves converging to Nusselt numbers around 8.5–9 for the elevated baffle location ($L = 0.8$). The lower fin lengths consistently outperform larger dimensional baffles across all fin locations, attributed to better utilization of the developing thermal boundary layer and convective currents near the bottom portion of annular domain. The effects of the NP volume fraction (ϕ) and fin length (δ) on thermal transport performance are reported in the bar graph (Figure 9) at $Ra = 10^6$, $\epsilon = 0.4$, $L = 0.5$, and $Da = 10^{-3}$. The parametric analysis elucidates that shorter fins ($\delta = 0.2$) consistently demonstrate superior thermal transport, with Nusselt numbers ranging from 6.29 to 6.82 across all NP concentrations. A moderate increase in heat transfer is observed with an increasing NP volume fraction, particularly for $\delta = 0.2$, where $\overline{Nu}$ increases from 6.29 ($\phi = 0$) to 6.82 ($\phi = 0.05$). However, this enhancement becomes less pronounced for longer fins ($\delta = 0.8$), where $\overline{Nu}$ values remain relatively lower (around 4.2–4.5). To consolidate the outcomes from these predictions, it may be suggested that the combination of shorter baffles with high-density NPs could enhance the thermal transport among other combinations.

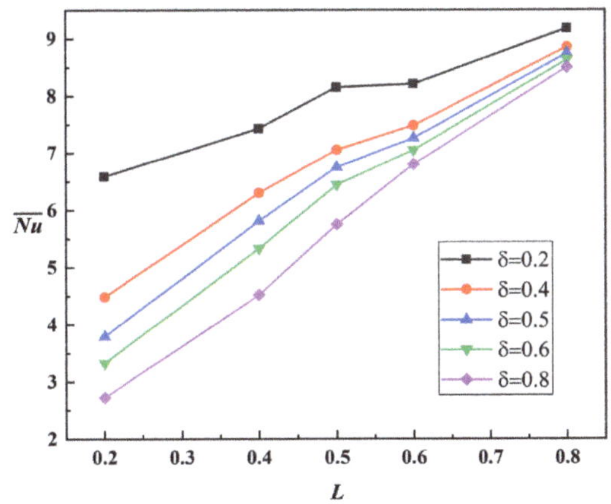

Figure 8. Thermal efficiency variations with fin dimensions and positions at $Ra = 10^6, \epsilon = 0.4$, $\phi = 0.04, Da = 10^{-2}$.

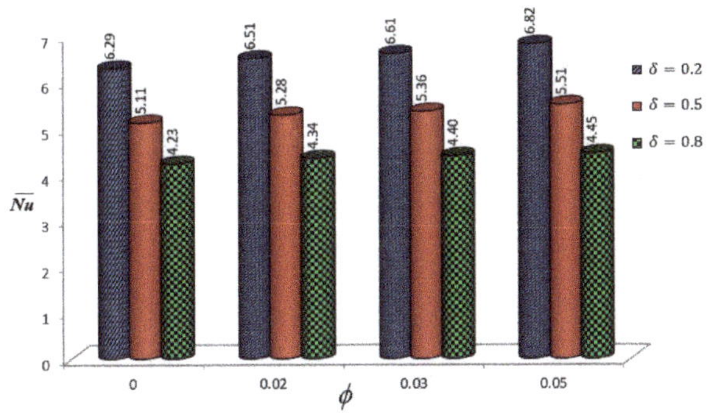

Figure 9. Examination of $\overline{Nu}$ sensitivity to variations in ϕ and δ for $Ra = 10^6, \epsilon = 0.4$, $L = 0.5$, $Da = 10^{-3}$.

Figure 10 reports the combined influences of the NP volume fraction (ϕ) and fin location (L) on the thermal transfer characteristics at $Ra = 10^6$, $\epsilon = 0.4$, $\delta = 0.5$, and $Da = 10^{-3}$. Fins positioned at $L = 0.2$ exhibit significantly enhanced heat transfer, with Nusselt numbers ranging from 7.29 to 7.93 across all NP concentrations. The addition of NPs shows a modest positive impact on heat transport, with the most pronounced enhancement observed for $L = 0.2$, where $\overline{Nu}$ increases from 7.29 ($\phi = 0$) to 7.93 ($\phi = 0.05$). However, fins positioned closer to the upper portion of the annular domain ($L = 0.8$) demonstrate consistently lower heat transfer rates ($\overline{Nu} \approx 2.5$–2.64), suggesting that positioning fins too close to the upper boundary restricts fluid circulation and thermal mixing. The intermediate fin position ($L = 0.5$) shows moderate performance, indicating optimal baffle placement is crucial for maximizing the combined benefits of fin-enhanced heat transfer and NF properties. The numerical predictions in Figure 11 demonstrate the interplay between Da and ϕ on thermal efficiency at $Ra = 10^6$ and $\epsilon = 0.4$. As expected, higher magnitude of Da ($Da = 10^{-1}$) yields substantially enhanced thermal transport rates, with average Nu ranging from 6.32 to 6.85, indicating augmented fluid permeability and consequently, higher convective transport. A moderate increment in the heat transport is observed with an increase in NP concentration across all Darcy numbers. However, for the low permeability case, ($Da = 10^{-5}$), the thermal transfer remains notably suppressed ($\overline{Nu} \approx 0.68$–0.77) despite increasing NP concentration, suggesting that the flow constriction dominates over the enhanced thermal conductivity impacts of NPs. The intermediate permeability case ($Da = 10^{-3}$) shows moderate heat transfer enhancement, highlighting the critical role of porous media permeability in determining the effectiveness of NP addition.

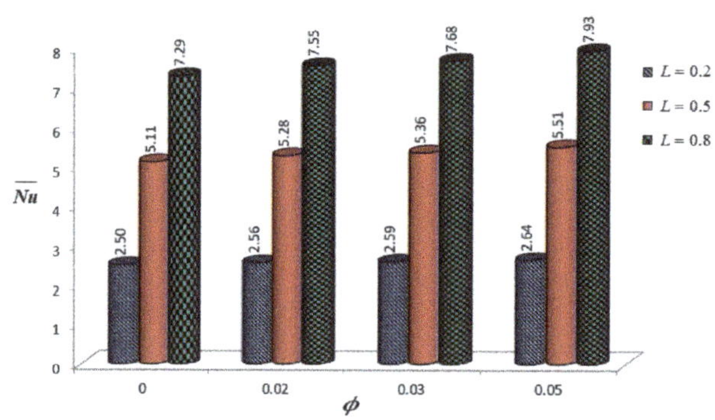

Figure 10. Examination of $\overline{Nu}$ sensitivity to variations in ϕ and L for $Ra = 10^6, \epsilon = 0.4$, $\delta = 0.5$, $Da = 10^{-3}$.

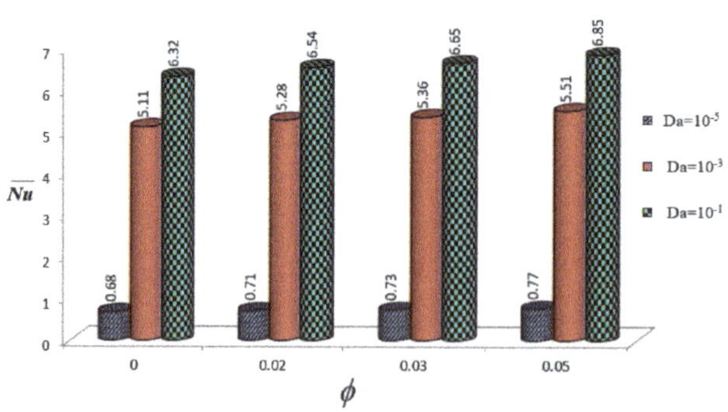

Figure 11. Thermal efficiency variations with the combined impacts of Da and ϕ at $Ra = 10^6, \epsilon = 0.4$, $\phi = 0.04$, $L = 0.5$.

4.2. Machine Learning Model

Predictive Models' Results

Table 4 presents a comparison of the training and testing performance for each model, considering R-squared (R^2), Mean Absolute Error (MAE), and Mean Absolute Percentage Error (MAPE). This detailed comparison allows for a thorough assessment of model generalization and potential overfitting.

Table 4. ML models' performance.

Model	Train R^2	Test R^2	Diff	Train MAE	Test MAE	Diff	Train MAPE	Test MAPE	Diff
Random Forest	0.9824	0.9152	0.0672	0.1555	0.3587	0.2032	0.0720	0.1956	0.1235
Gradient Boosting	**0.9938**	**0.9849**	**0.0089**	**0.1083**	**0.1913**	**0.0830**	**0.0375**	**0.0454**	**0.0080**
SVR	0.5553	0.6426	−0.0873	0.9670	0.8525	−0.1144	0.8359	0.5213	−0.3146
Ridge	0.3674	0.5048	−0.1374	1.6788	1.3265	−0.3523	0.9652	0.4099	−0.5553
ANN	0.5852	0.3044	0.2808	1.3718	1.6264	0.2546	0.6726	0.6621	−0.0106

Bold numbers indicate the best results.

The Gradient Boosting model shows the best performance, scoring a very high Test R^2 of 0.9849, with low Test MAE of 0.1913, and low Test MAPE of 0.0454. The small discrepancy between the training and testing metrics (R^2: 0.0089, MAE: 0.0830, MAPE: 0.0080) indicates very good generalization capability with no overfitting. The next best performance is the Random Forest model, which scored a Test R^2 of 0.9152, Test MAE of 0.3587, and Test MAPE of 0.1956. The Random Forest model does show slightly increased overfitting, in comparison to Gradient Boosting, with an R^2 of 0.0672, MAE of 0.2032, and MAPE of 0.1235. Overall, Random Forest still demonstrates good generalization. The results emphasize the strength of ensemble learning methods, specifically, Gradient Boosting, in generalizing complex non-linear relationships while providing good performance. Both of these ensemble methods improved performance when compared to SVR, Ridge, and ANN. It can be inferred that tree-based models are likely to be better suited for this area of application.

The ANN and Ridge Regression models exhibited evidence of overfitting as well. Although the ANN exhibited a large positive R^2 difference (0.2808), and an MAE difference (0.2546), the Ridge exhibited a negative R^2 difference (−0.1374), and a negative MAE difference (−0.3523). Furthermore, it is observed that there are negative differences in R^2, MAE, and MAPE for SVR and Ridge, indicating that both models performed better on the test set than on the training set. Overall, their performance is significantly lower than the ensemble methods described above. The poor performance of the ANN model demonstrates the complexity of the model and the inferences can be drawn that the structure of the ANN model network or the training process for the model were not optimal.

5. Conclusions

A comprehensive parametric analysis was conducted to examine BDC in an NF-saturated porous annular geometry having a circular hot baffle attached to the inner cylindrical surface. The computational results are supported by machine learning predictions to ensure the credibility of the numerical predictions. Through exhaustive numerical and machine learning analysis, the following significant findings are reported:

1. Both the baffle dimension and position significantly influence the fluid flow characteristics within the porous cavity, with longer baffles positioned at higher locations generally leading to more complex flow structures and thermal patterns.
2. The observations from the combined influences of the porosity and permeability of the porous material reveal a strong interplay between the Darcy number and porosity, which significantly influences both the flow characteristics and the thermal distribution

patterns, offering valuable insights for heat transfer applications and system design considerations.

3. Optimal heat transfer in the porous annular domain could be achieved through a combination of high permeability and shorter fins that do not cause severe restriction on the fluid movement.
4. The predictions suggest that shorter fins maintain better fluid circulation and mixing, while longer fins may create excessive flow resistance that counteracts the potential benefits of NP addition, even at higher NP concentrations.
5. The simulation predictions suggest that optimal fin placement is crucial for maximizing the combined benefits of fin-enhanced heat transfer and NF properties.
6. Despite using various models to obtain predictive accuracy, the comparative analysis showed that the Gradient Boosting model has an outstanding level of predictive accuracy (Test R^2 = 0.9849, Test MAE = 0.1913) and exhibited extensive generalization ability in comparison with Random Forest, Support Vector Regressor, Ridge, and Artificial Neural Network models.
7. The minor difference in metrics between the training and testing sets for Gradient Boosting (R^2 Diff = 0.0089) indicates that the model is robust to overfitting.
8. The results from this research strongly support the notion that ensemble tree-based models, specifically, Gradient Boosting models, are an effective means of accurately estimating the complex non-linear relationships being evaluated in this research, especially in comparison to linear, kernel-based approaches and neural networks.

Author Contributions: Conceptualization, methodology, software, and original draft preparation, S.M.; review and editing, ML model development and plagiarism reduction, A.S.; project administration review and editing, S.A.A.; preparation of graphs and literature review, P.G. All authors have read and agreed to the published version of the manuscript.

Funding: This work is supported by the Spanish Government under grants PID2023-150014OB-C21 and PID2023-150029NB-I00.

Data Availability Statement: The original contributions presented in the study are included in the article, further inquiries can be directed to the corresponding author.

Acknowledgments: The authors S.M. and A.S. acknowledge the support and encouragement from the University of Technology and Applied Sciences(UTAS)-Ibri, Oman.

Conflicts of Interest: The authors declare no conflicts of interest.

Nomenclature

A	aspect ratio
C_p	specific heat at constant pressure
D	annulus width (m)
Da	Darcy number
H	annulus height (m)
h	baffle location (m)
k	thermal conductivity (W/(m K))
K	permeability
l	length of baffle (m)
$\overline{Nu}$	average Nusselt number
p	liquid pressure (Pa)
Pr	Prandtl number
Ra	Rayleigh number
t^*	dimensional time (s)
t	dimensionless time
T	dimensionless temperature

L	dimensionless location
(r_i, r_o)	radius of inner and outer cylinders (m)
(R, Z)	non-dimensional radial and axial co-ordinates
(U, V)	non-dimensional velocity components in (R, Z) directions
Greek Letters	
α	thermal diffusivity (m^2/s)
β	thermal expansion coefficient (1/K)
ε	porosity
η	dimensionless length of baffle
ω	non-dimensional vorticity
θ	dimensional temperature (K)
λ	radius ratio
Abbrivations	
NF	nanofluid
NP	nanoparticle
TDR	thermal dissipation rate
BDC	buoyancy-driven convection

References

1. Choi, U.S. Enhancing Thermal Conductivity of Fluids with Nanoparticles, Developments and Application of Non–Newtonian Flows. *ASME J. Heat Transf.* **1995**, *66*, 99–105.
2. Nguyen, M.T.; Aly, A.M.; Lee, S. Natural convection in a non-Darcy porous cavity filled with Cu-water nanofluid using the characteristic-based split procedure in Finite-Element method. *Numer. Heat Transf. Part A Appl.* **2014**, *67*, 224–247. [CrossRef]
3. Alhajaj, Z.; Bayomy, A.M.; Saghir, M.Z.; Rahman, M.M. Flow of nanofluid and hybrid fluid in porous channels: Experimental and numerical approach. *Int. J. Thermofluids* **2020**, *1–2*, 100016. [CrossRef]
4. Abouali, O.; Falahatpisheh, A. Numerical investigation of natural convection of Al2O3 nanofluid in vertical annuli. *Heat Mass Transf.* **2009**, *46*, 15–23. [CrossRef]
5. Sankar, M.; Reddy, N.K.; Do, Y. Conjugate buoyant convective transport of nanofluids in an enclosed annular geometry. *Sci. Rep.* **2021**, *7*, 17122. [CrossRef]
6. Khan, S.A.; Siddiqui, M.A.; Asjad, M.; Khan, Z.A.; Husain, S. CFD simulation and optimization of natural convection in a vertical annulus with nanofluids. *Int. J. Therm. Sci.* **2023**, *185*, 108079. [CrossRef]
7. Scozia, R.; Frederick, R.L. Natural convection in slender cavities with multiple fins attached to an active wall. *Numer. Heat Transf. Part A* **1991**, *20*, 127–158. [CrossRef]
8. Facas, G.N. Natural convection in a cavity with fins attached to both vertical walls. *J. Thermophys. Heat Transf.* **1993**, *7*, 624–634. [CrossRef]
9. Shi, X.; Khodadadi, J.M. Laminar natural convection heat transfer in a differentially heated square cavity due to a thin fin on the hot wall. *ASME J. Heat Mass Transf.* **2003**, *125*, 624–634. [CrossRef]
10. Bilgen, E. Natural convection in cavities with a thin fin on the hot wall. *Int. J. Heat Mass Transf.* **2005**, *48*, 3493–3505. [CrossRef]
11. Kakaç, S.; Pramuanjaroenkij, A. Single-phase and two-phase treatments of convective heat transfer enhancement with nanofluids: A state-of-the-art review. *Int. J. Therm. Sci.* **2016**, *100*, 75–97. [CrossRef]
12. Hatami, M. Numerical study of nanofluids natural convection in a rectangular cavity including heated fins. *J. Mol. Liq.* **2017**, *233*, 1–8. [CrossRef]
13. Bakhti, F.Z.; Si-Ameur, M. A comparison of mixed convective heat transfer performance of nanofluids cooled heat sink with circular perforated pin fin. *Appl. Therm. Eng.* **2019**, *159*, 113819. [CrossRef]
14. Kolsi, L.; Oztop, H.F.; Al-Rashed, A.A.; Aydi, A.; Naceur, B.M.; Abu-Hamdeh, N. Control of heat transfer and fluid flow via a moving fin in a triangular enclosure filled with nanofluid. *Heat Transf. Res.* **2019**, *50*, 159–181. [CrossRef]
15. Shulepova, E.V.; Sheremet, M.A.; Oztop, H.F.; Abu-Hamdeh, N. Mixed convection of Al2O3–H2O nanoliquid in a square chamber with complicated fin. *Int. J. Mech. Sci.* **2020**, *165*, 105192. [CrossRef]
16. Hussein, A.K.; Ghodbane, M.; Said, Z.; Ward, R.S. The Effect of the Baffle Length on the Natural Convection in an Enclosure Filled with Different Nanofluids. *J. Therm. Anal. Calorim.* **2022**, *147*, 791–813. [CrossRef]
17. Khetib, Y.; Alahmadi, A.A.; Alzaed, A.; Azimy, H.; Sharifpur, M.; Cheraghian, G. Effect of Straight, Inclined and Curved Fins on Natural Convection and Entropy Generation of a Nanofluid in a Square Cavity Influenced by a Magnetic Field. *Processes* **2021**, *9*, 1339. [CrossRef]

18. Wang, D.; Hai, T. Effect of the Length and Thickness of Three Constant Temperature Baffles on the Natural Convection Heat Transfer of Nanofluid Flow inside an Enclosure Affected by a Magnetic Field. *Eng. Anal. Bound. Elem.* **2023**, *150*, 70–83. [CrossRef]
19. Abidi, A.; Sajadi, S.M. Impact of Fin and Hybrid Nanofluid on Hydraulic-Thermal Performance and Entropy Generation in a Solar Collector Using a Two-Phase Approach. *Eng. Anal. Bound. Elem.* **2023**, *156*, 311–320. [CrossRef]
20. Saha, T.; Islam, T.; Yeasmin, S.; Parveen, N. Thermal Influence of Heated Fin on MHD Natural Convection Flow of Nanofluids inside a Wavy Square Cavity. *Int. J. Thermofluids* **2023**, *18*, 100338. [CrossRef]
21. Ghurban, M.A.; Al-Farhany, K.; Olayemi, O.A. Numerical Investigation of Mixed Convection of non-Newtonian Fluid in a Vented Square Cavity with Fixed Baffle. *Heat Transf.* **2023**, *52*, 5381–5407. [CrossRef]
22. Kanimozhi, B.; Muthtamilselvan, M.; Al-Mdallal, Q.M.; Abdalla, B. Coupled Buoyancy and Marangoni Convection in a Hybrid Nanofluid-Filled Cylindrical Porous Annulus with a Circular Thin Baffle. *Eur. Phys. J. Spec. Top.* **2022**, *231*, 2645–2660. [CrossRef]
23. Nabwey, H.A.; Armaghani, T.; Azizimehr, B.; Rashad, A.M.; Chamkha, A.J. A Comprehensive Review of Nanofluid Heat Transfer in Porous Media. *Nanomaterials* **2023**, *13*, 937. [CrossRef] [PubMed]
24. Farhat, B.; Kaid, N.; Alqahtani, S.; Menni, Y.; Alshammari, B.M.; Kolsi, L. Finite Element Analysis of Laminar Natural Convection in a Differentially Heated Porous Cavity Using the Darcy–Brinkman Model. *Processes* **2024**, *12*, 1974. [CrossRef]
25. Mahalakshmi, T.; Nithyadevi, N.; Oztop, H. Numerical Study of Magnetohydrodynamic Mixed Convective Flow in a Lid-Driven Enclosure Filled with Nanofluid Saturated Porous Medium with Center Heater. *Therm. Sci.* **2017**, *23*, 1861–1873. [CrossRef]
26. Aly, A.M.; Raizah, Z.; Asai, M. Natural Convection from Heated Fin Shapes in a Nanofluid-Filled Porous Cavity Using Incompressible Smoothed Particle Hydrodynamics. *Int. J. Numer. Methods Heat Fluid Flow* **2019**, *29*, 4569–4597. [CrossRef]
27. Al-Farhany, K.; Al-Chlaihawi, K.K.; Al-Dawody, M.F.; Biswas, N.; Chamkha, A.J. Effects of Fins on Magnetohydrodynamic Conjugate Natural Convection in a Nanofluid-Saturated Porous Inclined Enclosure. *Int. Commun. Heat Mass Transf.* **2021**, *126*, 105413. [CrossRef]
28. Wang, L.; Wang, W.-W.; Cai, Y.; Liu, D.; Zhao, F.-Y. Mixed Convection and Heat Flow Characteristics in a Lid-Driven Enclosure with Porous Fins: Full Numerical Modeling and Parametric Investigations. *Numer. Heat Transf. Part A Appl.* **2019**, *77*, 361–390. [CrossRef]
29. Le, X.H.K.; Oztop, H.F.; Sheremet, M.A. Impact of porous fins on thermal convection in a differentially-heated cubical chamber. *J. Therm. Anal. Calorim.* **2025**, *20*, 1974. [CrossRef]
30. Qureshi, H.; Rani, S.; Altmeyer, S. Investigation of Marangoni Convective Flow of Hybrid Nanofluids In Darcy-Forchheimer Porous Medium. *J. Appl. Mater. Sci. Eng. Res.* **2024**, *8*, 1–14.
31. Mandal, D.K.; Biswas, N.; Manna, N.K.; Gorla, R.S.R.; Chamkha, A.J. Hybrid Nanofluid Magnetohydrodynamic Mixed Convection in a Novel W-Shaped Porous System. *Int. J. Numer. Methods Heat Fluid Flow* **2022**, *33*, 510–544. [CrossRef]
32. Mansour, M.A.; Bakier, M.A.Y. Magnetohydrodynamic Mixed Convection of TiO_2–Cu/Water between the Double Lid-Driven Cavity and a Central Heat Source Surrounding by a Wavy Tilted Domain of Porous Medium under Local Thermal Non-Equilibrium. *SN Appl. Sci.* **2023**, *5*, 51. [CrossRef]
33. Zheng, X.; Qi, Z. A Comprehensive Review of Offset Strip Fin and Its Applications. *Appl. Therm. Eng.* **2018**, *139*, 61–75. [CrossRef]
34. Jobby, A.; Khatamifar, M.; Lin, W. A Comprehensive Review on the Natural Convection Heat Transfer in Horizontal and Inclined Closed Rectangular Enclosures with Internal Objects at Various Heating Conditions. *Energies* **2025**, *18*, 950. [CrossRef]
35. Reddy, N.K.; Sankar, M. Buoyant Heat Transfer of Nanofluids in a Vertical Porous Annulus: A Comparative Study of Different Models. *Int. J. Numer. Methods Heat Fluid Flow* **2022**, *33*, 477–509. [CrossRef]
36. Sankar, M.; Swamy, H.A.K.; Do, Y.; Altmeyer, S. Thermal Effects of Nonuniform Heating in a Nanofluid-filled Annulus: Buoyant Transport versus Entropy Generation. *Heat Transf.* **2021**, *51*, 1062–1091. [CrossRef]

mathematics

MDPI

Article

Convection in a Rapidly Rotating Spherical Shell: Newton's Method Using Implicit Coriolis Integration

Juan Cruz Gonzalez Sembla [1], Camille Rambert [1], Fred Feudel [2] and Laurette S. Tuckerman [1,*]

1 PMMH, CNRS, ESPCI Paris, Université PSL, Sorbonne Université, Université de Paris, 75005 Paris, France; juan-cruz.gonzalez-sembla@espci.fr (J.C.G.S.); camille.rambert@espci.fr (C.R.)
2 Institut für Physik und Astronomie, Universität Potsdam, 14476 Potsdam, Germany; ffeudel@uni-potsdam.de
* Correspondence: laurette@pmmh.espci.fr

Abstract: Geophysical flows are characterized by rapid rotation. Simulating these flows requires small timesteps to achieve stability and accuracy. Numerical stability can be greatly improved by the implicit integration of the terms that are most responsible for destabilizing the numerical scheme. We have implemented an implicit treatment of the Coriolis force in a rotating spherical shell driven by a radial thermal gradient. We modified the resulting timestepping code to carry out steady-state solving via Newton's method, which has no timestepping error. The implicit terms have the effect of preconditioning the linear systems, which can then be rapidly solved by a matrix-free Krylov method. We computed the branches of rotating waves with azimuthal wavenumbers ranging from 4 to 12. As the Ekman number (the non-dimensionalized inverse rotation rate) decreases, the flows are increasingly axially independent and localized near the inner cylinder, in keeping with well-known theoretical predictions and previous experimental and numerical results. The advantage of the implicit over the explicit treatment also increases dramatically with decreasing Ek, reducing the cost of computation by as much as a factor of 20 for Ekman numbers of order of 10^{-5}. We carried out continuation for both the Rayleigh and Ekman numbers and obtained interesting branches in which the drift velocity remained unchanged between pairs of saddle–node bifurcations.

Keywords: rotating fluids; Krylov methods; preconditioning; bifurcation; rotating waves

MSC: 35B32; 37M20; 65F08; 65M70; 65N35; 65P30; 76E06; 76U60

1. Introduction

Convection in a rapidly rotating spherical shell subjected to differential heating or imposed heat flux and a radial gravity field is a standard model for planetary interiors. The onset of convection in this configuration has been extensively studied [1–8]. Due to the symmetry of the configuration, a primary Hopf bifurcation leads to traveling (rotating) waves [9–11], which take the form of fluid columns perpendicular to the axis of rotation, sometimes referred to as thermal Rossby waves [12–15]. Scaling laws have been derived for the critical Rayleigh number and for the azimuthal wavenumber for these patterns and their drifting frequencies [6] as a function of the Ekman number, which is the ratio of the viscous to the Coriolis force. A secondary Hopf bifurcation leads to modulated rotating waves, i.e., quasi-periodic patterns with an additional modulation frequency [16–20].

Although convection in astrophysics follows the same basic fluid-dynamical principles as convection in geophysics, our work is primarily relevant to geophysical applications, in which the density variations are sufficiently small that the fluid can be treated as

Boussinesq, the convection is due to temperature (rather than concentration) gradients, the domain is a spherical shell, and the Coriolis force is dominant. Concerning the physics of the problem, the balance of forces can be used to define various regimes, each with a different convective length and velocity scales. In particular, the Coriolis-inertial-buoyancy balance can be contrasted to a regime called viscous balance in which the viscous force replaces the inertial force [21–24]. Experimental and numerical studies have analyzed the effect of rotation on convection and on the generation of a magnetic field; these are reviewed in e.g., [12,15,23,25]. Some notable numerical papers incorporating these effects are [26], which describes a pioneering 3D code for solving the anelastic magnetohydrodynamic equations, and [27,28], which compare the performance of various codes on Boussinesq and anelastic convection-driven dynamo benchmark problems, respectively (the anelastic approximation lies between the Boussinesq approximation and the fully compressible equations, capturing some compressibility effects while filtering out fast sound waves). Laboratory experiments on radial gravity in a sphere are difficult to perform because they are affected by Earth's vertical gravity. For this reason, microgravity experiments called Geoflow and Atmoflow, respectively, have been placed on a space station to mimic radial convection in rotating spherical annuli within the Earth [29,30] and in the atmosphere [31].

Three-dimensional numerical simulations in a spherical geometry usually represent the velocity and magnetic fields in terms of poloidal and toroidal potentials, which reduce a 3D solenoidal field to two scalar fields. These potentials and the temperature are decomposed into spherical harmonics in the angular directions, with either Chebyshev polynomials or finite differences used in the radial direction. Chebyshev collocation methods lead to dense matrices, but sparse matrices can be obtained when using a Galerkin approach [32,33], resulting in lower time and memory requirements.

Rapid rotation leads to a large Coriolis force. The Coriolis force introduces coupling (of the velocity components and/or the spherical harmonics) and so it is usually treated explicitly in numerical codes. This leads to a significant limitation on the timestep. A natural approach is then to treat this term implicitly, leading to a more stable scheme; its implementation for finite difference or Chebyshev collocation discretizations in the radial direction is discussed in [34,35], respectively. The implicit treatment of the Coriolis term has been successfully implemented by [36–39] in a planar geometry and by [20,33,40,41] in a spherical geometry.

Another form of numerical computation is continuation, i.e., the computation of steady states, traveling waves, or other periodic states independently of their stability via Newton's or a related method. Although unstable solutions cannot be observed experimentally, they are interesting because they form a framework for understanding the stable solutions, which in turn are accessible to experiment with.

In this work, we describe the implementation and capabilities of a pair of numerical codes—two drivers relying on a common set of subroutines—that incorporate an implicit treatment of the Coriolis force to carry out both timestepping and also continuation. We will illustrate, test, and compare the codes on the thermally driven rotating waves. We carried out numerical continuation in both Rayleigh and Ekman numbers. We found interesting examples of branches which contain saddle–node bifurcations separating plateaus in drift frequency. Our numerical algorithm uses the basic framework described in [18,19,35,42,43] and the spherical harmonic library of [44]. The research which is closest to ours is that of [20,45–47], who, like us, have carried out implicit timestepping and continuation for convection in a rotating spherical shell and explored various interesting parameter regimes. There are a number of differences between our continuation method and theirs, some of which have been analyzed in [48] and which we will discuss after we have described our numerical methods.

In Section 2, we describe the problem, governing equations and non-dimensional parameters in addition to introducing rotating wave solutions of different azimuthal symmetries. The numerical methods, including spatial discretization, Newton, and path-following methods are detailed in Section 3. Continuation results are described in Section 4, while timing comparisons and timestepping results are presented in Section 5. We discuss and provide a conclusion to our results in Sections 6 and 7.

2. Physical Description

2.1. Governing Equations

We study classical Rayleigh–Bénard convection in a spherical fluid shell rotating with constant angular velocity Ω about the z axis, as illustrated in Figure 1. The shell is heated from within by imposing a temperature difference ΔT between the inner and outer spherical boundaries. Lengths are non-dimensionalized with the gap size d, so that the dimensionless outer and inner radii are r_{out} and $r_{\text{in}} = r_{\text{out}} - 1$, respectively. The aspect ratio can be specified via r_{out} or via $\eta \equiv r_{\text{in}}/r_{\text{out}} = (r_{\text{out}} - 1)/r_{\text{out}}$. Time is scaled by the viscous diffusion time d^2/ν, where ν is the kinematic viscosity and the velocity is scaled by the viscous diffusion velocity ν/d. Measuring temperature from a reference temperature T_0 at which the mass density is ρ_0, we non-dimensionalize pressure by $\rho_0\nu$, and temperature by ΔT.

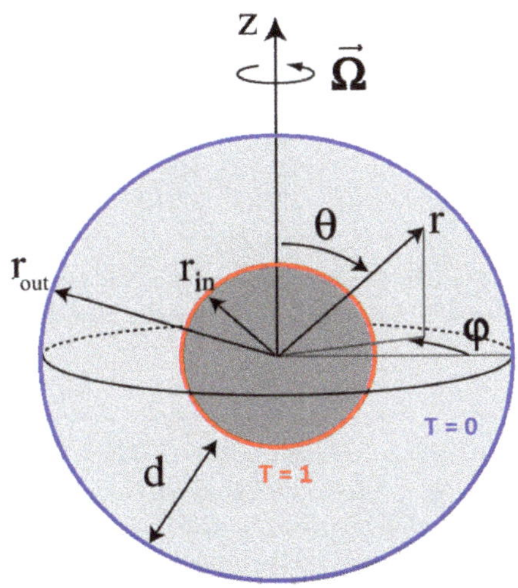

Figure 1. Geometry. The domain is the spherical annulus between an inner and outer sphere of radius r_{in} and r_{out} whose temperatures are fixed at $T = 1$ and $T = 0$. Both spheres rotate around the z axis with angular velocity Ω. Figure taken and adapted from [49].

The gravitational acceleration g is assumed to be proportional to the distance r from the center of the sphere (as is the case for self-gravity in the interior of a spherical body with constant mass density) and is thus of the form $g = -(g_o/r_{\text{out}})r$, where g_o is the acceleration at radius r_{out}. The resulting non-dimensional Boussinesq equations read

$$\text{Ek}\left[\frac{\partial \boldsymbol{U}}{\partial t} + (\boldsymbol{U} \cdot \nabla)\boldsymbol{U} - \nabla^2 \boldsymbol{U}\right] = -\nabla P + \text{Ra}\, T \frac{\boldsymbol{r}}{r_{\text{out}}} - 2\boldsymbol{e}_z \times \boldsymbol{U} \tag{1a}$$

$$\frac{\partial T}{\partial t} + \boldsymbol{U} \cdot \nabla T = \frac{1}{\text{Pr}} \nabla^2 T \tag{1b}$$

$$\boldsymbol{\nabla} \cdot \boldsymbol{U} = 0 \tag{1c}$$

When the density is constant, the gravitational and centrifugal forces can be written as gradients and included in the pressure gradient. Variable density leads to a non-gradient portion of these forces. The non-gradient part arising from gravity drives the convection. We make the common assumption in the geophysics of neglecting the non-gradient part arising from the centrifugal force [15,47]; see [15,50,51] for examples of the effect of centrifugal buoyancy.

The non-dimensional parameters used in Equation (1a) above are the Ekman, Prandtl, and Rayleigh numbers:

$$\mathrm{Ek} \equiv \frac{\nu}{\Omega d^2}, \quad \mathrm{Pr} \equiv \frac{\nu}{\kappa}, \quad \mathrm{Ra} = \mathrm{Ra}_{\mathrm{rot}} \equiv \frac{d\alpha g_o \Delta T}{\Omega \nu} \tag{2}$$

where κ is the thermal diffusivity and α is the thermal expansion coefficient. The Rayleigh number used here is adapted to the rotating case and is related to the conventional thermal Rayleigh number $\mathrm{Ra}_{\mathrm{therm}}$ by

$$\mathrm{Ra}_{\mathrm{therm}} \equiv \frac{d^3 \alpha g_0 \Delta T}{\kappa \nu} = \frac{d\alpha g_o \Delta T}{\Omega \nu} \frac{\Omega d^2}{\nu} \frac{\nu}{\kappa} = \mathrm{Ra}_{\mathrm{rot}} \frac{\mathrm{Pr}}{\mathrm{Ek}} \tag{3}$$

In what follows, we will denote $\mathrm{Ra}_{\mathrm{rot}}$ merely by Ra. No-slip and fixed-temperature boundary conditions are applied at the inner and outer radii:

$$\boldsymbol{U}(r_{\mathrm{in}}) = 0 \quad \boldsymbol{U}(r_{\mathrm{out}}) = 0 \tag{4a}$$

$$T(r_{\mathrm{in}}) = 1 \quad T(r_{\mathrm{out}}) = 0 \tag{4b}$$

and the conductive solution is

$$\boldsymbol{U}_{\mathrm{cond}} = 0, \quad T_{\mathrm{cond}}(r) = \frac{r_{\mathrm{out}}\, r_{\mathrm{in}}}{r} - r_{\mathrm{in}} \tag{5}$$

Following the benchmark study [27], we set the Prandtl number to $\mathrm{Pr} = 1$ and the radii to $r_{\mathrm{out}} = 20/13$ and $r_{\mathrm{in}} = 7/13$ (so that $\eta = 7/20 = 0.35$) throughout the investigation and we will vary Ek and Ra.

2.2. Overview

The first states to appear at the onset of convection are rotating waves. We denote these by RW_M, where M is the azimuthal wavenumber of the rotating wave. Figure 2a,b, modeled on those in [18], display properties of some of these rotating wave solutions for $\mathrm{Ek} = 10^{-3}$. Four traveling waves are shown, with azimuthal wavenumbers from $M = 2$ to $M = 5$. At $\mathrm{Ek} = 10^{-3}$, RW_4 is the first in Rayleigh number to bifurcate, and therefore, it is the only one which is stable at onset. The drift frequency, i.e., the frequency relative to the imposed frequency Ω, decreases as Ra increases, from prograde (faster than Ω) to retrograde (slower than Ω). These results were obtained via timestepping simulations starting from the initial conditions of the form $\cos(M\varphi)$.

Figure 3 shows the qualitative evolution of the rotating waves as Ek is decreased from 10^{-2} to 10^{-5}: the flow is increasingly stronger near the inner sphere and the azimuthal wavenumber increases. These two properties are related: the radial interval over which the convection is most active decreases, and the azimuthal wavelength decreases as well [6,41]. RW_8 appeared naturally when performing timestepping simulations from an initial condition of the form $\cos(4\varphi)$ at $\mathrm{Ek} = 10^{-4}$, as did RW_{12} at $\mathrm{Ek} = 3 \times 10^{-5}$. This result was then used as input for a path-following computation to obtain RW_{12} at $\mathrm{Ek} = 10^{-5}$. The same techniques were applied to obtain RW_4 at $\mathrm{Ek} = 10^{-2}$ starting from RW_4 at $\mathrm{Ek} = 10^{-3}$. Figure 4 gives a more detailed visualization of an RW_4 state.

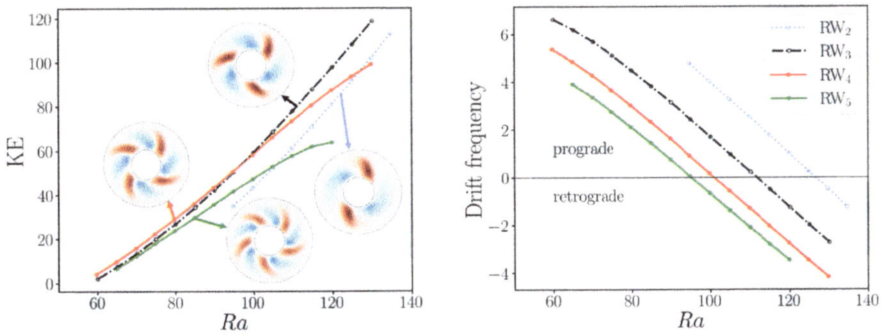

(a) (b)

Figure 2. (**a**) Bifurcation diagram of convection in a rotating spherical annulus for Ek $= 10^{-3}$. Branches RW_2 (blue), RW_3 (black), RW_4 (red), and RW_5 (green) are shown. (**a**) Kinetic energy density. (**b**) Drift frequency. The drift frequencies for each rotating wave decreases from prograde (faster than imposed velocity Ω) to retrograde (slower than Ω) with increasing Ra with the same slope. The resolution used for these simulations was $(N_r, N_\theta, N_\varphi \times M) = (46, 72, 128 \times 1)$.

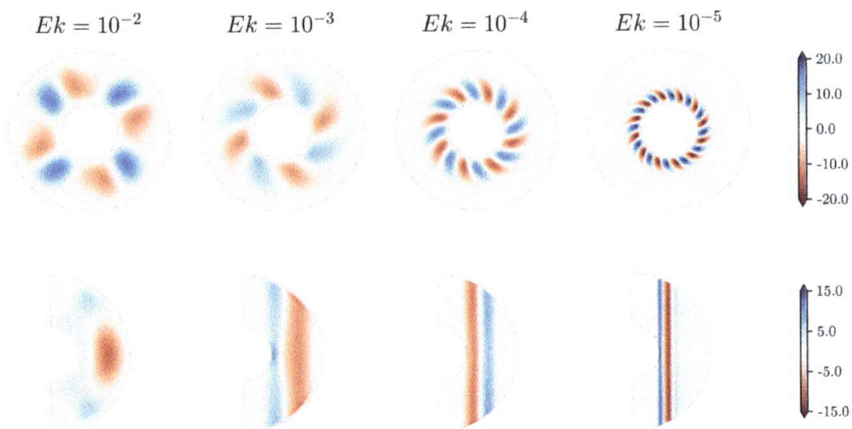

Figure 3. Velocity fields of rotating waves as the Ekman number is reduced. The above shows RW_4 for Ek $= 10^{-2}$ and $Ra = 140$; RW_4 for Ek $= 10^{-3}$ and $Ra = 77$; RW_8 for Ek $= 10^{-4}$ and $Ra = 88$; and RW_{12} for Ek $= 10^{-5}$ and $Ra = 126$. A state with azimuthal wavenumber M has M convection cells, forming M Taylor columns. All of these states have an approximate kinetic energy density of 25. For each field, the radial velocity U_r on the equatorial plane (**top**) and the azimuthal velocity U_φ on a meridional plane (**bottom**) are shown. As Ek decreases, the convective region becomes more confined near the inner sphere and the flow becomes almost axially independent, according to the Taylor–Proudman theorem. The resolutions used for these simulations were $(N_r, N_\theta, N_\varphi \times M) = (46, 72, 32 \times 4)$ for RW_4 at both Ek $= 10^{-2}$ and Ek $= 10^{-3}$; $(60, 100, 28 \times 8)$ for RW_8; and $(90, 184, 32 \times 12)$ for RW_{12}.

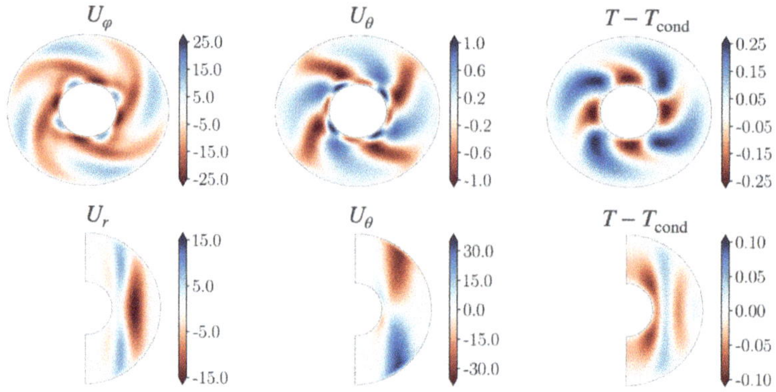

Figure 4. Visualizations of the components of RW_4 at $Ek = 10^{-3}$ and $Ra = 140$. **Top**: equatorial plane. **Bottom**: meridional plane. The resolution used here was $(N_r, N_\theta, N_\varphi \times M) = (46, 72, 32 \times 4)$.

3. Numerical Methods

3.1. Spatial Representation

The velocity is decomposed into toroidal and poloidal potentials e and f such that

$$\boldsymbol{U}(r,\theta,\varphi,t) = \boldsymbol{\nabla}\times e\,\boldsymbol{e}_r + \boldsymbol{\nabla}\times\boldsymbol{\nabla}\times f\boldsymbol{e}_r \tag{6}$$

These potentials and the temperature are expanded in spherical harmonics $Y_l^m(\theta,\varphi)$ and Chebyshev polynomials T_k of the shifted radius $x \equiv (2r - (r_{\text{out}} + r_{\text{in}}))/(r_{\text{out}} - r_{\text{in}})$.

$$f(r,\theta,\varphi,t) = \sum_{k,l,m} f_{k,l,m}(t) T_k(x) Y_l^m(\theta,\varphi) \tag{7}$$

To carry out transformations to and from the spherical harmonic space, we use the `SHTns` library [44]. This is a highly efficient code that uses the `FFTW` library to perform fast transformations to and from Fourier space, and the recursion relations presented in [52] for an optimized computation of the associated Legendre polynomials. Although the library allows for multithreaded computations as well as GPU offloading, these capabilities were not used in the present work. This library has promising scalability prospects for computations in massively parallel clusters, as demonstrated in the `XSHELLS` and `MagIC` codes [53,54]. Furthermore, our code agrees with the non-magnetic benchmark proposed in [27] and the results presented in [18], validating our numerical method as well as our choice of using the `SHTns` library.

De-aliasing in the r direction is carried out according to the $3/2$ rule, whereas in the θ and φ directions, it is performed by `SHTns`. To achieve this, the library determines a suitable number of physical points based on the nonlinear order of the equations to be solved (two in this case) with the aim of maximizing the efficiency of the FFT algorithm. Moreover, for solutions which have azimuthal periodicity $2\pi/M$, we restrict our calculations to a segment of the sphere $0 \le \varphi < 2\pi/M$, or, equivalently, to those whose Fourier expansions contain only multiples of the wavenumber M; this is easily implemented using options in `SHTns`. Lastly, we will denote the number of gridpoints in r, θ and φ as N_r, N_θ and $N_\varphi \times M$, respectively. The resolutions chosen for the simulations are similar to those that have been shown to be adequate in the benchmark paper [27] and in more recent studies [7,20,55]. The spatial resolutions are given in the captions of each of the figures.

The radial component of the curl and of the double curl of Equation (1a) are taken, leading to

$$\sum_{l,m} \frac{l(l+1)}{r^2} \mathrm{Ek}\left(\frac{\partial}{\partial t} - L_l\right) e_{l,m}(r,t) Y_l^m(\theta,\varphi) = \boldsymbol{e_r} \cdot \boldsymbol{\nabla} \times \boldsymbol{F} \tag{8a}$$

$$-\sum_{l,m} \frac{l(l+1)}{r^2} \mathrm{Ek}\left(\frac{\partial}{\partial t} - L_l\right) L_l f_{l,m}(r,t) Y_l^m(\theta,\varphi) = \boldsymbol{e_r} \cdot \boldsymbol{\nabla} \times \boldsymbol{\nabla} \times \boldsymbol{F} \tag{8b}$$

where

$$L_l \equiv \frac{\partial^2}{\partial r^2} - \frac{l(l+1)}{r^2} \quad \text{and} \quad \boldsymbol{F} \equiv \mathrm{Ek}\,(\boldsymbol{U} \cdot \nabla)\boldsymbol{U} - \nabla P + \frac{Ra}{r_{\text{out}}} T\,\boldsymbol{r} - 2\boldsymbol{e}_z \times \boldsymbol{U} \tag{9}$$

Equations (8a) and (8b) are decoupled in ℓ, m and in potential (e vs. f), and so their discrete versions involve block-diagonal matrices, with an $N_r \times N_r$ block for each (l, m) pair, as in Figure 5a. Boundary conditions (4a) on $\boldsymbol{U}$ become

$$e_{lm} = f_{lm} = df_{lm}/dr = 0 \quad \text{at } r_{\text{in}}, r_{\text{out}} \tag{10}$$

The number of boundary conditions on e and f matches the fact that Equation (8a) for e is of second order in r while Equation (8b) for f is of fourth order in r. The boundary conditions are imposed by replacing the last two rows of Equation (8a) or the last four rows of Equation (8b), corresponding to the highest Chebyshev polynomials. See, for example, [35,56].

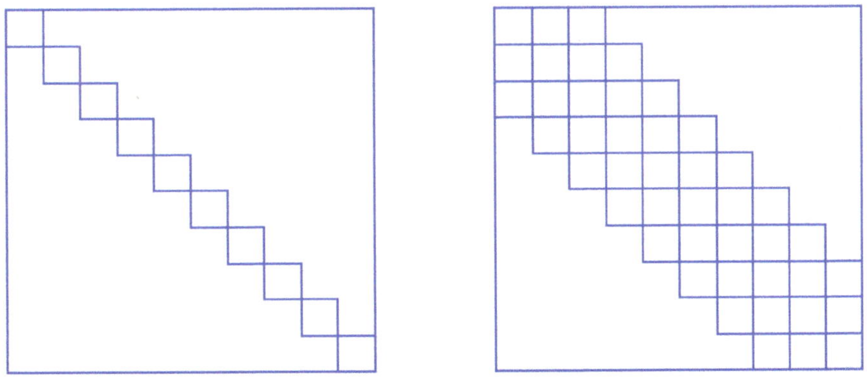

(a) (b)

Figure 5. (**a**) Block-diagonal matrix. (**b**) Block-pentadiagonal matrix.

The temperature field is also expanded in Chebyshev polynomials and spherical harmonics like Equation (7). Its evolution is governed by the discretized form of Equation (1b) and the boundary conditions in Equation (4b) on the temperature are imposed straightforwardly on the rows corresponding to the last two Chebyshev polynomials.

3.2. Implicit Coriolis Integration

To carry out the implicit integration of the Coriolis term [35], we include the Coriolis force in the left-hand-side and remove it from **F**, leading to

$$\begin{aligned}&\sum_{m,l}\left[\frac{l(l+1)}{r^2}\mathrm{Ek}\left(\frac{\partial}{\partial t}-L_l\right)-\frac{2im}{r^2}\right]e_{lm}(r,t)Y_l^m(\theta,\varphi)\\&+\frac{2}{r^2}\left(\frac{l(l+1)}{r}-\frac{\partial}{\partial r}\right)f_{lm}(r,t)\sin\theta\frac{d}{d\theta}Y_l^m(\theta,\varphi)\\&+2\frac{l(l+1)}{r^2}\left(\frac{2}{r}-\frac{\partial}{\partial r}\right)f_{lm}(r,t)\cos\theta\, Y_l^m(\theta,\varphi)=\boldsymbol{e_r}\cdot\boldsymbol{\nabla}\times\boldsymbol{F}^{\text{implicit}}\end{aligned}\tag{11a}$$

$$\begin{aligned}&\sum_{m,l}-\left[\frac{l(l+1)}{r^2}\mathrm{Ek}\left(\frac{\partial}{\partial t}-L_l\right)-\frac{2im}{r^2}\right]L_l f_{\mathrm{lm}}(r,t)Y_l^m(\theta,\varphi)\\&+\frac{2}{r^2}\left(\frac{l(l+1)}{r}-\frac{\partial}{\partial r}\right)e_{lm}(r,t)\sin\theta\frac{d}{d\theta}Y_l^{|m|}(\theta,\varphi)\\&+2\frac{l(l+1)}{r^2}\left(\frac{2}{r}-\frac{\partial}{\partial r}\right)e_{lm}(r,t)\cos\theta\, Y_l^m(\theta,\varphi)=\boldsymbol{e_r}\cdot\boldsymbol{\nabla}\times\boldsymbol{\nabla}\times\boldsymbol{F}^{\text{implicit}}\end{aligned}\tag{11b}$$

where

$$\boldsymbol{F}^{\text{implicit}}\equiv\mathrm{Ek}\,(\boldsymbol{U}\cdot\nabla)\boldsymbol{U}-\nabla P+\frac{\mathrm{Ra}}{r_{\text{out}}}T\,\boldsymbol{r}\tag{12}$$

The recursion relations of the Legendre polynomials

$$\sin\theta\frac{d}{d\theta}P_l^{|m|}=\frac{l(l-|m|+1)}{2l+1}P_{l+1}^{|m|}-\frac{(l+|m|)(l+1)}{2l+1}P_{l-1}^{|m|}\tag{13a}$$

$$\cos\theta P_l^{|m|}=\frac{l-|m|+1}{2l+1}P_{l+1}^{|m|}+\frac{(l+|m|)}{2l+1}P_{l-1}^{|m|}\tag{13b}$$

together with

$$Y_l^m(\theta,\varphi)=N_l^mP_l^m(\cos\theta)e^{im\varphi}\qquad N_l^m=\sqrt{(2-\delta_{m0})(2l+1)\frac{(l-m)!}{l+m)!}}\tag{14}$$

can be used to transform Equations (11a) and (11b) into

$$\begin{aligned}&\sum_{m,l}Y_l^m(\theta,\varphi)\left\{\left[\frac{l(l+1)}{r^2}\mathrm{Ek}\left(\frac{\partial}{\partial t}-L_l\right)-\frac{2im}{r^2}\right]e_{lm})r,t)\right.\\&+\frac{2}{r^2}\frac{(l-1)(l+1)(l-|m|)}{2l-1}\left[\frac{l}{r}-\frac{\partial}{\partial r}\right]\frac{N_{l-1}^m}{N_l^m}f_{l-1,m}(r,t)\\&\left.+\frac{2}{r^2}\frac{l(l+2)(l+1+|m|)}{2l+3}\left[-\frac{(l+1)}{r}-\frac{\partial}{\partial r}\right]\frac{N_{l+1}^m}{N_l^m}f_{l+1,m}(r,t)\right\}=\boldsymbol{e_r}\cdot\boldsymbol{\nabla}\times\boldsymbol{F}^{\text{implicit}}\end{aligned}\tag{15a}$$

$$\begin{aligned}&\sum_{m,l}Y_l^m(\theta,\varphi)\left\{-\left[\frac{l(l+1)}{r^2}\mathrm{Ek}\left(\frac{\partial}{\partial t}-L_l\right)-\frac{2im}{r^2}\right]L_lf_{lm}(r,t)\right.\\&+\frac{2}{r^2}\frac{(l-1)(l+1)(l-|m|)}{2l-1}\left[\frac{l}{r}-\frac{\partial}{\partial r}\right]\frac{N_{l-1}^m}{N_l^m}e_{l-1,m}(r,t)\\&\left.+\frac{2}{r^2}\frac{l(l+2)(l+1+|m|)}{2l+3}\left[-\frac{(l+1)}{r}-\frac{\partial}{\partial r}\right]\frac{N_{l+1}^m}{N_l^m}e_{l+1,m}(r,t)\right\}=\boldsymbol{e_r}\cdot\boldsymbol{\nabla}\times\boldsymbol{\nabla}\times\boldsymbol{F}^{\text{implicit}}\end{aligned}\tag{15b}$$

Appendix A presents further details of these computations. In contrast with Equations (8a) and (8b), Equations (15a) and (15b) are coupled in several ways:

- The spectral coefficients $e_{\rm lm}$ and $f_{\rm lm}$ both appear in both equations.
- While each m can be treated independently, components ℓ, $\ell+1$, and $\ell-1$ are coupled.
- The real and imaginary parts of $e_{\rm lm}$ and $f_{\rm lm}$ are coupled via the imaginary coefficient $2im/r^2$.

However, two decoupled classes of coefficients appear, with one class containing coefficients with odd l for e_l and even l for f_l and a second class with the opposite property. For example, in Equation (15a), the real component of e_{lm} is coupled to its imaginary component and to the real parts of $f_{l\pm1,m}$ (with opposite parity to l) and in Equation (15b), the real component of f_{lm} is coupled to its imaginary component and to the real parts of $e_{l\pm1,m}$. For each class, the sums in Equations (15a) and (15b) are represented by a block pentadiagonal matrix, as illustrated in Figure 5b.

3.3. *Newton Method*

We represent our system of governing equations schematically by

$$\frac{\partial \boldsymbol{U}}{\partial t} = \mathcal{N}(\boldsymbol{U}) + \mathcal{L}\boldsymbol{U} \tag{16}$$

For our problem, $\boldsymbol{U}$ corresponds to the poloidal and toroidal fields e and f and the temperature T. For explicit or implicit Coriolis integration, $\mathcal{N}(\boldsymbol{U})$ corresponds to the right-hand-sides of Equations (8a) and (8b) or of Equations (11a) and (11b), respectively. $\mathcal{L}\boldsymbol{U}$ corresponds to minus the left-hand-sides of the same equations with the time derivative omitted (the correspondence is imperfect, since $\partial/\partial t$ does not act directly on $\boldsymbol{U}$.)

We represent our timestepping code schematically by the following implicit–explicit Euler method:

$$\begin{aligned} &\boldsymbol{U}(t+\Delta t) = \boldsymbol{U}(t) + \Delta t(\mathcal{N}(\boldsymbol{U}(t)) + \mathcal{L}\boldsymbol{U}(t+\Delta t)) \\ \Longrightarrow\ &\boldsymbol{U}(t+\Delta t) = \mathcal{B}(\boldsymbol{U}(t)) \equiv (I-\Delta t\mathcal{L})^{-1}(I+\Delta t\mathcal{N})\boldsymbol{U}(t) \end{aligned} \tag{17}$$

where $\mathcal{L}$ is linear (though $\mathcal{N}$ does not need to be nonlinear). Steady states are solutions to

$$0 = \mathcal{A}(\boldsymbol{U}) \equiv \mathcal{N}(\boldsymbol{U}) + \mathcal{L}\boldsymbol{U} \tag{18}$$

or, alternatively

$$0 = \boldsymbol{U}(t+\Delta t) - \boldsymbol{U}(t) \tag{19}$$

where $\boldsymbol{U}$ is a solution to the continuous-time differential Equation (16). Surprisingly, Equation (19) is also a criterion for stationarity when $\boldsymbol{U}(t+\Delta t)$ is calculated via the timestepping scheme Equation (17) *for any value of* Δt, as can be seen from

$$\begin{aligned} (\mathcal{B}-I)(\boldsymbol{U}(t)) = \boldsymbol{U}(t+\Delta t) - \boldsymbol{U}(t) &= (I-\Delta t\mathcal{L})^{-1}(I+\Delta t\mathcal{N})\boldsymbol{U}(t) - \boldsymbol{U}(t) \\ &= (I-\Delta t\mathcal{L})^{-1}(I+\Delta t\mathcal{N} - (I-\Delta t\mathcal{L}))\boldsymbol{U}(t)) \\ &= \underbrace{(I-\Delta t\mathcal{L})^{-1}\Delta t}_{\mathcal{P}(\Delta t)}\underbrace{(\mathcal{N}+\mathcal{L})}_{\mathcal{A}}\boldsymbol{U}(t) \end{aligned} \tag{20}$$

Thus, $\mathcal{B}-I = \mathcal{P}(\Delta t)\mathcal{A}$ and so roots of $\mathcal{A}$ of Equation (18) can be found by computing roots of $\mathcal{B}-I$, which is simply the difference between two large consecutive timesteps. Note that Equation (20) does not use Taylor series; Δt can be of any size. Indeed, for Δt

large, $\mathcal{P}(\Delta t) \to -\mathcal{L}^{-1}$ acts as a preconditioner (approximate inverse) for $\mathcal{A}$, whose poor conditioning is due to that of $\mathcal{L}$.

Finding the roots of Equation (20) via Newton's method requires the solution of the linear system

$$(\mathcal{B}_{\boldsymbol{U}} - I)\boldsymbol{u} = (\mathcal{B} - I)\boldsymbol{U} \tag{21}$$

where $\boldsymbol{U}$ is the current estimate and $\mathcal{B}_{\boldsymbol{U}}$ is the Jacobian of $\mathcal{B}$ evaluated at $\boldsymbol{U}$. The linear Jacobian operator $\mathcal{B}_{\boldsymbol{U}}$ acting on $\boldsymbol{u}$ is derived from $\mathcal{B}$ by modifying the nonlinear operator $\mathcal{N}$. We recall that $\boldsymbol{U}$ represents $(\boldsymbol{U}, T)$ and $\boldsymbol{u}$ represents $(\boldsymbol{u}, \tau)$ where τ is a temperature perturbation. To form $\mathcal{N}_{\boldsymbol{U}}$, we replace the nonlinear terms in Equations (1a) and (1b) as follows:

$$(\boldsymbol{U} \cdot \boldsymbol{\nabla})\boldsymbol{U} \Longrightarrow (\boldsymbol{U} \cdot \boldsymbol{\nabla})\boldsymbol{u} + (\boldsymbol{u} \cdot \boldsymbol{\nabla})\boldsymbol{U} \tag{22a}$$

$$\boldsymbol{U} \cdot \boldsymbol{\nabla} T \Longrightarrow \boldsymbol{U} \cdot \boldsymbol{\nabla}\tau + \boldsymbol{u} \cdot \boldsymbol{\nabla} T \tag{22b}$$

These substitutions produce $\mathcal{N}_{\boldsymbol{U}}$, which is then used in Equation (17) to form $\mathcal{B}_{\boldsymbol{U}}$. In addition, homogeneous boundary conditions must be applied to the perturbations $\boldsymbol{u}$ and τ instead of the inhomogeneous boundary conditions Equation (4). We emphasize that the operations on both sides of Equation (21) are just the ordinary and the linearized timestepping operators $\mathcal{B}$ and $\mathcal{B}_{\boldsymbol{U}}$.

We solve Equation (21) using a Krylov method such as GMRES [57]. In such matrix-free methods, one only needs to provide the right-hand-side $(\mathcal{B} - I)\boldsymbol{U}$ for the current estimate, and a routine which carries out the *action* of $(\mathcal{B}_{\boldsymbol{U}} - I)$ on any vector $\boldsymbol{u}$. The computational cost of a Newton step can be measured by the number of such actions (i.e., GMRES iterations) taken by the Krylov method, since the right-hand-side remains constant throughout the step. The number of GMRES iterations required is low if $(\mathcal{B}_{\boldsymbol{U}} - I) = \mathcal{P}(\Delta t)\mathcal{A}$ is well conditioned; it is for this reason that we take Δt large. Once the decrement $\boldsymbol{u}$ is determined by solving Equation (21), it is subtracted from $\boldsymbol{U}$ to form an improved estimate. We accept $\boldsymbol{u}$ as the decrement if the linear system Equation (21) is solved by GMRES to relative accuracy 10^{-10}. For Newton's method, we accept $\boldsymbol{U}$ as a steady state, i.e., a solution to Equation (19), if $||(\mathcal{B} - I)\boldsymbol{U}|| < 10^{-7}$. Similar values of this tolerance have been used in [20]. In addition, solutions found via Newton's method are far more accurate than those found by timestepping, which is usually halted when a solution remains constant to three to five significant digits.

The method described above is called *Stokes preconditioning*. It was first applied to calculate bifurcation diagrams in spherical Couette flow [58,59] and subsequently to a wide variety of hydrodynamic problems, e.g., [60–67] and even to Bose–Einstein condensation [68,69]. In Stokes preconditioning, Δt no longer plays the role of a timestep but serves to better condition the system of linear equations in each Newton step. We investigated the effect of the choice of Δt on Newton solving with Stokes preconditioning in [48,58] and on the computation of eigenvalues by a similar method in [70]. In these articles, time has been non-dimensionalized by the advective time, and the usual value used in timestepping is $\Delta t \approx 0.01$. An increase in the value of Δt from 0.01 to 0.1 and then to 10 leads to a decrease in the required CPU-time for convergence GMRES by 1–2 orders of magnitude per Δt decade until an asymptotic limit of $\Delta t \approx 100$ or 1000 is reached. We emphasize that the final result is independent of the choice of Δt: only the time taken for convergence is affected. In the current study, we use the value $\Delta t = 200$ for Newton solving.

The name of the method comes from the fact that the linear operator $\mathcal{L}$ which is integrated implicitly in Equation (17) is usually the viscous term that occurs in Stokes equation. This preconditioning becomes less powerful as the Reynolds number increases and other terms begin to dominate the viscous term; this effect was demonstrated and measured quantitatively in [48]. Hence, it is beneficial to include as many possible other terms in $\mathcal{L}$, as long as they are linear and can be inverted directly. It is for this reason that we have included the Coriolis force in $\mathcal{L}$, using the equations derived in Section 3.2. In Section 5, we will compare the cost of computations using Newton's method with implicit vs. explicit Coriolis integration for various values of the Ekman number by comparing the number of GMRES iterations necessary for each.

3.4. Traveling Waves

Newton's method can also be used to compute traveling waves in the same way. Azimuthal rotating waves satisfy $\boldsymbol{U}(\varphi,t) = \tilde{\boldsymbol{U}}(\varphi - Ct) = \tilde{\boldsymbol{U}}(\tilde{\varphi})$, where C is an unknown wavespeed. Thus, $\partial_t \boldsymbol{U} = -C\partial_{\tilde{\varphi}}\tilde{\boldsymbol{U}}$. Substituting into Equation (16) and dropping the tildes leads to

$$0 = \mathcal{N}(\boldsymbol{U}) + C\partial_\varphi \boldsymbol{U} + \mathcal{L}\boldsymbol{U} \tag{23}$$

The explicit portion of the timestep is augmented to include $C\partial_\varphi$ as well as $\mathcal{N}$:

$$\boldsymbol{U}(t+\Delta t) = (I - \Delta t\mathcal{L})^{-1}\big(I + \Delta t(\mathcal{N} + C\partial_\varphi)\big)\boldsymbol{U}(t) \tag{24}$$

If $\boldsymbol{U}$ is expressed in terms of spherical harmonics in which the φ dependence is trigonometric, the action of $C\partial_\varphi$ on a Fourier component $\boldsymbol{U}_m$ is merely $C\partial_\varphi \boldsymbol{U}_m = Cim\boldsymbol{U}_m$.

To use Newton's method to determine the unknown field $\boldsymbol{U}$ and wavespeed C, we substitute $\boldsymbol{U} \to \boldsymbol{U} - \boldsymbol{u}$ and $C \to C - c$ into Equation (23):

$$0 = \mathcal{N}(\boldsymbol{U} - \boldsymbol{u}) + (C - c)\partial_\varphi(\boldsymbol{U} - \boldsymbol{u}) + \mathcal{L}(\boldsymbol{U} - \boldsymbol{u}) \tag{25}$$

Expanding around $(\boldsymbol{U}, C)$ and truncating at first order leads to the linear system that must be solved for the decrements $(\boldsymbol{u}, c)$:

$$(\mathcal{N}_{\boldsymbol{U}} + C\partial_\varphi + \mathcal{L})\boldsymbol{u} + c\partial_\varphi \boldsymbol{U} = (\mathcal{N} + C\partial_\varphi + \mathcal{L})(\boldsymbol{U}) \tag{26}$$

The preconditioner remains $\mathcal{P}(\Delta t) = (I - \Delta t\mathcal{L})^{-1}\Delta t$ with large Δt, since $\mathcal{L}$ continues to be responsible for the large condition number of Equation (26).

$$\mathcal{P}(\Delta t)\big[(\mathcal{N}_{\boldsymbol{U}} + C\partial_\varphi + \mathcal{L})\boldsymbol{u} + c\,\partial_\varphi \boldsymbol{U}\big] = \mathcal{P}(\Delta t)(\mathcal{N} + C\partial_\varphi + \mathcal{L})(\boldsymbol{U}). \tag{27}$$

An additional equation must be added to the system to compensate for the additional unknown. We choose a phase condition, more specifically we require the imaginary part of a single component (temperature, toroidal or poloidal field; radial and angular and azimuthal mode) of $\boldsymbol{u}$ be zero, i.e., that the corresponding *phase component* (whose index we shall call J) of $\boldsymbol{U}$ remains unchanged.

This simple choice suggests a trick for retaining the size of the unknown $\boldsymbol{u}$ rather than using augmented fields, since $\boldsymbol{u}_J$ is no longer an unknown. The routine which acts on $(\boldsymbol{u}, c)$ is defined such that c is stored in $\boldsymbol{u}_J$. At the beginning of an action, c is extracted, $\boldsymbol{u}_J$ is set to zero, and the explicit part of the action on $\boldsymbol{u}$ is carried out. Then, we multiply the stored value of $\partial_\varphi \boldsymbol{U}$ by c and add the result to the explicit part of the action. When the Krylov method converges and returns $\boldsymbol{u}$, we must again extract c from $\boldsymbol{u}_J$, after which $\boldsymbol{u}_J$ is set to zero. Effectively, although C and c have been added to the unknowns for the Newton method and for the linear equation, $\boldsymbol{U}_J$ and $\boldsymbol{u}_J$ are no longer unknowns.

3.5. Continuation

We compute solutions along a branch via Newton's method as described above. We do not impose additional equations, such as requiring a new solution along the branch to be a certain distance from a prior solution or that the increment along the branch must be perpendicular to some direction. Therefore, the only additional ingredients that must be introduced to discuss continuation are the choice of initial estimate for each solution along the branch and the parameters that are prescribed for the Newton iteration.

If the continuation is in the Rayleigh number, we increment or decrement this parameter according to the number of Newton iterations required for convergence in the previous step as follows [64]:

$$Ra^{(i+1)} = Ra^{(i)} + \Delta Ra = Ra^{(i)} + \alpha(Ra^{(i)} - Ra^{(i-1)}) \tag{28}$$

where $\mathrm{Ra}^{(i)}$, $\mathrm{Ra}^{(i-1)}$ denote the Rayleigh numbers used in the two previous continuation steps, ΔRa is the increment or decrement, and α is defined by

$$\alpha = \frac{N^{\mathrm{opt}} + 1}{N^{(i)} + 1} \tag{29}$$

N^{opt} is the target number of Newton iterations. If $N^{(i)} = N^{\mathrm{opt}}$, then ΔRa remains unchanged, whereas ΔRa is reduced (increased) if $N^{(i)} > (<) N^{\mathrm{opt}}$. The choice of N^{opt} is guided by two considerations. The first is the level of sampling desired along the branch. The second is economy: a smaller value of α will engender more values of Ra, but each calculation will be faster. For our computations, we fixed N^{opt} to be between 4 and 6.

To choose an initial estimate $\boldsymbol{U}$ for the next solution along a branch at $\mathrm{Ra}^{(i+1)}$, first-order and even zero-th order extrapolation (i.e., using just the previously computed field) can be used to follow a smooth and monotonically varying branch. However, quadratic extrapolation is essential for going around turning points. Lagrange interpolation uses the three previous Rayleigh numbers $\mathrm{Ra}^{(i)}$, $\mathrm{Ra}^{(i-1)}$, $\mathrm{Ra}^{(i-2)}$ and the new Rayleigh number $\mathrm{Ra}^{(i+1)}$ from Equation (28) to determine coefficients a, b, c such that

$$Ra^{(i+1)} = aRa^{(i)} + bRa^{(i-1)} + cRa^{(i-2)}. \tag{30a}$$

We then use a, b, c to form a new estimate of the solution by setting

$$\boldsymbol{U}^{(i+1)} = a\boldsymbol{U}^{(i)} + b\boldsymbol{U}^{(i-1)} + c\boldsymbol{U}^{(i-2)} \tag{30b}$$

Newton iterations are then used to refine $\boldsymbol{U}$ until the norm of Equation (23) is 10^{-7}. This procedure requires saving the three previous solution vectors and Rayleigh numbers.

3.6. Turning Points

We now turn to the more complicated matter of extrapolating near saddle–node bifurcations, at which $\boldsymbol{U}$ ceases to be a single-valued function of Ra. The code detects that the current step is in the vicinity of a turning point by comparing the relative changes between the solution vector $\boldsymbol{U}$, and the Rayleigh number, i.e., we compare

$$\left|\frac{\Delta U_J}{U_J}\right| \equiv \left|\frac{U_J^{(i)} - U_J^{(i-1)}}{U_J^{(i)}}\right| \quad \text{with} \quad \gamma\left|\frac{\Delta Ra}{Ra}\right| \equiv \gamma\left|\frac{Ra^{(i)} - Ra^{(i-1)}}{Ra^{(i)}}\right| \tag{31}$$

where J is the index denoting the element of the solution vector $U^{(i)}$ of the highest absolute value and γ is a constant factor that makes the two magnitudes comparable. For our computations, we fixed this constant to be between 10 and 100.

Since the normal form of a saddle–node bifurcation at $(\mu, x) = (0, 0)$ is $\dot{x} = \mu - x^2$, dependent variables $(x, \boldsymbol{U})$ vary like the square root of the control parameter $(\mu, \text{Ra} - Ra_c)$ near a turning point. Consequently, as the current solution approaches a turning point, the relative difference $|\Delta U_J / U_J|$ increases until it is greater than $\gamma|\Delta Ra/Ra|$. It is at this stage that the code switches to extrapolating quadratically, using the component U_J as the independent variable instead of the Rayleigh number. This allows ΔRa to change sign and the continuation to go around the turning point. We replace Equations (28) and (30a) by analogous equations in $\boldsymbol{U}_J$ to determine $\boldsymbol{U}_J^{(i+1)}$ and a, b, c, and then replace Equation (30) by

$$U_j^{(i+1)} = aU_j^{(i)} + bU_j^{(i-1)} + cU_j^{(i-2)} \text{ for } j \neq J \text{, and} \tag{32a}$$

$$Ra^{(i+1)} = aRa^{(i)} + bRa^{(i-1)} + cRa^{(i-2)} \tag{32b}$$

to set the estimate of the new solution. Note that we have only changed the method of determining the initial guess. Ra remains fixed to $\text{Ra}^{(i+1)}$ during the Newton step, while all the elements of $\boldsymbol{U}$ are allowed to vary.

Continuation follows in this manner until eventually $|\Delta \boldsymbol{U}_J / \boldsymbol{U}_J|$ exceeds $\gamma|\Delta Ra/Ra|$, at which point the code switches back to using the Rayleigh number as the independent variable. The parameter γ can be obtained by analyzing the behavior of the continuation near a turning point. Indeed, if γ is too large, then the code will continue to use Ra as the independent variable past the point at which there is no solution for the next continuation step, and Newton's method will not converge. Should this situation arise, the continuation can be restarted at the last converged solution using a suitably reduced value of γ. Although the parameter γ is necessary for comparing $|\Delta U_J / U_J|$ and $|\Delta Ra/Ra|$ and thus for determining when to switch continuation variables, its value has no influence on the location of the turning point or of the solution branch. The choice of γ only affects the speed of continuation, as we determined by varying its value near a turning point. See also [64].

4. Branch Following

4.1. Continuation in Rayleigh Number

Our first computations with the implicit Coriolis method validated the new code by comparing the branches it produced for $\text{Ek} = 10^{-3}$ with those in [18], which were obtained using an entirely different continuation code. These branches were presented in Figure 2 above. As explained in Section 3, to search for solutions having an M azimuthal periodicity, we perform our computations in a fraction of the annulus of azimuthal width $2\pi/M$. The solutions are computed independently of their stability; most of the solutions we compute are unstable, either within the restricted domain $0 \leq \varphi < 2\pi/M$, or to instabilities which break this restriction such as rotating waves with a different M.

We then used the continuation code to compute branches of rotating waves at lower values of the Ekman number. Fixing the Ekman number, we carried out continuation in Rayleigh number Ra. Most of the branches that we computed showed no unusual features, varying smoothly and monotonically down to their threshold at a supercritical Hopf bifurcation. However, a few branches presented some interesting non-monotonic behavior, which we show in order to display the capacities of our code. Figure 6 tracks the Rayleigh-number dependence of the RW_4 branch for $\text{Ek} = 3.53 \times 10^{-5}$. This branch consists of three smooth regions that are separated from one another by short intervals which each contain two saddle–node bifurcations and rapid changes in drift frequency.

We also computed an RW_8 branch for $Ek = 1.26 \times 10^{-5}$, as shown in Figure 7. Indeed, for this value of Ek, rotating waves with an azimuthal wavenumber of 8 are more appropriate, i.e., more likely to be stable. This branch also contains a plateau in drift frequency adjacent to a short interval at $Ra \approx 159$ of rapid change delimited by two saddle–node bifurcations. These rapid rises and plateaus in drift frequency should have a physical or at least a phenomenological explanation, but we have not yet been able to find one.

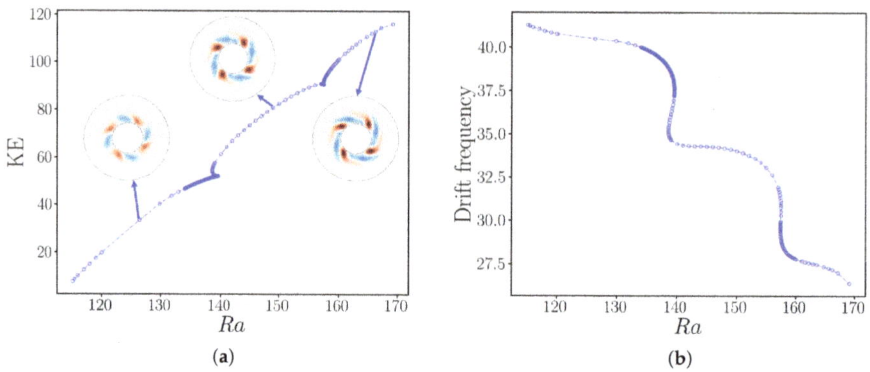

Figure 6. Bifurcation diagram of rotating wave RW_4 for $Ek = 3.53 \times 10^{-5}$ as a function of Ra. (**a**) Kinetic energy. (**b**) Drift frequency. The branch contains three long smooth regions of almost constant drift frequency separated by two short intervals (at $Ra \approx 140$ and $Ra \approx 158$) of rapid change containing saddle–node bifurcations. The resolution used for this computation was $(N_r, N_\theta, N_\varphi \times M) = (60, 80, 40 \times 4)$.

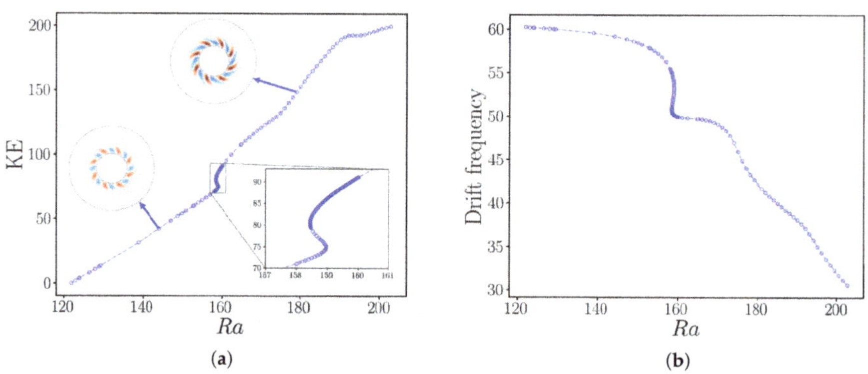

Figure 7. Bifurcation diagram of rotating wave RW_8 for $Ek = 1.26 \times 10^{-5}$ as a function of Ra. (**a**) Kinetic energy. (**b**) Drift frequency. The branch contains a single interval of rapid change at $Ra \approx 159$. The resolution used for this computation was $(N_r, N_\theta, N_\varphi \times M) = (68, 100, 28 \times 8)$.

4.2. Continuation in Ekman Number and in Resolution

We adapted our method to follow branches in Ekman number, varying Ek on a logarithmic scale. We replace Ra with $\log_{10}(Ek)$ in Equation (28) as follows:

$$\begin{aligned}\log_{10}(\mathrm{Ek}^{(i+1)}) &= \log_{10}(\mathrm{Ek}^{(i)}) + \Delta[\log_{10}(\mathrm{Ek})] \\ &= \log_{10}(\mathrm{Ek}^{(i)}) + \alpha(\log_{10}(\mathrm{Ek}^{(i)}) - \log_{10}(\mathrm{Ek}^{(i-1)}))\end{aligned} \tag{33}$$

where the computation of α remains as in Equation (29). In this case, we used $N^{\mathrm{opt}} = 3$ for all of the simulations. Furthermore, in order to go around turning points, we now compare $|\Delta \boldsymbol{U}_j / \boldsymbol{U}_j|$ and $\gamma|\Delta[\log_{10}(\mathrm{Ek})]/\log_{10}(\mathrm{Ek})|$, where we chose γ between 400 and 500.

Apart from these minor changes, there are several major differences between performing continuation in Ekman and Rayleigh numbers. The first is that the matrices that represent the left-hand-sides of Equations (8a) and (8b) or Equations (15a) and (15b) must be recomputed every time a new value of Ek is chosen. Indeed, while the Rayleigh number only appears in the right-hand side of these equations, Ek, is also present in the diffusion terms, which are treated implicitly regardless of how the Coriolis term is handled. This means that extra work must be performed at the beginning of every continuation step.

Secondly, as the Ekman number is decreased, the critical Rayleigh number for the onset of convection increases. That is, rotation stabilizes the configuration against convection. A classic result [3] is that the critical value of the usual thermal Rayleigh number $\mathrm{Ra}_{\mathrm{therm}}$ varies like $\mathrm{Ek}^{-4/3}$, so that the critical value of our rotational Rayleigh number $\mathrm{Ra}_{\mathrm{rot}} = \mathrm{Ra}_{\mathrm{therm}}\mathrm{Ek}/\mathrm{Pr}$ varies like $\mathrm{Ek}^{-1/3}/\mathrm{Pr}$. Therefore, instead of keeping Ra fixed, we have increased Ra every time we decrease Ek, so as to remain at approximately the same distance from the convective threshold.

Third, as the simulation ventures towards lower Ekman numbers, the fields require a higher resolution. This is clearly seen from the visualizations in Figure 3, which show that the radial extent and azimuthal wavelength decrease with decreasing Ek. To achieve this, grid refinement is introduced in the code such that the spectral resolution is increased by 20% whenever under-resolution is detected in the Chebyshev or the spherical harmonic modes. This is performed by introducing a threshold for the amplitude ratio between the mode of highest absolute value and of highest wavenumber. When this ratio exceeds the threshold, the code calls a grid refinement subroutine which first deallocates the previous grid, then creates a new one using the new resolution and finally represents the fields from the last continuation step on this new grid by filling in the new modes with zero.

This procedure, called Fourier interpolation [71,72], involves no loss of accuracy or stability. The most recent Newton step is then recomputed, using the representation with the finer resolution as an initial condition, and the path following continues as intended. Most of our runs were carried out with an under-resolution threshold (ratio of the highest-amplitude mode to that of the highest wavenumber) of 10^{-6}. Decreasing this threshold to 10^{-7} led to minimal gains in accuracy at a high cost in CPU time.

Figure 8 shows the result of continuation in Ek. (Recall that Ra is kept proportional to $\mathrm{Ek}^{-1/3}$.) This branch showed three coexisting solutions over the range $4 \times 10^{-5} \lesssim \mathrm{Ek} \lesssim 6 \times 10^{-5}$. Our grid refinement algorithm increased the resolution by about 20% in r and by 50% in θ and φ. We emphasize that most continuations showed monotonic behavior and we have deliberately chosen to present those that did not.

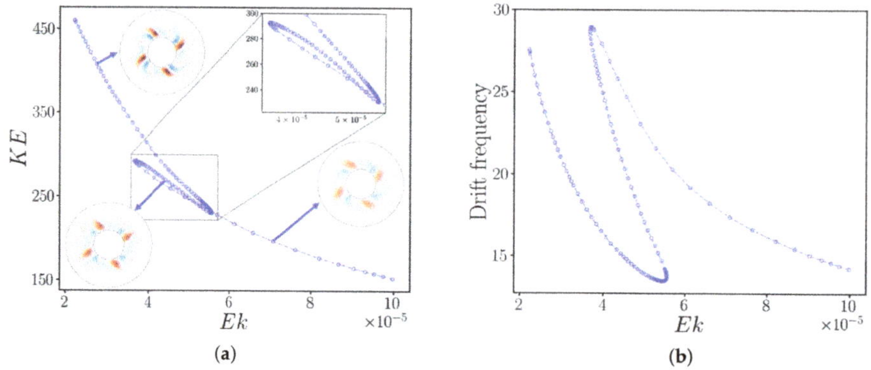

Figure 8. Bifurcation diagram of the rotating wave RW_4 as a function of Ek, while fixing $\mathrm{Ra} = 6.5 \times \mathrm{Ek}^{-1/3}$. (**a**) Kinetic energy. (**b**) Drift frequency. Three solution branches exist over the range $4 \times 10^{-5} \lesssim \mathrm{Ek} \lesssim 6 \times 10^{-5}$. The resolutions used for this computation ranged from $(N_r, N_\theta, N_\varphi \times M) = (68, 92, 48 \times 4)$ to $(80, 136, 70 \times 4)$.

5. Timing Comparisons

Newton's method is very fast, typically requiring 3–10 iterations. The bottleneck in applying Newton's method to systems of partial differential equations is always the solution of the linear systems. In our case, this is quantified by the total number of GMRES iterations necessary to compute a new state along the branch. We find that the number of iterations depends on the Ekman number, but is fairly independent of the Rayleigh number. We therefore average the number of GMRES iterations over all the points computed in a branch for a fixed Ekman number. We do this for the Newton method with both implicit and explicit Coriolis to produce the curves in Figures 9–11 for RW_4, RW_8, and RW_{12}. The ratio of the number of GMRES iterations between the explicit and implicit methods ranges from 2, for RW_4 at $\mathrm{Ek} = 3 \times 10^{-2}$, to 20 for RW_{12} at $\mathrm{Ek} = 3 \times 10^{-5}$. This ratio would surely continue to increase as Ek decreases, but the explicit Coriolis calculation became prohibitively expensive below $\mathrm{Ek} = 3 \times 10^{-5}$. Figure 9 also demonstrates that carrying out the calculation in the restricted domain $0 \leq \varphi \leq 2\pi/M$ requires fewer GMRES iterations (in addition to each iteration being at least M times faster).

Measuring the economy realized in timestepping is more problematic. Because explicit integration effectively approximates a decaying exponential by a polynomial, it displays artificial temporal divergence, i.e., numerical instability, if the timestep is too large. Because implicit integration instead approximates the exponential by a decaying rational function, the timestep is not constrained by stability. The timestep is, however, still constrained by accuracy. A particularly demanding criterion for judging accuracy is the wavespeed [73]. We compute the relative errors in wavespeeds $C_{\mathrm{error}} \equiv (C_{\Delta t} - C_{\mathrm{exact}})/C_{\mathrm{exact}}$, where C_{exact} is obtained from Newton's method and hence has no timestepping error. Figure 12 presents the relative errors as a function of Ek and Δt, with the other parameters set to the values below the figure. C_{error} obtained from the explicit and implicit methods are the same or very close for the same value of Δt. C_{error} increases like $(\Delta t)^2$, indicating that both time-integration methods are second-order in time. Indeed, for timestepping, we have not used the first-order scheme given in Equation (17) and used for our Newton algorithm, but a second-order method combining Runge–Kutta and a predictor–corrector scheme, as described in [35].

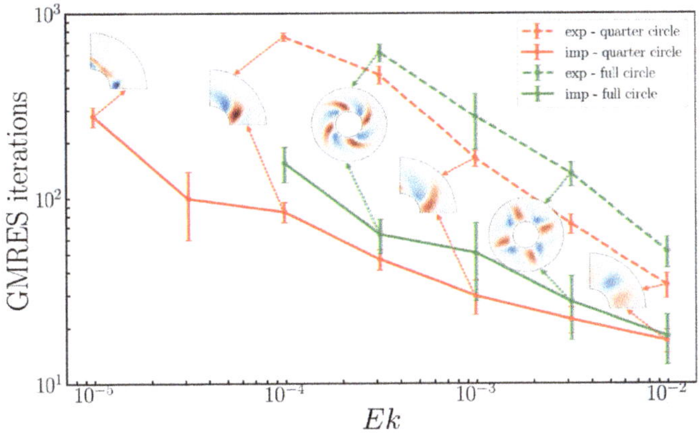

Figure 9. Total number of matrix–vector actions required by nested Newton-GMRES algorithm to compute RW_4 as a function of Ek with explicit (dashed) and implicit (solid) implementation of Coriolis force. An average is taken over a branch of Ra values. The number of actions required by the explicit algorithm is always greater than that required by the implicit algorithm, with the ratio between them increasing from approximately 2 at $\text{Ek} = 10^{-2}$ to approximately 9 at $\text{Ek} = 10^{-4}$. Using the full domain $0 \leq \varphi < 2\pi$ (green) instead of the reduced domain $0 \leq \varphi < \pi/2$ (red) increases the number of GMRES iterations, as well as the cost of each iteration. On average, the full domain requires 1.5 times more actions than the reduced domain counterpart. The explicit algorithm is prohibitively time-consuming for $\text{Ek} < 10^{-4}$. The resolutions used in this case were $(N_r, N_\theta, N_\varphi \times M) = (46, 72, 128 \times 1)$ for the computations in the full circle and from $(46, 72, 32 \times 4)$ to $(76, 80, 40 \times 4)$ for those in the quarter circle.

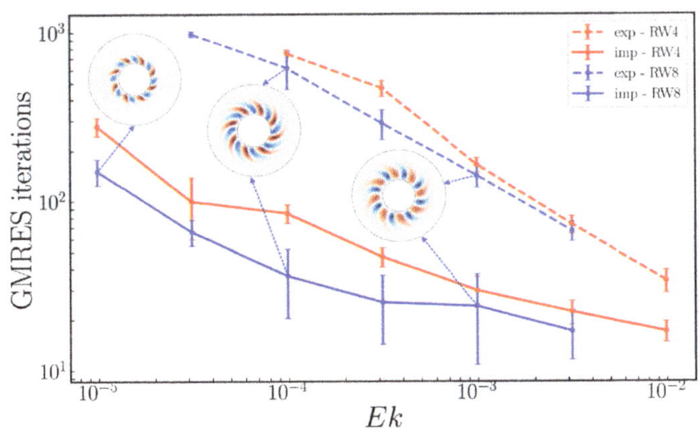

Figure 10. Total number of matrix–vector actions required by the nested Newton-GMRES algorithm to compute RW_4 (red) and RW_8 (blue) as a function of Ek with an explicit (dashed) and implicit (solid) implementation of Coriolis force. For clarity, the insets show the full domain, although the computations are carried out in reduced domains $0 \leq \varphi < 2\pi/M$. An average is taken over many values of Ra. The number of actions required by the explicit algorithm is always greater than that required by the implicit algorithm, with the ratio between them increasing from approximately 4 at $\text{Ek} = 3 \times 10^{-3}$ to 15 at $\text{Ek} = 3 \times 10^{-5}$, below which the explicit algorithm is prohibitively time-consuming. The resolutions used for the RW_8 computations ranged from $(N_r, N_\theta, N_\varphi \times M) = (64, 100, 28 \times 8)$ to $(76, 124, 32 \times 8)$.

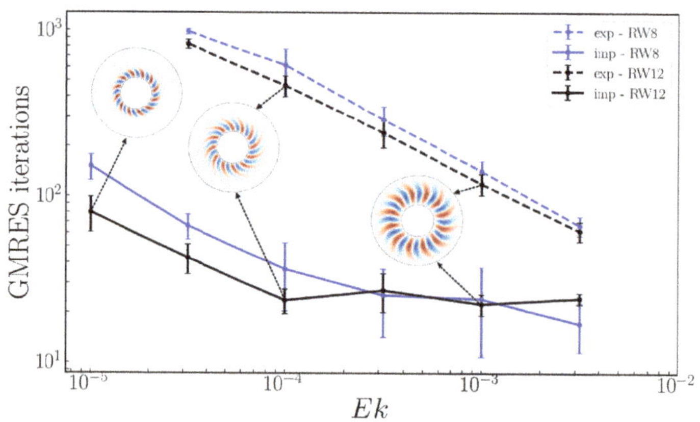

Figure 11. Total number of matrix–vector actions required by the nested Newton-GMRES algorithm to compute RW_{12} (black) and RW_8 (blue) as a function of Ek with explicit (dashed) and implicit (solid) implementation of Coriolis force. For clarity, the insets show the full domain, although the computations are carried out in reduced domains $0 \le \varphi < 2\pi/M$. An average is taken over a branch of Ra values. The number of actions required by the explicit algorithm is always greater than that required by the implicit algorithm, with the ratio between them increasing from approximately 2.5 for $\mathrm{Ek} = 3 \times 10^{-3}$ to 20 for $\mathrm{Ek} = 3 \times 10^{-5}$, below which the explicit algorithm fails. The resolutions used for the RW_8 computations ranged from $(N_r, N_\theta, N_\varphi \times M) = (60, 112, 20 \times 12)$ to $(90, 184, 32 \times 12)$.

For each Ek, there is a minimum Δt above which the explicit Coriolis simulation diverges in time. This value of Δt is indicated in Figure 12 for each Ekman number as the left endpoint of an arrow and also in Table 1. Above this value of Δt, implicit Coriolis timestepping must be used. But eventually, Δt is so large that the results of the implicit method are too inaccurate to be useful. As an upper limit for the implicit method, we make the arbitrary choice that the relative error on C_{error} must be less than 2%. These limiting values of large Δt are indicated as the right endpoints of the arrows in Figure 12 and in Table 1. Hence, for each Ek, there is a large range of Δt-values that can be used only for implicit timestepping and whose error does not exceed 2%. For example, for $\mathrm{Ek} = 10^{-5}$, the allowable timestep (<2% error) for the implicit Coriolis method is almost 20 times that at which the explicit method diverges. These ranges are given in Table 1. Fitting to the two smaller values of Ek, both endpoints of the range are approximately proportional to Ek: the explicit method diverges for $\Delta t \gtrsim 0.5\ \mathrm{Ek}^{1.1}$ while the error for the implicit method remains less than 2% for $\Delta t \lesssim 0.8\ \mathrm{Ek}^{0.9}$. If a 2% error in the wavespeed is considered to be too large, the data in Figure 12 can be used to determine the largest Δt that achieves the desired error, by drawing a horizontal line at the desired level. Although these results are specific to the parameter values and flows that we have simulated, they imply that implicit Coriolis integration can be orders of magnitude faster as Ek decreases, enabling the simulation of convection in a spherical annulus at low Ekman numbers.

Table 1. Parameters used for testing and useful range of Δt for implicit timestepping.

					Δt		
Ek	**Ra**	M	$(N_r, N_\theta, N_\varphi \times M)$	C_{exact}	**Explicit Diverges**	**2% Error**	**Ratio**
10^{-3}	120	4	$(46, 72, 32 \times 4)$	-2.7647	4.0×10^{-4}	1.1×10^{-3}	3
10^{-4}	130	8	$(60, 80, 40 \times 4)$	3.9998	2.0×10^{-5}	1.9×10^{-4}	9
10^{-5}	140	12	$(76, 136, 24 \times 4)$	51.2817	1.6×10^{-6}	2.8×10^{-5}	17

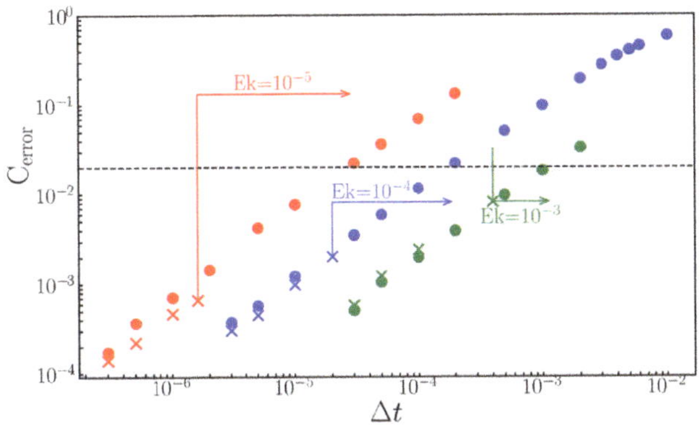

Figure 12. Accuracy of the time-dependent calculation of rotating waves RW_M as a function of timestep Δt using implicit (circles) and explicit (crosses) timestepping of the Coriolis term. Shown here is the relative error $C_{error} \equiv |(C_{\Delta t} - C_{exact})/C_{exact}|$ of the drift velocity as a function of the timestep for various sets of parameter values (see table) where C_{exact} is calculated via Newton's method. Both the explicit and implicit methods are second order in time, with $C_{error} \sim \Delta t^2$. Vertical lines indicate the limiting Δt above which explicit timestepping diverges and cannot be used. The horizontal dashed line indicates $C_{error} = 2\%$. The arrows designate the range of Δt for which implicit timestepping is advantageous: it does not diverge and C_{error} remains less than 2%. An approximate fit yields the range $0.5 \times \mathrm{Ek}^{1.1} \lesssim \Delta t \lesssim 0.8 \times Ek^{0.9}$. See Table 1.

We studied the transition to chaos for $\mathrm{Ek} = 5 \times 10^{-6}$. Explicit Coriolis timestepping requires $\Delta t \lesssim 5 \times 10^{-7}$. Using the implicit method with 5 Δt and then 10 Δt allowed us to simulate five or 10 times longer and to tentatively confirm the temporally chaotic behavior we observed with the explicit method. If we wish to study this phenomenon further, we will decrease Δt in order to obtain more accurate results.

As discussed in Section 3.2, treating the Coriolis term implicitly requires the use of block pentadiagonal matrices rather than block diagonal matrices. However, the additional cost is negligible. Part of the reason for this is that, in pseudospectral methods, the cost of carrying out the nonlinear terms (or the linearized nonlinear terms), more specifically the transforms to and from spectral space, is by far the most time-consuming portion of the calculation. Thus, the cost of a timestep is barely increased by the implicit treatment of the Coriolis term. In timestepping, if Δt can be increased by a factor of 100 (assuming the accuracy is still acceptable), then the simulation to the same final time costs (almost exactly) 100 times less. In Newton's method, if 10 times fewer actions of the Jacobian (i.e., linearized timesteps) are required for a Newton step, then the computation will be (almost exactly) 10 times faster.

6. Discussion

6.1. Differences with Other Methods

We now describe the differences between Stokes preconditioning and the method used in [20,45–47] for convection in rotating spheres, as well as in [74–78] for other hydrodynamic problems. These authors seek steady states or traveling waves as roots of $\boldsymbol{U}(t+T) - \boldsymbol{U}(t)$, where $\boldsymbol{U}(t+T)$ is computed from $\boldsymbol{U}(t)$ by carrying out many timesteps, each with a small Δt; we therefore call this the integration method. In contrast, although Equations (19) and (20) would seem to imply that we too seek roots of $\boldsymbol{U}(t+T) - \boldsymbol{U}(t)$, this is not at all the case. In the Stokes preconditioning method, we compute $\boldsymbol{U}(t+T)$ from $\boldsymbol{U}(t)$ by carrying out a single very large implicit–explicit Euler timestep Equation (17), with a timestep $\Delta t = T$ that is so large that the difference $\boldsymbol{U}(t+\Delta t) - \boldsymbol{U}(t)$ no longer approximates the time derivative. Via Equation (20), it turns out that this difference is a preconditioned version of the operator whose roots are sought by our method, namely $\mathcal{L} + \mathcal{N}$, preconditioned by $\mathcal{L}$. Both methods solve the linear systems that are the core of Newton's method via GMRES, which relies on the repeated actions of the Jacobian. For the integration method, the action of the Jacobian consists of integrating the linearized equations via many small timesteps, while for us, it consists of taking a single large linearized timestep. Here, there is a trade-off. Despite the preconditioning displayed by Equation (20), the Jacobian resulting from Stokes preconditioning is less well conditioned than that which results from taking many small linearized timesteps, and so more Jacobian actions are required for GMRES to converge to a solution of our linear system Equation (21). However, each action costs less, since it consists of only a single timestep. This trade-off—number of actions vs. timesteps per action—can be quantified via the total number of timesteps required to compute a steady state or a traveling wave. For wall-bounded shear flows in the transitional regime, we have found that the Stokes preconditioning method is faster than the integration method by a factor of 11 for plane Couette flow and by a factor of 35 for pipe flow; see [48] for details. We have not carried out a timing comparison of the integration and the Stokes preconditioning method for convection in rotating spheres.

Although the Stokes preconditioning method is much faster (at least in the cases and the parameter regimes that we have studied), the integration method has the considerable advantage of being far more general. The Stokes preconditioning method is only capable of computing steady states or traveling waves, while the integration method can compute periodic orbits of all kinds, including, for example, modulated rotating waves, standing waves, or pulsing states.

A specific difference between our implementation of implicit Coriolis integration and that of [20,40,41,45–47] is that we solve the linear systems arising from the implicit treatment of the diffusive and Coriolis terms directly via block pentadiagonal LU decomposition and backsolving, whereas [20,40,41,45–47] use Krylov methods to solve these systems. Time-integration using the explicit, implicit, and semi-implicit treatment of the Coriolis term is compared by [40]. Our strategy is to solve linear systems directly as much as possible and to resort to Krylov methods only to invert the full Jacobian.

6.2. Relevance for Geophysics

One might wonder about the applicability of this achievement to geophysical research. We begin by discussing the relevance of calculating traveling waves via Newton's method. Small Ekman numbers, like large Reynolds numbers, are associated with chaos and turbulence, not with the regularity and periodicity of traveling waves, which, moreover, are almost invariably unstable. The Boussinesq and Navier–Stokes equations generally contain a very large number of solution branches, most of which are partly or completely unstable, e.g., [64,75–81]. This profusion of states, sometimes called exact coherent structures, has become the focus of extensive research, motivated by the idea [82,83] that turbulence could be viewed from a dynamical systems perspective as a collection of trajectories ricocheting between periodic orbits along their unstable directions, a kind of deterministic analogue of ergodic theory. Our Newton solver would enable the application of this line of research to geophysical flows. More generally, unstable states can cast light on the origin and organization of turbulent states; in one of the best known examples, ghostly Taylor vortices exist in even highly turbulent Taylor–Couette flow [84–87] and the unstable underlying vortices may even reproduce the mean properties of the turbulent flow [88].

We now turn to the relevance for geophysics of implicit Coriolis timestepping with large timesteps. Constraints on timesteps (whether for stability or accuracy) arise from the different physical forces in the equations. In rapidly rotating fluids, the Coriolis force generates inertial waves, which have a large range of frequencies and are continually generated and damped. Using a timestep that greatly exceeds the constraint for resolving inertial waves can be considered analogous to using the incompressible Navier–Stokes equations (or the anelastic approximation), which act to filter out the high-frequency sound waves [38,39].

Using values of Δt at which implicit Coriolis timestepping is possible but inaccurate can also help to explore the large parameter space. The most economical procedure is to carry out a preliminary large-scale survey with a coarse spatial resolution and a large timestep. Interesting regions can then be accurately simulated using finer resolutions and smaller timesteps.

Previous research by two of the authors [18,19,42,43] originated in the context of the Geoflow consortium, centered on microgravity experiments meant to mimic convective flows within the Earth [29,30]. These experiments were run in the Fluid Science Laboratory facility located in the European Space Agency's Columbus laboratory on the International Space Station. The computations in [18,19,42,43] used an explicit treatment of the Coriolis force and could not be continued to Ekman numbers smaller than 10^{-4}. Geoflow has been succeeded by Atmoflow [31], whose purpose is to mimic convective flows in the atmosphere. We hope to use the new code to carry out computations relevant to AtmoFlow and to be able to achieve lower Ekman numbers.

7. Conclusions

We have developed a pair of codes for simulating thermal convection in a rotating spherical fluid shell that relies on an implicit treatment of the Coriolis force. The numerical cost of this improvement is quite manageable: the block diagonal matrix systems which arise from the implicit treatment of the diffusive terms must be replaced by block penta-diagonal matrix systems, which can still be solved by block banded LU decomposition and backsolving. Once implemented in a timestepping code, implicit integration with a very large pseudo-timestep ($\Delta t = 200$) can be leveraged to precondition the large linear systems that are the core of Newton's method. When only the diffusive terms are treated implicitly, this is known as Stokes preconditioning; the method developed here could be called Stokes-and-Coriolis preconditioning.

We demonstrated this method's capabilities by carrying out continuation in Rayleigh number at various values of the Ekman number on the order of 10^{-5} for rotating waves with azimuthal wavenumbers 4, 8, and 12. We found several intriguing examples of branches containing plateaus in drift frequency, separated by intervals of rapid change delimited by pairs of saddle-node bifurcations. The physical, or at least phenomenological, reasons for these properties remain to be discovered. We have also implemented continuation in the Ekman number, spaced logarithmically, in which we automatically measure and increase the resolution as needed. We are unaware of any previous examples of continuation in the Ekman number or with automatic resolution adjustment in the literature.

We have measured the economy that is realized by the implicit treatment of the Coriolis force. For Newton's method, the advantage of the implicit over the explicit treatment is dramatic. For example, the explicit algorithm takes 20 times as many GMRES iterations (and hence 20 times as much CPU time) as the implicit method to compute states on the RW_{12} branch at $Ek = 3 \times 10^{-5}$. For lower Ekman numbers, the explicit method takes an unmanageable number of GMRES iterations, making it impossible to use in practice.

For timestepping, the advantage of the implicit over the explicit treatment is equally spectacular. For computing rotating waves at $Ek = 10^{-5}$, the implicit algorithm can reasonably use timesteps that are almost 20 times past the temporal stability limit, meaning that simulations in this regime can be 20 times faster than if an explicit method were used. In conclusion, the implicit treatment of the Coriolis force greatly improves the efficiency of computations in the low Ekman number regime.

Author Contributions: Conceptualization, L.S.T.; Methodology, J.C.G.S.; Software, J.C.G.S. and C.R.; Validation, J.C.G.S. and C.R.; Investigation, J.C.G.S. and F.F.; Writing—original draft, L.S.T.; Writing—review & editing, J.C.G.S. and F.F.; Visualization, J.C.G.S.; Supervision, L.S.T. All authors have read and agreed to the published version of the manuscript.

Funding: The calculations for this work were performed using high performance computing resources provided by the Grand Equipement National de Calcul Intensif (GENCI) at the Institut du Développement et des Ressources en Informatique Scientifique (IDRIS, CNRS) through Grant No. A0162A01119.

Data Availability Statement: Code availability: the code is in active development and fully available under the GNU General Public License v2.0 on the Github repository https://github.com/JuanSembla/spherical_code_pmmh, accessed on 30 March 2025.

Acknowledgments: We gratefully acknowledge Alan Riquier for programming assistance and we thank Adrian van Kan, Benjamin Favier, and Rainer Hollerbach for helpful discussions.

Conflicts of Interest: The authors declare no conflicts of interest.

Appendix A

Here, we present the intermediate calculations leading from Equations (11a) and (11b) to Equations (15a) and (15b). Using Equation (14), the recursion relations Equation (13) for the associated Legendre polynomials can be rewritten in terms of the spherical harmonics as

$$\sin\theta \frac{d}{d\theta} Y_l^{|m|} = \frac{l(l-|m|+1)}{2l+1} \frac{N_l^m}{N_{l+1}^m} Y_{l+1}^{|m|} - \frac{(l+|m|)(l+1)}{2l+1} \frac{N_l^m}{N_{l-1}^m} Y_{l-1}^{|m|} \tag{A1a}$$

$$\cos\theta\, Y_l^{|m|} = \frac{l-|m|+1}{2l+1} \frac{N_l^m}{N_{l+1}^m} Y_{l+1}^{|m|} + \frac{(l+|m|)}{2l+1} \frac{N_l^m}{N_{l-1}^m} Y_{l-1}^{|m|} \tag{A1b}$$

Applying Equation (A1) to Equation (11a) leads to

$$\begin{aligned}
&\boldsymbol{e_r}\cdot\boldsymbol{\nabla}\times\boldsymbol{F}^{\text{implicit}} \\
&= \sum_{m,l}\left[\frac{l(l+1)}{r^2}\mathrm{Ek}\left(\frac{\partial}{\partial t}-L_l\right)-\frac{2im}{r^2}\right]e_{lm}Y_l^m \\
&\quad+\frac{2}{r^2}\left(\frac{l(l+1)}{r}-\frac{\partial}{\partial r}\right)f_{lm}\left[\frac{l(l-|m|+1)}{2l+1}\frac{N_l^m}{N_{l+1}^m}Y_{l+1}^{|m|}-\frac{(l+|m|)(l+1)}{2l+1}\frac{N_l^m}{N_{l-1}^m}Y_{l-1}^{|m|}\right] \\
&\quad+2\frac{l(l+1)}{r^2}\left(\frac{2}{r}-\frac{\partial}{\partial r}\right)f_{lm}\left[\frac{l-|m|+1}{2l+1}\frac{N_l^m}{N_{l+1}^m}Y_{l+1}^{|m|}+\frac{(l+|m|)}{2l+1}\frac{N_l^m}{N_{l-1}^m}Y_{l-1}^{|m|}\right]
\end{aligned}$$

Grouping terms in $Y_{l+1}^{|m|}$ and $Y_{l-1}^{|m|}$, we obtain

$$\begin{aligned}
&= \sum_{m,l}\left[\frac{l(l+1)}{r^2}\mathrm{Ek}\left(\frac{\partial}{\partial t}-L_l\right)-\frac{2im}{r^2}\right]e_{lm}Y_l^m \\
&\quad+\frac{2}{r^2}\frac{l(l-|m|+1)}{2l+1}\left[\left(\frac{l(l+1)}{r}-\frac{\partial}{\partial r}\right)+(l+1)\left(\frac{2}{r}-\frac{\partial}{\partial r}\right)\right]\frac{N_l^m}{N_{l+1}^m}f_{lm}Y_{l+1}^m \\
&\quad+\frac{2}{r^2}\frac{(l+|m|)(l+1)}{2l+1}\left[-\left(\frac{l(l+1)}{r}-\frac{\partial}{\partial r}\right)+l\left(\frac{2}{r}-\frac{\partial}{\partial r}\right)\right]\frac{N_l^m}{N_{l-1}^m}f_{lm}Y_{l-1}^m
\end{aligned}$$

$$\begin{aligned}
&= \sum_{m,l}\left[\frac{l(l+1)}{r^2}\mathrm{Ek}\left(\frac{\partial}{\partial t}-L_l\right)-\frac{2im}{r^2}\right]e_{lm}Y_l^m \\
&\quad+\frac{2}{r^2}\frac{(l-|m|+1)l(l+2)}{2l+1}\left[\frac{(l+1)}{r}-\frac{\partial}{\partial r}\right]\frac{N_l^m}{N_{l+1}^m}f_{lm}Y_{l+1}^m \\
&\quad+\frac{2}{r^2}\frac{(l+|m|)(l+1)(l-1)}{2l+1}\left[-\frac{l}{r}-\frac{\partial}{\partial r}\right]\frac{N_l^m}{N_{l-1}^m}f_{lm}Y_{l-1}^m
\end{aligned}$$

Finally, changing the names of the indices so that all terms correspond to the same spherical harmonic Y_l^m, we obtain Equation (15a):

$$
\begin{aligned}
=\sum_{m,l} Y_l^m \Bigg\{ & \left[\frac{l(l+1)}{r^2}\mathrm{Ek}\left(\frac{\partial}{\partial t}-L_l\right)-\frac{2im}{r^2}\right] e_{lm} \\
& +\frac{2}{r^2}\frac{(l-1)(l+1)(l-|m|)}{2l-1}\left[\frac{l}{r}-\frac{\partial}{\partial r}\right]\frac{N_{l-1}^m}{N_l^m} f_{l-1,m} \\
& +\frac{2}{r^2}\frac{(l+1+|m|)l(l+2)}{2l+3}\left[-\frac{(l+1)}{r}-\frac{\partial}{\partial r}\right]\frac{N_{l+1}^m}{N_l^m} f_{l+1,m} \Bigg\}
\end{aligned}
\tag{A2}
$$

The same calculations can be applied to Equation (11b) to obtain Equation (15b):

$$
\begin{aligned}
& \boldsymbol{e}_r \cdot \boldsymbol{\nabla}\times\boldsymbol{\nabla}\times \boldsymbol{F}^{\text{implicit}} \\
& =\sum_{m,l} - \left[\frac{l(l+1)}{r^2}\mathrm{Ek}\left(\frac{\partial}{\partial t}-L_l\right)-\frac{2im}{r^2}\right] L_l f_{\mathrm{lm}} Y_l^m \\
& \quad +\frac{2}{r^2}\left(\frac{l(l+1)}{r}-\frac{\partial}{\partial r}\right) e_{lm}\left[\frac{l(l-|m|+1)}{2l+1}\frac{N_l^m}{N_{l+1}^m}Y_{l+1}^{|m|}-\frac{(l+|m|)(l+1)}{2l+1}\frac{N_l^m}{N_{l-1}^m}Y_{l-1}^{|m|}\right] \\
& \quad +2\frac{l(l+1)}{r^2}\left(\frac{2}{r}-\frac{\partial}{\partial r}\right) e_{lm}\left[\frac{l-|m|+1}{2l+1}\frac{N_l^m}{N_{l+1}^m}Y_{l+1}^{|m|}+\frac{(l+|m|)}{2l+1}\frac{N_l^m}{N_{l-1}^m}Y_{l-1}^{|m|}\right]
\end{aligned}
$$

$$
\begin{aligned}
& =\sum_{m,l} - \left[\frac{l(l+1)}{r^2}\mathrm{Ek}\left(\frac{\partial}{\partial t}-L_l\right)-\frac{2im}{r^2}\right] L_l f_{lm} Y_l^m \\
& \quad +\frac{2}{r^2}\frac{l(l-|m|+1)}{2l+1}\left[\left(\frac{l(l+1)}{r}-\frac{\partial}{\partial r}\right)+(l+1)\left(\frac{2}{r}-\frac{\partial}{\partial r}\right)\right]\frac{N_l^m}{N_{l+1}^m} e_{lm} Y_{l+1}^m \\
& \quad +\frac{2}{r^2}\frac{(l+|m|)(l+1)}{2l+1}\left[-\left(\frac{l(l+1)}{r}-\frac{\partial}{\partial r}\right)+l\left(\frac{2}{r}-\frac{\partial}{\partial r}\right)\right]\frac{N_l^m}{N_{l-1}^m} e_{lm} Y_{l-1}^m
\end{aligned}
$$

$$
\begin{aligned}
& =\sum_{m,l} - \left[\frac{l(l+1)}{r^2}\mathrm{Ek}\left(\frac{\partial}{\partial t}-L_l\right)-\frac{2im}{r^2}\right] L_l f_{lm} Y_l^m \\
& \quad +\frac{2}{r^2}\frac{l(l-|m|+1)(l+2)}{2l+1}\left[\frac{(l+1)}{r}-\frac{\partial}{\partial r}\right]\frac{N_l^m}{N_{l+1}^m} e_{lm} Y_{l+1}^m \\
& \quad +\frac{2}{r^2}\frac{(l+|m|)(l+1)(l-1)}{2l+1}\left[-\frac{l}{r}-\frac{\partial}{\partial r}\right]\frac{N_l^m}{N_{l-1}^m} e_{lm} Y_{l-1}^m
\end{aligned}
$$

$$
\begin{aligned}
=\sum_{m,l} Y_l^m \Bigg\{ & -\left[\frac{l(l+1)}{r^2}\mathrm{Ek}\left(\frac{\partial}{\partial t}-L_l\right)-\frac{2im}{r^2}\right] L_l f_{lm} \\
& +\frac{2}{r^2}\frac{(l-1)(l-|m|)(l+1)}{2l-1}\left[\frac{l}{r}-\frac{\partial}{\partial r}\right]\frac{N_{l-1}^m}{N_l^m} e_{l-1,m} \\
& +\frac{2}{r^2}\frac{(l+1+|m|)(l+2)l}{2l+3}\left[-\frac{(l+1)}{r}-\frac{\partial}{\partial r}\right]\frac{N_{l+1}^m}{N_l^m} e_{l+1,m} \Bigg\}
\end{aligned}
\tag{A3}
$$

References

1. Chandrasekhar, S. *Hydrodynamic and Hydromagnetic Stability*; Oxford University Press: Oxford, UK, 1961.
2. Roberts, P.H. On the thermal instability of a rotating-fluid sphere containing heat sources. *Phil. Trans. R. Soc. Lond. A* **1968**, *263*, 93–117.
3. Busse, F. Thermal instabilities in rapidly rotating systems. *J. Fluid Mech.* **1970**, *44*, 441–460. [CrossRef]

4. Zhang, K.K.; Busse, F.H. On the onset of convection in rotating spherical shells. *Geophys. Astrophys. Fluid Dyn.* **1987**, *39*, 119–147. [CrossRef]
5. Jones, C.A.; Soward, A.M.; Mussa, A.I. The onset of thermal convection in a rapidly rotating sphere. *J. Fluid Mech.* **2000**, *405*, 157–179. [CrossRef]
6. Dormy, E.; Soward, A.; Jones, C.; Jault, D.; Cardin, P. The onset of thermal convection in rotating spherical shells. *J. Fluid Mech.* **2004**, *501*, 43–70. [CrossRef]
7. Net, M.; Garcia, F.; Sánchez, J. On the onset of low-Prandtl-number convection in rotating spherical shells: Non-slip boundary conditions. *J. Fluid Mech.* **2008**, *601*, 317–337. [CrossRef]
8. Skene, C.S.; Tobias, S.M. Weakly nonlinear analysis of the onset of convection in rotating spherical shells. *Geophys. Astrophys. Fluid Dyn.* **2024**, 1–22. [CrossRef]
9. Ruelle, D. Bifurcations in the presence of a symmetry group. *Arch. Rat. Mech. Anal.* **1973**, *51*, 136–152. [CrossRef]
10. Ecke, R.; Zhong, F.; Knobloch, E. Hopf bifurcation with broken reflection symmetry in rotating Rayleigh-Bénard convection. *Europhys. Lett.* **1992**, *19*, 177. [CrossRef]
11. Chossat, P.; Lauterbach, R. *Methods in Equivariant Bifurcations and Dynamical Systems*; World Scientific: Singapore, 2000.
12. Busse, F. Convective flows in rapidly rotating spheres and their dynamo action. *Phys. Fluids* **2002**, *14*, 1301–1314. [CrossRef]
13. Hindman, B.W.; Jain, R. Radial trapping of thermal Rossby waves within the convection zones of low-mass stars. *Astrophys. J.* **2022**, *932*, 68. [CrossRef]
14. Dormy, E. Rapidly Rotating Magnetohydrodynamics and the Geodynamo. *Annu. Rev. Fluid Mech.* **2025**, *57*. [CrossRef]
15. Pothérat, A.; Horn, S. Seven decades of exploring planetary interiors with rotating convection experiments. *Comptes Rendus Phys.* **2025**, *25*, 233.
16. Zhang, K. Convection in a rapidly rotating spherical shell at infinite Prandtl number: Transition to vacillating flows. *Phys. Earth Planet. Inter.* **1992**, *72*, 236–248. [CrossRef]
17. Simitev, R.; Busse, F. Patterns of convection in rotating spherical shells. *New J. Phys.* **2003**, *5*, 97. [CrossRef]
18. Feudel, F.; Seehafer, N.; Tuckerman, L.S.; Gellert, M. Multistability in rotating spherical shell convection. *Phys. Rev. E* **2013**, *87*, 023021. [CrossRef]
19. Feudel, F.; Tuckerman, L.S.; Gellert, M.; Seehafer, N. Bifurcations of rotating waves in rotating spherical shell convection. *Phys. Rev. E* **2015**, *92*, 053015. [CrossRef]
20. Garcia, F.; Net, M.; Sánchez, J. Continuation and stability of convective modulated rotating waves in spherical shells. *Phys. Rev. E* **2016**, *93*, 013119. [CrossRef]
21. Cardin, P.; Olson, P. Chaotic thermal convection in a rapidly rotating spherical shell: Consequences for flow in the outer core. *Phys. Earth Planet. Inter.* **1994**, *82*, 235–259. [CrossRef]
22. Aubert, J.; Brito, D.; Nataf, H.C.; Cardin, P.; Masson, J.P. A systematic experimental study of rapidly rotating spherical convection in water and liquid gallium. *Phys. Earth Planet. Inter.* **2001**, *128*, 51–74. [CrossRef]
23. Jones, C.A. Thermal and compositional convection in the outer core. *Core Dyn.* **2007**, *8*, 131–185.
24. Aurnou, J.M.; Horn, S.; Julien, K. Connections between nonrotating, slowly rotating, and rapidly rotating turbulent convection transport scalings. *Phys. Rev. Res.* **2020**, *2*, 043115. [CrossRef]
25. Olson, P. Laboratory experiments on the dynamics of the core. *Phys. Earth Planet. Inter.* **2011**, *187*, 139–156. [CrossRef]
26. Glatzmaier, G.A. Numerical simulations of stellar convective dynamos. I. the model and method. *J. Comput. Phys.* **1984**, *55*, 461–484. [CrossRef]
27. Christensen, U.; Aubert, J.; Cardin, P.; Dormy, E.; Gibbons, S.; Glatzmaier, G.; Grote, E.; Honkura, Y.; Jones, C.; Kono, M.; et al. A numerical dynamo benchmark. *Phys. Earth Planet. Inter.* **2001**, *128*, 25–34. [CrossRef]
28. Jones, C.; Boronski, P.; Brun, A.; Glatzmaier, G.; Gastine, T.; Miesch, M.; Wicht, J. Anelastic convection-driven dynamo benchmarks. *Icarus* **2011**, *216*, 120–135. [CrossRef]
29. Futterer, B.; Krebs, A.; Plesa, A.C.; Zaussinger, F.; Hollerbach, R.; Breuer, D.; Egbers, C. Sheet-like and plume-like thermal flow in a spherical convection experiment performed under microgravity. *J. Fluid Mech.* **2013**, *735*, 647–683. [CrossRef]
30. Zaussinger, F.; Haun, P.; Szabo, P.S.B.; Travnikov, V.; Al Kawwas, M.; Egbers, C. Rotating spherical gap convection in the GeoFlow International Space Station (ISS) experiment. *Phys. Rev. Fluids* **2020**, *5*, 063502. [CrossRef]
31. Travnikov, V.; Egbers, C. Numerical investigation of atmospherelike flows in a spherical geometry. *Phys. Rev. E* **2021**, *104*, 065110. [CrossRef]
32. Tuckerman, L.S. Transformations of matrices into banded form. *J. Comput. Phys.* **1989**, *84*, 360–376. [CrossRef]
33. Marti, P.; Calkins, M.; Julien, K. A computationally efficient spectral method for modeling core dynamics. *Geochem. Geophys. Geosystems* **2016**, *17*, 3031–3053. [CrossRef]
34. Kuang, W.; Bloxham, J. Numerical modeling of magnetohydrodynamic convection in a rapidly rotating spherical shell: Weak and strong field dynamo action. *J. Comput. Phys.* **1999**, *153*, 51–81. [CrossRef]

35. Hollerbach, R. A spectral solution of the magneto-convection equations in spherical geometry. *Int. J. Numer. Methods Fluids* **2000**, *32*, 773–797. [CrossRef]
36. Sprague, M.; Julien, K.; Knobloch, E.; Werne, J. Numerical simulation of an asymptotically reduced system for rotationally constrained convection. *J. Fluid Mech.* **2006**, *551*, 141–174. [CrossRef]
37. Stellmach, S.; Hansen, U. An efficient spectral method for the simulation of dynamos in Cartesian geometry and its implementation on massively parallel computers. *Geochem. Geophys. Geosyst.* **2008**, *9*.
38. Julien, K.; van Kan, A.; Miquel, B.; Knobloch, E.; Vasil, G. Rescaled Equations of Fluid Motion for Well-Conditioned Direct Numerical Simulations of Rapidly Rotating Convection. *arXiv* **2024**, arXiv:2410.02702.
39. van Kan, A.; Julien, K.; Miquel, B.; Knobloch, E. Bridging the Rossby number gap in rapidly rotating thermal convection. *J. Fluid Mech.* **2025**, *1010*, A42. [CrossRef]
40. García González, F.; Net Marcé, M.; Garcia-Archilla, B.; Sánchez Umbría, J. A comparison of high-order time integrators for thermal convection in rotating spherical shells. *J. Comput. Phys.* **2010**, *229*, 7997–8010. [CrossRef]
41. Garcia, F.; Sánchez, J.; Dormy, E.; Net, M. Oscillatory Convection in Rotating Spherical Shells: Low Prandtl Number and Non-Slip Boundary Conditions. *SIAM J. Appl. Dyn. Syst.* **2015**, *14*, 1787–1807. [CrossRef]
42. Feudel, F.; Bergemann, K.; Tuckerman, L.S.; Egbers, C.; Futterer, B.; Gellert, M.; Hollerbach, R. Convection patterns in a spherical fluid shell. *Phys. Rev. E* **2011**, *83*, 046304. [CrossRef]
43. Feudel, F.; Tuckerman, L.S.; Zaks, M.; Hollerbach, R. Hysteresis of dynamos in rotating spherical shell convection. *Phys. Rev. F* **2017**, *2*, 053902. [CrossRef]
44. Schaeffer, N. Efficient spherical harmonic transforms aimed at pseudospectral numerical simulations. *Geochem. Geophys. Geosyst.* **2013**, *14*, 751–758. [CrossRef]
45. Sánchez, J.; Net, M.; Garcıa-Archilla, B.; Simó, C. Newton–Krylov continuation of periodic orbits for Navier–Stokes flows. *J. Comput. Phys.* **2004**, *201*, 13–33. [CrossRef]
46. Garcia, F.; Sánchez, J.; Net, M. Antisymmetric Polar Modes of Thermal Convection in Rotating Spherical Fluid Shells at High Taylor Numbers. *Phys. Rev. Lett.* **2008**, *101*, 194501. [CrossRef]
47. Sánchez, J.; Garcia, F.; Net, M. Computation of azimuthal waves and their stability in thermal convection in rotating spherical shells with application to the study of a double-Hopf bifurcation. *Phys. Rev. E* **2013**, *87*, 033014. [CrossRef]
48. Tuckerman, L.S.; Langham, J.; Willis, A. Order-of-magnitude speedup for steady states and traveling waves via Stokes preconditioning in Channelflow and Openpipeflow. In *Computational Modelling of Bifurcations and Instabilities in Fluid Dynamics*; Springer: Berlin/Heidelberg, Germany, 2018; pp. 3–31.
49. Gastine, T.; Wicht, J.; Barik, A.; Duarte, L. Formulation of the (magneto)-hydrodynamics Problem. Available online: https://magic-sph.github.io/ (accessed on 30 May 2025).
50. Marques, F.; Mercader, I.; Batiste, O.; Lopez, J.M. Centrifugal effects in rotating convection: Axisymmetric states and three-dimensional instabilities. *J. Fluid Mech.* **2007**, *580*, 303–318. [CrossRef]
51. Satake, H.; Tagawa, T. Influence of Centrifugal Buoyancy in Thermal Convection within a Rotating Spherical Shell. *Symmetry* **2022**, *14*, 2021. [CrossRef]
52. Ishioka, K. A New Recurrence Formula for Efficient Computation of Spherical Harmonic Transform. *J. Meteorol. Soc. Jpn.* **2018**, *96*, 241–249. [CrossRef]
53. Schaeffer, N.; Jault, D.; Nataf, H.C.; Fournier, A. Turbulent geodynamo simulations: A leap towards Earth's core. *Geophys. J. Int.* **2017**, *211*, 1–29. [CrossRef]
54. Lago, R.; Gastine, T.; Dannert, T.; Rampp, M.; Wicht, J. MagIC v5. 10: A two-dimensional message-passing interface (MPI) distribution for pseudo-spectral magnetohydrodynamics simulations in spherical geometry. *Geosci. Model Dev.* **2021**, *14*, 7477–7495. [CrossRef]
55. Garcia, F.; Sánchez, J.; Net, M. Numerical simulations of thermal convection in rotating spherical shells under laboratory conditions. *Phys. Earth Planet. Inter.* **2014**, *230*, 28–44. [CrossRef]
56. Gottlieb, D.; Orszag, S.A. *Numerical Analysis of Spectral Methods: Theory and Applications*; SIAM: Philadelphia, PA, USA, 1977.
57. Saad, Y.; Schultz, M.H. GMRES: A generalized minimal residual algorithm for solving nonsymmetric linear systems. *SIAM J. Sci. Stat. Comput.* **1986**, *7*, 856–869. [CrossRef]
58. Tuckerman, L.S. Steady-state solving via Stokes preconditioning; Recursion relations for elliptic operators. In Proceedings of the 11th International Conference on Numerical Methods in Fluid Dynamics, Williamsburg, VA, USA, 27 June 1988; Springer: Berlin/Heidelberg, Germany, 1989; pp. 573–577.
59. Mamun, C.K.; Tuckerman, L.S. Asymmetry and Hopf bifurcation in spherical Couette flow. *Phys. Fluids* **1995**, *7*, 80–91. [CrossRef]
60. Bergeon, A.; Henry, D.; Benhadid, H.; Tuckerman, L.S. Marangoni convection in binary mixtures with Soret effect. *J. Fluid Mech.* **1998**, *375*, 143–177. [CrossRef]
61. Nore, C.; Tuckerman, L.S.; Daube, O.; Xin, S. The 1:2 mode interaction in exactly counter-rotating von Kármán swirling flow. *J. Fluid Mech.* **2003**, *477*, 51–88. [CrossRef]

62. Meca, E.; Mercader, I.; Batiste, O.; Ramírez-Piscina, L. Blue sky catastrophe in double-diffusive convection. *Phys. Rev. Lett.* **2004**, *92*, 234501. [CrossRef]
63. Batiste, O.; Knobloch, E.; Alonso, A.; Mercader, I. Spatially localized binary-fluid convection. *J. Fluid Mech.* **2006**, *560*, 149–158. [CrossRef]
64. Borońska, K.; Tuckerman, L.S. Extreme multiplicity in cylindrical Rayleigh-Bénard convection. II. Bifurcation diagram and symmetry classification. *Phys. Rev. E* **2010**, *81*, 036321. [CrossRef]
65. Mercader, I.; Batiste, O.; Alonso, A.; Knobloch, E. Convectons, anticonvectons and multiconvectons in binary fluid convection. *J. Fluid Mech.* **2011**, *667*, 586–606. [CrossRef]
66. Beaume, C.; Bergeon, A.; Kao, H.C.; Knobloch, E. Convectons in a rotating fluid layer. *J. Fluid Mech.* **2013**, *717*, 417–448. [CrossRef]
67. Torres, J.F.; Henry, D.; Komiya, A.; Maruyama, S. Bifurcation analysis of steady natural convection in a tilted cubical cavity with adiabatic sidewalls. *J. Fluid Mech.* **2014**, *756*, 650–688. [CrossRef]
68. Huepe, C.; Metens, S.; Dewel, G.; Borckmans, P.; Brachet, M.E. Decay rates in attractive Bose-Einstein condensates. *Phys. Rev. Lett.* **1999**, *82*, 1616. [CrossRef]
69. Huepe, C.; Tuckerman, L.S.; Métens, S.; Brachet, M.E. Stability and decay rates of nonisotropic attractive Bose-Einstein condensates. *Phys. Rev. A* **2003**, *68*, 023609. [CrossRef]
70. Tuckerman, L.S. Laplacian preconditioning for the inverse Arnoldi method. *Commun. Comput. Phys.* **2015**, *18*, 1336–1351. [CrossRef]
71. Lanczos, C. Trigonometric interpolation of empirical and analytical functions. *J. Math. Phys.* **1938**, *17*, 123–199. [CrossRef]
72. Trefethen, L.N. *Spectral Methods in MATLAB*; SIAM: Philadelphia, PA, USA, 2000.
73. Marcus, P.S. Simulation of Taylor-Couette flow. Part 1. Numerical methods and comparison with experiment. *J. Fluid Mech.* **1984**, *146*, 45–64. [CrossRef]
74. Duguet, Y.; Pringle, C.C.; Kerswell, R.R. Relative periodic orbits in transitional pipe flow. *Phys. Fluids* **2008**, *20*, 114102. [CrossRef]
75. Gibson, J.F.; Halcrow, J.; Cvitanović, P. Equilibrium and travelling-wave solutions of plane Couette flow. *J. Fluid Mech.* **2009**, *638*, 243–266. [CrossRef]
76. Zheng, Z.; Tuckerman, L.S.; Schneider, T.M. Natural convection in a vertical channel. Part 1. Wavenumber interaction and Eckhaus instability in a narrow domain. *J. Fluid Mech.* **2024**, *1000*, A28. [CrossRef]
77. Zheng, Z.; Tuckerman, L.S.; Schneider, T.M. Natural convection in a vertical channel. Part 2. Oblique solutions and global bifurcations in a spanwise-extended domain. *J. Fluid Mech.* **2024**, *1000*, A29. [CrossRef]
78. Zheng, Z.; Tuckerman, L.S.; Schneider, T.M. Natural convection in a vertical channel. Part 3. Bifurcations of many (additional) unstable equilibria and periodic orbits. *arXiv* **2025**, arXiv:2504.05524.
79. Schmiegel, A. Transition to Turbulence in Linearly Stable Shear Flows. Ph.D. Thesis, Philipps-Universität Marburg, Marburg, Germany, 1999. Available online: http://archiv.ub.uni-marburg.de/diss/z2000/0062/ (accessed on 30 May 2025).
80. Pringle, C.C.; Duguet, Y.; Kerswell, R.R. Highly symmetric travelling waves in pipe flow. *Phil. Trans. R. Soc. Lond. A* **2009**, *367*, 457–472. [CrossRef]
81. Borońska, K.; Tuckerman, L.S. Extreme multiplicity in cylindrical Rayleigh-Bénard convection. I. Time dependence and oscillations. *Phys. Rev. E* **2010**, *81*, 036320. [CrossRef] [PubMed]
82. Cvitanovic, P.; Eckhardt, B. Periodic orbit expansions for classical smooth flows. *J. Phys. A-Math.* **1991**, *24*, L237. [CrossRef]
83. Kawahara, G.; Uhlmann, M.; Van Veen, L. The significance of simple invariant solutions in turbulent flows. *Annu. Rev. Fluid Mech.* **2012**, *44*, 203–225. [CrossRef]
84. Lathrop, D.P.; Fineberg, J.; Swinney, H.L. Transition to shear-driven turbulence in Couette-Taylor flow. *Phys. Rev. A* **1992**, *46*, 6390. [CrossRef] [PubMed]
85. Dong, S. Direct numerical simulation of turbulent Taylor–Couette flow. *J. Fluid Mech.* **2007**, *587*, 373–393. [CrossRef]
86. Huisman, S.G.; Van Der Veen, R.C.; Sun, C.; Lohse, D. Multiple states in highly turbulent Taylor–Couette flow. *Nat. Commun.* **2014**, *5*, 3820. [CrossRef]
87. Grossmann, S.; Lohse, D.; Sun, C. High-Reynolds number Taylor-Couette turbulence. *Annu. Rev. Fluid Mech.* **2016**, *48*, 53–80. [CrossRef]
88. Eckhardt, B.; Doering, C.R.; Whitehead, J.P. Exact relations between Rayleigh-Bénard and rotating plane Couette flow in two dimensions. *J. Fluid Mech.* **2020**, *903*, R4. [CrossRef]

mathematics

MDPI

Article

Accurate Implementation of Rotating Magneto-Hydrodynamics in a Channel Geometry Using an Influence Matrix Method

Jean-Clément Ringenbach [1,*], Steven M. Tobias [2,*] and Tobias M. Schneider [1,*]

1 Emergent Complexity in Physical Systems, École Polytechnique Fédérale de Lausanne, 1015 Lausanne, Switzerland
2 School of Physics & Astronomy, University of Edinburgh, James Clerk Maxwell Building, Edinburgh EH9 3FD, UK
* Correspondence: jean-clement.ringenbach@epfl.ch (J.-C.R.); s.tobias@ed.ac.uk (S.M.T.); tobias.schneider@epfl.ch (T.M.S.)

Abstract: We numerically study wall-bounded convectively driven magneto-hydrodynamic (MHD) flows subject to rotation in a Cartesian periodic channel. For the accurate treatment of the rotating MHD equations, we develop a pseudo-spectral simulation code with accurate treatment of boundary conditions for both velocity and magnetic fields. The solenoidal condition on the magnetic field is enforced by the addition of a fictitious magnetic pressure. This allows us to employ an influence matrix method with tau correction for the treatment of velocity and magnetic fields subject to Robin boundary conditions at the confining walls. We validate the developed method for the specific case of no slip velocity and perfectly conducting magnetic boundary conditions. The validation includes the accurate reproduction of linear stability thresholds and of turbulent statistics. The code shows favorable parallel scaling properties.

Keywords: MHD; influence matrix; DNS; dynamo; ChannelFlow

MSC: 76W05; 76M22

1. Introduction

Many phenomena in geophysical and astrophysical contexts involve the interaction of turbulent, conducting fluid flows with magnetic fields. A prime example is the magnetic fields of stars and planetary objects, where convectively driven flows of conducting fluids, subject to the rotation of their astrophysical bodies, are believed to generate self-sustained dynamos. This is the case for stars [1], rocky planets [2], gas giants and moons [3].

Such phenomena including self-sustained dynamos often occur in the highly nonlinear turbulent regime; therefore, characterizing and describing the physical mechanism in this regime is aided by augmenting linear and weakly nonlinear approaches with a fully nonlinear description. A fully nonlinear description, in this context, may refer either to an accurate direct numerical simulation or the identification and tracking of non-chaotic so-called invariant solutions, including equilibria and periodic orbits. The latter approach, in the context of a dynamical systems description of the flow, carries the promise that tracking invariant solutions in parameter space can provide insights into the parameter dependence of various phenomena [4]. This has been notably accomplished in turbulent, non-magnetic shear flows [5,6], and some invariant solutions have also been found in spherical shell dynamo solutions [7,8].

While studying convection in an astrophysical context suggests the consideration of spherical shell domains, many important phenomena only involve scales that are small compared with the radius of curvature of such a shell, so that they can also be studied in rotating plane layer models within the f-plane approximation. In particular, the increase in heat transport due to dynamo effect, which is often discussed in relation to a possible explanation for the existence of self-sustained dynamos in rapidly rotating systems, is also observed within Cartesian domains [9,10].

We, consequently, also consider the well-established model of a doubly periodic box of a conducting convective fluid layer at a prescribed latitude, as illustrated in Figure 1, representing a slab of a convective region where curvature effects are neglected. The flow is convectively driven, subject to rotation and potentially imposed external magnetic fields. The imposed fields may represent the large-scale fields surrounding the portion of the astrophysical object considered—such as a stellar convection zone or convective planetary interiors.

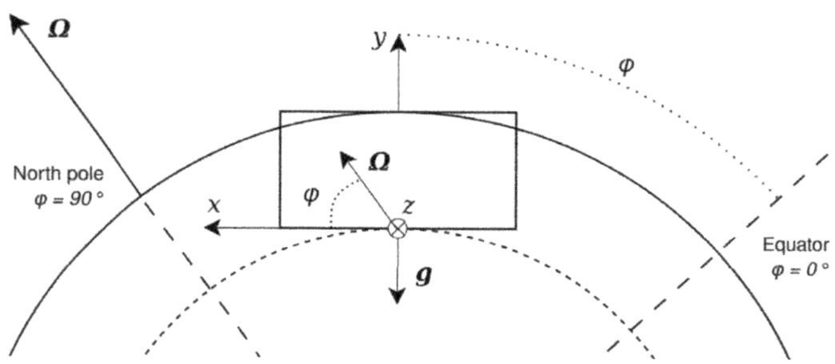

Figure 1. Interpretation of the channel geometry as the portion of an astrophysical body's convective rotating flow chosen at a specific latitude angle ϕ. At the north pole, the rotation vector $\boldsymbol{\Omega}$ is vertical, and it is horizontal at the equator.

The discussed flow problem has been extensively studied using linear stability analysis [11], investigating the destabilizing and stabilizing effects of rotation and imposed fields on thermally driven convection, and using nonlinear simulations [12,13]. The widely accepted hypothesis is that magnetic fields enhance turbulent convection, leading to stronger field generation until saturation and increased heat transport. This is analogous to the fact that, in the linear regime, the interaction between imposed magnetic fields and rotation can induce instabilities that enable convection, which would not occur in the non-rotating non-magnetic case [14].

To study such flow problems using fully nonlinear approaches, and in order to specifically lay the foundation for a dynamical systems description based on exact invariant solutions, we present a highly accurate numerical solver for the MHD equations. To benefit from the superior approximation properties of a spectral discretization, we consider the geometry of a doubly periodic box, which allows us to study the coupling mechanisms between convectively driving, magnetic fields and rotation that control MHD flows in astrophysical contexts.

Here, we specifically present a high-accuracy pseudo-spectral MHD scheme that precisely handles boundary conditions at confining walls using the influence matrix method [15]. We introduce a fictitious magnetic pressure in the induction equation and apply an extended influence matrix method with Tau correction and Robin boundary conditions to handle both the velocity and magnetic fields, ensuring incompressibility and magnetic solenoidality at machine-precision accuracy. These methods are implemented in a parallel fashion on top of the existing C++ ChannelFlow 2.0 code [16,17]. Our code demonstrates good parallel scaling and is validated against results from the literature. With its accuracy, parallel scaling and straightforward interfacing with Newton-based shooting methods, we expect the code to allow us to efficiently compute and track unstable equilibrium and periodic orbit solutions of the nonlinear MHD equations.

2. Materials and Methods

2.1. Equations and Control Parameters

We consider a channel, periodic in the streamwise (x) and spanwise (z) directions and wall-bounded in the vertical (y) direction.

Specifically, we consider a spatial domain $\mathcal{D} = [0, L_x) \times [a, b] \times [0, L_z) \subset \mathbb{R}^3$ depicted in Figure 2. The velocity, magnetic, temperature and pressure fields

$$\begin{aligned} \boldsymbol{U}(\boldsymbol{x},t) &: \mathcal{D} \times \mathbb{R}^+ \to \mathbb{R}^3, & \boldsymbol{B}(\boldsymbol{x},t) &: \mathcal{D} \times \mathbb{R}^+ \to \mathbb{R}^3, \\ T(\boldsymbol{x},t) &: \mathcal{D} \times \mathbb{R}^+ \to \mathbb{R}, & P(\boldsymbol{x},t) &: \mathcal{D} \times \mathbb{R}^+ \to \mathbb{R}, \end{aligned}$$

are governed by the standard magnetohydrodynamics (MHD) equations for a conducting, convectively driven incompressible Newtonian fluid subject to rotation

$$\nabla \cdot \boldsymbol{U} = 0, \tag{1}$$

$$\nabla \cdot \boldsymbol{B} = 0, \tag{2}$$

$$\frac{\partial \boldsymbol{U}}{\partial t} + \boldsymbol{U} \cdot \nabla \boldsymbol{U} + \Omega \hat{e}_\Omega \times \boldsymbol{U} = -\nabla P + \lambda(\nabla \times \boldsymbol{B}) \times \boldsymbol{B} + \nu \nabla^2 \boldsymbol{U} + \left(\beta + T_{ref} - T\right)\hat{e}_g, \tag{3}$$

$$\frac{\partial \boldsymbol{B}}{\partial t} = \nabla \times (\boldsymbol{U} \times \boldsymbol{B}) + \eta \nabla^2 \boldsymbol{B}, \tag{4}$$

$$\frac{\partial T}{\partial t} + \boldsymbol{U} \cdot \nabla T = \kappa \nabla^2 T. \tag{5}$$

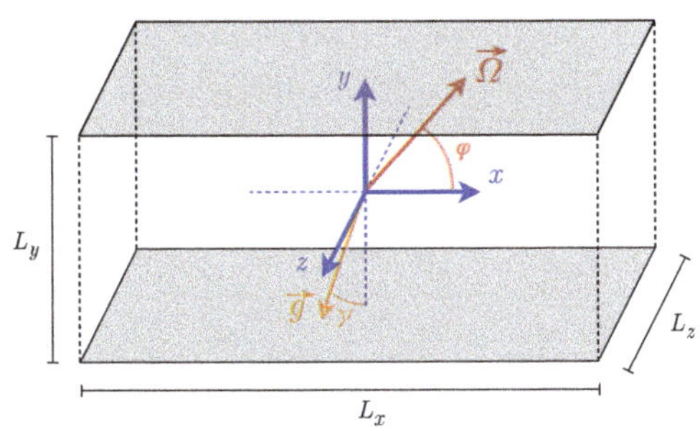

Figure 2. Domain-considered, doubly periodic in the two horizontal directions and wall-bounded in the vertical one. The streamwise direction (x) has an extent of L_x, the spanwise direction (z) has an extent of L_z and the vertical direction (y) has an extent of $L_y = b - a$.

Here, we provide the nondimensional formulation, with (1) and (2) indicating constraints enforcing the incompressibility of the fluid, and the absence of magnetic monopoles, also called the solenoidal condition. Equation (3) describes momentum balance incorporating coupling to temperature under the Boussinesq approximation, the Coriolis force and the Lorentz force yielding the coupling to the magnetic field. The induction in Equation (4) captures the diffusion and generation of magnetic fields through charges advected by the fluid flow. It is derived from the Maxwell equations neglecting relativistic terms and assuming Ohm's law $\vec{j} = \sigma(\boldsymbol{E} + \boldsymbol{U} \times \boldsymbol{B})$, where σ is the electrical conductivity [18]. The MHD equations are completed by the temperature advection and diffusion in (5). The parameters

$\Omega, \lambda, \nu, \beta, \eta$ and κ indicate rotation strength, magnetic coupling, momentum diffusivity, hydrostatic pressure, magnetic diffusivity and thermal diffusivity. The unit vectors are

$$\hat{e}_g(\gamma_x) = -\sin(\gamma_x)\hat{e}_x - \cos(\gamma_x)\hat{e}_y, \qquad \hat{e}_\Omega(\phi) = \cos(\phi)\hat{e}_x + \sin(\phi)\hat{e}_y, \tag{6}$$

with γ_x and ϕ indicating the angles in the $(\hat{e}_x, \hat{e}_y)$ plane between $\hat{e}_y$ and gravity, and between $\hat{e}_x$ and the rotation vector, as shown in Figure 2. In an astrophysical context, the former accounts for gravity inclination due, for instance, to the ellipsoidity of the body, and the latter represents the latitude at which the system is defined on (see Figure 1).

The governing MHD equations have been rendered nondimensional using the following length, time, temperature, mass and magnetic field scales:

$$L^* = H_0^*, \qquad t^* = H_0^*/U_0^*, \qquad T^* = \Delta T_0^*, \qquad M^* = \rho_0^* H_0^{*3}, \qquad B^* = B_0^*, \tag{7}$$

where the star * denotes dimensional quantities. The length scale H_0^* is the vertical extent of the domain. For the time scale, we choose common free-fall units with the free-fall velocity U_0^* (see below). We allow the scale for the magnetic field strength to be chosen dependent on the specific MHD problem considered. If an external magnetic field is imposed, this imposed field provides the natural magnetic scale [19,20]. Without an imposed external field, a velocity-based scale such as one based on the Alfvén velocity $U_0^* = B_0^*/\sqrt{\rho_0^*\mu_0^*}$ is more appropriate [9,21]. This is the difference between dynamo calculations and magneto-convection calculations.

$$U_0^* = \sqrt{g^*\alpha^*\Delta T_0^* H_0^*}, \qquad B_0^* = U_0^*\sqrt{\rho_0^*\mu_0^*} \;\text{ or }\; B_0^*. \tag{8}$$

The choice of scales (7)–(8) yields the classical dimensionless numbers

$$\mathrm{Ra} = \frac{g^*\alpha^*\Delta T_0^* H_0^{*3}}{\kappa^*\nu^*}, \quad \mathrm{Ek} = \frac{\nu^*}{\Omega^* H_0^{*2}}, \quad \mathrm{Pr} = \frac{\nu^*}{\kappa^*}, \quad \mathrm{Pr}_m = \frac{\nu^*}{\eta^*}, \quad \mathrm{Q} = \frac{B_0^{*2} H_0^{*2}}{\rho_0^*\mu_0^*\nu^*\eta^*}, \tag{9}$$

with Ra the Rayleigh number, Ek the Ekman number, Pr the Prandtl number, Pr_m the magnetic Prandtl number and Q the Chandrasekhar number. The control parameters of the Equations (3)–(5) are expressed in terms of classical dimensionless numbers as

$$\Omega = \frac{2}{\mathrm{Ek}}\sqrt{\frac{\mathrm{Pr}}{\mathrm{Ra}}}, \qquad \lambda = \frac{\mathrm{Q\,Pr}}{\mathrm{Ra\,Pr}_m}, \qquad \nu = \sqrt{\frac{\mathrm{Pr}}{\mathrm{Ra}}}, \tag{10}$$

$$\beta = \frac{1}{\alpha^*\Delta T_0^*}, \qquad \eta = \frac{1}{\mathrm{Pr}_m}\sqrt{\frac{\mathrm{Pr}}{\mathrm{Ra}}}, \qquad \kappa = \frac{1}{\sqrt{\mathrm{Pr\,Ra}}}. \tag{11}$$

For the periodic domain, there are in total 10 control parameters, including the 2 angles (6) the 6 nondimensional parameters (10) and the domain sizes L_x, L_z. As a note, when performing dynamo calculations, the magnetic scale (8) is velocity-based, which consequently removes one control parameter as

$$B_0^* = U_0^*\sqrt{\rho_0^*\mu_0^*} \qquad \Longrightarrow \qquad \mathrm{Q} = \frac{\mathrm{Ra\,Pr}_m}{\mathrm{Pr}} \qquad \Longrightarrow \qquad \lambda = 1. \tag{12}$$

Regarding boundary conditions (BCs), the velocity field is subject to no-slip no-penetrating BCs, the magnetic field is subject to perfectly conducting BCs and the temperature field is isothermal on the boundary

$$\boldsymbol{U}(\boldsymbol{x},t)\Big|_{y=a,b} = (U_{a,b}, 0, W_{a,b}), \qquad T(\boldsymbol{x},t)\Big|_{y=a,b} = T_{a,b},$$
$$\boldsymbol{B}(\boldsymbol{x},t)\cdot\hat{e}_y\Big|_{y=a,b} = B_v, \qquad \partial_y \boldsymbol{B}(\boldsymbol{x},t)\cdot\hat{e}_{x,z}\Big|_{y=a,b} = 0, \tag{13}$$

where $U_{a,b}, W_{a,b}$ are the top and bottom horizontal wall velocities, B_v is the vertical component of the imposed magnetic field and $T_{a,b}$ are the top and bottom wall temperatures. The two horizontal directions are periodic, so

$$F(\boldsymbol{x} + nL_x\hat{e}_x + mL_z\hat{e}_z, t) = F(\boldsymbol{x}, t), \ \forall n, m \in \mathbb{Z}, \tag{14}$$

with F being associated to each component of the various fields. The pressure is constrained as have a zero mean.

2.2. Perturbative Formulation

The velocity, magnetic, temperature and pressure gradient fields are decomposed into a stationary vertical-dependent base state and a deviation from this base state. The base states do not need to be solutions of the governing equations. They must, however, satisfy the generally inhomogeneous boundary conditions, and the vector-valued base states of the velocity and magnetic fields need to be divergence-free. In the following, deviation fields are denoted in lowercase and total fields in uppercase. Base states are indicated in uppercase with a zero index. The decompositions are formally written as

$$\boldsymbol{U}(\boldsymbol{x},t) = U_0(y)\hat{e}_x + V_0\hat{e}_y + W_0(y)\hat{e}_z + \boldsymbol{u}(\boldsymbol{x},t), \tag{15}$$
$$\boldsymbol{B}(\boldsymbol{x},t) = B_{0,x}(y)\hat{e}_x + B_{0,y}\hat{e}_y + B_{0,z}(y)\hat{e}_z + \boldsymbol{b}(\boldsymbol{x},t), \tag{16}$$
$$T(\boldsymbol{x},t) = T_0(y) + \theta(\boldsymbol{x},t), \tag{17}$$
$$\nabla P(\boldsymbol{x},t) = \Pi_x(y)\hat{e}_x + \Pi_y(y)\hat{e}_y + \Pi_z(y)\hat{e}_z + \nabla p(\boldsymbol{x},t). \tag{18}$$

It is relevant in magnetoconvection to consider a constant magnetic field imposed on the system. In this case, we choose the magnetic scale to be the norm of the imposed field. Consequently, the dimensionless form of the imposed vector field is a unit vector that can be parametrized as

$$\boldsymbol{B}_0 = \sin\vartheta \sin\varphi\, \hat{e}_x + \cos\vartheta\, \hat{e}_y + \sin\vartheta\cos\varphi\, \hat{e}_z, \tag{19}$$

with $\vartheta \in [0, \pi]$ and $\varphi \in [0, 2\pi)$. The boundary conditions of the perturbative formulation of the equations are then

$$\boldsymbol{U}_0(y)\Big|_{y=a,b} = (U_{a,b}, 0, W_{a,b}), \qquad \boldsymbol{u}(\boldsymbol{x},t)\Big|_{y=a,b} = \boldsymbol{0}, \tag{20}$$
$$\boldsymbol{B}_0(y)\cdot\hat{e}_y\Big|_{y=a,b} = B_v, \qquad \boldsymbol{b}(y)\cdot\hat{e}_y\Big|_{y=a,b} = 0, \tag{21}$$
$$\partial_y \boldsymbol{B}_0(\boldsymbol{x},t)\cdot\hat{e}_{x,z}\Big|_{y=a,b} = 0, \qquad \partial_y \boldsymbol{b}(\boldsymbol{x},t)\cdot\hat{e}_{x,z}\Big|_{y=a,b} = 0, \tag{22}$$
$$T_0(y)\Big|_{y=a,b} = T_{a,b}, \qquad \theta(\boldsymbol{x},t)\Big|_{y=a,b} = 0. \tag{23}$$

The governing equations for the perturbations are obtained by inserting the base states into Equations (1)–(5), yielding

$$\nabla\cdot\boldsymbol{u} = 0, \tag{24}$$
$$\nabla\cdot\boldsymbol{b} = 0, \tag{25}$$

$$\frac{\partial \boldsymbol{u}}{\partial t} + \boldsymbol{U} \cdot \nabla \boldsymbol{U} + \Omega \hat{e}_\Omega \times \boldsymbol{U} - \lambda(\nabla \times \boldsymbol{B}) \times \boldsymbol{B} = -\nabla p + \nu \nabla^2 \boldsymbol{u} - \theta \hat{e}_g$$
$$+ \left[-\Pi_x(y) + \nu \frac{\partial^2 U_0(y)}{\partial y^2} - \beta \sin \gamma_x + \sin \gamma_x \left(T_0(y) - T_{ref} \right) \right] \hat{e}_x$$
$$+ \left[-\Pi_y(y) - \beta \cos \gamma_x + \cos \gamma_x \left(T_0(y) - T_{ref} \right) \right] \hat{e}_y + \left[-\Pi_z(y) + \nu \frac{\partial^2 W_0(y)}{\partial y^2} \right] \hat{e}_z, \quad (26)$$

$$\frac{\partial \boldsymbol{b}}{\partial t} - \nabla \times (\boldsymbol{U} \times \boldsymbol{B}) = \eta \nabla^2 \boldsymbol{b} + \left[\eta \frac{\partial^2 B_{0,x}(y)}{\partial y^2} \right] \hat{e}_x + \left[\eta \frac{\partial^2 B_{0,z}(y)}{\partial y^2} \right] \hat{e}_z, \quad (27)$$
$$\frac{\partial \theta}{\partial t} + \boldsymbol{U} \cdot \nabla T = \kappa \nabla^2 \theta + \left[\kappa \frac{\partial^2 T_0(y)}{\partial y^2} \right]. \quad (28)$$

2.3. Enforcing Magnetic Solenoidality Through a Fictitious Pressure

The divergence-free constraints for both the velocity and magnetic fields must be satisfied at all times. The momentum equation introduces divergence, which is readily observed when taking the divergence of (3):

$$\frac{\partial}{\partial t}(\nabla \cdot \boldsymbol{U}) = \nu \nabla^2 (\nabla \cdot \boldsymbol{U}) - \nabla^2 P - \nabla(\boldsymbol{U} \cdot \nabla) \cdot \boldsymbol{U} + \Omega \hat{e}_\Omega \cdot \nabla \times \boldsymbol{U}$$
$$- \lambda \left(\boldsymbol{B} \cdot \nabla^2 \boldsymbol{B} + (\nabla \times \boldsymbol{B})^2 \right) - \nabla T \cdot \hat{e}_g. \quad (29)$$

Pressure acts as a Lagrange multiplier in the momentum equation, enforcing the incompressibility constraint. While numerically handling pressure as a Lagrange multiplier for incompressibility is a challenging problem, precise methods have been developed to address it, as we will discuss below. In contrast, the induction equation does not generate divergence of the magnetic field, as

$$\frac{\partial}{\partial t}(\nabla \cdot \boldsymbol{B}) = \eta \nabla^2 (\nabla \cdot \boldsymbol{B}). \quad (30)$$

The vanishing divergence of the initial field is, therefore, propagated in time and, thus, ensuring a divergence-free initial magnetic field should be sufficient to satisfy the solenoidality of the magnetic field. However, in a numerical discretization with the finite resolution of double precision arithmetic, a straightforward implementation of the induction equation would generate a small divergence in the magnetic field. Over time, this divergence would accumulate, ultimately leading to nonphysical fields. To address this issue, we introduce a fictitious pressure $p_b(\boldsymbol{x}, t) : \mathcal{D} \times \mathbb{R}^+ \to \mathbb{R}$ into the induction equation, which acts as a Lagrange multiplier enforcing the solenoidal constraint [22]. Analytically, this pressure is obviously constant and can be chosen as zero due to gauge invariance. With this addition, the perturbative induction Equation (27) is modified as follows:

$$\frac{\partial \boldsymbol{b}}{\partial t} - \nabla \times (\boldsymbol{U} \times \boldsymbol{B}) = -\nabla p_b + \eta \nabla^2 \boldsymbol{b} + \left[\eta \frac{\partial^2 B_{0,x}(y)}{\partial y^2} \right] \hat{e}_x + \left[\eta \frac{\partial^2 B_{0,z}(y)}{\partial y^2} \right] \hat{e}_z. \quad (31)$$

2.4. Spatial and Temporal Discretization

Because of the double periodicity and wall-bounded nature of our problem, we choose a spectral discretization using Fourier × Chebyshev × Fourier in the $\hat{e}_x, \hat{e}_y$ and $\hat{e}_z$ directions. The use of Chebyshev polynomials in the vertical direction makes the collocation points denser near the boundaries, which allows a fine resolution of boundary layer phenomena. Also, spectral transforms in Chebyshev polynomials can make use of fast Fourier transform

(FFT) algorithms, which are computationally efficient. The domain is now considered in a discretized version $\mathcal{D}^d$ defined as

$$\mathcal{D}^d = \left\{ \boldsymbol{x}^d = (x_{n_x}, y_{n_y}, z_{n_z}) : x_n = \frac{nL_x}{N_x},\ y_n = \cos\left(\frac{n\pi}{N_y - 1}\right),\ z_n = \frac{nL_z}{N_z} \right\}, \tag{32}$$

with $N_{x,y,z}$ the number of collocation points in the corresponding direction and $n_{x,y,z} \in [0, N_{x,y,z} - 1] \subset \mathbb{N}$. The temperature field as well as velocity and magnetic field components taken at discrete time-steps n_t are expressed as $f^{n_t}(\boldsymbol{x^d}) : \mathcal{D}^d \to \mathbb{R}$. The forward and backward Fourier–Chebyshev spectral transformations $\widetilde{f}(\boldsymbol{k}) = \mathcal{F}(f(\boldsymbol{x}^d))(\boldsymbol{k})$ and $f(\boldsymbol{x}^d) = \mathcal{F}^{-1}(\widetilde{f}(\boldsymbol{k}))(\boldsymbol{x}^d)$ are defined as

$$\widetilde{f}(\boldsymbol{k}) = \frac{p_{n_y}}{N_x N_y N_z} \sum_{n_x=0}^{N_x-1} \sum_{n_y=0}^{N_y-1} \sum_{n_z=0}^{N_z-1} f(\boldsymbol{x}^d)\, T_{k_y}(y_{n_y}) \exp\left(-2\pi i \left(\frac{k_x x_{n_x}}{L_x} + \frac{k_z z_{n_z}}{L_z}\right)\right), \tag{33}$$

$$f(\boldsymbol{x}^d) = \sum_{k_x=1-N_x/2}^{N_x/2} \sum_{k_y=0}^{N_y-1} \sum_{k_z=1-N_z/2}^{N_z/2} \widetilde{f}(\boldsymbol{k}) T_{k_y}(y_{n_y}) \exp\left(2\pi i \left(\frac{k_x x_{n_x}}{L_x} + \frac{k_z z_{n_z}}{L_z}\right)\right), \tag{34}$$

$$\boldsymbol{k} = (k_x, k_y, k_z) : k_{x,z} \in \left[1 - \frac{N_{x,z}}{2}, \frac{N_{x,z}}{2}\right] \subset \mathbb{Z},\ k_y \in [0, N_y - 1] \subset \mathbb{N}, \tag{35}$$

where $p_m = 2 - \delta_{0m}$ is a Chebyshev normalization term and $T_m(y)$ is the mth Chebyshev polynomial of the first kind rescaled on $[a, b] \subset \mathbb{R}$.

For time-stepping the equations, we must decide which terms to treat explicitly or implicitly. Nonlinear terms must be handled explicitly, while linear terms are preferably treated implicitly for stability reasons, though they can also be handled explicitly. We refer by a slight misuse of language to the implicitly-treated terms as linear operators $\mathcal{L}_f$ and to the explicitly-treated ones as nonlinear operators $\mathcal{N}_f$. In this notation, f is associated to the governing equation of the deviation fields $\boldsymbol{u}, \boldsymbol{b}$ and θ. The Equations (26), (28) and (31) are transformed into spectral space, with the explicitly and implicitly-treated terms grouped together as

$$\frac{\partial \widetilde{\boldsymbol{u}}}{\partial t} = \widetilde{\boldsymbol{\mathcal{L}}}_u(\widetilde{\boldsymbol{u}}, \widetilde{p}) - \widetilde{\boldsymbol{\mathcal{N}}}_u\left(\widetilde{\boldsymbol{U}}, \widetilde{\boldsymbol{B}}, \widetilde{\theta}\right), \tag{36}$$

$$\frac{\partial \widetilde{\boldsymbol{b}}}{\partial t} = \widetilde{\boldsymbol{\mathcal{L}}}_b\left(\widetilde{\boldsymbol{b}}, \widetilde{p}_b\right) - \widetilde{\boldsymbol{\mathcal{N}}}_b\left(\widetilde{\boldsymbol{U}}, \widetilde{\boldsymbol{B}}\right), \tag{37}$$

$$\frac{\partial \widetilde{\theta}}{\partial t} = \widetilde{\mathcal{L}}_\theta\left(\widetilde{\theta}\right) - \widetilde{\boldsymbol{\mathcal{N}}}_\theta\left(\widetilde{\boldsymbol{U}}, T\right). \tag{38}$$

The linear operators are defined as

$$\widetilde{\boldsymbol{\mathcal{L}}}_u(\widetilde{\boldsymbol{u}}, \widetilde{p}) = \nu \widetilde{\nabla}^2 \widetilde{\boldsymbol{u}} - \widetilde{\nabla} \widetilde{p}, \qquad \widetilde{\boldsymbol{\mathcal{L}}}_b\left(\widetilde{\boldsymbol{b}}, \widetilde{p}_b\right) = \eta \widetilde{\nabla}^2 \widetilde{\boldsymbol{b}} - \widetilde{\nabla} \widetilde{p}_b, \qquad \widetilde{\mathcal{L}}_\theta\left(\widetilde{\theta}\right) = \kappa \widetilde{\nabla}^2 \widetilde{\theta}, \tag{39}$$

and the nonlinear ones as

$$\begin{aligned} \widetilde{\boldsymbol{\mathcal{N}}}_u\left(\widetilde{\boldsymbol{U}}, \widetilde{\boldsymbol{B}}, \widetilde{\theta}\right) &= \mathcal{F}\left(\mathcal{F}^{-1}\left(\widetilde{\boldsymbol{U}}\right) \cdot \mathcal{F}^{-1}\left(\widetilde{\nabla} \widetilde{\boldsymbol{U}}\right)\right) + \Omega \hat{e}_\Omega \times \widetilde{\boldsymbol{U}} \\ &\quad - \lambda \mathcal{F}\left(\mathcal{F}^{-1}\left(\widetilde{\nabla} \times \widetilde{\boldsymbol{B}}\right) \times \mathcal{F}^{-1}\left(\widetilde{\boldsymbol{B}}\right)\right) + \widetilde{\theta} \hat{e}_g + \widetilde{\boldsymbol{C}}_u, \end{aligned} \tag{40}$$

$$\widetilde{\boldsymbol{\mathcal{N}}}_b\left(\widetilde{\boldsymbol{U}}, \widetilde{\boldsymbol{B}}\right) = \widetilde{\nabla} \times \mathcal{F}\left(\mathcal{F}^{-1}\left(\widetilde{\boldsymbol{U}}\right) \times \mathcal{F}^{-1}\left(\widetilde{\boldsymbol{B}}\right)\right) + \widetilde{\boldsymbol{C}}_b \tag{41}$$

$$\widetilde{\boldsymbol{\mathcal{N}}}_\theta\left(\widetilde{\boldsymbol{U}}, \widetilde{T}\right) = \mathcal{F}\left(\mathcal{F}^{-1}\left(\widetilde{\boldsymbol{U}}\right) \cdot \mathcal{F}^{-1}\left(\widetilde{\nabla} \widetilde{T}\right)\right) + \widetilde{C}_\theta, \tag{42}$$

where $\widetilde{\nabla}, \widetilde{\nabla}\cdot, \widetilde{\nabla}\times$ and $\widetilde{\nabla}^2 \equiv \widetilde{\nabla} \cdot \widetilde{\nabla}$ are the spectral gradient, divergence, curl and Laplacian operators, and $\widetilde{C}_u, \widetilde{C}_b$ and $\widetilde{C}_\theta$ are constants representing the Fourier–Chebyshev transform of the bracket terms in Equations (26), (28) and (31). The rotation and temperature coupling terms are treated explicitly, so that the structure of the time-stepping schemes used follows an unified notation [23]. The time-stepping momentum equation is

$$\nu \frac{\partial^2 \hat{\boldsymbol{u}}^{n+1}}{\partial y^2} - D_\nu \hat{\boldsymbol{u}}^{n+1} - \hat{\nabla} \hat{p}^{n+1} = \hat{\boldsymbol{R}}_u \left(\hat{\boldsymbol{u}}, \hat{\boldsymbol{b}}, \hat{\theta}\right)^{n,n-1,\ldots}, \quad D_\nu = \frac{\chi}{\Delta t} + 4\pi^2 \nu \left(\frac{k_x^2}{L_x^2} + \frac{k_z^2}{L_z^2}\right), \tag{43}$$

where $\hat{\boldsymbol{R}}_u \left(\hat{\boldsymbol{u}}, \hat{\boldsymbol{b}}, \hat{\theta}\right)^{n,n-1,\ldots}$ refers to explicitly-treated terms of the momentum equation together with their time-step dependence, and χ is a time-stepping scheme-dependent constant. The time-stepping schemes considered are the ones presented in [23]. As a note, the fields $\hat{u}, \hat{b}, \hat{\theta}, \hat{p}$ and $\hat{p}_b$ are functions of y only. Similar unified notation is also applicable to the induction Equation (37) and to the temperature Equation (38) yielding the time-stepping induction and time-stepping temperature equations

$$\eta \frac{\partial^2 \hat{\boldsymbol{b}}^{n+1}}{\partial y^2} - D_\eta \hat{\boldsymbol{b}}^{n+1} - \hat{\nabla} \hat{p}_b^{n+1} = \hat{\boldsymbol{R}}_b \left(\hat{\boldsymbol{u}}, \hat{\boldsymbol{b}}\right)^{n,n-1,\ldots}, \quad D_\eta = \frac{\chi}{\Delta t} + 4\pi^2 \eta \left(\frac{k_x^2}{L_x^2} + \frac{k_z^2}{L_z^2}\right), \tag{44}$$

$$\kappa \frac{\partial^2 \hat{\theta}^{n+1}}{\partial y^2} - D_\kappa \hat{\theta}^{n+1} = \hat{R}_\theta \left(\hat{\boldsymbol{u}}, \hat{\theta}\right)^{n,n-1,\ldots}, \quad D_\kappa = \frac{\chi}{\Delta t} + 4\pi^2 \kappa \left(\frac{k_x^2}{L_x^2} + \frac{k_z^2}{L_z^2}\right). \tag{45}$$

The addition of fictitious pressure in (31) has the technical advantage of making the time-stepping induction Equation (44) identical to the time-stepping momentum Equation (43) substituting η for ν, $\boldsymbol{b}$ for $\boldsymbol{u}$, p_b for p and swapping "forcing" terms $\hat{R}$. The following section is dedicated to the presentation of an influence matrix method with tau correction used to solve both Equations (43) and (44) enforcing the divergence-free conditions, subject to the BCs (20)–(23).

2.5. Influence Matrix with Robin Boundary Conditions

With the addition of fictitious magnetic pressure, the numerical problems of time-stepping momentum (43) and time-stepping induction Equation (44) are identical. The accurate treatment of the former is achieved using a tau correction and influence matrix method [15]. If the magnetic field had the same BCs as the velocity field, the same method could be used. However, magnetic fields are subject to BCs involving a mix of Dirichlet and Neumann BCs on their different components. Consequently, we present a generalized tau correction and influence matrix method for more general BCs.

2.5.1. Tau Correction Method

The fields present in the time-stepping momentum (43) and induction (44) equations are expressed as expansions on a finite Chebyshev basis. The function space spanned by the finite Chebyshev basis is not guaranteed to contain a solution satisfying the equations together with the associated BCs. The tau method enables the elimination of solution components that do not lie within the span of the expansion basis [24]. The time-stepping momentum and induction equations are augmented by adding monomials from the Chebyshev expansion basis, each weighted by a prefactor known as a tau constant or tau correction. The number of added monomials must match the number of boundary conditions and consists of the highest-degree elements of the Chebyshev expansion basis. The time-stepping momentum and induction equations each have two BCs, so we need to add two tau corrections into each equation. The tau corrections quantify the portion of the solution that is not captured due to discretization on a finite Chebyshev basis, and they are expected to decrease exponentially as the Chebyshev expansion basis size is increased.

2.5.2. Extended Influence Matrix Method

Solving the time-stepping momentum Equation (43) requires finding velocity and pressure fields that satisfy the equation, along with velocity BCs, under the divergence-free constraint. Similarly, solving the time-stepping induction Equation (44) requires finding magnetic and fictitious pressure fields that satisfy the equation, along with magnetic BCs, under the divergence-free constraint. In both cases, the difficulty arises from the absence of BCs for the pressure and fictitious pressure fields. For Dirichlet BCs, the influence matrix introduced by [15] is a precise and efficient method to solve (43). It uses the linear superposition of specific velocity and pressure field decompositions to derive BCs for pressure that are equivalent to enforcing the incompressibility condition.

Since magnetic fields have mixed BCs for their different components, the original influence matrix methodology does not transfer directly. Furthermore, other types of BCs, such as free-slip, open channel, or finite-slip BCs, are also relevant for velocity fields [25,26], in addition to Dirichlet conditions. We, thus, present an extension of the influence matrix method, with the tau correction inherently applied, that is applicable to Robin BCs. These BCs may be directly relevant for certain flow situations, and they include both Dirichlet and Neumann conditions as special cases. Since the numerical problems for the time-stepping momentum and induction equations are identical, we will describe the method for the time-stepping momentum equation here. However, exactly the same treatment applies to the time-stepping of the induction equation.

Robin BCs for a field $f : \mathcal{D} \to \mathbb{R}$ are generically expressed as follows:

$$B^R_{a,b}(f) \equiv \alpha^f_{a,b} f\Big|_{y=a,b} + \beta^f_{a,b} \frac{\partial f}{\partial y}\Big|_{y=a,b} - \gamma^f_{a,b} = 0, \tag{46}$$

where the coefficients $\alpha^u_{a,b}$, $\beta^u_{a,b}$ and $\gamma^u_{a,b}$ depend on the boundary $y = a, b$ as well as on the field component. As shown in [27], for a velocity field subject to the Robin BCs

$$B^R_{1;a,b}(u) = \alpha^u_{a,b} u\Big|_{y=a,b} + \beta^u_{a,b} \frac{\partial u}{\partial y}\Big|_{y=a,b} - \gamma^u_{a,b} = 0, \tag{47}$$

$$B^R_{1;\,a,b}(v) = \alpha^v v\Big|_{y=a,b} + \beta^v \frac{\partial v}{\partial y}\Big|_{y=a,b} - \gamma^v = 0, \tag{48}$$

$$B^R_{1;a,b}(w) = \alpha^w_{a,b} w\Big|_{y=a,b} + \beta^w_{a,b} \frac{\partial w}{\partial y}\Big|_{y=a,b} - \gamma^w_{a,b} = 0, \tag{49}$$

if the Robin BC coefficients of the horizontal components of velocity satisfy

$$\alpha^u_a = \alpha^w_a \equiv \alpha_a, \qquad \alpha^u_b = \alpha^w_b \equiv \alpha_b, \qquad \beta^u_a = \beta^w_a \equiv \beta_a, \qquad \beta^u_b = \beta^w_b \equiv \beta_b, \tag{50}$$

then the incompressibility condition at the boundaries required by the influence matrix method [23,28] becomes equivalent to $B^R_{2;\,a,b}(v) = \alpha_{a,b} v'\big|_{y=a,b} + \beta_{a,b} v''\big|_{y=a,b} = 0$, where the primes denote vertical derivatives. Equation (43) has to be solved for each pair of horizontal Fourier modes (k_x, k_z). In order to do so, it is useful to express all fields in terms of Chebyshev expansions and construct for each pair (k_x, k_z) a new system. This new system is obtained by taking the divergence of the time-stepping momentum or induction equation, as well as its y-component, as

$$\mathcal{A} : \begin{cases} p^{(2)}_m - k^2 p_m = d_m(\mathbf{R}) - b^{(1)}_m, & m = 0, \dots, N_y - 2 \quad (51) \\ \nu v^{(2)}_m - D_\nu v_m - p^{(1)}_m = -R_{y,m} + b_m, & m = 0, \dots, N_y - 2 \quad (52) \\ B^R_{1;\,a,b}(v) = 0,\ B^R_{2;\,a,b}(v) = 0, & (53) \end{cases}$$

where the m index refers to the mth coefficient of the Chebyshev expansion, $k^2 = k_x^2 + k_z^2$, $\boldsymbol{R}$ refers to the right-hand side of (43), d_m represents the mth Chebyshev coefficient of the divergence of a given field, b is a tau correction such that $b_m = 0\ \forall m \in [0, N_y - 2]$, R_y is the y component or $\boldsymbol{R}$, the (i) exponent refers to the Chebyshev coefficients of the ith derivative of a given field, $B^R_{1;\,a,b}(v)$ is the system BC of v at $y = a, b$ and $B^R_{2;\,a,b}(v)$ is the BC of v at $y = a, b$ due to incompressibility evaluated at the boundaries. Note that the hats are dropped for the sake of notation clarity.

Following [23], the system (51)–(53) can be decomposed into an $\widetilde{\mathcal{A}}$ and an $\bar{\mathcal{A}}$ problem, with the fields also decomposed in the same way as

$$p_m = \widetilde{p}_m + \bar{p}_m, \qquad v_m = \widetilde{v}_m + \bar{v}_m, \qquad b_m = \widetilde{b}_m + \bar{b}_m, \tag{54}$$

$$\widetilde{\mathcal{A}} : \begin{cases} \widetilde{p}_m^{(2)} - k^2 \widetilde{p}_m = r_m, & m = 0, \ldots, N_y - 2 \qquad (55) \\ \nu \widetilde{v}_m^{(2)} - D_\nu \widetilde{v}_m - \widetilde{p}_m^{(1)} = -R_{y,m} + \widetilde{b}_m, & m = 0, \ldots, N_y - 2 \qquad (56) \\ B^R_{1;\,a,b}(\widetilde{v}) = 0,\ \widetilde{p}(a, b) = 0, & \qquad (57) \end{cases}$$

$$\bar{\mathcal{A}} : \begin{cases} \bar{p}_m^{(2)} - k^2 \bar{p}_m = -b_m^{(1)}, & m = 0, \ldots, N_y - 2 \qquad (58) \\ \nu \bar{v}_m^{(2)} - D_\nu \bar{v}_m - \bar{p}_m^{(1)} = \bar{b}_m, & m = 0, \ldots, N_y - 2 \qquad (59) \\ B^R_{1;\,a,b}(\bar{v}) = 0,\ B^R_{2;\,a,b}(\bar{v}) = -B^R_{2;\,a,b}(\widetilde{v}), & \qquad (60) \end{cases}$$

where $r_m = d_m(\boldsymbol{R})$. Furthermore, $\widetilde{b}_m$ and $\bar{b}_m$ have the same property as b_m, to be only non-zero for $m = N_y - 1$ and $m = N_y$, and $\widetilde{b}_m$ is evaluated as

$$\widetilde{b}_m = \nu \widetilde{v}_m^{(2)} - D_\nu \widetilde{v}_m - \widetilde{p}_m^{(1)} + R_{y,m},\ \ m \in \{N_y - 1, N_y\}. \tag{61}$$

The $\bar{\mathcal{A}}$ problem is solved by linear superposition for each field

$$\bar{\phi}_m = \sum_{l=1}^{4} \xi_l \bar{\phi}_{l,m}\,, \tag{62}$$

with $\bar{\phi}_m$ and $\bar{\phi}_{l,m}$ being associated to $\bar{p}_m, \bar{v}_m, \bar{b}_m, b_m$, and to their "$_{l,m}$" variants. The four associated $\bar{\mathcal{A}}_l$ systems that need to be solved are

$$\bar{\mathcal{A}}_l : \begin{cases} \bar{p}_{l,m}^{(2)} - k^2 \bar{p}_{l,m} = -b_{l,m}^{(1)}, & m = 0, \ldots, N_y - 2 \qquad (63) \\ \nu \bar{v}_{l,m}^{(2)} - D_\nu \bar{v}_{l,m} = \bar{p}_{l,m}^{(1)} + \bar{b}_{l,m}, & m = 0, \ldots, N_y - 2 \qquad (64) \\ B^R_{1;\,a,b}(\bar{v}_l) = 0,\ \bar{p}_l(a, b) = q_l^{a,b}, & \qquad (65) \end{cases}$$

with $q_l^a = \delta_{1l}$, $q_l^b = \delta_{2l}$, $b_{l,N_y} = \delta_{3l}$, $b_{l,N_y-1} = \delta_{4l}$, and the tau correction $\bar{b}_{l,m}$ evaluated as

$$\bar{b}_{l,m} = \nu \bar{v}_{l,m}^{(2)} - D_\nu \bar{v}_{l,m} - \bar{p}_{l,m}^{(1)},\ \ l \in \{1, 2, 3, 4\},\ m \in \{N_y - 1, N_y\}. \tag{66}$$

The coefficients ξ_l are determined enforcing the $B^R_{2;a,b}(v)$ BC of system $\bar{\mathcal{A}}$ as well as the compatibility of the tau corrections between the systems $\bar{\mathcal{A}}$ and $\widetilde{\mathcal{A}}$, resulting in the following relations:

$$\sum_{l=1}^{4} \xi_l \left[\alpha_a \bar{v}'_{l,m}(a) + \beta_a \bar{v}''_{l,m}(a)\right] = -\alpha_a \widetilde{v}'_m(a) - \beta_a \widetilde{v}''_m(a), \tag{67}$$

$$\sum_{l=1}^{4} \xi_l \left[\alpha_b \bar{v}'_{l,m}(b) + \beta_b \bar{v}''_{l,m}(b)\right] = -\alpha_b \widetilde{v}'_m(b) - \beta_b \widetilde{v}''_m(b), \tag{68}$$

$$\sum_{l=1}^{4} \xi_l \left[b_{l,N_y-1} - \bar{b}_{l,N_y-1}\right] = \widetilde{b}_{N_y-1}, \tag{69}$$

$$\sum_{l=1}^{4} \xi_l \left[b_{l,N_y} - \bar{b}_{l,N_y}\right] = \widetilde{b}_{N_y}. \tag{70}$$

In terms of implementation, the four $\bar{\mathcal{A}}_l$ problems are solved during the preprocessing stage since they are independent of the time-dependent forcing term, $\boldsymbol{R}$. As a result, all terms in brackets on the left-hand side of Equations (67)–(70) are consolidated into a matrix, which is inverted during preprocessing. This inverted matrix is referred to as the generalized influence matrix. During time-stepping of the momentum equation, the $\widetilde{\mathcal{A}}$ problem is solved at each time-step, allowing evaluation of the right-hand side of Equations (67)–(70), after which the ξ_l coefficients are obtained through a matrix-vector multiplication. Finally, the solutions to the $\bar{\mathcal{A}}$ problem are recovered from the $\bar{\mathcal{A}}_l$ systems using (62). The solutions of the $\mathcal{A}$ problem are then obtained by combining the solutions of the $\widetilde{\mathcal{A}}$ and $\bar{\mathcal{A}}$ problems using (54).

The horizontal components of the velocity field can be easily solved once the pressure is known. By considering the first and third components of the time-stepping momentum Equation (43) along with the Robin boundary conditions (47) and (49), we are left with two Helmholtz equations to solve for two fields, both of which have explicit boundary conditions.

As a note, if the divergence of the $\boldsymbol{R}$ term in (51) is assumed to be exactly zero (which does not occur numerically), the pressure becomes a linear function of y. Due to the Dirichlet boundary conditions in the $\widetilde{\mathcal{A}}$ problem, $\widetilde{p}$ is zero, and $p = \bar{p}$, which is, then, solely determined by the tau corrections. If the simulation program lacks a mechanism to remove or compensate for divergence generation in the momentum equation, the error's order of magnitude is increased from 10^{-15} to 10^{-7} [29].

2.6. Implementation of the Methods

The method described above is implemented within ChannelFlow 2.0 [16,17], an open-source parallelized pseudo-spectral code originally designed accurate simulations of transitionary turbulence in a channel geometry. It is written in C++ and uses the Message-Passing Interface (MPI) library [30] for computation parallelization. It is designed in an efficient and modular way, utilizing virtual classes to define all components of the solver [31]. Thereby, the code can be extended beyond its original capabilities, specifically, including extensions involving additional fields. It has already been extended to solve visco-elastic flows [32] and inclined Rayleigh–Bénard convection (ILC) [6,33,34].

In addition to time-steppers, ChannelFlow also includes a Newton solver library and a dynamical system interface (DSI) class that is designed to map any physical system implemented into ChannelFlow to a generic autonomous dynamical system $\dot{x}(t) = f(x(t))$. This enables the use of invariant solution tracking, which eventually aims to be utilized in the MHD context.

The rotating MHD Equations (24)–(28), together with the methods presented above, are implemented in a new MHD module for ChannelFlow.

The presented method involves solving Helmholtz equations, which are numerically formulated as a quasi-tridiagonal system of equations for Dirichlet or Neumann BCs or, instead, as a quasi-pentadiagonal system of equations for Robin BCs [28].

3. Validation and Benchmark Results

To assess the reliability and performance of the code, we first reproduce linear stability theory results for the onset of convection when rotation and imposed magnetic fields are present. Then, we test the fully nonlinear case by comparing turbulent DNS statistics (including boundary layer phenomenology) with the results from the literature. Thirdly, the accuracy of the time-stepper is checked against the magnetic energy equation. Finally, we assess the parallel scaling of the code and compare the performance with a pure convection problem without magnetic fields.

3.1. Linear Stability Analysis

The first test consists in reproducing linear stability results using the nonlinear solver. In the specific case of rotating MHD, the system can be subject to rotation and/or imposed magnetic fields. The separate stabilizing effect of rotation and imposed magnetic field are studied. In order to do so, the results from linear stability analysis presented in [11] are used. The rotation, imposed magnetic field and gravity all act in the $\hat{e}_y$ direction, so $\gamma_x = 0$, $\phi = 0$ and $\vartheta = 0$ in Equations (6) and (19). The base states used for these calculations are the laminar solution for velocity with static walls, hydrostatic pressure and an adverse temperature gradient [33]. When the conductive state is unstable, the field deviations experience an exponential growth with an exponent corresponding to the eigenvalue of the fastest growing eigenmode. When the conductive state is stable, the field deviations experience an exponential decay with exponent corresponding to the slowest decaying eigenmode. In the case of a marginally stable conductive state, the field deviations should remain constant, although practically, we always observe a non-zero growth/decay rate.

Simulations are run at equal, slightly higher and slightly lower Ra values compared to the expected Ra_c for given Q or Ek values from [11], starting from a random field whose L2-norm is set to 10^{-4}. The resulting growth rates are measured and used to quadratically interpolate the critical Rayleigh number Ra_c at which the conductive state is marginally stable. It should be noted that in the case where all obtained growth rates are strictly positive or negative, additional simulations are performed at lower/higher Ra such that the three interpolant growth rates do not all have the same sign. In addition, the grid is refined and/or the integration time-step is reduced, until the predicted Ra_c stabilizes. The results are displayed in Table 1.

Table 1. Linear stability tests against linear stability theory [11], using the same rounding. Grid size values represent $N_x \times N_y \times N_z$, and the Taylor number is related to the Ekman number as Ta = $4/\mathrm{Ek}^2$.

Parameter	a_c	Theoretical Ra_c	Obtained Ra_c	Rel. Error	Grid Size
–	3.117	1707.762	1707.762	6×10^{-8}	$32 \times 31 \times 32$
–	8.00	7084.51	7084.51	1×10^{-8}	$32 \times 31 \times 32$
Ta = 5000	4.25	3468.6	3468.6	8×10^{-5}	$32 \times 31 \times 32$
Ta = 500	3.30	1940.3	1940.3	1×10^{-8}	$32 \times 31 \times 32$
Ta = 10^5	7.20	16,721	16,720	7×10^{-5}	$32 \times 31 \times 32$
Ta = 10^{10}	55.5	3.4574×10^7	3.4498×10^7	6×10^{-3}	$48 \times 47 \times 48$
Q = 100	4.00	3757.3	3757.3	5×10^{-6}	$64 \times 33 \times 64$
Q = 1000	5.80	17,103	17,103	3×10^{-6}	$64 \times 63 \times 64$
Q = 10^4	8.66	124,508	124,509	1×10^{-5}	$64 \times 63 \times 64$

In every test performed, the results closely match the theoretical predictions. It is important to note that the theoretical critical Rayleigh numbers are only exact for Rayleigh–Bénard Convection without external magnetic fields or rotation. Otherwise, the values given in [11] are approximations, albeit accurate ones, derived using test functions. Consequently, the criterion for relative error is stringent, and achieving a zero error is understandably unrealistic.

3.2. Direct Numerical Simulation Statistics

We want to compare DNS statistics of our code in the turbulent regime, including boundary layer phenomenology resolution, with a study which uses the same no-slip, perfectly conducting and isothermal BCs that are used in our problem (20)–(23). In [35], several direct numerical simulations (DNS) for various sets of BCs are presented. This study is based on a modified version of the code presented in [36], which uses poloidal–toroidal decomposition for the magnetic field. The simulation n°9 utilizes the same BCs as implemented and tested here. With their choice of parameters $\mathrm{Ra} = 5 \times 10^8, \mathrm{Ek} = 10^{-5}, \mathrm{Pr} = 1, \mathrm{Pr}_m = 2.5, \phi = \pi/2, \gamma_x = 0$, $L_x = L_z = 1, a = -0.5$ and $b = 0.5$, the statistically averaged root mean-square (rms) profiles of vertical and horizontal magnetic fields are computed as

$$B_h = \sqrt{\langle B_y^2 \rangle}, \qquad B_v = \sqrt{\langle B_x^2 + B_z^2 \rangle}. \tag{71}$$

The horizontal and vertical velocity rms values are computed in the same manner. Since the nondimensionalization used in [35] is based on the thermal diffusion length-scale of the system H_0^{*2}/κ^*, we need to convert non-dimensional magnetic field values from free-fall time unit to thermal time unit measurements. Velocities expressed in units of free-fall time need to be multiplied by $\sqrt{\mathrm{Ra}\,\mathrm{Pr}} \approx 22{,}361$, and magnetic fields—based on the free-fall velocity—need to be multiplied by $\sqrt{\mathrm{Ra}\,\mathrm{Pr}_m\,/\,\mathrm{Pr}} \approx 35{,}355$. Figure 3 is a reproduction of Figure 6c,f of [35]. It depicts the above-mentioned rms velocity and magnetic field values, scaled to be expressed in the thermal diffusion time units. While the simulation presented in [35] employed a grid with $(N_x, N_y, N_z) = (288, 256, 288)$, we choose a coarser grid which resolution reduced by a factor of two in each direction, resulting in $(N_x, N_y, N_z) = (144, 127, 144)$. This grid reduction is chosen to speed up the simulation, and since the results are already matching within their statistical errors, additional simulations using a finer grid seem unnecessary. The integration time-step is set to $\Delta t = 2.5 \times 10^{-3}$. We compute averages over 2000 snapshots, separeted by a quarter free-fall time unit. As evidenced by the comparison in Figure 3, the rms values of both magnetic fields are almost indistinguishable between our DNS and the the reference simulation from [35]. This good agreement is observed both in the Ekman layer, where the horizontal rms velocity profile experiences strong gradients, and in the bulk. Despite the fundamentally different approach for enforcing the magnetic field to remain divergence free, the validation data clearly lie within one standard deviation of the rms values we computed.

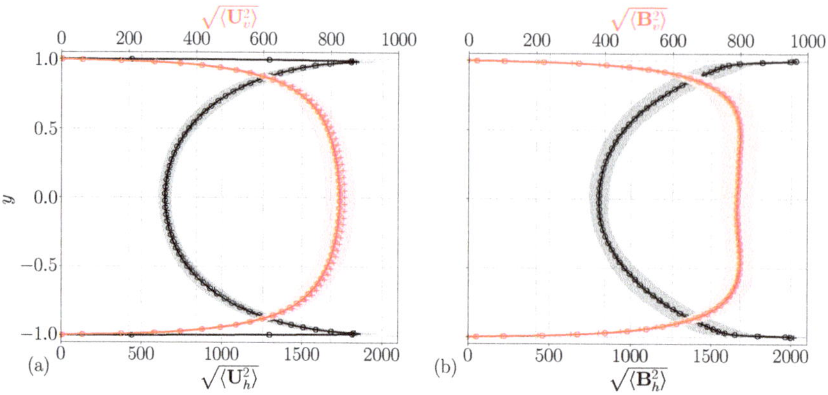

Figure 3. (**a**) U_h and U_v are the horizontal and vertical rms values of velocity. (**b**) B_h and B_v are the horizontal and vertical rms values of the magnetic field, respectively. Horizontal velocity and magnetic field rms values are depicted in black, and vertical rms values in red. All fields in this figure are scaled to thermal time-scale. Circles represent our simulation data and pluses the data of [35]. The lightly-colored bands are the statistical standard deviations. For visibility reasons, only every second points is marked with a circle whereas the reference figure, with a grid twice refined in each direction, shows one every four points.

3.3. Energy Equation

To further test the accuracy of our time-stepping scheme, we check the consistency with global conservation law, relating the rate of change of mean magnetic energy to fields themselves. The magnetic energy equation is obtained by multiplying Equation (31) by $\boldsymbol{B}$, and taking its spatial average yielding an expression for the rate of change of the nondimensionalized magnetic energy as

$$\frac{1}{2}\frac{\partial}{\partial t}\left\langle \boldsymbol{B}^2 \right\rangle = -\left\langle \boldsymbol{U}\cdot(\nabla\times\boldsymbol{B})\times\boldsymbol{B} \right\rangle - \eta\left\langle (\nabla\times\boldsymbol{B})^2 \right\rangle \tag{72}$$

where $\langle\cdot\rangle \equiv \frac{1}{L_x L_z(b-a)}\iiint_{\mathcal{D}} \cdot\, dxdydz$ is a spatial average over the whole domain. We assume that there are no imposed magnetic fields in (21); hence, the p_b surface term vanishes. To check the accuracy at which our numerical scheme satisfies this global conservation law, we compute the rate of change of the magnetic energy on the left-hand side and the terms on the right-hand side independently. Here, derivatives and spatial averages are computed spectrally, while the time derivative of the mean magnetic energy is approximated by centered differences. As shown in Figure 4, the time derivative approximation of the magnetic energy closely matches the sum of the kinetic energy transfer term and ohmic heating term. The relative error is of 10^{-3}. This error can be rationalized by the lack of precision in the approximation of the time derivative of $\langle \boldsymbol{B}^2\rangle$. Note that the actual time-stepping code is based on a much more accurate third-order Adams–Bashforth scheme with backwards differentiation [23,37].

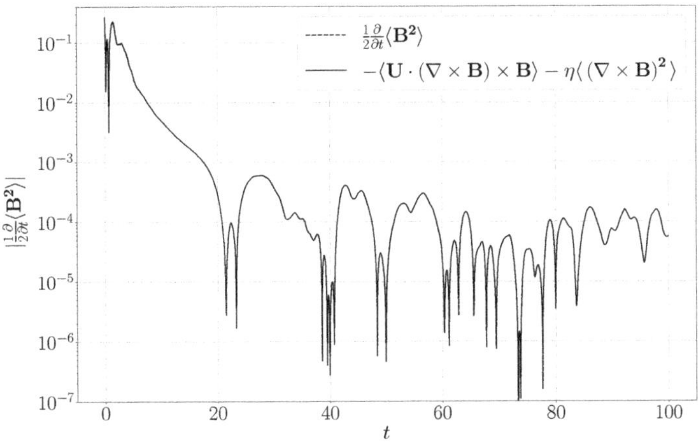

Figure 4. Absolute value of the time derivative of magnetic energy, approximated by centered differences as well as by the sum of components on the right-hand side of (72). The geometrical parameters used for this simulation are $L_x = L_z = 5, a = -0.5$ and $b = 0.5$, the physical ones are $\mathrm{Ra} = 5 \times 10^5, \mathrm{Ek} = 2 \times 10^{-2}, \mathrm{Pr} = 1, \mathrm{Pr}_m = 1, \gamma_x = 0$ and $\phi = \pi/2$. The grid size is set to $(N_x, N_y, N_z) = (48, 47, 48)$ and the integration time-step to $\Delta t = 2.5 \times 10^{-3}$.

3.4. Code Benchmarks

Two different types of benchmark are run to assess the scalability of the code. Both of them use the same physical and numerical parameters for all tests, only varying either the number of processes allocated to it or the grid size of the simulated fields. All the simulations are run on a compute node of the JED cluster (SCITAS, EPFL), which consists in 72 cores of Intel Xeon Platinum 8360Y CPU @ 2.40 GHz, 512 GB of memory and 3.2 TB of NVMe storage [38]. The geometrical parameters used are $L_x = 1$, $L_z = 1$ and $a = -0.5$, $b = 0.5$, and the physical ones are $\mathrm{Ra} = 10^6$, $\mathrm{Pr} = 1$, $\mathrm{Pr}_m = 1$, $\mathrm{Ek} = 10^{-2}$, $\gamma_x = 0$ and $\phi = \pi/2$. The wall velocities are kept to zero, and an adverse temperature gradient is maintained as the temperature base state. The numerical integration time-step Δt is set to 10^{-3}, and the code is compiled using the `mpicxx` compiler issued by Intel.

We first test the strong scaling of our code. The grid size is kept fixed at $(N_x, N_y, N_z) = (128, 127, 144)$, which represents approximately 2.34×10^6 collocation points. The number of MPI processes allocated to the simulation together with the spatial distribution $n_p[n_{px}, n_{pz}]$ are $1[1,1], 2[1,2], 8[4,2], 12[4,3], 16[4,4], 24[4,6], 32[8,4], 48[8,6], 64[8,8]$ and $72[8,9]$. Ideally, the distribution of processes should be as close as possible to the same number in each periodic direction such that the load on each process is equal, but these distributions are solely chosen for benchmarking. The left panel of Figure 5 shows the variation in the mean elapsed time integrating all the fields $\boldsymbol{u}, \boldsymbol{b}, \theta, p$ and p_b as the number of MPI processes increases from 1 to 72. For comparison, the same benchmark is performed using identical relevant parameters with another ChannelFlow-based code (ILC) that handles the same domain without rotation and magnetic fields and that has been thoroughly tested [6,33].

The dependence of the elapsed time on the number of processes is similar for both cases, the MHD code scaling as $\Delta t^{\mathrm{MHD}}_{\mathrm{elapsed}} \propto n_p^{-0.91}$ and the ILC code as $\Delta t^{\mathrm{ILC}}_{\mathrm{elapsed}} \propto n_p^{-0.85}$. An ensemble average carried over the mean elapsed times of both cases shows that the MHD code runs 1.9 times slower than the ILC one. With a rough estimate, the MHD and ILC codes, respectively, handle nine and five similar scalar-like fields. Therefore, in principle, the MHD code cannot run faster than $9/5 = 1.8$ times the runtime of the ILC code. The fact that our code runs only 1.9 times slower is notable, as it indicates that the additional couplings in the equations are not computationally expensive.

The second benchmark assesses weak scaling, keeping the number of MPI processes as well as their distribution fixed to $n_p[n_{px}, n_{pz}] = 72[8,9]$. The grid size is varied as $(Nx, Ny, Nz) = (16,15,18), (32,31,36), (64,63,72), (128,127,144), (192,191,216), (256,255,288), (384,383,432)$ and $(512,511,588)$. In the right panel of Figure 5, the mean time per time-step is plotted with respect to the grid size. The scaling of performance with respect to the number of points n_g is found to be $\Delta t^{\mathrm{MHD}}_{\mathrm{elapsed}} \propto n_g^{0.87}$ in the configuration described above.

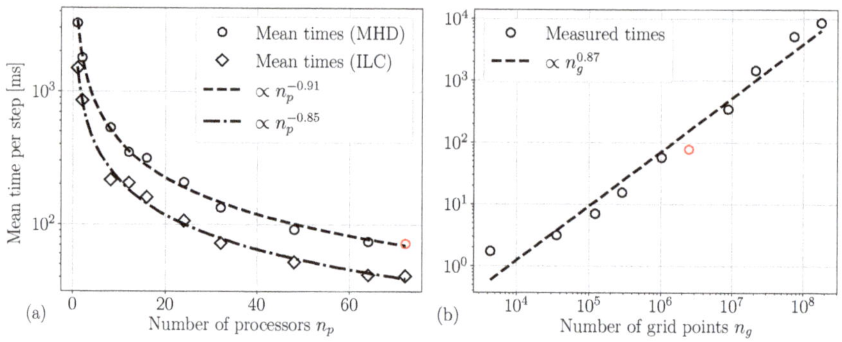

Figure 5. (**a**) Mean time spent per time-step as a function of the number of MPI processes used. For comparison purposes, mean times are shown both for the MHD code and for the ILC code. The relative standard deviations range from 15 to 1%. (**b**) Mean time spent per time-step as a function of the grid size. The standard deviation is of the order of 100% for the lower grid sizes, as fluctuations on such of a short duration have a strong influence, and reaches values of around 0.5% for larger grid sizes. On both panels, the red circle corresponds to the same simulation case of $n_p = 72$ and $n_g = 128 \times 127 \times 144 \approx 2.34 \times 10^6$.

4. Conclusions and Discussion

We have developed an accurate pseudo-spectral numerical code for the simulation of rotating and convection-driven flow of a conducting Newtonian fluid in a double-periodic wall-bounded domain. The code is based on a primitive variable formulation of the MHD equations and uses a fictitious magnetic pressure to enforce the solenoidal condition of the magnetic field. An extension of the classical influence matrix method with tau correction is derived for general Robin boundary conditions and applied to both velocity and magnetic fields. The accurate scheme is implemented in C++, extending the functionality of the existing parallelized open-source ChannelFlow 2.0 software. Our implementation has been tested against linear stability theory in different scenarios with either imposed magnetic fields or rotation. We successfully reproduced previous results on the statistics of turbulent flows and observed very good agreement when compared to a simulation using an alternative approach for enforcing the magnetic field to remain divergence free. Lastly, the accuracy of the time-marching scheme has been demonstrated by validating it against the analytically derived magnetic energy equation. Additionally, we ran benchmarks demonstrating solid weak and strong scaling of our code. Since the numerical code is (a) accurate, (b) shows favorable parallel scaling, (c) can handle general Robin boundary conditions for both the velocity and magnetic field and (d) can easily interface with Newton-based shooting methods, we expect it to enable the identification and tracking of invariant solutions of rotating MHD in a plane layer.

We believe that the construction of this code opens up the possibility for increased understanding of the interaction of convection with magnetic field in situations relevant to geophysical and astrophysical fluid dynamics, where rotation plays an important role. The local geometry, considered here, is often utilized for modeling turbulent interactions; the accurate and efficient methods described here, coupled with the possibility of the detection of exact nonlinear solutions, will enable us to determine better the nature of transport and dynamo action in such rotating magnetized systems as the interior of planets and stars.

Author Contributions: Methodology, J.-C.R.; Software, J.-C.R.; Writing—original draft, J.-C.R.; Writing—review & editing, S.M.T. and T.M.S.; Supervision, T.M.S. All authors have read and agreed to the published version of the manuscript.

Funding: This work was supported by the European Research Council (ERC) under the European Union's Horizon 2020 research and innovation programme (grant no. 865677).

Data Availability Statement: The data that support the findings of this study are available from the corresponding author upon reasonable request.

Conflicts of Interest: The authors declare no conflicts of interest. The funders had no role in the design of the study; in the collection, analyses, or interpretation of data; in the writing of the manuscript; or in the decision to publish the results.

References

1. Hathaway, D.H. The Solar Cycle. *Living Rev. Sol. Phys.* **2015**, *12*, 4. [CrossRef]
2. McElhinny, M.W.; Senanayake, W.E. Paleomagnetic evidence for the existence of the geomagnetic field 3.5 Ga ago. *J. Geophys. Res.* **1980**, *85*, 3523–3528. [CrossRef]
3. Kivelson, M.G.; Khurana, K.K.; Volwerk, M. The Permanent and Inductive Magnetic Moments of Ganymede. *Icarus* **2002**, *157*, 507–522. [CrossRef]
4. Ashtari, O.; Schneider, T.M. Identifying invariant solutions of wall-bounded three-dimensional shear flows using robust adjoint-based variational techniques. *J. Fluid Mech.* **2023**, *977*, A7. [CrossRef]
5. Nagata, M. Three-dimensional finite-amplitude solutions in plane Couette flow: Bifurcation from infinity. *J. Fluid Mech.* **1990**, *217*, 519–527. [CrossRef]
6. Reetz, F.; Schneider, T.M. Invariant states in inclined layer convection. Part 1. Temporal transitions along dynamical connections between invariant states. *J. Fluid Mech.* **2020**, *898*, A22. [CrossRef]
7. Feudel, F.; Tuckerman, L.S.; Zaks, M.; Hollerbach, R. Hysteresis of dynamos in rotating spherical shell convection. *Phys. Rev. Fluids* **2017**, *2*, 053902. [CrossRef]
8. Skene, C.S.; Marcotte, F.; Tobias, S.M. On nonlinear transitions, minimal seeds and exact solutions for the geodynamo. *arXiv* **2024**, arXiv:2411.05499v2. [CrossRef]
9. Naskar, S.; Pal, A. Direct numerical simulations of optimal thermal convection in rotating plane layer dynamos. *J. Fluid Mech.* **2022**, *942*, A37. [CrossRef]
10. Stellmach, S.; Hansen, U. Cartesian convection driven dynamos at low Ekman number. *Phys. Rev. E* **2004**, *70*, 056312. [CrossRef]
11. Chandrasekhar, S. *Hydrodynamic and Hydromagnetic Stability*; Oxford University Press: London, UK, 1961.
12. Weiss, N.O.; Proctor, M.R.E. *Magnetoconvection*; Cambridge University Press: Cambridge, UK, 2014.
13. Cooper, R.G.; Bushby, P.J.; Guervilly, C. Subcritical dynamos in rapidly rotating planar convection. *Phys. Rev. Fluids* **2020**, *5*, 113702. [CrossRef]
14. Roberts, P.H. Diffusive instabilities in magnetohydrodynamic convection. In *Les Instabilitiés Hydrodynamiques en Convection Libre, Forcée et Mixte*; Legros, J.C., Platten, J.K., Eds.; Springer: Berlin/Heidelberg, Germany, 1978; pp. 102–111.
15. Kleiser, L.; Schumann, U. Treatment of Incompressibility and Boundary Conditions in 3-D Numerical Spectral Simulations of Plane Channel Flows. In Proceedings of the Third GAMM—Conference on Numerical Methods in Fluid Mechanics, Cologne, Germany, 10–12 October 1979; Hirschel, E.H., Ed.; Vieweg+Teubner Verlag: Wiesbaden, Germany, 1980; pp. 165–173.
16. ChannelFlow 2.0. Available online: https://www.channelflow.ch/ (accessed on 27 March 2025).
17. Gibson, J.F.; Reetz, F.; Azimi, S.; Ferraro, A.; Kreilos, T.; Schrobsdorff, H.; Farano, M.; Yesil, A.F.; Schütz, S.S.; Culpo, M.; et al. Channelflow 2.0. 2019, *manuscript in preparation*.
18. Chen, F.F. *Introduction to Plasma Physics and Controlled Fusion*, 3rd ed.; Springer: Cham, Switzerland, 2015.
19. Arter, W. Nonlinear Convection in an Imposed Horizontal Magnetic Field. *Geophys. Astrophys. Fluid Dyn.* **1983**, *25*, 259–292. [CrossRef]

20. Weiss, N.O. Convection in an imposed magnetic field. Part 1. The development of nonlinear convection. *J. Fluid Mech.* **1981**, *108*, 247–272. [CrossRef]
21. Tobias, S.M. The turbulent dynamo. *J. Fluid Mech.* **2021**, *912*, P1. [CrossRef]
22. Bader, S.H.; Zhu, Z. AFiD-MHD: A finite difference method for magnetohydrodynamic flows. *J. Comput. Phys.* **2005**, *523*, 113658. [CrossRef]
23. Peyret, R. *Spectral Methods for Incompressible Viscous Flow*; Applied Mathematical Sciences; Springer: New York, NY, USA, 2002; Volume 148.
24. Tenam, R. *Navier-Stokes Equations: Theory and Numerical Analysis*, 3rd ed.; American Mathematical Society: Providence, RI, USA, 2001.
25. Eriksson, K.; Estep, D.; Hansbo, P.; Johnson, C. *Computational Differential Equations*; Cambridge University Press: Cambridge, UK, 1996.
26. Min, T.; Kim, J. Effects of hydrophobic surface on skin-friction drag. *Phys. Fluids* **2004**, *16*, L55–L58. [CrossRef]
27. Liu, X. Extension of Kleiser & Schumann's influence-matrix method for generalized velocity boundary conditions. *J. Comput. Phys.* **2011**, *230*, 7911–7916.
28. Canuto, C.; Hussaini, Y.M.; Quarteroni, A.; Zang, T.A. *Spectral Methods in Fluid Dynamics*; Springer: Berlin/Heidelberg, Germany, 1988.
29. Tuckerman, L.S. Divergence-free Velocity Fields in Nonperiodic Geometries. *J. Comput. Phys.* **1989**, *80*, 403–441. [CrossRef]
30. Message Passing Interface Forum. *MPI: A Message-Passing Interface Standard*, Version 3.1; High Performance Computing Center Stuttgart (HLRS): Stuttgart, Germany, 2015.
31. Reetz, F.; Kreilos, T.; Schneider, T.M. Exact invariant solution reveals the origin of self-organized oblique turbulent-laminar stripes. *Nat. Commun.* **2019**, *10*, 2277. [CrossRef]
32. Ferraro, A. Exploiting Marginal Stability in Slow-Fast Quasilinear Dynamical Systems. Ph.D. Thesis, EPFL, Lausanne, Switzerland, 2022.
33. Reetz, F. Turbulent Patterns in Wall-Bounded Shear Flows: Invariant Solutions and Their Bifurcations. Ph.D. Thesis, EPFL, Lausanne, Switzerland, 2019.
34. Zheng, Z.; Tuckerman, L.S.; Schneider, T.M. Natural convection in a vertical channel. Part 2. Oblique solutions and global bifurcations in a spanwise-extended domain. *J. Fluid Mech.* **2024**, *1000*, A29. [CrossRef]
35. Kolhey, P.; Stellmach, S.; Heyner, D. Influence of boundary conditions on rapidly rotating convection and its dynamo action in a plane fluid layer. *Phys. Rev. Fluids* **2022**, *7*, 043502. [CrossRef]
36. Stellmach, S.; Hansen, U. An efficient spectral method for the simulation of dynamos in Cartesian geometry and its implementation on massively parallel computers. *Geochem. Geophys. Geosystems* **2008**, *9*, Q05003. [CrossRef]
37. Gibson, J.F. ChannelFlow User Guide 0.9.18 2009. Available online: http://channelflow.org/dokuwiki/doku.php?id=docs (accessed on 25 November 2024).
38. SCITAS JED Documentation, EPFL. Available online: https://scitas-doc.epfl.ch/supercomputers/jed/ (accessed on 14 November 2024).

mathematics

MDPI

Article

Buoyant Convective Thermal Transport in a Discretely Heated–Cooled Porous Parallelogrammic Configuration Saturated with Nanofluids: A Tiwari and Das Approach

Vishwanatha Shivakumar [1,2,3], Vinay C. Veeranna [1,2], Mani Sankar [2,4,*], Sebastian A. Altmeyer [5] and Abdulrahman Al Maqbali [6]

1 VTU Research Center, Department of Mathematics, JSS Academy of Technical Education, Dr. Vishnuvardhan Road, Bangalore 560060, India; s.vishwanatha@jainuniversity.ac.in (V.S.); vinaycv@jssateb.ac.in (V.C.V.)
2 Research Center, Visvesvaraya Technological University, Belagavi 590018, India
3 Department of Mathematics, Faculty of Engineering and Technology, Jain Deemed-to-be-University, Kanakapura Taluk, Ramanagaram District, Bangalore 562112, India
4 College of Computing and Information Science, University of Technology and Applied Sciences, Ibri 516, Oman
5 Department of Physics, Aerospace Division, Universitat Politècnica de Catalunya—Barcelona Tech, 08034 Barcelona, Spain; sebastian.andreas.altmeyer@upc.edu
6 Department of Basic and Applied Sciences, College of Applied and Health Sciences, A'Sharqiyah University, P.O. Box 42, Ibra 400, Oman; abdulrahman.almaqbali@asu.edu.om
* Correspondence: sankar.mani@utas.edu.om

Abstract: The strategic positioning of heating and cooling segments within complex non-rectangular geometries has emerged as a critical engineering challenge across multiple industries in thermal management systems for electronic components. This analysis presents a numerical inspection of buoyancy-driven convective flow and thermal transport mechnisms of nanofluids in a parallelogrammic porous geometry. A single discrete heating–cooling segment has been placed along the slanting surfaces of the geometry. The mathematical model is formulated utilizing Darcy's law, incorporating the Tiwari and Das approach to characterize the thermophysical properties of the nanofluid. The governing model equations corresponding to the physical process are solved numerically using finite-difference-based alternating direction implicit (ADI) and successive line over-relaxation (SLOR) techniques. Computational simulations are performed for various parametric conditions, including different nanoparticle volume fractions ($\phi = 0$–0.05), Rayleigh numbers ($Ra = 10^1$–10^3), and parallelogram geometry (α) and sidewall (γ) tilting angles ($-45^\circ \leq \alpha \leq +45^\circ$ and $-45^\circ \leq \gamma \leq +45^\circ$), while examining the effect of discrete thermal locations. The results reveal a significant decrement in thermal transfer rates with an increasing nanoparticle concentration, particularly at higher Rayleigh numbers. The skewness of the parallelogrammic boundaries is found to substantially influence flow patterns and thermal transport characteristics compared to conventional rectangular enclosures. Further, the discrete placement of heating and cooling sources creates unique thermal plumes that modify circulation patterns within the domain. The predictions suggest profound insights for optimizing thermal management systems by employing nanofluids in non-rectangular porous configurations, with potential applications in geothermal energy extraction, electronic cooling systems, and thermal energy storage devices.

Keywords: Tiwari and Das model; buoyancy-driven convection; nanofluid-saturated porous envelope; inclined parallelogram geometry; discrete thermal boundary conditions; porous media; numerical method

MSC: 80A19; 80M20; 35G61; 76D05; 65H10; 65M06

https://doi.org/10.3390/math13213516

1. Introduction

Buoyancy-assisted flow motion and thermal transport processes in finite-shaped porous domains represent a critical area of thermal science with profound practical applications. Unlike open-domain flows, convection within bounded porous geometries manifest distinct flow structures, thermal stratification, and recirculation zones, which, in turn, fundamentally alter heat transport mechanisms. In addition, finite-spaced porous geometries represent a critical engineering configuration that maximizes thermal performance in space-constrained applications, such as electronic cooling, building technology, and industrial processes, to mention a few [1,2]. Finite-shaped domains fall into two broad categories: regular-shaped and non-regular-shaped geometries. Non-regular geometries serve unique specialized applications across various engineering disciplines. These irregular domains present significant analytical challenges, particularly due to the fact that their boundaries typically do not align with the coordinate axes. Additionally, they create complex gravitational force interactions from their unconventional shapes. Applications such as biomedical engineering, aerospace components, electronics cooling systems, and energy systems frequently feature intricate geometrical configurations. These characteristics make thermal fluid analysis in non-regular domains particularly demanding in computational studies. Among various non-rectangular conduits, a parallelogrammic domain has potential implementations, such as thermal diodes, compact heat exchangers, the cooling of electronic equipment, and solar thermal systems. The early experimental and theoretical studies on thermal transport in this geometry are from Seki et al. [3] and Hyun and Choi [4]. Later, Baïri and co-researchers [5,6] performed a combined numerical and experimental investigation on transient buoyant-assisted flow and thermal mechanisms in a uniformly and discretely heated–cooled parallelogram-shaped section to comprehend critical thermal behavior patterns, with a particular emphasis on avionics. Thermosolutal transport phenomena in parallelogram-shaped configurations have garnered substantial interest for understanding the complex interplay between thermal and solutal mechanisms under various conditions, particularly numerical examination of mixed convection in ventilated parallelogrammic domains [7] with an air–CO_2 mixture, while more recent investigations [8] have extended this work to thermo–solutal–magnetoconvection in tilted porous parallelogrammic domains with discrete heated–cooled segments. It should be noted that the above discussed studies primarily focused on conventional fluids.

The electronics cooling of industrial components faced growing thermal management challenges that could not be adequately addressed by conventional fluids. This led to the development of novel fluids, coined as "nanofluids," a breakthrough innovation by Choi and colleagues [9]. These specialized fluids consist of nano-sized particles (NPs) dispersed within a base fluid. Their superior heat transfer properties make them particularly valuable for meeting the highly demanding cooling requirements of modern electronic components. Ghalambaz et al. [10] studied convective motion of Cu–water nanofluids (NFs) within the parallelogrammic-shaped porous domain using the Darcy assumption by adopting the Tiwari and Das approach [11]. They predicted that the presence of NPs in the porous structure deteriorated thermal transfer rates due to increased viscosity, despite enhanced thermal conductivity, this effect being more pronounced in low-porosity media and at negative tilt angles. Later, Alsabery et al. [12] analyzed transient buoyant convection in an NF-saturated oblique porous geometry and observed an enhanced thermal dissipation for a thermal non-equilibrium model compared to thermal equilibrium conditions, with water–Ag NF showing superior performance among the four NPs considered. Hussein and Mustafa [13] numerically investigated buoyant-assisted convection in an open parallelogram-shaped cavity with localized bottom heating and observed that the optimal thermal dissipation transfer occurs with the heat source near the left wall at a 60° inclination. A non-homogeneous model for combined free-forced convection in a skewed enclosure revealed elevated thermal transport compared to the homogeneous model, while demonstrating that smaller NPs provide superior thermal transfer performance compared to larger ones [14]. Magneto-mixed convection inside a vented parallelogrammic configuration with injection or suction mechanisms has been examined by Bhuiyan et al. [15]. Their analysis demonstrated enhanced thermal dissipation rates with higher Richardson numbers, while the Hartmann number serves as an effective control parameter for regulating thermal transport phenomena. Yasin et al. [16] investigated magneto-mixed convection in a corrugated parallelogram configuration with a partially heated lower boundary. Their finite element simulation revealed the dominance of forced convective motion at low Richardson numbers, while enhancing the wall undulation amplitude elevates thermal dissipation rates. Recently, Humayoun et al. [17] examined buoyancy-assisted convection inside a porous parallelogram-structured domain under non-uniform temperature conditions. Their predictions revealed enhanced thermal transfer rates with higher Rayleigh and Prandtl numbers and larger inclination angles that decreased with higher Darcy numbers. The above investigations primarily focus on the buoyancy-assisted convection of different NFs in parallelogram-shaped configurations with various constraints, such as magnetic fields, porosity, and curved and vented boundaries.

Among the diverse finite-sized configurations, a differently heated square or rectangular porous domain filled with different NFs demonstrates significant practical relevance across numerous industrial applications. In this direction, Oztop and Abu-Nada [18] numerically examined convective thermal transport in a partially heated rectangular enclosure filled with three different (Cu, Al_2O_3, and TiO_2) NFs. Their results revealed that thermal dissipation elevates with NP concentration, and that the enhancement is more pronounced at low aspect ratios, with Cu NPs providing the maximum heat dissipation improvement. Buoyant-driven convection in square porous domains filled with diverse nanofluids has been investigated by employing Darcy's law, but different approaches have been used, such as Buongiorno's model [19] and Tiwari and Das' model [20]. Their predictions demonstrated that the relative difference in thermal conductivity between nanoparticles and porous media is the key factor determining heat transfer improvement. Alsabery and collaborators [21,22] performed numerical experiments on buoyant thermal transport in porous-NF systems with sinusoidal thermal constraints using finite difference methodology. In their studies of both an inclined square enclosure with a porous NF layer and conjugate thermal transfer with finite wall thickness, they demonstrated that heat transport enhancement varied significantly with geometry inclination angle, porous layer thickness, wall properties, and nanoparticle type, while non-uniform heating substantially increased the overall thermal transfer performance. In our earlier work [23] we numerically analyzed the thermal effects caused by non-uniform heating with a focus on buoyant transport versus entropy generation. The results strongly support the notion that ensemble-tree-based models, specifically gradient boosting models, are an effective means of accurately estimating complex non-linear relationships, especially in comparison to linear, kernel-based approaches and neural networks. Chamkha and Selimefendigil [24] numerically investigated magneto-convection and entropy generation in a square NF-filled porous domain with corrugated walls. They observed that increasing corrugation frequency reduced thermal transfer rates, while the magnetic force suppressed the heat transfer for both flat and corrugated boundaries.

Using Buongiorno's two-phase model, Alhashash [25] investigated the buoyant motion of nanoliquid in a square porous chamber with a partially heated cylinder. The results showed that thermal transfer rates decreased with increasing heated surface area, but increased with higher NP concentrations. Abed and Al-Damook [26] examined convective transport mechanisms in a square NF-filled porous domain containing three heated tubes. The multi-objective optimization approach suggested an enhanced heat dissipation through the proper selection of geometric and thermophysical parameters. Azad et al. [27] examined the rotational influence of a hot tube on magneto-hydrothermal mechanisms in a square conduit with a localized source containing CNT–water NF and reported an enhanced flow circulation and overall thermal performance with the cylinder's rotational speed. Investigations inside a shallow chamber packed with metal foam and nano-enhanced PC material reveal that metal foam significantly outperforms nanoparticles for thermal dissipation, with a complete melting time significantly reduced as the foam filling ratio increases [28]. Lakshmi et al. [29] numerically examined the buoyant transport of Cu–water NF within a porous square conduit with different orientations of a centrally located heated rod. Their findings demonstrated that the inclined rod configuration exhibited superior thermal performance compared to horizontal and vertical orientations. Mixed convection in a lid-driven porous configuration with TiO_2–water NF revealed that increasing NP volume fraction elevated thermal transfer at lower concentrations, while magnetic field intensity significantly influenced both heat transfer and entropy generation [30]. Vigneshwari et al. [31] investigated the unsteady magneto-convection of TiO_2-H_2O NF in a partially heated–cooled square porous domain and observed enhanced thermal transport rates with an increase in the heat source/sink parameter.

Researchers have also thoroughly documented how porous structures influence flow dynamics and heat transport performance within diverse irregular geometries, primarily due to the widespread implementation of such configurations across numerous engineering and industrial applications [32–34]. An exhaustive review was conducted on buoyant-assisted convection phenomena and the associated thermal transfer characteristics of NFs in various geometries, providing an extensive analysis of the impacts of parameters like Rayleigh, Darcy, and Hartman numbers and NF volume fraction [35,36]. Recent investigations have expanded the understanding of NF convection behavior in locally heated porous domains under various constraints, as evidenced in works examining convection in tilted wavy porous geometries with localized heating [37], square conduits with Casson hybrid nanofluids with classical [38] and sinusoidal heat flux [39], MHD convection in partially cross-heated NF-loaded geometries [40], and vibrational effects on thermosolutal free convection phenomena [41]. Based on a comprehensive review of the established literature concerning diverse porous configurations containing NFs, significant research gaps remain unexplored in understanding the effects of complex geometry, coupled modeling, and discrete thermal boundary conditions. Specifically, no previous studies have investigated the combined influences of the following:

(a) Investigation of parallelogrammic geometry with simultaneous cavity inclination (α) and sidewall tilting (γ), creating a unique double-inclination configuration that has not been previously studied.
(b) Implementation of discrete heating/cooling source–sink pairs on inclined walls of the parallelogram, departing from conventional uniform heating or discrete heating on vertical walls.
(c) Integration of a Darcy porous medium framework with a Tiwari and Das nanofluid model for this specific geometric and thermal configuration.

Despite the relevance of such geometry in numerous engineering applications, the effects of orientation angles on buoyant transport characteristics within this domain remain unexplored. This study addresses this knowledge gap by conducting a systematic numerical investigation to elucidate the influence of combined inclination angles and the enclosure, as well as the sidewall, on buoyancy-driven convection and the associated thermal transport mechanisms in a parallelogrammic porous geometry. The primary objective is to establish quantitative relationships between geometric parameters, thermal boundary conditions, and resultant heat dissipation phenomena in this complex configuration.

2. Mathematical Framework

2.1. Description of Geometry

Our analysis examines a porous domain shaped as a parallelogram, illustrated in Figure 1, with its key dimensions and orientation in the Cartesian reference frame. The geometry, characterized by dimensions L (width) and H (height), is oriented at an angle α with the $x-$axis. The thermal boundary conditions feature a thermal source and sink located on the opposing inclined surfaces. Specifically, there is a higher-temperature source (Th) on the left slanted surface and a lower-thermal sink (Tc) on the opposite slated surface. The remaining boundary segments maintain thermal insulation (adiabatic) conditions. The current analysis intends to investigate the positional impact of these thermal boundaries on the flow structure, temperature distributions, and heat transport efficiency. The working medium within the enclosure consists of Cu-H_2O NF saturating the porous structure. We employ the following simplifying assumptions in our analysis:

- The fluid follows the Boussinesq approximation. This approximation is valid when density variations remain small (typically <5–10%) compared to the reference density, which is satisfied for moderate temperature differences in water-based fluids [1,20]
- The fluid maintains incompressibility. Water-based nanofluids have very low compressibility and, in particular, copper nanoparticles further reduce compressibility [1,10]
- The fluid experiences negligible effects from viscous heating and inertial forces within the porous matrix.
- The porous medium is assumed to be homogeneous and isotropic with constant porosity ($\epsilon = 0.9$) and permeability throughout the enclosure. The medium is fully saturated with NF under local thermal equilibrium (LTE) conditions between the solid matrix and fluid phases.
- Fluid motion is modeled with Darcy's law. Darcy's law is applicable to our study based on (i) the moderate Rayleigh number range maintaining low-velocity flows within Darcy's validity domain, and (ii) Darcy's law being successfully validated for nanofluid flows in porous media in similar studies [10,20].
- NF properties are characterized using the Tiwari and Das [11] formulation, which treats the nanofluid as a homogeneous mixture with effective thermophysical properties. This is a widely used model in the literature [10,29].

The present study focuses specifically on the low Rayleigh number regime ($10^1 \leq Ra \leq 10^3$), where the Darcy model accurately represents the momentum transport in porous geometry. This parameter range encompasses numerous practical applications and serves as a fundamental baseline for understanding buoyancy-assisted convective motions before extending to more complex, higher Ra regimes that require extended porous media models. The current study systematically analyzes the parameter space where the Darcy model is physically appropriate and well-established in the literature [1,10,20].

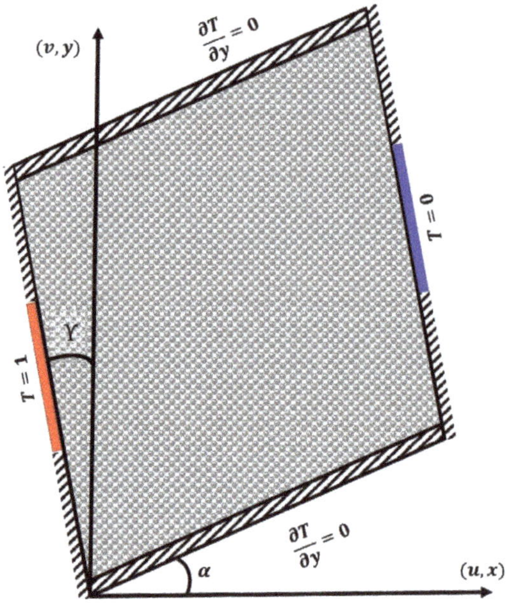

Figure 1. Geometrical configuration with coordinate system and thermal boundary conditions.

2.2. Governing Model Equations

For an incompressible Boussinesq NF-saturated porous parallelogram-shaped domain, applying Darcy's law and the Tiwari and Das NF model, and employing all the above assumptions, the governing model equations within a tilted NF-infused porous parallelogrammic domain in Cartesian coordinates can be represented as the following:

$$\frac{\partial u}{\partial x} + \frac{\partial v}{\partial y} = 0, \tag{1}$$

$$\frac{\mu_{nf}}{K} u = -\left[\frac{\partial p}{\partial x} + g(\rho\beta)_{nf} \sin\alpha\right], \tag{2}$$

$$\frac{\mu_{nf}}{K} v = -\left[\frac{\partial p}{\partial y} + g(\rho\beta)_{nf} \cos\alpha\right], \tag{3}$$

$$\sigma\frac{\partial T}{\partial t} + u\frac{\partial T}{\partial x} + v\frac{\partial T}{\partial y} = \alpha_{mnf}\left(\frac{\partial^2 T}{\partial x^2} + \frac{\partial^2 T}{\partial y^2}\right) \tag{4}$$

In the above model equations, the symbols represent physical quantities: K represents the permeability constant, **g** corresponds to gravitational force, p stands for pressure, and ρ stands for density. The coefficient β characterizes the volumetric expansion constant, μ quantifies dynamic viscosity, k measures thermal conductivity, and C_p defines the heat capacity under isobaric conditions. The NF properties utilized in this investigation are provided in Table 1 [10,20]. In these relations, the parameter ϕ represents the homogeneous NP concentration and the indices "nf", "p", and "f" denote the properties associated with the NF mixture, NPs, and base-fluid, respectively. Also, these expressions are restricted only to spherical NPs and not applicable to any other shapes of NPs. Table 2 summarizes the thermophysical characteristics of three components: the H_2O, NF, and material comprising the porous medium [10,20].

Table 1. Properties and the corresponding correlations of NFs.

Property	Correlation
Viscosity (Brinkman model)	$\mu_{\mathrm{nf}} = \dfrac{\mu_f}{(1-\phi)^{2.5}}$
Heat capacity (mixture model)	$(\rho C_p)_{\mathrm{nf}} = (1-\phi)(\rho C_p)_{\mathrm{f}} + \phi(\rho C_p)_{\mathrm{p}}$
Thermal conductivity (Maxwell model)	$\dfrac{k_{\mathrm{nf}}}{k_{\mathrm{f}}} = \dfrac{k_{\mathrm{p}} + 2k_{\mathrm{f}} - 2\phi(k_{\mathrm{f}} - k_{\mathrm{p}})}{k_{\mathrm{p}} + 2k_{\mathrm{f}} + \phi(k_{\mathrm{f}} - k_{\mathrm{p}})}$
Thermal expansion constant (linear mixing rule)	$(\rho\beta)_{\mathrm{nf}} = (1-\phi)(\rho\beta)_{\mathrm{f}} + \phi(\rho\beta)_{\mathrm{p}}$

Table 2. Physical properties of H_2O, Cu, and porous materials.

Properties	H_2O	Cu	Glass Balls
C_P ($\mathrm{J \cdot K^{-1} \cdot kg^{-1}}$)	4179	385	840
ρ ($\mathrm{m^{-3} \cdot kg}$)	997.1	8933	2700
k ($\mathrm{W \cdot K^{-1} \cdot m^{-1}}$)	0.613	400	1.05
$\alpha \times 10^{-7}$ ($\mathrm{m^2/s}$)	1.47	1163.1	4.63
$\beta \times 10^{-5}$ ($\mathrm{K^{-1}}$)	21	1.67	0.9

For the energy equation in the porous medium, we have the following relations from Nield and Bejan [1]:

$$\begin{aligned} (\rho c_p)_{\mathrm{m}} &= (1-\epsilon)(\rho c_p)_{\mathrm{s}} + \epsilon(\rho c_p)_{\mathrm{f}}, \\ k_{\mathrm{m}} &= (1-\epsilon)k_{\mathrm{s}} + \epsilon k_{\mathrm{f}}, \end{aligned} \tag{5}$$

Here, ϵ refers to porosity and the indices m, f, and s denote the H_2O-saturated porous structure, fluid, and solid regions of the porous material, respectively. The physical properties of the NF-saturated porous material are determined by integrating the relationships documented in Table 1 with Equation (5). Through this integration, the characteristic parameters of the NF-saturated porous structure can be established as follows [10,20]:

$$\begin{aligned} (\rho C_p)_{\mathrm{mnf}} &= \epsilon(\rho C_p)_{\mathrm{nf}} + (1-\epsilon)(\rho C_p)_{\mathrm{s}} = (\rho C_p)_{\mathrm{m}}\left[1 - \epsilon\phi\frac{(\rho C_p)_{\mathrm{f}} - (\rho C_p)_{\mathrm{p}}}{(\rho C_p)_{\mathrm{m}}}\right], \\ k_{\mathrm{mnf}} &= \epsilon k_{\mathrm{nf}} + (1-\epsilon)k_{\mathrm{s}} = k_{\mathrm{m}}\left\{1 - \frac{3\epsilon\phi k_{\mathrm{f}}(k_{\mathrm{f}} - k_{\mathrm{p}})}{k_{\mathrm{m}}[k_{\mathrm{p}} + 2k_{\mathrm{f}} + \phi(k_{\mathrm{f}} - k_{\mathrm{p}})]}\right\}, \\ \alpha_{\mathrm{mnf}} &= \frac{k_{\mathrm{mnf}}}{(\rho C_p)_{\mathrm{nf}}} \end{aligned} \tag{6}$$

where the index "mnf" refers to the NF-saturated porous structure. The relations presented in (6) establish the novel empirical formulations characterizing the thermal properties of NF-infused porous media. Unlike conventional approaches documented in previous studies that primarily focus on interplay between the base fluid and NPs, the current expressions emphasize the crucial influence of the porous material's solid matrix. By accounting for the interrelationships among all three components of the system, such as the base fluid, NPs, and porous matrix structure, the current formulations enable significantly enhanced precision in modeling flow analysis and thermal transport phenomena of NFs within porous systems [10,19,20].

By eliminating the pressure gradient terms through cross-differentiation of momentum Equations (2) and (3) and introducing the stream function $\psi^*(x,y)$ in the form $u = \dfrac{\partial\psi^*}{\partial y}$, $v = -\dfrac{\partial\psi^*}{\partial x}$, satisfying the continuity Equation (1), the modified momentum equation is

$$\frac{\mu_{mnf}}{K}\left[\frac{\partial^2\psi^*}{\partial x^2}+\frac{\partial^2\psi^*}{\partial y^2}\right]=g(\rho\beta)_{nf}\left[\frac{\partial T}{\partial y}\sin\alpha-\frac{\partial T}{\partial x}\cos\alpha\right] \tag{7}$$

Due to the tilted sidewalls of the parallelogrammic domain, we have adapted the following geometric coordinate transformation, utilized by many researchers [42,43], to reshape the physical domain into a square geometry:

$$X = x - y\,tan\,\gamma \text{ and } Y = y. \tag{8}$$

Finally, the following dimensionless transformations are utilized:

$$\xi=\frac{X}{L},\eta=\frac{Y}{H\cos\gamma},\tau=\frac{t\alpha_{mnf}}{\sigma LH\cos\gamma},\psi=\frac{\psi^*}{\alpha_{mnf}},\theta=\frac{(T-T_c)}{T_h-T_c} \tag{9}$$

Employing the above coordinate transformation (8) and dimensionless transformations (9), the modified governing model (momentum and energy) equations assume the following form:

$$\frac{\partial^2\psi}{\partial\xi^2}-2\frac{sin\gamma}{A}\frac{\partial^2\psi}{\partial\xi\partial\eta}+\frac{1}{A^2}\frac{\partial^2\psi}{\partial\eta^2}=RaH(\phi)\cos^2\gamma\left(\left[\frac{1}{Acos\gamma}\frac{\partial\theta}{\partial\eta}-tan\gamma\frac{\partial\theta}{\partial\xi}\right]sin\alpha-cos\alpha\frac{\partial\theta}{\partial\xi}\right), \tag{10}$$

$$\frac{\partial\theta}{\partial\tau}+\frac{\partial\psi}{\partial\eta}\frac{\partial\theta}{\partial\xi}-\frac{\partial\psi}{\partial\xi}\frac{\partial\theta}{\partial\eta}=\frac{A}{cos\gamma}\left[\frac{\partial^2\theta}{\partial\xi^2}-2\frac{sin\gamma}{A}\frac{\partial^2\theta}{\partial\xi\partial\eta}+\frac{1}{A^2}\frac{\partial^2\theta}{\partial\eta^2}\right]. \tag{11}$$

The dimensionless form of the differential equations shown above provides a mathematical framework describing the physical phenomena being examined in this study, incorporating the following relevant dimensionless parameters:

$Ra=\frac{gK(\rho\beta)_f\Delta\theta L}{\mu_f\alpha_m}$, the Rayleigh number, and $H(\phi)=\frac{H_1\cdot H_2}{H_3}(1-\phi)^{2.5}$, $A=\frac{H}{L}$, the aspect ratio, where $H_1=\left[1-\phi+\frac{\phi(\rho\beta)_p}{(\rho\beta)_f}\right]$, $H_2=\left[1-\phi+\frac{\phi(\rho C_p)_p}{(\rho C_p)_f}\right]$ and $H_3=\left[1-\frac{3\epsilon\phi k_f(k_f-k_p)}{k_m[k_p+2k_f+\phi(k_f-k_p)]}\right]$.

2.3. Temporal and Spatial Boundary Specifications

The dimensionless supporting constraints by utilizing (8) and (9) are

$$\psi=0,\begin{cases}\theta=1 & \text{at source}\\ \dfrac{\partial\theta}{\partial\eta}=0 & \text{at adiabatic section}\end{cases}\quad \text{at } \xi=0$$

$$\psi=0,\begin{cases}\theta=0 & \text{at sink}\\ \dfrac{\partial\theta}{\partial\eta}=0 & \text{at adiabatic section}\end{cases}\quad \text{at } \xi=1 \tag{12}$$

$$\psi=0, A\sin\gamma\frac{\partial\theta}{\partial\xi}-\frac{\partial\theta}{\partial\eta}=0,\quad \text{at } \eta=0 \text{ and } A$$

2.4. Thermal Transport Parameter

The rate of thermal dissipation from the source is estimated through the following relation:

$$\overline{Nu}=-\frac{k_{mnf}}{k_f}\frac{1}{\delta}\int_{L-\frac{\delta}{2}}^{L+\frac{\delta}{2}}Nu\,d\eta,\ \text{ where } Nu=\frac{1}{\cos\gamma}\left(\frac{\sin\gamma}{A}\frac{\partial\theta}{\partial\eta}-\frac{\partial\theta}{\partial\xi}\right) \tag{13}$$

Here $\overline{Nu}$ and Nu are the overall and local Nusselt numbers, respectively.

3. Computational Procedure

The computational approach utilizes finite difference discretization with a combination of a time-splitting methodology and line-based over-relaxation algorithms to achieve numerical convergence. The solution procedure employs the following:

(a) Time-splitting technique: The energy equation is solved using the ADI scheme, where the time increment is split into two halves, with each part treating derivatives in one direction implicitly. This method is explained below by considering the energy equation.
(b) Line over-relaxation: For the stream function equation, the SLOR method is utilized, which enhances convergence compared to point-by-point methods. This method is illustrated in the following momentum equation.
(c) Discretization: Forward and central differencing are utilized for temporal and diffusion terms.
(d) Grid independence: A uniform grid of 126 × 126 is chosen after several trails with various grids from 51 × 51 to 201 × 201.
(e) Numerical integration: Simpson's rule is adopted to evaluate the overall $\overline{Nu}$

3.1. Implementation of ADI Technique

The energy equation in terms of the stream function ψ is given by

$$\frac{\partial \theta}{\partial \tau}+\frac{\partial \psi}{\partial \eta}\frac{\partial \theta}{\partial \xi}-\frac{\partial \psi}{\partial \xi}\frac{\partial \theta}{\partial \eta}=\frac{A}{\cos\gamma}\left[\frac{\partial^2\theta}{\partial \xi^2}-\frac{2\sin\gamma}{A}\frac{\partial^2\theta}{\partial \xi\partial \eta}+\frac{1}{A^2}\frac{\partial^2\theta}{\partial \eta^2}\right] \tag{14}$$

For the time derivative, the forward difference is used and the diffusion terms are approximated by central differences.

$$\frac{\theta_{i,j}^{n+\frac{1}{2}}-\theta_{i,j}^{n}}{\Delta\tau/2}+\left(\frac{\psi_{i,j+1}-\psi_{i,j-1}}{2\Delta\eta}\right)\left(\frac{\theta_{i+1,j}^{n+\frac{1}{2}}-\theta_{i-1,j}^{n+\frac{1}{2}}}{2\Delta\xi}\right)-\left(\frac{\psi_{i+1,j}-\psi_{i-1,j}}{2\Delta\xi}\right)\left(\frac{\theta_{i,j+1}^{n}-\theta_{i,j-1}^{n}}{2\Delta\eta}\right)=$$
$$\frac{A}{\cos\gamma}\left\{\left(\frac{\theta_{i-1,j}^{n+\frac{1}{2}}-2\theta_{i,j}^{n+\frac{1}{2}}+\theta_{i+1,j}^{n+\frac{1}{2}}}{(\Delta\xi)^2}\right)-\frac{2\sin\gamma}{A}\left(\frac{\theta_{i+1,j+1}^{n}-\theta_{i+1,j-1}^{n+\frac{1}{2}}-\theta_{i-1,j+1}^{n}+\theta_{i-1,j-1}^{n+\frac{1}{2}}}{4\Delta\xi\Delta\eta}\right)\right.$$
$$\left.+\frac{1}{A^2}\left(\frac{\theta_{i,j-1}^{n}-2\theta_{i,j}^{n}+\theta_{i,j+1}^{n}}{(\Delta\eta)^2}\right)\right\}$$

Upon rearranging the terms in the above equation, we get

$$A_1\theta_{i-1,j}^{*}+B_1\theta_{i,j}^{*}+C_1\theta_{i+1,j}^{*}=E_1\theta_{i,j-1}^{n}+F_1\theta_{i,j}^{n}+G_1\theta_{i,j+1}^{n}+H_1 \tag{15}$$

where

$$A_1=-\frac{\beta}{4}(\psi_{i,j+1}-\psi_{i,j-1})-\frac{A}{\cos\gamma};\ B_1=\frac{2}{\lambda}-\frac{2A}{\cos\gamma}$$
$$C_1=\frac{\beta}{4}(\psi_{i,j+1}-\psi_{i,j-1})-\frac{A}{\cos\gamma};\ E_1=-\frac{\beta}{4}(\psi_{i+1,j}-\psi_{i-1,j})+\frac{\beta^2}{A\cos\gamma}$$
$$F_1=\frac{2}{\lambda}-\frac{2\beta^2}{A\cos\gamma};\ G_1=\frac{\beta}{4}(\psi_{i+1,j}-\psi_{i-1,j})-\frac{\beta^2}{A\cos\gamma}$$
$$H_1=-\frac{\beta\tan\gamma}{2}\left(\theta_{i+1,j+1}^{n}-\theta_{i+1,j-1}^{n+\frac{1}{2}}-\theta_{i-1,j+1}^{n}+\theta_{i-1,j-1}^{n+\frac{1}{2}}\right)$$

Equation (15) is a tri-diagonal system for the variable $\theta^*_{i,j}$ that can be inverted by utilizing the Thomas algorithm.

For the II half-time increment, the variables $\theta^{n+1}_{i,j}$ are computed from the following equation:

$$\begin{aligned}&\left.\frac{\partial\theta}{\partial\tau}\right|^{n+\frac{1}{2}}_{i,j}+\left.\frac{\partial\psi}{\partial\eta}\frac{\partial\theta}{\partial\xi}\right|^{n+\frac{1}{2}}_{i,j}-\left.\frac{\partial\psi}{\partial\xi}\frac{\partial\theta}{\partial\eta}\right|^{n+1}_{i,j}\\&=\frac{A}{\cos\gamma}\left\{\left.\frac{\partial^2\theta}{\partial\xi^2}\right|^{n+\frac{1}{2}}_{i,j}-\frac{2\sin\gamma}{A}\left.\frac{\partial^2\theta}{\partial\xi\partial\eta}\right|^{n+\frac{1}{2}}_{i,j}+\frac{1}{A^2}\left.\frac{\partial^2\theta}{\partial\eta^2}\right|^{n+1}_{i,j}\right\}\end{aligned}\tag{16}$$

Replacing the time derivative by the forward difference and the convective and diffusion terms by central difference approximations in (16), as explained in the first-half time step, the following finite difference equation can be obtained:

$$A_2\theta^{n+1}_{i,j-1}+B_2\theta^{n+1}_{i,j}+C_2\theta^{n+1}_{i,j+1}=E_2\theta^*_{i-1,j}+F_2\theta^*_{i,j}+G_2\theta^*_{i+1,j}+H_2\tag{17}$$

where

$$\begin{aligned}A_2&=\frac{\beta}{4}(\psi_{i+1,j}-\psi_{i-1,j})-\frac{\beta^2}{A\cos\gamma};\ B_2=\frac{2}{\lambda}+\frac{2\beta^2}{A\cos\gamma}\\C_2&=-\frac{\beta}{4}(\psi_{i+1,j}-\psi_{i-1,j})-\frac{\beta^2}{A\cos\gamma};\ E_2=\frac{\beta}{4}(\psi_{i,j+1}-\psi_{i,j-1})+\frac{A}{\cos\gamma}\\F_2&=\frac{2}{\lambda}-\frac{2A}{\cos\gamma};\ G_2=-\frac{\beta}{4}(\psi_{i,j+1}-\psi_{i,j-1})+\frac{A}{\cos\gamma}\\H_2&=-\frac{\beta\tan\gamma}{2}\left(\theta^{n+\frac{1}{2}}_{i+1,j+1}-\theta^{n+1}_{i+1,j-1}-\theta^{n+\frac{1}{2}}_{i-1,j+1}+\theta^{n+1}_{i-1,j-1}\right)\end{aligned}$$

Equation (17), which is implicit in the η-direction, is a tri-diagonal system in the unknown $\theta^{n+1}_{i,j}$ that can be solved in a similar manner.

3.2. Implementation of SLOR Technique

We consider the momentum equation in terms of the stream function in the following form:

$$\frac{1}{A^2}\frac{\partial^2\psi}{\partial\eta^2}-\frac{2\sin\gamma}{A}\frac{\partial^2\psi}{\partial\xi\partial\eta}+\frac{\partial^2\psi}{\partial\xi^2}=Ra\,H(\phi)\cdot\cos^2\gamma\left\{\left(\frac{1}{A\cos\gamma}\frac{\partial\theta}{\partial\eta}-\tan\gamma\frac{\partial\theta}{\partial\xi}\right)\sin\alpha-\cos\alpha\frac{\partial\theta}{\partial\xi}\right\}$$

Applying central difference quotients, the discretized equation becomes

$$\begin{aligned}&(\psi_{i+1,j}-2\psi_{i,j}+\psi_{i-1,j})-\frac{\beta}{2A}\sin\gamma(\psi_{i+1,j+1}-\psi_{i+1,j-1}-\psi_{i-1,j+1}+\psi_{i-1,j-1})\\&+\frac{\beta^2}{A^2}(\psi_{i,j+1}-2\psi_{i,j}+\psi_{i,j-1})=Ra\,H(\phi)\cos^2\gamma\left[\left(\frac{\Delta\xi\,\beta}{2A\cos\gamma}\left(\theta^{n+1}_{i,j+1}-\theta^{n+1}_{i,j-1}\right)\right.\right.\\&\left.\left.+\frac{\Delta\xi\,\tan\gamma}{2}\left(\theta^{n+1}_{i+1,j}-\theta^{n+1}_{i-1,j}\right)\right)\sin\alpha-\frac{\cos\alpha}{2}\Delta\xi\left(\theta^{n+1}_{i+1,j}-\theta^{n+1}_{i-1,j}\right)\right]\end{aligned}$$

where $\beta=\frac{\Delta\xi}{\Delta\eta}$. This can be written as

$$A_1\,\psi_{i-1,j}+B_1\,\psi_{i,j}+C_1\,\psi_{i+1,j}=E_1$$

where

$$
\begin{aligned}
A_1 &= C_1 = 1 \\
B_1 &= -2 - 2\frac{\beta^2}{A^2} \\
E_1 &= \frac{\beta}{2A}\sin\gamma\left(\psi_{i+1,j+1} - \psi_{i+1,j-1} - \psi_{i-1,j+1} + \psi_{i-1,j-1}\right) \\
&\quad + Ra\,H(\phi)\cos^2\gamma\left(\left[\frac{\Delta\xi\,\beta}{2A\cos\gamma}\left(\theta^{n+1}_{i,j+1} - \theta^{n+1}_{i,j-1}\right)\right.\right. \\
&\quad \left.\left.+\frac{\Delta\xi\tan\gamma}{2}\left(\theta^{n+1}_{i+1,j} - \theta^{n+1}_{i-1,j}\right)\right]\sin\alpha - \frac{\cos\alpha}{2}\Delta\xi\left(\theta^{n+1}_{i+1,j} - \theta^{n+1}_{i-1,j}\right)\right) \\
&\quad - \frac{\beta^2}{A^2}\left(\psi_{i,j+1} + \psi_{i,j-1}\right)
\end{aligned}
$$

The computational procedure utilized for estimating the stream function and thermal distribution repeats cyclically until achieving the specified convergence threshold:

$$
\frac{|\chi^{n+1}_{i,j} - \chi^{n}_{i,j}|}{|\chi^{n+1}_{i,j}|} \leq \Gamma \tag{18}
$$

Within this convergence requirement, the variable χ represents either ψ or θ, with indices i and j corresponding to spatial coordinates in the (ξ,η) computational domain. The superscript n indicates the temporal iteration step, while Γ defines the tolerance limit for convergence. A mesh refinement analysis was conducted by systematically varying the mesh densities from 51×51 to 161×161 points (see Table 3). The numerical values of $\overline{Nu}$ were monitored across these mesh configurations to ensure computational accuracy and solution stability. Following comprehensive assessment of these mesh sensitivity trials, the final computations were executed using a 161×161 grid distributions.

Table 3. Grid independence analysis at $Ra = 10^3$, $\alpha = 45°$, $\phi = 0.05$, $\epsilon = 0.2$, $\gamma = 30°$, and $L = 0.5$.

Grid Size	$\overline{Nu}$	Relative Difference
51×51	25.508976744	
		0.03236
101×101	24.680709289	
		0.01467
161×161	24.317631546	
		0.00213
201×201	24.265793436	
		0.00001
251×251	24.265551151	

3.3. Validation

To establish computational reliability, we rigorously validated our in-house numerical code against the benchmark results published by Sheremet et al. [20] for buoyant convection in a uniformly heated porous square domain. The validation cases were configured with specific parameters (inclination angle, $\alpha = 0°$, sidewall angle, $\gamma = 0°$) for two distinct porous matrices—aluminum foam and glass ball packing—and the geometry was filled with Cu-H_2O nanofluid. Figure 2 illustrates a comparative analysis of both NF-convective flow and thermal contours among our estimations and the simulations of Sheremet et al. [20], and the results demonstrate excellent agreement. Beyond the qualitative comparison, we also conducted additional simulations to validate our quantitative predictions by comparing the average Nusselt number values with those reported by Saeid and Pop [44] and Baytas [42] for buoyancy-assisted convection in a porous square conduit. For this validation, we set $\gamma = 0$, $\alpha = 0$, and $\phi = 0$ to match the reference conditions. As displayed in Table 4, our current predictions demonstrate excellent agreement with the established results for a square porous enclosure using the Darcy model. This comprehensive validation confirms the accuracy of our numerical approach for the NF-saturated porous domain, providing a solid foundation for the subsequent parametric analysis.

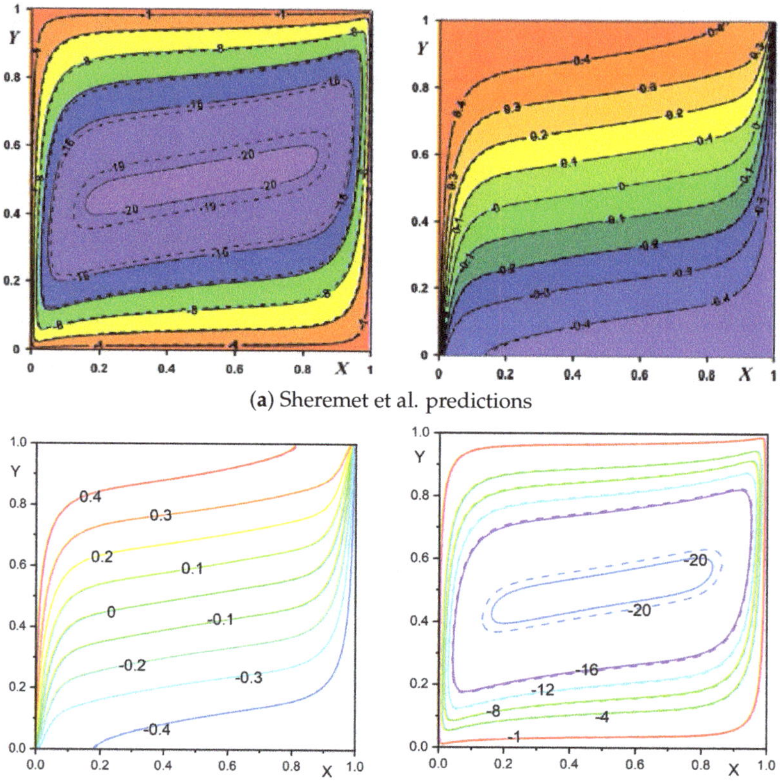

(**a**) Sheremet et al. predictions

(**b**) Present predictions

Figure 2. Benchmarking present predictions (**b**) against the established results of Sheremet et al. [20] (**a**) for $Ra = 10^3$, $\phi = 0.05$, $\epsilon = 0.5$, $\alpha = 0°$, and $\gamma = 0°$. Solid lines (aluminum foam) and glass balls (dashed lines) as porous structures.

Table 4. Comparison of average Nusselt number values with literature findings for $\gamma = 0$, $\alpha = 0$, and $\phi = 0$.

Ra	Saeid and Pop [44]	Baytas [42]	Present Study
100	3.002	3.160	3.102
1000	13.726	14.060	13.914
10,000	43.953	48.330	42.316

4. Results and Discussion

Here, we present the comprehensive illustrations of buoyancy-assisted convection in an NF-saturated porous structure within an inclined parallelogrammic geometry subjected to discrete thermal boundary conditions. The thermal–hydraulic characteristics of the setup are systematically investigated through computational simulations by resolving the coupled momentum and energy transport equations. Flow patterns and thermal distributions are visualized via streamline and isotherm contours, while heat transfer performance is quantified through estimating the average Nusselt number at the discrete thermal source. The computational domain consists of an oriented parallelogrammic space with localized heating and cooling elements positioned on opposing tilted sidewalls. The simulations were performed with fixed structural parameters (aspect ratio $A = 1$ and porosity $\epsilon = 0.9$) while systematically varying the following thermophysical and geometric parameters:

Rayleigh number (Ra): $10^1 \leq Ra \leq 10^3$
Source length (δ): 0.2 and 0.5
Source position (L): 0.3, 0.5 and 0.7
Enclosure inclination angle (α): $-45^\circ \leq \alpha \leq 45^\circ$
Sidewall inclination angle (γ): $-30^\circ \leq \gamma \leq 30^\circ$
Nanoparticle volume fraction (ϕ): $0 \leq \phi \leq 0.05$

4.1. Enclosure Orientation Impact on Hydrodynamic Flow and Thermal Transport

Figure 3 depicts the influence of the geometry inclination angle (α) on the flow structure and thermal pattern inside the parallelogrammic geometry with a discrete thermal source–sink. The predictions were obtained with fixed parameters of $Ra = 10^3$, $\gamma = 30^\circ$, $\delta = 0.2$, $L = 0.5$, and $\phi = 0.04$. The streamline structure reveals a progressive enhancement in flow circulation intensity with a change in geometry tilting angle. At $\alpha = -45^\circ$ (Figure 3a), a relatively weak clockwise convective motion is observed with an extreme flow circulation rate of approximately -2.2. The hydrodynamic flow exhibits a primary circulation cell with secondary vortices near the geometric corners due to collective influences of discrete thermal conditions and geometrical inclination. When the enclosure is horizontal ($\alpha = 0^\circ$, Figure 3b), the circulation intensity increases moderately, with the stream function value reaching -6.7 and a more organized flow structure concentrated toward the central region. The most profound flow enhancement occurs at $\alpha = 45^\circ$ (Figure 3c), where the maximum stream function value elevated to approximately -16.1, indicating an approximate 7−fold increase in circulation strength compared to the $\alpha = -45^\circ$ configuration. The isotherm distributions exhibit the corresponding changes in thermal characteristics across three different inclination angles. For $\alpha = -45^\circ$, the isotherms are marginally distorted and spread throughout the geometry, indicating thermal boundary layer formation and predominantly a conduction-dominated transport. At $\alpha = 0^\circ$, the isotherms exhibit a moderate shift toward the central region, indicating the enhanced convective transport. For the $\alpha = 45^\circ$ configuration, the thermal contours cluster near the thermal source with reduced thermal boundary layer thickness near both the source and sink. Further, a more pronounced horizontal stratification can be observed in the core region, indicating superior convective mixing and thermal transport efficiency.

A comprehensive analysis of the global transport rate ($\overline{Nu}$) sensitivity to variations in Ra and the geometry inclination angle (α) is presented in Figure 4 with fixed parameters $\gamma = 30^\circ$, $\delta = 0.2$, and $L = 0.5$. The graph demonstrates a vivid correlation between the improvement in thermal dissipation and the increasing magnitudes of both Ra and α. For all magnitudes of Ra, the global Nu exhibits a monotonic increase as the tilt angle transitions from negative (-45°) to positive ($+45^\circ$) inclinations, with a pronounced enhancement observed in the range of $-20^\circ \leq \alpha \leq 20^\circ$. At $Ra = 10^3$, $\overline{Nu}$ increases approximately six-fold from $\alpha = -45^\circ$ to $\alpha = 45^\circ$, whereas at $Ra = 10^2$, the enhancement is very modest. An examination of thermal energy dissipation characteristics comparing pure water (H_2O) as the reference medium (depicted by solid curves) against NFs with volume concentration $\phi = 0.05$ (represented by dotted curves) demonstrates that NFs continuously exhibit a reduced performance relative to H_2O for all parameter settings. Specifically, at $\alpha = 45^\circ$, the NF demonstrates an 8.6% reduction in mean Nusselt number for $Ra = 10^3$. Similarly, at $Ra = 5 \times 10^2$ and $Ra = 10^2$, the NF manifests a 13.0% and 12.5% decline in heat dissipation rate, respectively. This paradoxical deterioration suggests that, despite the enhanced thermal conductivity of NFs, the accompanying viscosity enhancement hinders the formation of stronger convection cells, particularly in the buoyancy-driven flow regime at higher Ra values, an anomalous behavior predicted in the earlier literature [10,20] for a similar model.

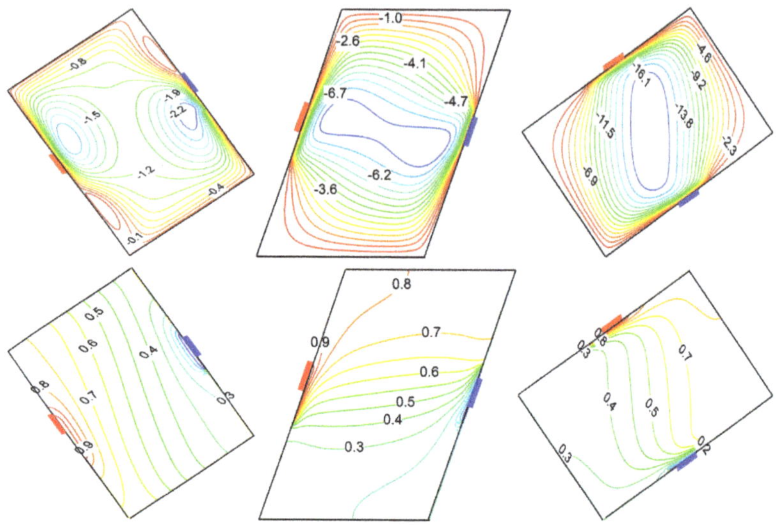

(a) (b) (c)

Figure 3. Effect of geometry inclination on streamlines (**top row**) and isotherms (**bottom row**) for $\phi = 0.04$, $Ra = 10^3$, $\gamma = 30°$, $\delta = 0.2$, $L = 0.5$. (**a**) $\alpha = -45°$. (**b**) $\alpha = 0°$. (**c**) $\alpha = 45°$.

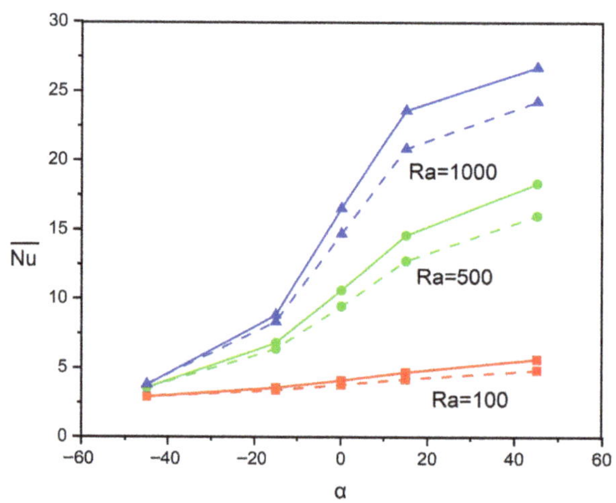

Figure 4. Inspection of $\overline{Nu}$ dependency on variations in Ra and α for $\gamma = 30°$, $\delta = 0.2$, $L = 0.5$. Continuous curves correspond to H_2O and dashed curves represent NF ($\phi = 0.05$).

Figure 5 presents a critical evaluation of the $\overline{Nu}$ variation in the combined impacts of sidewall tilting (γ) as well as cavity inclination (α) with fixed parameters $Ra = 10^3$, $\delta = 0.2$, $L = 0.5$, and $\phi = 0.05$. The observation reveals the complex interactions between these two geometric parameters that profoundly influence thermal dissipation performance. For all three orientations of γ, the magnitude of $\overline{Nu}$ remains comparatively low (≈3–4) at $\alpha = -45°$, indicating minimal dependence on sidewall tilting at negative geometry inclinations where buoyancy effects are substantially suppressed. As α increases toward positive values, thermal transport enhancement becomes pronounced and geometrically dependent, with all configurations exhibiting an increase in $\overline{Nu}$. The square domain ($\gamma = 0°$) demonstrates superior performance, achieving the highest $\overline{Nu}$ value (≈24.5) at $\alpha = 15°$ and reaching a constant value. Notably, the negatively tilted parallelogram ($\gamma = -30°$) exhibits non-monotonic behavior, while the positively tilted configuration ($\gamma = 30°$) demonstrates continuous enhancement, achieving the maximum heat transfer rate at $\alpha = 45°$.

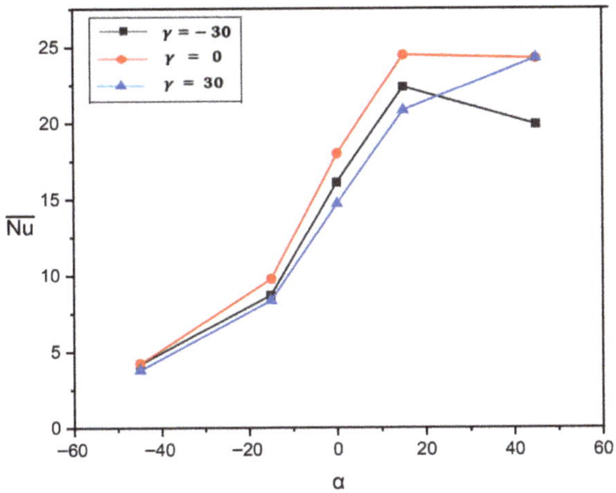

Figure 5. Inspection of $\overline{Nu}$ dependency on combined influences of γ and α for $Ra = 10^3, \delta = 0.2$, $L = 0.5$, $\phi = 0.05$.

4.2. Thermal Source–Sink Position and Dimension Impact on Hydrodynamic Flow and Thermal Transport

Figure 6 illustrates the positional (L) influence of the thermal source–sink on velocity and temperature distributions for a smaller dimension ($\delta = 0.2$). The top row displays streamline contours while the bottom row represents the corresponding isotherms by considering three source positions: $L = 0.3$, $L = 0.5$, and $L = 0.7$. The streamline pattern reveals a complex bi-cellular flow structure at $L = 0.3$, with counter-rotating vortices of unequal strength, where the primary vortex ($\psi_{min} = -3.1$) dominates the upper region and a secondary vortex ($\psi_{min} = -2.5$) appears near the bottom sink. As the source–sink shifts to a central position ($L = 0.5$), the flow reorganizes into a more symmetric bi-cellular pattern with two distinct counter-rotating cells of comparable intensity ($\psi_{min} = -3.2$ for both), positioned diagonally across the enclosure and located near the source and sink. Further shifting the source to $L = 0.7$, the flow transforms into a distinctly asymmetric pattern characterized by a smaller eddy ($\psi_{min} = -2.1$) in the upper region and a larger, more intense, dominating eddy ($\psi_{min} = -2.7$) at the lower portion. The corresponding isotherms demonstrate a progressive transformation from steep, concentrated gradients near the source and sink regions at $L = 0.3$ to more uniformly distributed thermal fields at $L = 0.7$. In particular, at the lower positioning of source ($L = 0.3$), the isotherms exhibit significant clustering near the bottom left and top right regions, indicating intense local heat transport. As L increases to 0.5 and subsequently to 0.7, the thermal stratification becomes more balanced throughout the geometry, with progressively more uniform gradients between the source and the sink-placed boundaries. Figure 7 elucidates the significant influence of thermal source–sink location on velocity and temperature distributions for an extended thermal source–sink length of $\delta = 0.5$. Unlike the previous case with a shorter source–sink length ($\delta = 0.2$), this configuration with an extended source–sink length generates the strong single-eddy flow patterns across all source positions, albeit with significant variations in intensity and structure. At $L = 0.35$, the streamline distribution exhibits a strong uni-cellular structure with a maximum intensity of $\psi_{min} = -18.0$ concentrated in the lower portion. As the source position moves further ($L = 0.5$ and $L = 0.65$), the circulation core shifts toward the middle and upper regions with a slightly increased intensity ($\psi_{min} = -18.2$ and -18.1) while maintaining similar structural characteristics. The corresponding isotherms demonstrate parallel evolutionary behavior, transitioning from a moderately stratified thermal field at $L = 0.35$ to increasingly distorted patterns at higher source positions. This progression vividly demonstrates that, with an extended thermal source length ($\delta = 0.5$), the source–sink position exerts a profound influence on flow morphology and thermal transport characteristics.

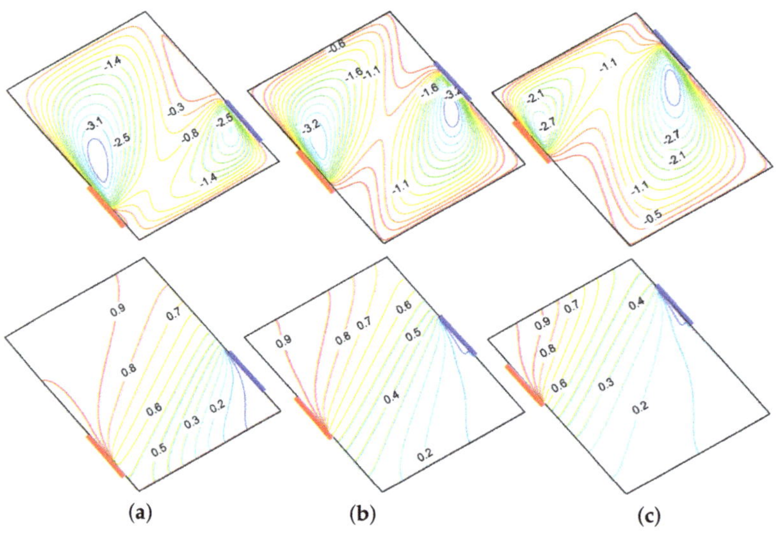

Figure 6. Influence of source–sink arrangement on streamlines (**top row**) and isotherms (**bottom row**) for $\phi = 0.04$, $Ra = 10^3$, $\delta = 0.2$, $\gamma = 15°$, $\alpha = -30°$. (**a**) $L = 0.3$. (**b**) $L = 0.5$. (**c**) $L = 0.7$.

Figure 8 depicts the evolution of $\overline{Nu}$ for different magnitudes of Ra and thermal source–sink locations (L) with $\gamma = 15°$, $\delta = 0.2$, and $\alpha = 30°$. The estimation presents a comparative analysis of $\overline{Nu}$ between H_2O (dashed lines) and NF with $\phi = 0.05$ (solid lines). For all magnitudes of Rayleigh numbers ($Ra = 10^2$, 5×10^2, and 10^2), the global Nu reveals a declining trend as the source–sink position shifts upward from $L = 0.3$ to $L = 0.7$, indicating that lower source–sink placements promote a more efficient heat dissipation rate. This trend is most pronounced at lower Rayleigh numbers, where the thermal efficiency decreases by approximately 54% for $Ra = 10^2$ to 28% for $Ra = 10^3$ as L increases from 0.3 to 0.7. With regard to the inclusion of NPs, the base fluid (H_2O) consistently outperforms NF across all conditions. This enhancement is particularly significant for the middle position ($L = 0.5$), where the improvement reaches approximately 9.8%, 11.8%, and 9.1% for $Ra = 10^3$, 5×10^2, and 10^2 respectively, compared to the lower enhancement percentages observed at $L = 0.3$. The superior performance at lower source–sink positions can be attributed to the favorable alignment of the buoyancy-driven convection patterns with the thermal gradient when the heat source is positioned near the bottom of the inclined wall. The outcomes in Figure 9 illustrate the sensitivity of the thermal transfer rate performance to variations in the thermal source–sink dimension (δ) across different Rayleigh numbers. Analysis of the prediction reveals that the $\overline{Nu}$ consistently decreases as the thermal source length (δ) increases from 0.2 to 1.0 in all Rayleigh numbers, indicating that a shorter thermal source–sink efficiently promotes higher heat dissipation. Quantitatively, the heat dissipation efficiency decreases by approximately 33% for $Ra = 1000$, 35% for $Ra = 500$, and 20% for $Ra = 100$ as δ increases from 0.2 to 1.0. The comparative performance between NFs and water reveals that H_2O (base fluid) consistently outperforms NFs at all source lengths, with enhancement ranging from 10 to 17%.

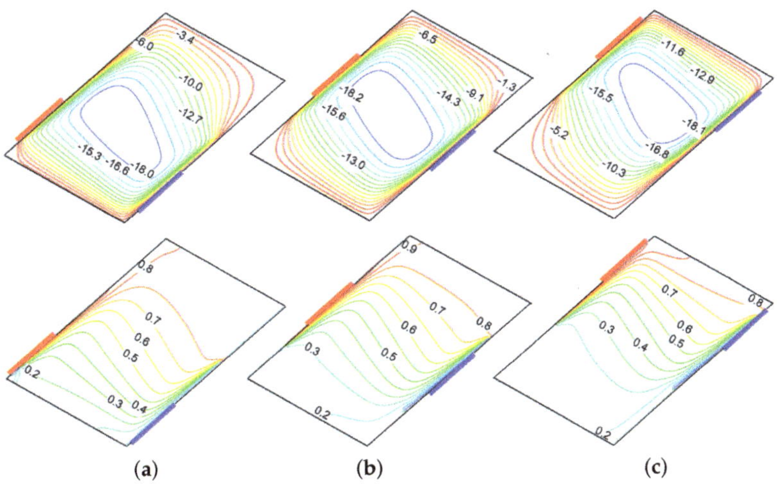

Figure 7. Influence of source–sink arrangement on streamlines (**top row**) and isotherms (**bottom row**) for $\phi = 0.04$, $Ra = 10^3$, $\gamma = 30°$, $\alpha = 30°$, $\delta = 0.5$. (**a**) $L = 0.35$. (**b**) $L = 0.5$. (**c**) $L = 0.65$.

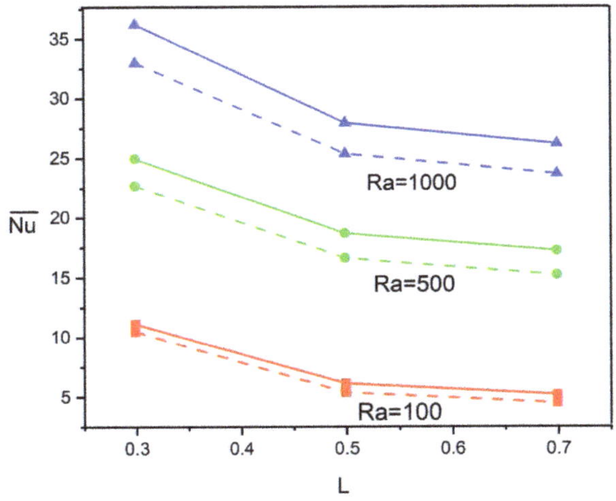

Figure 8. Heat dissipation rate variations with thermal source locations and $Ra = 10^3$ at $\gamma = 15°$, $\delta = 0.2$, $\alpha = 30°$. Continuous curves correspond to H_2O and dashed curves represent NF ($\phi = 0.05$).

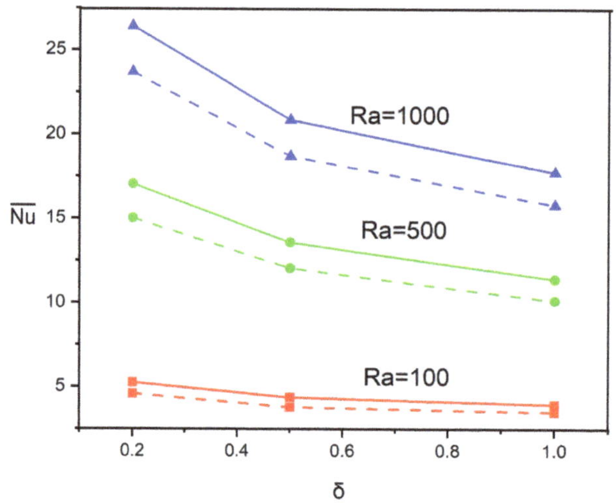

Figure 9. Inspection of $\overline{Nu}$ dependency on variations in δ and Ra for $L = 0.5$, $\gamma = 30°$, $\alpha = 30°$. Continuous curves correspond to H_2O and dashed curves represent NF ($\phi = 0.05$).

4.3. Influence of Ra and γ on Hydrodynamic Motion and Heat Transport

Figure 10 portrays the influence of sidewall orientation (γ) on flow and thermal patterns at $Ra = 10^3$, with parameters $L = 0.5$, $\delta = 0.2$, $\alpha = 30°$, and $\phi = 0.04$ fixed. The upper row displays streamlines while the bottom row represents isotherms for three distinct configurations: $\gamma = -30°$, $\gamma = 0°$, and $\gamma = 30°$. The streamline structure reveals a strong clockwise rotating cell that dominates the flow field in all three geometries, driven by the thermal buoyancy forces between the source (red segment on left wall) and sink (blue segment on right wall). The circulation intensity is considerably influenced by the sidewall orientation, with maximum stream function values of approximately -11.5 for $\gamma = -30°$, -11.7 for $\gamma = 0°$, and -14.0 for $\gamma = 30°$. This progressive augmentation elucidates that the positive sidewall tilt ($\gamma = 30°$) elevates convective circulation by approximately 20% compared to the negative tilt configuration. The corresponding isotherms demonstrate substantial deformation from the conduction-dominated pattern, confirming the prevalence of convective heat transfer. As γ increases from $-30°$ to $30°$, the isotherms exhibit increased clustering near the source and sink regions, particularly evident in the $\gamma = 30°$ case, where temperature gradients are most pronounced. These observations collectively demonstrate that the parallelogrammic configuration with a positive sidewall orientation ($\gamma = 30°$) provides the optimal thermal performance among the three orientations investigated due to its favorable alignment with the buoyancy-driven flow dynamics.

Figure 11 demonstrates the impact of sidewall orientation (γ) on thermal efficiency for diverse magnitudes of Ra in the tilted parallelogrammic geometry with fixed parameters $L = 0.5$, $\delta = 0.2$, and $\alpha = 30°$. The overall thermal dissipation rate ($\overline{Nu}$) exhibits a non-monotonic variation with γ across all examined Rayleigh numbers. As γ varies across $\pm 30°$, heat dissipation efficiency declines, with the reduction more pronounced at positive tilt angles. For $Ra = 10^3$, the thermal dissipation rate reaches its maximum at $\gamma = 0°$, with the base-fluid ($\phi = 0$) achieving $\overline{Nu} \approx 28$ compared to the NF ($\phi = 0.05$) $\overline{Nu} \approx 26$, indicating an approximately 7.7% enhancement. For $Ra = 5 \times 10^2$, similar behavior is predicted with peak values occurring near $\gamma = 0°$, where H_2O demonstrates an approximately 11.4% improvement over NFs ($\overline{Nu} \approx 19.5$ versus $\overline{Nu} \approx 17.5$). For the lower $Ra = 10^2$ considered in this analysis, the predictions exhibit less sensitivity to γ variations, with maximum values slightly shifted toward $\gamma = -10°$ and the base fluid maintaining an approximately

13.3% enhancement across the examined tilt range. Notably, the thermal performance declines at extreme tilt angles ($\gamma = \pm 30^\circ$), and it appears to be more significant as the magnitude of Ra increases, suggesting that an optimal configuration becomes more critical at higher convection intensities.

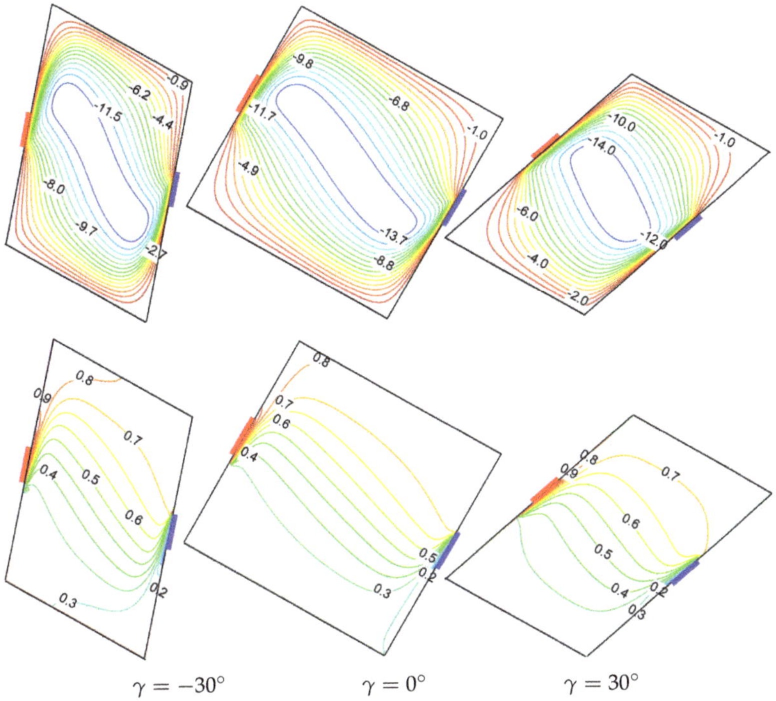

Figure 10. Sidewall tilt angle impact on streamlines (**top row**) and isotherms (**bottom row**) for $L = 0.5, \delta = 0.2, \alpha = 30^\circ, \phi = 0.04, Ra = 10^3$.

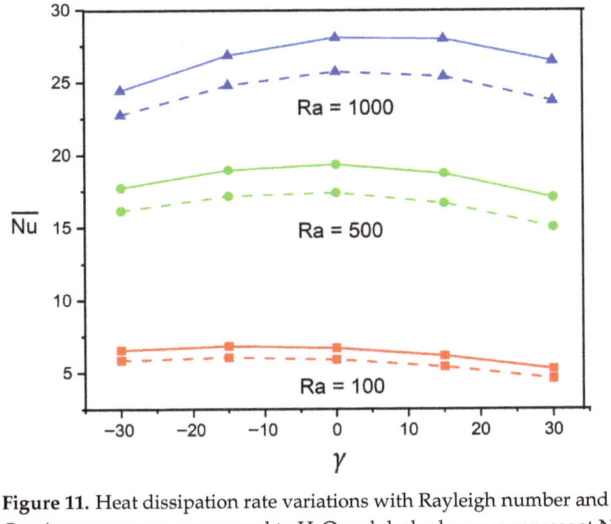

Figure 11. Heat dissipation rate variations with Rayleigh number and γ at $L = 0.5, \delta = 0.2, \alpha = 30^\circ$. Continuous curves correspond to H_2O and dashed curves represent NF ($\phi = 0.05$).

4.4. Impact of *Ra* and ϕ on Hydrodynamic Flow and Thermal Transport

Figure 12 displays the profound physical transformations in terms of NF buoyant flow and thermal distributions with Rayleigh number variation for H_2O as well as NF. At $Ra = 10^2$, a weak single-eddy circulation exists with $\psi_{max} \approx -2.2$, indicating that buoyancy forces marginally exceeding viscous resistance and thermal distribution contours exhibit a near-conduction regime characterized by almost upright equally spaced isotherms. The fundamental transition in heat transport processes occurs at $Ra = 5 \times 10^2$, where the convective motion begins to dominate, accompanied by the intensive streamline, which increases more than five-fold ($\psi_{max} \approx -8.2$). This is further evidenced by significant isotherm distortion as the buoyant fluid motion proactively transports thermal energy across the geometry. The convection-dominant phenomenon is further amplified at $Ra = 10^3$, where the circulation rate intensifies substantially ($\psi_{max} \approx -12.0$) with a pronounced change in the vortex direction, while isotherms develop distinctive thermal boundary layers near active walls. The physical emphasis of these transformations could be interpreted as the progressive shift from molecular-level heat transport to bulk fluid transport as the driving mechanism. In addition, the substantial thinning of the thermal boundary layer has been predicted at $Ra = 10^3$, where sharp thermal gradients form adjacent to the thermal source and sink, which dramatically elevates the local thermal transport rates.

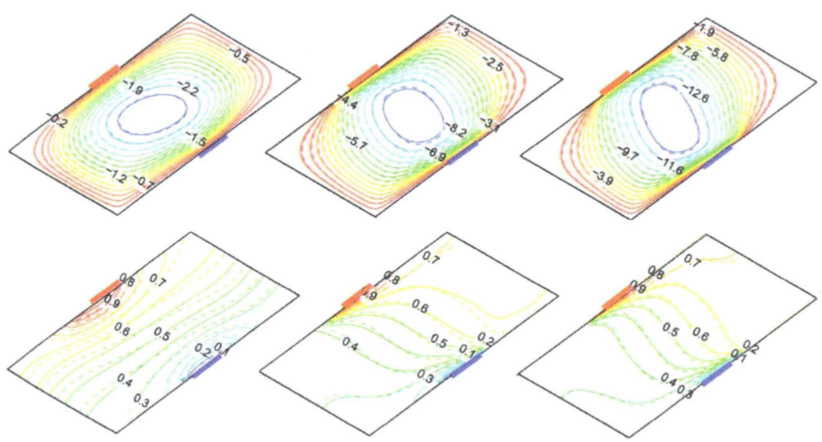

$Ra = 10^2$ $\quad$ $Ra = 5 \times 10^2$ $\quad$ $Ra = 10^3$

Figure 12. Streamlines (**top row**) and isotherms (**bottom row**) for diverse magnitudes of *Ra* at $L = 0.5, \delta = 0.2, \alpha = 30°, \gamma = 45°$. Continuous curves correspond to H_2O and dashed curves represent NF ($\phi = 0.04$).

Figure 13 elucidates the thermophysical mechanisms governing heat dissipation in a discretely heated–cooled tilted parallelogrammic geometry as functions of NP concentration (ϕ) and Rayleigh number (*Ra*) at fixed geometric parameters ($\gamma = 30°$, $L = 0.5$, $\alpha = 30°$). A counterintuitive thermal phenomenon has been noticed where enhancing NP concentration consistently reduces heat transport efficiency at all examined *Ra* values, contradicting the conventional comprehension that elevated thermal conductivity from NPs improves the thermal transport. This contradictory prediction reveals the dominance of viscosity effects over conductivity enhancement in deaccelerating the buoyant-assisted motion, and a similar prediction was made in previous investigations [10,20]. The elevated viscosity from the addition of NP suppresses flow mobility and consequently reduces the convective transport mechanisms. Further, the thermal source–sink dimension (δ) induces a substantial impact on heat dissipation dynamics, with the smaller heat source–sink ($\delta = 0.2$)

consistently evidencing superior thermal efficiency compared to the larger source–sink ($\delta = 0.5$) across all parametric combinations. This enhancement in $\overline{Nu}$ can be attributed to concentrated thermal gradients generated by the smaller source, which in turn amplify the local buoyancy-driven flows and develop stronger convection currents. In accordance with established predictions, the Ra exhibits the most pronounced impact on the thermal dissipation mechanism, with $\overline{Nu}$ increasing approximately five-fold from $Ra = 10^2$ to $Ra = 10^3$ for pure fluid ($\phi = 0$), characterizing the significant progression from a conduction-dominated thermal regime to a convection-prevalent thermal state. In particular, the negative slope of $\overline{Nu}$ versus ϕ steepens with an increase in Ra, demonstrating that the suppression effect of NPs becomes more detrimental at higher magnitudes of Ra where buoyant convection would otherwise be more vigorous.

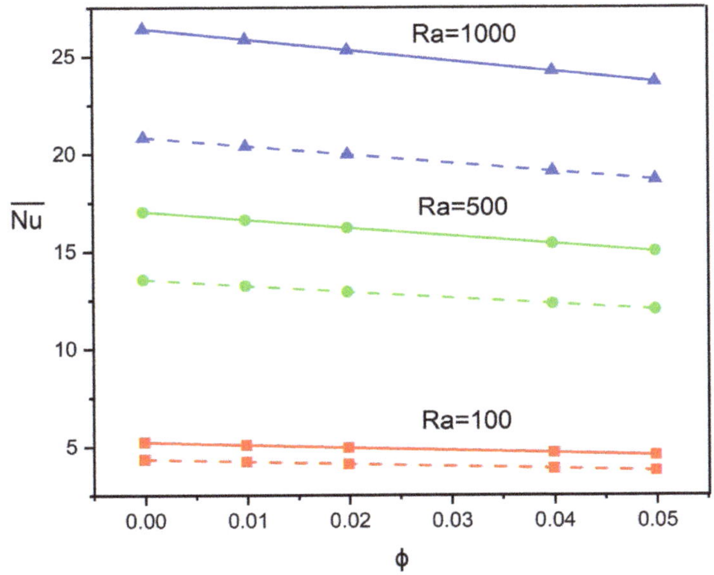

Figure 13. Heat dissipation rate variations with collective influences of Ra and ϕ at $\gamma = 30°$, $L = 0.5$, $\alpha = 30°$. Dashed curves correspond to $\delta = 0.5$ and continuous curves represent smaller source dimension $\delta = 0.2$.

5. Conclusions

A comprehensive numerical investigation has been conducted to elucidate the characteristics of buoyancy-driven convective phenomena and associated thermal transport mechanisms within an NF-saturated porous parallelogrammic geometry. The geometry also incorporates strategically positioned discrete thermal source and sink elements, presenting a configuration with significant practical relevance. The systematic parametric analysis encompassing diverse physical and geometrical parameters has yielded quantifiable insights into the governing flow and transport phenomena. The salient observations and important conclusions derived from this investigation are enumerated as follows:

1. Thermal source–sink positioning predominantly influences the convective flow patterns and thermal performance, with intermediate positions ($L = 0.5$) generating the most energetic flow structures, while extreme locations ($L = 0.7$) promote more uniform thermal distributions.
2. The complex interaction between sidewall orientation (γ) and enclosure tilting (α) reveals a significant influence on thermal transport behavior. The optimal geometric

configuration transitions from $\gamma = 0^\circ$ at moderate cavity inclinations to $\gamma = 30^\circ$ at high positive inclinations (α), suggesting that alignment between the buoyancy-driven flow direction and the enclosure geometry becomes increasingly critical as α approaches 45°. These findings demonstrate that strategic manipulation of γ and α can produce substantial thermal performance improvements.

3. Source–sink configuration optimization shows that positioning thermal elements closer to the bottom wall ($L = 0.3$) and using smaller dimensions ($\delta = 0.2$) substantially enhance thermal efficiency, with improvements of approximately 38% and 45%, respectively, at higher Rayleigh numbers.
4. Nanofluid thermal transport consistently exhibits a reduction compared to the base fluid across all examined parameters, with the most pronounced degradation occurring at higher magnitudes of Ra and moderate inclination angles, mainly attributed to competing impacts among the thermal conductivity enhancement and viscosity-induced circulation dampening.
5. Sidewall orientation (γ) sensitivity demonstrates optimal performance at near-rectangular configurations ($\gamma \approx 0^\circ$ to 10°), with a 7–12% heat transfer decline toward extreme inclinations, intensifying at higher Rayleigh numbers, with $Ra = 10^3$ showing the most pronounced variation.
6. Optimal thermal performance is achieved through strategic combinations of higher Rayleigh numbers, appropriate source-s-ink arrangements, positive enclosure tilting, and favorable geometric inclinations that enhance the buoyancy-driven convection.
7. The current predictions provide fundamental insights for optimizing thermal management systems in porous media applications and highlight the complex interplay among geometric parameters, fluid properties, and thermal transport mechanisms in an inclined parallelogrammic geometry.
8. It is worth mentioning that the present study is conducted within the framework of the Darcy model, which limits the investigation to Rayleigh numbers below 10^4. The range of Rayleigh numbers ($Ra = 10^1$–10^3) represents the complete validity domain of the Darcy approximation, where viscous forces dominate and inertial effects remain negligible. While higher magnitudes of Ra are indeed encountered in many practical applications, their investigation would necessitate the adoption of non-Darcy models. Future studies should extend this analysis to the non-Darcy regime using appropriate porous media formulations to capture the behavior at higher Ra values.

Author Contributions: Conceptualization and original draft preparation, M.S.; review and editing, S.A.A.; project administration, methodology, and software, V.C.V.; preparation of graphs and literature review, V.S.; plagiarism reduction and validation, A.A.M. All authors have read and agreed to the published version of the manuscript.

Funding: This work is supported by the University of Technology and Applied Sciences(UTAS)-Ibri, Oman, under the Internal Research Funding project No. IRG-IBRI-25-49 and Spanish Government under grants PID2023-150014OB-C21 and PID2023-150029NB-I00.

Data Availability Statement: The raw data supporting the conclusions of this article will be made available by the authors on request.

Acknowledgments: The authors, V.C.V. and V.S., express their gratitude to JSSATE, Bangalore, VTU, Belagavi and FET, Jain Deemed-to-be University, Ramanagaram, India. M.S. acknowledges the support and encouragement by the University of Technology and Applied Sciences, Ibri, Oman.

Conflicts of Interest: The authors declare no conflicts of interest.

Nomenclature

The following abbreviations are used in this manuscript:

A	aspect ratio
g	gravitational acceleration (m/s^2)
H	height of the enclosure (m)
L	width of the enclosure (m)
k	thermal conductivity $(W/(mK))$
K	permeability constant (m^2)
Nu	local Nusselt number
$\overline{Nu}$	average Nusselt number
p	pressure
Ra	Rayleigh number
t	dimensional time (s)
T	temperature (K)
T_c	sink temperature
T_h	source temperature
(u, v)	velocity components in the x and y direction
(x, y)	Cartesian coordinates (m)
(X, Y)	transformed coordinates
L	source position
C_p	heat capacity
Greek Letters	
α	Cavity inclination
δ	source length
γ	sidewall inclination angle
μ	dynamic viscosity (Kg/ms)
ϕ	nanoparticle volume fraction
ρ	fluid density (kg/m^3)
σ	heat capacity ratio
(ξ, η)	dimensionless transformed coordinates
τ	dimensionless time
θ	dimensional temperature
ψ^*	stream function
ψ	dimensionless stream function
β	thermal expansion coefficient $(1/K)$
$\Delta\theta$	temperature difference K
ϵ	porosity
Subscripts	
f	base fluid
nf	nanofluid
p	nanoparticle
m	porous structure
mnf	nanofluid porous structure
Abbreviations	
ADI	alternating direction implicit
$SLOR$	successive line over-relaxation
NF	nanofluid
NP	nanoparticle

References

1. Nield, D.A.; Bejan, A. *Convection in Porous Media*, 5th ed.; Springer: Cham, Switzerland, 2017.
2. Vafai, K. *Handbook of Porous Media*, 3rd ed.; CRC Press: Boca Raton, FL, USA, 2015.

3. Seki, N.; Fukusako, S.; Yamaguchi, A. An Experimental Study of Free Corrective Heat Transfer in a Parallelogrammic Enclosure. *ASME J. Heat Mass Transf.* **1983**, *105*, 433–439. [CrossRef]
4. Hyun, J.M.; Choi, B.S. Transient Natural Convection in a Parallelogram-Shaped Enclosure. *Int. J. Heat Fluid Flow* **1990**, *11*, 129–134. [CrossRef]
5. Baïri, A.; De María, J.M.G.; Laraqi, N. Transient Natural Convection in Parallelogrammic Enclosures with Isothermal Hot Wall. Experimental and Numerical Study Applied to on-Board Electronics. *Appl. Therm. Eng.* **2010**, *30*, 1115–1125. [CrossRef]
6. Baïri, A.; De María, J.M.G. Nu–Ra–Fo Correlations for Transient Free Convection in 2D Convective Diode Cavities with Discrete Heat Sources. *Int. J. Heat Mass Transf.* **2012**, *57*, 623–628. [CrossRef]
7. Gupta, N.; Nayak, A.K. Performance Evaluation of Coolant Air with Buoyancy in a Parallelogrammic Mixed Displacement Ventilated System. *Int. J. Mech. Sci.* **2018**, *149*, 38–53. [CrossRef]
8. Ravindra, P.; Sankar, M.; Rasappan, S.; Majrafi, W.A.A.; Rajan, P.; Kumar, S.S. Double-Diffusive Magnetoconvection in a Tilted Porous Parallelogrammic Domain with Discrete Heated-Cooled Segments: Leveraging Machine Learning and CFD Approach. *Results Eng.* **2025**, *27*, 105921. [CrossRef]
9. Choi, U.S. Enhancing Thermal Conductivity of Fluids with Nanoparticles. In Proceedings of the ASME 1995 International Mechanical Engineering Congress and Exposition, San Francisco, CA, USA, 12–17 November 1995; Volume 66, pp. 99–105. [CrossRef]
10. Ghalambaz, M.; Sheremet, M.A.; Pop, I. Free Convection in a Parallelogrammic Porous Cavity Filled with a Nanofluid Using Tiwari and Das' Nanofluid Model. *PLoS ONE* **2015**, *10*, e0126486. [CrossRef]
11. Tiwari, R.K.; Das, M.K. Heat transfer augmentation in a two-sided lid-driven differentially heated square cavity utilizing nanofluids. *Int. J. Heat Mass Transf.* **2007**, *50*, 2002–2018. [CrossRef]
12. Alsabery, A.I.; Saleh, H.; Hashim, I.; Siddheshwar, P.G. Transient Natural Convection Heat Transfer in Nanoliquid-Saturated Porous Oblique Cavity Using Thermal Non-Equilibrium Model. *Int. J. Mech. Sci.* **2016**, *114*, 233–245. [CrossRef]
13. Hussein, A.K.; Mustafa, A.W. Natural Convection in Fully Open Parallelogrammic Cavity Filled with Cu–Water Nanofluid and Heated Locally from Its Bottom Wall. *Therm. Sci. Eng. Prog.* **2017**, *1*, 66–77. [CrossRef]
14. Nayak, R.K.; Bhattacharyya, S.; Pop, I. Effects of Nanoparticles Dispersion on the Mixed Convection of a Nanofluid in a Skewed Enclosure. *Int. J. Heat Mass Transf.* **2018**, *125*, 908–919. [CrossRef]
15. Bhuiyan, A.H.; Munshi, M.J.H.; Alim, M.A.; Alam, M.S. MHD Effect on Mixed Convection Heat Transfer of Cu-Water Nanofluid in a Vented Parallelogrammic Cavity with Injection or Suction. *AIP Conf. Proc.* **2019**, *2121*, 070008. [CrossRef]
16. Yasin, A.; Ullah, N.; Nadeem, S.; Ghazwani, H.A. Numerical Simulation for Mixed Convection in a Parallelogram Enclosure: Magnetohydrodynamic (MHD) and Moving Wall-Undulation Effects. *Int. Commun. Heat Mass Transf.* **2022**, *135*, 106066. [CrossRef]
17. Shahid, H.; Sajida, M.; Khan, W.A.; Ahmad, F. Analysis of Heat Transfer in a Parallelogram-Shaped Cavity with Porous Medium under Non-Uniform Temperature. *Alex. Eng. J.* **2024**, *95*, 204–223. [CrossRef]
18. Oztop, H.F.; Abu-Nada, E. Numerical study of natural convection in partially heated rectangular enclosures filled with nanofluids. *Int. J. Heat Fluid Flow* **2008**, *29*, 1326–1336. [CrossRef]
19. Groşan, T.; Revnic, C.; Pop, I.; Ingham, D.B. Free Convection Heat Transfer in a Square Cavity Filled with a Porous Medium Saturated by a Nanofluid. *Int. J. Heat Mass Transf.* **2015**, *87*, 36–41. [CrossRef]
20. Sheremet, M.A.; Grosan, T.; Pop, I. Free Convection in a Square Cavity Filled with a Porous Medium Saturated by Nanofluid Using Tiwari and Das' Nanofluid Model. *Transp. Porous Media* **2015**, *106*, 595–610. [CrossRef]
21. Alsabery, A.I.; Chamkha, A.J.; Saleh, H.; Hashim, I. Natural Convection Flow of a Nanofluid in an Inclined Square Enclosure Partially Filled with a Porous Medium. *Sci. Rep.* **2017**, *7*, 2357. [CrossRef]
22. Alsabery, A.I.; Chamkha, A.J.; Saleh, H.; Hashim, I.; Chanane, B. Effects of Finite Wall Thickness and Sinusoidal Heating on Convection in Nanofluid-Saturated Local Thermal Non-Equilibrium Porous Cavity. *Phys. A Stat. Mech. Its Appl.* **2017**, *470*, 20–38. [CrossRef]
23. Sankar, M.; Swamy, H.A.K.; Do, Y.; Altmeyer, S. Thermal Effects of Nonuniform Heating in a Nanofluid-filled Annulus: Buoyant Transport versus Entropy Generation. *Heat Transf.* **2021**, *51*, 1062–1091. [CrossRef]
24. Chamkha, A.J.; Selimefendigil, F. MHD Free Convection and Entropy Generation in a Corrugated Cavity Filled with a Porous Medium Saturated with Nanofluids. *Entropy* **2018**, *20*, 846. [CrossRef] [PubMed]
25. Alhashash, A. Natural Convection of Nanoliquid from a Cylinder in Square Porous Enclosure Using Buongiorno's Two-Phase Model. *Sci. Rep.* **2020**, *10*, 143. [CrossRef] [PubMed]
26. Abed, W.M.; Al-Damook, A. Optimal Characteristics of Natural Convection in a Square Porous-Nanofluid-Filled Enclosure Containing Three Tubes. *Numer. Heat Transf. Part A Appl.* **2023**, *85*, 1706–1729. [CrossRef]
27. Azad, A.K.; Hasan, M.J.; Karim, M.F.; Alam, E.M.M.; Rahman, M.M. Rotational Effect of a Cylinder on Hydro-Thermal Characteristics in a Partially Heated Square Enclosure Using CNT-Water Nanofluid. *Heliyon* **2023**, *9*, e22744. [CrossRef]

28. Bondareva, N.S.; Sheremet, M.A. Numerical Simulation of Heat Transfer Performance in an Enclosure Filled with a Metal Foam and Nano-Enhanced Phase Change Material. *Energy* **2024**, *296*, 131123. [CrossRef]
29. Lakshmi, C.V.; Sireesha, M.; Venkatadri, K.; Fazuruddin, S.; Arigela, S. Natural convection of nanofluid flow in a porous enclosure with isothermal heated plate: A Tiwari and Das nanofluid model. *Int. J. Thermofluids* **2025**, *27*, 101238. [CrossRef]
30. Al-Kaby, R.N.; Abdulhaleem, S.M.; Hameed, R.H.; Yasiry, A. Mixed Convection Heat Transfer and Fluid Flow of Nanofluid/Porous Medium under Magnetic Field Influence. *Appl. Sci.* **2025**, *15*, 1087. [CrossRef]
31. Vigneshwari, S.; Reddappa, B.; Sumithra, A.; Kumar, B.R.; Öztop, H.F. Thermal and Flow Dynamics of Unsteady MHD Nanofluid Convection in a Partially Heated Porous Cavity. *J. Therm. Anal. Calorim.* **2025**, *150*, 5601–5616. [CrossRef]
32. Younis, O.; Alizadeh, M.; Hussein, A.K.; Ali, B.; Biswal, U.; Malekshah, E.H. MHD Natural Convection and Radiation over a Flame in a Partially Heated Semicircular Cavity Filled with a Nanofluid. *Mathematics* **2022**, 10, 1347. [CrossRef]
33. Kim, H.; Thirumalaisamy, K.; Venkatadri, K. Computational Analysis of Magnetohydrodynamic Buoyancy-Driven Flow and Thermal Transmission within a Circular Dome-Shaped Porous Enclosure Using Finite Difference Scheme. *Int. J. Numer. Methods Heat Fluid Flow* **2025**, *35*, 1642–1679. [CrossRef]
34. Ali, A.; Ayaz, M.; Ahmad, Z.; Marei, A.M. Analysis of Entropy Generation in Magnetohydrodynamic Convective Flow of Nanofluids within a Wavy Trapezoidal Enclosure: A Brinkmann-Forchheimer Model Using Finite Element Method. *Case Stud. Therm. Eng.* **2025**, *73*, 106719. [CrossRef]
35. Izadi, S.; Armaghani, T.; Ghasemiasl, R.; Chamkha, A.J.; Molana, M. A Comprehensive Review on Mixed Convection of Nanofluids in Various Shapes of Enclosures. *Powder Technol.* **2019**, *343*, 880–907. [CrossRef]
36. Abdulkadhim, A.; Abed, I.M.; Said, N.M. An Exhaustive Review on Natural Convection within Complex Enclosures: Influence of Various Parameters. *Chin. J. Phys.* **2021**, *74*, 365–388. [CrossRef]
37. Sivanandam, S.; Cheong, H.T.; Thangaraj, A. Numerical Study on Free Convection in an Inclined Wavy Porous Cavity with Localized Heating. *Modelling* **2025**, *6*, 30. [CrossRef]
38. Qureshi, H.; Rani, S.; Altmeyer, S. Investigation of Marangoni Convective Flow of Hybrid Nanofluids In Darcy-Forchheimer Porous Medium. *J. Appl. Mater. Sci. Eng. Res.* **2024**, *8*, 1–14. [CrossRef]
39. Ahlawat, A.; Sharma, M.K.; Ghachem, K.; Alshammari, B.M.; Kolsi, L. Impacts of Sinusoidal Heat Flux and Embraced Heated Rectangular Cavity on Natural Convection within a Square Enclosure Partially Filled with Porous Medium and Casson-Hybrid Nanofluid. *Open Phys.* **2025**, *23*, 20250142. [CrossRef]
40. Marfouk, A.; Mansour, A.; Hasnaoui, A.; Amahmid, A.; Hasnaoui, M. MHD Free Convection in an Enclosure Loaded with Nanofluid and Partially Cross-Heated. *J. Appl. Fluid Mech.* **2025**, *18*, 1720–1734. [CrossRef]
41. Sayyou, H.; Belabid, J.; Öztop, H.F.; Allali, K. Vibrational effects on thermosolutal free convection of $Cu - Al_2O_3$ /water nanofluids in a partially heated and salted square porous enclosure. *J. Mol. Liq.* **2025**, *423*, 126990. [CrossRef]
42. Baytas, A.C.; Pop, I. Free Convection in Oblique Enclosures Filled with a Porous Medium. *Int. J. Heat Mass Transf.* **1999**, *42*, 1047–1057. [CrossRef]
43. Jagadeesha, R.D.; Prasanna, B.M.R.; Sankar, M. Numerical Simulation of Double Diffusive Magnetoconvection in an Inclined Parallelogrammic Porous Enclosure with an Internal Heat Source. *Mater. Today Proc.* **2017**, *4*, 10544–10548. [CrossRef]
44. Saeid, N.H.; Pop, I. Transient free convection in a square cavity filled with a porous medium. *Int. J. Heat Mass Transf.* **2004**, *47*, 1917–1924. [CrossRef]

MDPI AG
Grosspeteranlage 5
4052 Basel
Switzerland
Tel.: +41 61 683 77 34

Mathematics Editorial Office
E-mail: mathematics@mdpi.com
www.mdpi.com/journal/mathematics

www.ingramcontent.com/pod-product-compliance
Lightning Source LLC
Chambersburg PA
CBHW061607210926
51850CB00009B/2249
9783725860593